Women and Law
in Late Antiquity

Women and Law
in Late Antiquity

ANTTI ARJAVA

CLARENDON PRESS · OXFORD

Oxford University Press, Walton Street, Oxford OX2 6DP

Oxford New York
Athens Auckland Bangkok Bogota Bombay
Buenos Aires Calcutta Cape Town Dar es Salaam
Delhi Florence Hong Kong Istanbul Karachi
Kuala Lumpur Madras Madrid Melbourne
Mexico City Nairobi Paris Singapore
Taipei Tokyo Toronto
and associated companies in
Berlin Ibadan

Oxford is a trade mark of Oxford University Press

Published in the United States
by Oxford University Press Inc., New York

British Library Cataloguing in Publication Data
Data available

Library of Congress Cataloging in Publication Data
Women and law in late antiquity / Antti Arjava.
Includes bibliographical references and index.
1. Women—Legal status, laws, etc.—Europe—History. 2. Women-
-Legal status, laws, etc. (Roman law) 3. Women—Europe—Social
conditions. I. Title
KJC1019.A96 1996 346.401'34—dc20 95–53235
[344.06134]
ISBN 0–19–815233–7 (pbk)

1 3 5 7 9 10 8 6 4 2

Printed in Great Britain on acid-free paper by
Bookcraft (Bath) Ltd., Midsomer Norton

PREFACE

THERE are many people who think that men should not write women's history. Nevertheless, I have ventured to spend eight years studying women in late antiquity. Although I have tried my best to avoid any male bias, I am the first to confess that there is very little in my work which might be called feminist insight. I hope that someone else will be able to make good this deficiency in the future.

Iiro Kajanto first suggested the topic to me and later encouraged me to continue. Päivi Setälä introduced me to women's studies in the classical world. My special gratitude is due to Paavo Castrén, who promoted the study of late antiquity in Finland and led the research programme in which the major part of this work was written. Over the years he has been an unfailing and inspiring support. Christer Bruun, Jaakko Frösén, Maarit Kaimio, Unto Paananen, Olli Salomies, and Heikki Solin read drafts of the manuscript and supplied a wealth of useful comments. Heikki Kotila shared my office, kept me good company, and discussed my topic as a theologian. The Department of Classical Philology at the University of Helsinki has been an ideal place to work. All my colleagues there contributed to a pleasant atmosphere and offered their help whenever I needed it.

It would have been very difficult to write a study like this without succour from the best experts all over the world. I owe an inestimable debt to Gillian Clark, Judith Evans Grubbs, Jane F. Gardner, and Pauline Stafford, who all read through the whole manuscript, corrected dozens of errors, opened new avenues of approach, and helped me generously in every possible way. Judith Evans Grubbs allowed me to see her study on Constantine's marriage legislation still in typescript, and I could only partially indicate in the footnotes how much I owe to her work. Roger S. Bagnall, Katrinette Bodarwé, Suzanne Dixon, Tim Parkin, and Richard P. Saller sent their valuable comments on individual chapters. Many people, among them Joëlle Beaucamp,

Jan Bremmer, Elizabeth A. Clark, Marie-Thérèse Raepsaet-Charlier, and Anja Wieber-Scariot, supplied me with works that I would otherwise not have found. Margot Stout Whiting patiently corrected stylistic errors in the manuscript. Of course, none of the persons mentioned should be held responsible for remaining errors.

My work was made possible by a five-year research grant from the Academy of Finland, and by grants from the Finnish Cultural Foundation and the Emil Aaltonen Foundation. Effective research is impossible without a well–stocked library, and I must express my appreciation of the Helsinki University Library and the History and Philology Library, with their excellent staffs, who could supply almost every book and periodical I needed to see.

Finally, I acknowledge my indebtedness to the legal historian I know best: my wife Anu Pylkkänen. Her book on women in seventeenth-century Finland was an indirect source of inspiration. Our two daughters, Heini and Tuire (neither of whom had been born when the work begun), have made me believe that Roman fathers loved their daughters very much. I attach great value to the efficient Finnish day-care system, which enables male and female scholars alike to enjoy the pleasures of both academic work and happy family life. That is an achievement which my small country can be proud of.

A.A

Helsinki
October 1995.

CONTENTS

Abbreviations   ix

Note on Translations   xii

1. Historical Setting and Sources   1

   Introduction   1
   From Antiquity to the Early Middle Ages   3
   Sources   8

2. Fathers and Children   28

   Giving a Child in Marriage   29
   Paternal Power and Adult Children   41
   Dowry and Inheritance   52
   Summary and Conclusions   73

3. Mothers and Children   76

   Motherhood and Population Policy   77
   Mothers' Rights and Duties   84
   Maternal Kin and Inheritance   94
   Summary and Conclusions   108

4. Married Women   111

   Guardianship of Women   112
   Husbands and Wives   123
   Economic Independence   133
   Summary and Conclusions   154

5. Separation and Single Life   157

   Christian Asceticism   157
   Widowhood and Remarriage   167
   Divorce   177
   Summary and Conclusions   189

6. Sexual Relations outside Marriage   193

   Marital Infidelity   193
   Concubinage   205
   Sexual Affairs of Unmarried Women   217
   Summary and Conclusions   228

7. Women and the Society of Men   230

   Restraints and Privileges   231
   Women in Public   243
   Summary and Conclusions   254

8. General Conclusions   257

   Bibliography   267

   Glossary of Latin Legal Terms   290

   Index of Sources   295

   Subject Index   303

ABBREVIATIONS

THE abbreviations of ancient authors and their works follow the system used in the *Thesaurus Linguae Latinae* and should be clear. For the epigraphical and papyrological sources standard abbreviations have been used. The main legal sources and the most important series of patristic texts are listed below.

CCL   *Corpus Christianorum, series Latina*

CE   *Codex Euricianus*, ed. K. Zeumer, in MGH Legum Sectio I:1 (Hanover, Leipzig, 1902)

CG   *Epitome Codicis Gregoriani Wisigothica*, in FIRA ii. 655–64

CI   *Codex Iustinianus*, ed. P. Krueger, in *Corpus Iuris Civilis*, ii, 11th edn. (Berlin, 1954)

Coll.   *Mosaicarum et Romanarum legum collatio*, in FIRA ii. 541–89

Cons.   *Consultatio veteris cuiusdam iurisconsulti*, in FIRA ii. 591–613

CSEL   *Corpus Scriptorum Ecclesiasticorum Latinorum*

CT   *Codex Theodosianus*, ed. Th. Mommsen, in *Theodosiani Libri XVI cum Constitutionibus Sirmondianis et Leges Novellae ad Theodosianum pertinentes*, i (repr. Hildesheim 1990). Translated by C. Pharr, *The Theodosian Code* (Princeton, 1952)

D.   *Digesta*, ed. Th. Mommsen and P. Krueger, in *Corpus Iuris Civilis*, i, 17th edn. (Berlin, 1963). Translated by A. Watson *et al.*, *The Digest of Justinian* (Philadelphia, 1985)

ER   *Edictum Rothari*, ed. F. Beyerle, in *Leges Langobardorum* 643–866, Germanenrechte, NF, Westgermanisches Recht, 9; 2nd edn. (Witzenhausen, 1962)

ET   *Edictum Theoderici*, in FIRA ii. 681–710

FIRA   *Fontes Iuris Romani Anteiustiniani*, i–iii. Ad usum scholarum ediderunt S. Riccobono, J. Barrera, C.

Ferrini, J. Furlani, V. Arangio-Ruiz, 2nd edn. (Florence, 1940)

Form./F.   *Formulae Merowingici et Karolini Aevi*, ed. K. Zeumer, in MGH Legum Sectio V (Hanover, 1886)

FV   *Fragmenta quae dicuntur Vaticana*, in FIRA ii. 460–540

GE   *Gai Institutionum epitome*, in FIRA ii. 229–57

GI   *Gai Institutionum commentarii quattuor*, in FIRA ii. 3–192. Translated by W. M. Gordon and O. F. Robinson, *The Institutes of Gaius* (Ithaca, NY, 1988)

Inst.   *Iustiniani Institutiones*, ed. P. Krueger, in *Corpus Iuris Civilis*, i, 17th edn. (Berlin, 1963)

LB   *Lex Burgundionum*, ed. L. R. de Salis, in MGH Legum Sectio I:2 (Hanover, 1892)

LL   *Liutprandi Leges*, ed. F. Beyerle, in *Leges Langobardorum* 643–866, Germanenrechte, NF, Westgermanisches Recht, 9; 2nd edn. (Witzenhausen, 1962)

LRB   *Lex Romana Burgundionum*, ed. L. R. de Salis, in MGH Legum Sectio I:2 or FIRA ii. 711–50

LRib   *Lex Ribuaria*, ed. F. Beyerle and R. Buchner, in MGH Legum Sectio I:3. 2 (Hanover, 1954)

LRV   *Lex Romana Visigothorum*, ed. G. Haenel (Leipzig, 1849)

LV   *Lex Visigothorum*, ed. K. Zeumer, in MGH Legum Sectio I:1 (Hanover, Leipzig, 1902)

MGH   *Monumenta Germaniae Historica*

Nov.   *Iustiniani Novellae*, ed. R. Schoell and G. Kroll, in *Corpus Iuris Civilis*, iii, 8th edn. (Berlin, 1963)

NTh   *Leges Novellae Divi Theodosii (Valentiniani, Maior-*
(etc.)   *iani, etc.)*, ed. P. M. Meyer, in *Theodosiani Libri XVI cum Constitutionibus Sirmondianis et Leges Novellae ad Theodosianum pertinentes*, ii (repr. Hildesheim 1990). Translated by C. Pharr, *The Theodosian Code* (Princeton, 1952)

PA   *Pactus Alamannorum*, ed. K. Lehmann, in MGH Legum Sectio I:5. 1 (Hanover, 1888)

Pard.   *Diplomata, Chartae, Epistolae, Leges aliaque instrumenta ad res Gallo-Francicas spectantia*, i–ii, ed. J. M. Pardessus (Paris, 1843–9)

PG   *Patrologiae cursus completus, series Graeca,* ed. J. P. Migne

PL   *Patrologiae cursus completus, series Latina,* ed. J. P. Migne

PLS   *Pactus Legis Salicae,* ed. K. A. Eckhardt, in MGH Legum Sectio I:4. 1 (Hanover, 1962)

PS   *Sententiarum receptarum libri quinque, qui vulgo Julio Paulo adhuc tribuuntur,* in FIRA ii. 317–417
The *Interpretationes* of the *Sententiae* are found in LRV 338–444, or in M. Kaser and F. Schwartz (eds.), *Die Interpretatio zu den Paulussentenzen* (Cologne, Graz, 1956)

SC   *Sources Chrétiennes*

UE   *Tituli XXVIII ex corpore Ulpiani, qui vulgo D. Ulpiano adhuc tribuuntur,* in FIRA ii. 259–301

NOTE ON TRANSLATIONS

For the Digest, the Institutes of Gaius, the Theodosian Code, and the Theodosian *Novellae* I have used the translations mentioned above. The long translations from Jerome's letters 54 and 77 are reprinted by permission of the publishers and the Loeb Classical Library from St Jerome, *Select Letters*, tr. F. A. Wright (Cambridge, Mass.; Harvard University Press, 1933). The translations from the Institutes of Gaius, tr. W. M. Gordon and O. F. Robinson (1988), are reprinted by permission of Cornell University Press and Gerald Duckworth & Co Ltd, and the translations from the Theodosian Code, tr. Clyde Pharr (1952), by permission of Princeton University Press. Other translations are my own, unless otherwise indicated.

I

Historical Setting and Sources

I. INTRODUCTION

In political and religious history, late antiquity marks the end of one world and the beginning of another. The Roman empire slowly disintegrated, Christianity prevailed over other religions, and classical antiquity gave way to the dark ages. In the end, Germanic kings held sway over western Europe.

My intention is to find out how these developments affected the status of women. This is not first and foremost a study in legal history. The main source material is composed of legal texts because there is no other group of evidence which one could follow continuously from the early empire through the pivotal but enigmatic third century up to the beginning of the early middle ages. During late antiquity, other traditional literature dwindled away, and was replaced by the works of Christian bishops and monks. The latter are by no means to be neglected, but they are difficult to compare with earlier material. In the midst of political and religious upheavals, Roman law was a well-established institution, which preserved its mainly secular character. In this study it will gradually appear that from the standpoint of most women late antiquity was not a period of radical change. In particular, the influence of Christianity has been greatly exaggerated.

For the purpose of my study, it is not relevant to define the beginning and end of late antiquity. I will take late antiquity in its widest possible sense, and I will pay close attention to the immediately preceding period. In order to understand some phenomena, we have to begin as early as the reign of Augustus. On the other hand, we shall follow some developments as late as the reign of Charlemagne. But the bulk of the evidence discussed comes from between the second and the seventh centuries.

Many exhaustive studies have already been written on the life of Roman women.[1] Until very recently late antiquity has received little attention, and a general comparison between the early and the later empire is still lacking.[2] In fact, there is some difficulty in defining *Roman* women in late antiquity. During the first two centuries AD most Roman citizens lived in Italy. Even those who dwelt in the provinces could be taken to represent the most Romanized part of the population. In late antiquity things were totally different. Roman citizenship had been granted to all inhabitants of the empire in AD 212 (the *Constitutio Antoniniana*). From then on most people had Roman names and were, in theory, bound by Roman law. In practice, however, provincial communities had their distinct social and demographic structures. A Briton on a misty island and a Syrian on the desert's edge were both Romans but not similar Romans. Could they really know how they were expected to act as Roman men and women? Were they eventually Romanized, or did they themselves have an influence on Roman law and culture? Did the general population have any knowledge of legal matters? These questions will often recur in the present study.

From the late third century, the Roman empire was usually divided into two or more parts. As time went on, legal development took different courses in the east and in the west. The eastern legislation of Justinian in the sixth century has a special value because of its sheer volume and the historical information which it gives. However, this is not going to be a systematic account of Byzantine law.[3] From the sixth century the present work follows more closely developments in the west, in so far as there is anything to follow. In the early middle ages we encounter new problems: the old Roman population fades from sight, and the very meagre written evidence we have about this period tells more about the ruling Germanic minority. The sources become abundant only in the Carolingian period. Thus it seems that no

[1] For the principate, see above all Gardner (1986); Dixon (1988; 1992); Treggiari (1991a); and for senatorial women, the works of Raepsaet-Charlier, listed in the Bibliography.

[2] See esp. Beaucamp (1990; 1992a); Clark (1993); other useful works are Thraede (1972); Evans Grubbs (1995); and Krause (1991; 1994a–c). The latter appeared when the present study was almost finished.

[3] For that, readers may be referred to Beaucamp (1990, with 1992a).

comprehensive history of women in the dark ages can ever be written, at least not in the sense familiar to ancient historians.[4]

This work is very much about property. Juridical sources inevitably focus on the material side of life. Most legal rules directly or indirectly regulate movements of property. Thus, they are vital for the upper classes but often irrelevant for the poor. Although morality and ideology are not without interest, in general they exert less influence on law than considerations of power and property. Even norms for sexual behaviour have much more to do with financial interests than legal historians have tended to think. Sex leads to children, children are potential heirs, and inheritance was the single most important way to transfer private property in the Roman empire.

The central theme of this study is change—or the lack of it. How did the legal and social position of Roman women change during the period which is called late antiquity? However, as women cannot be separated from the rest of society, this question inevitably leads us to consider the evolution of the Roman family, of Roman law, and of Roman society itself.

2. FROM ANTIQUITY TO THE EARLY MIDDLE AGES

Christians and Pagans

During the third century the Christian church had been tolerated at best and often persecuted. Early in the next century, the emperor Constantine officially recognized the expanding religion. Gradually the church accumulated both political power and material wealth. It met with stiff resistance in the countryside and was long despised by the senatorial aristocracy, but by the end of the fourth century Christianity was declared the sole accepted faith by the emperor Theodosius I. Politically, the Christian victory was soon complete.

For a long time it was believed that this religious change had a dramatic effect on legal and social developments in the Roman empire. For example, it was claimed that Christian teaching

---

[4] The most important general survey so far is Wemple (1981); see also Ganshof (1962); and many recent collections of articles, e.g. Affeldt and Kuhn (1986); Affeldt (1990); Goetz (1991); the individual contributions are listed separately in the Bibliography.

rapidly permeated the whole of late Roman law.[5] It is my impression that in a less exaggerated form the idea still survives. Many scholars tend to see Christianity as a major factor influencing Roman social behaviour and especially Roman family law.

It is clear that culturally and socially the Christianized empire was very different from the world which had been ruled by pagan emperors. It is equally clear that Christianity itself was only one factor in this metamorphosis. The origins of many new phenomena can be seen long before their breakthrough, and that would be the case much more often if the third century were not so poorly illuminated by our extant sources. To take just one trivial example, Christian emperors used to grant a general amnesty to convicted criminals at Easter (CT 9. 38). It is easy to see here a Christian virtue put into practice. However, general amnesties on memorable days had been known already in the early third century (D. 48. 16. 8–9). It was only the timing of amnesties, not the practice itself, which derived from Christian influence. In this case as in many others, Christianization of Roman society was rather superficial.

When it has proved difficult to demonstrate clear changes in Roman thought or behaviour, some scholars have tried to evade the problem by speaking about a 'new spirit', which permeated traditional ideas, such as opinions about married life. In other words, they do not actually claim that the patterns of thought changed, just that a new Christian justification was given to them.[6] An even simpler conclusion emerged from a study on pagan and Christian personal letters in papyri: 'The Christian influence is to be sought first and foremost in the vocabulary and phrases . . . whereas the sentiments expressed do not really change.'[7]

Can Christian teaching explain any social or legal changes in the later Roman empire? Were Christian morals different from secular morals and, if they were, did they affect the ways in which people lived and acted? Could the same changes have happened

---

[5] An extreme example of this argument was Biondi (1952–4).

[6] See e.g. Gaudemet (1969) 348; Delling (1959*b*) 703.

[7] Joxe (1959) 419, see also her amusing quotations from earlier scholars, 413–14.

even without Christianity? There is at present no simple and generally applicable answer to those questions.[8]

One major difficulty arises from the definition of 'Christianity' itself. We habitually give that name to a mixture of traditions which was formed in late antiquity. The similarities between Christian and pagan ethics have led many scholars to consider Christian morality simply a subspecies of 'hellenistic' or 'oriental' morality. Christianization has also been linked with the appearance of middle-class or provincial attitudes, as opposed to the urban upper-class perspective, which dominates our sources in the early empire.[9]

Depending on personal experience and religious conviction, each scholar may entertain a different idea of 'real' or 'original' Christian teaching. Inevitably, this is also reflected in the notion of 'Christian influence'. Both the subordination of women and their recent emancipation have been thought harmonious with Christian teaching or even necessitated by it.

Thus it is not easy to find an independent Christian factor which could explain historical developments in Roman society. It is hardly sufficient to identify in the Bible a suitable maxim which appears to have been adopted in late antiquity. True, Jesus disapproved of divorce, and Constantine tried to forbid it. On the other hand, Jesus disapproved of material wealth, but Constantine did nothing to prevent his subjects from amassing riches. There must have been some contributing factors which made certain biblical precepts acceptable to Roman lawgivers while others were silently forgotten. Moreover, in many western societies today divorce is not considered to be irreconcilable with Christian faith, demonstrating that religious authority alone is rarely sufficient to determine ethical norms in a community.

All these are serious but not insurmountable obstacles to our investigation. The present work will adopt a very materialistic view of reality.[10] It is not easy to study Roman women's religious convictions. Their life on earth is at issue, not their fate after

---

[8] For the more recent discussion, see e.g. Ehrhardt (1955); Gaudemet (1962; 1969: 341–57; 1978); Forlin Patrucco (1976) 158–60; Cantalamessa (1976); Veyne (1978); Frend (1984) 569–71; Sargenti (1985); Cameron (1986); MacMullen (1986b); Brown (1987) 259–67; Brundage (1987) 1–5; Nocera (1988); Evans Grubbs (1995).

[9] See e.g. Ehrhardt (1955) 137–8, 185; Brown (1987) 259–67; Evans Grubbs (1995), 330–42.   [10] Such a view is rejected by e.g. Cantalamessa (1976) 458.

death. I cannot tell if Christian women in late antiquity were more content with their lives than their pagan grandmothers had been, and I wonder if anyone can. But I do attempt to discover if the men and women of Christian Rome behaved in a different way because they had adopted the new faith, and if the Christian emperors gave different laws for the same reason.

Romans and Barbarians

According to a recent estimate, over 200 different explanations have been offered for the 'decline and fall' of the Roman empire.[11] It would be fatuous to attempt here even a short description of that very long and complex process. There were conflicting tendencies, and the pace of development varied between regions, especially between east and west. As we all know (though contemporaries did not), after the year 395 the two halves of the empire were never to be united again. The western half soon got into increasing internal and external troubles. It ceased to exist within a century, while the eastern state survived for another millennium. The impact of the Islamic conquests from the seventh century onward falls outside the scope of this study.

In the west, the fifth century was marked by a collapse of central authority. The imperial government was no longer able to maintain law and order in the provinces. Rural communities were dominated by rich landlords and local bishops. For many centuries of Mediterranean history, the countryside had supported a prosperous culture in the cities. Now the unequal relationship was broken, and there were no more material preconditions for an advanced urban civilization.

These were internal developments in the western Roman empire, but they coincided with violent external upheavals. Germanic nations had been ravaging the western provinces from the beginning of the fifth century. The last western Roman emperor was deposed in 476. At that time the former imperial territory had split up into several smaller realms under Germanic kings. In Italy the Ostrogoths established a fairly stable government, which collapsed half a century later when Justinian's

---

[11] For good full presentations, see Jones (1964); Demandt (1989); Cameron (1993*a* and 1993*b*), with up-to-date bibliographies.

reconquest devastated Italy. Only a little later the Langobards invaded from the north. Thus in the sixth century western Europe was divided into Visigothic Spain, Frankish (Merovingian) Gaul, and a battlefield which was called Italy. Anglo-Saxon Britain in the fifth and sixth centuries is little known.

From the viewpoint of women's history, these political and military feats (or disasters) have only limited relevance. Nowhere did the Germans make up more than a tiny fraction of the population, except in north-eastern Gaul, the Frankish heartland.[12] Southern Gaul remained for a long time almost unaffected by them. The indigenous rural population continued to live as they had done for generations, speaking Latin and paying their taxes to the new rulers. Although their imperial governors turned into royal officials, people certainly did not change their habits in one night, and still less when their Visigothic and Burgundian superiors were replaced by Frankish lords. In fact, we do not know if their lives changed at all.

The process of the Germanic settlement is an obscure and controversial issue, and its details need not concern us here. In all new states the Germans constituted the ruling class. Although the kings adopted what was left of the administrative system, the central power remained weak. Descendants of the old Roman nobility now ruled their subjects simply as landowners and bishops. At first they despised their new long-haired neighbours, but as their financial privileges were preserved they did not put up any real resistance.[13]

The indigenous populations retained their cultural and legal autonomy. They were expected to observe old Roman law while the Germanic newcomers chose to codify their own customs separately (see below). Thus the legal system was based on a personal, not territorial, principle. It would be misleading to speak generally of the legal position of women in the early middle ages because there were in fact two separate sections of the society which followed different traditions. The existing evidence focuses on the Germanic élite. Inevitably, no treatise upon early medieval women can provide much concrete informa-

---

[12] See e.g. King (1972) 6; Geary (1988) 114–15.
[13] See Jones (1964) 248–65; Goffart (1980) e.g. 206–22; Thompson (1982) 23–37, 92–4, 100–9, 176–82, 212–16, 251–5; Geary (1988) 25, 28–38, 88–95; Wood (1990).

tion about the Romanic population. Of course, intermarriage and close contacts gradually closed the gap. Exactly how it happened remains shrouded in mystery: this period is not called the dark ages for nothing.[14] When the peoples of western Europe reappear from the shadows in the ninth century, the process has advanced so far that the original population groups can no longer be identified.

The transition from one economic and social system to another had the most far-reaching consequences for inhabitants in the old imperial territory. The ancient culture had been based on urban life, commerce, and a well developed division of labour. In the new agrarian feudal setting both men, women, and the family as a social unit faced different tasks and living conditions. The change was felt primarily by the upper and middle classes. The overwhelming majority of Roman citizens had always lived in the countryside, farming at subsistence level and observing their own traditional customs. For them the decline and fall of the Roman empire was a less significant phenomenon.

3. SOURCES

Roman Law as a Historical Source

In the Roman republic laws (*leges*), in the original sense of the word, were passed in people's assemblies (*comitia, concilium plebis*). This traditional method of law-making had in practice fallen into desuetude by the early empire. Resolutions of the senate (*senatusconsulta*) survived somewhat longer, at least to the Severan age. In the final stage of their history they tended to fuse with imperial legislation, as they were often proposed by the emperor himself. The third main source of classical Roman law was the praetor's edict. It had developed casuistically over centuries by slow accumulation and modernization. This more progressive set of rules helped Roman citizens to evade the more primitive precepts of their earliest law, the Twelve Tables, which was never formally abrogated. In the early second century the praetor's edict, too, was stabilized (*edictum perpetuum*).

Such was Roman law in the middle of the second century, the

---

[14] On this issue Wemple (1981) should be read with caution, e.g. 31, 49–50, 189–90; cf. also Ganshof (1962) 7–8; Rouche (1987) 417.

heyday of the empire, when the period of study for this work begins. At that time the famous textbook of Roman law, the Institutes of Gaius, was written. Nothing more is known about this mysterious work, not even the full name of its author. It has come down to us nearly complete and without later amendments, something which is rare and extremely valuable in a Roman legal source. It offers a clear and basically reliable picture of the contemporary legal situation, against which later developments can be measured.

After Gaius' time there were two principal methods for reshaping the legal system: juristic writings and imperial constitutions. The first of these, the opinions of the jurisprudents, were not actually new laws but only new interpretations and applications of existing principles. They could disagree on individual points. The lawyers not only gave their advice in specific cases but they also wrote extensive commentaries on various topics. Sometimes it is difficult to believe that the complex problems which they so scrupulously discussed had other than theoretical value. But on the whole their works create an impression of reality. Their activity reached its peak under the Severan emperors in the late second and early third centuries and declined soon after.

Naturally these jurisprudents came from the educated classes, and they were increasingly imperial officials of equestrian background. Thus they were very much the same men as were also involved in the drafting of imperial constitutions. It seems, however, that in their role as juridical experts they could act quite independently. Perhaps this was because the emperors were not personally interested in private law and there was no clearly worked-out imperial policy to develop it. On the other hand, it would be interesting to know if these imperial bureaucrats had values and interests different from those of the old senatorial aristocracy, which had dominated law-making up to the early empire. But such differences are difficult to demonstrate.

Few writings of the imperial jurists have been preserved intact. They are mainly known through the *Corpus Iuris Civilis*, the great collection of Roman law which was compiled in the sixth century for the emperor Justinian. Its largest section, the Digest, includes a vast number of quotations from the famous classical lawyers. But Justinian did not want a historical document. His commissioners carefully removed or modified ('interpolated') all passages which were not consonant with sixth century law.[15] Sometimes these changes are easy to detect but mostly they are not.

No problem riddles the study of Roman law more than this. If one wants to show that nothing changed from the second century to the sixth, one upholds the authenticity of most Digest passages. On the other hand, if one craves for impressive changes, it is easy to discard all contrary evidence as later interpolations.[16] Roughly speaking, the first half of the twentieth century was marked by an eager hunt for interpolations: they were 'detected' everywhere by everyone. Today scholars tend to be more cautious.[17]

In this work I have no more objective criteria for discerning interpolations than anyone else, but I start from the assumption that the old texts were changed only where it was absolutely necessary and where the alterations were small in relation to the main argument of the passage. Otherwise its inclusion would hardly have been justified at all. Why would Justinian have chosen to excerpt ancient texts for his great codification, a very cumbersome task, if his lawyers had still been compelled to rewrite everything? Unfortunately, this is only a rule of thumb, and we have to accept the fact that many important pieces of evidence always remain unreliable.

The last major source of Roman law, the imperial constitutions, is the most important for late antiquity. In the beginning, they were not first and foremost intended as a means to change existing law. A governor might request the emperor to give legal advice or to decide an individual case or a private citizen might send a written petition (*libellus*) describing a juridic problem and asking for help. The emperor was expected to answer them through a rescript. Such petitions were surprisingly common at least from the second century onward. They came from all parts of the empire and from all echelons of society, even from slaves.

---

[15] For these working principles, see the introductory constitutions, which are habitually known by their initial words, *Tanta* 10; *Haec* 2; *Summa* 3; *Cordi* 3.
[16] A shining example of this is Biondi (1952–4), e.g. ii. 220–1, 224–5.
[17] A vast literature exists for this topic, see e.g. Kaser (1972 and 1979); Wieacker (1988) 154–82, with further bibliography.

Significantly, there are over six hundred extant rescripts which were sent to women, about a quarter of the total preserved.[18]

The emperors usually wrote their answer (*subscriptio*) on the bottom of the petition. It was necessarily short, summing the situation up in a few words and not repeating all the details which were included in the petition itself. Now the problem is that when these imperial rescripts were collected, filed, and arranged for future use the original petition was not preserved. The *subscriptio* contained enough information for the needs of a Roman lawyer. For a modern historian the loss of the original *libellus* is irksome: a full description of the circumstances would have been much more interesting than the emperor's blunt answer, often containing rather trivial legal instructions.

Rescripts to private citizens form the bulk of our legal material in the third century. They are all the more valuable because so few other sources exist for that period. The rescripts were collected for the first time and published in the Gregorian and Hermogenian Codes in the 290s. That is why we have so many of them precisely from the time of the Diocletianic tetrarchy. It is evident that the material was mainly gathered from the archives of the eastern chancellery, while Diocletian's western colleagues were hardly represented at all. True, this cannot be securely demonstrated: the place of issue has often not been preserved, and the rescripts always have the names of all emperors attached, irrespective of their real provenance. But it is safe to assume that they reflect social and legal conditions mainly in the eastern part of the Roman empire.[19]

The practice of answering petitions obviously continued in the fourth century. Unfortunately, very few have been preserved because rescripts to private persons were not included in the Theodosian Code, which is our main source for the period (see below). Three examples are casually attested in 364-5. As it happens, two of them are addressed to women. But by and large it seems that the emperors now preferred to disseminate more extensive enactments. Such *constitutiones generales*, often called the edicts, had a long history behind them but they do not seem

---

[18] Petitions from women are discussed by Huchthausen (1974; 1976); and Sternberg (1985). For rescripts in general, see e.g. Millar (1977) 240-52, 537-49; Turpin (1991).   [19] See e.g. Mitteis (1891) 11-12; Huchthausen (1976) 56-7.

to have been very common before the tetrarchic period. From the fourth century onward they were the sole source of new Roman law.[20]

The change from rescripts to edicts is very important in two respects. First, the rescripts always, even in their summary form, reflected actual problems which some private citizens had faced. Through them we catch glimpses into the life of many ordinary inhabitants of the empire. The edicts, on the other hand, had wider publicity in mind and strove for generalizations. The difference would be less marked if we had the edicts in their original form: they usually had an extensive preamble describing the real-life circumstances which had led the emperor to promulgate a new edict. Alas, in their present state these preambles have usually been cut out. As in the case of *libelli*, later collectors wanted to preserve only the legal substance, not any details of purely historical interest. Sometimes only a sentence may remain out of a long constitution.[21]

Secondly, the edicts display a new imperial interest in legislation. The rescripts had been only reactions to private petitions or to enquiries from officials. They were mainly new interpretations or adaptations, sometimes just brief explanations of existing law. Of course they set legal precedents for similar cases, in so far as they were published or could be effectively filed in the imperial chancellery, but in any case they reflect the very passive attitude which most second- and third-century emperors took towards legal change. The edicts may also have been called forth by reports from officials or by appeals from private citizens. But they show a far greater tendency towards active legislating. If the emperor's attention was drawn to a particular legal or social problem, he no longer hesitated to promulgate a general edict which solved it not only in this individual case but once and for all. And as the edicts were made public they instantly reshaped the law. Of course, in practice most people in the empire never heard about them and continued to live as before.

[20] For the survival of private rescripts, see Cons. 9. 2, 5–6; FV 33–4, 287; P.Oxy. lv. 3820 (*c.*340); Symm. *rel.* 39. 3 (384/5); and cf. CT 1. 1–2. See also Millar (1977) 252–9; Turpin (1985; 1991: 114–18).

[21] Occasionally the original is still extant and can be compared with later versions, cf. e.g. Coll. 6. 4 with CI 5. 4. 17; or FV 249 with Cons. 9. 13; CT 8. 12. 1, 3. 30. 2; CI 5. 37. 21, 8. 53. 25.

The Gregorian and Hermogenian Codes, which contained third-century rescripts, have not been preserved themselves. A large part of their material was included in the Justinian Code, another main section of the sixth-century *Corpus Iuris Civilis*. There are a few independent smaller collections, but by far the greatest part of our information comes through Justinian. Thus, very much as in the case of the Digest, the authenticity of the third-century evidence is not always above suspicion.

For the fourth and fifth centuries we are in a much better position. Imperial edicts since the reign of Constantine were collected and published in 438 in the Theodosian Code. It was divided into sixteen books, consisting of thematic titles. Unlike the later Justinian Code, it did not harmonize old laws by interpolating them: inside the titles texts were arranged chronologically and new constitutions simply overruled old ones. They were usually shortened, and sometimes individual laws were broken up and assigned to different titles, but the existing parts are mainly authentic.[22]

Of course, after 438 new laws were again passed both in the east and in the west. They were called *novellae* and were not inserted into the Theodosian Code but published separately. Several smaller collections of them have been preserved. These constitutions are especially valuable because they survive entirely in their original form, showing also the extensive preambles which have been lost in the Theodosian Code. The last extant western edict dates from the year 468. Eastern laws up to 534 can be found in the Justinian Code and later ones in the collection of Justinian's own *novellae*.

When the *Corpus Iuris Civilis* officially replaced other collections in the east, most copies of the older collections were destroyed. Consequently, we have only a few western manuscripts of the Theodosian Code. The first five books were covered by a sole codex, which was called manuscript T and was lost in a fire in 1904. It was so fragmentary that only about one-third of the original text has been preserved.[23] Some of the gaps have been filled from a later collection which was made in 506 in the Visigothic dominions (the *Breviarium Alaricianum*, see below). It

---

[22] See CT 1. 1. 5; Honoré (1986) 156–63; cf. also e.g. Matthews (1993); Sirks (1993).   [23] Mommsen, in his introduction to CT, pp. xxxviii ff.

is simply an abridged version of the Theodosian Code. As far as we know, the compilers incorporated into it only authentic material from the Code. However, they avoided obsolete laws, and whole titles were passed over in silence. Where the *Breviarium* can be compared with the text of manuscript T it is easy to see that it omits a great part of the original constitutions.[24] In particular, all changes in imperial policy remain concealed. Anyone reading the printed edition of the Theodosian Code is liable to get a very distorted picture of those topics which were discussed in the first books, for example family law. We shall often return to this problem in later chapters.

As the imperial constitutions form the bulk of our source material, it is natural to ask who wrote them. Was the emperor personally involved or were the laws only formally issued under his name? This question has been much discussed in recent times. There are many texts that clearly show the emperor deciding cases in person. He had a council of jurists around him but he was not bound by their opinion.[25] On the other hand, stylistic analysis indicates that it was someone else who drafted the texts: certain periods of distinctive style can be discerned and they seldom coincide with imperial reigns. In the third century the person behind the laws was probably the secretary *a libellis*, who was often a famous jurist, like Papinian, Ulpian, or Modestine. Later the task was assigned to the imperial quaestor.[26]

Most laws that are discussed in this study had little direct political significance, and the status of women as such was hardly a contentious issue inside the imperial administration. However, subjects like inheritance, sexual behaviour, and family law in general could be of great importance in the long term. It is possible and indeed probable that some emperors pursued a deliberate policy in regard to them, especially if they had a long reign and could devote their time to something beyond mere power struggles. Augustus, Constantine, and Justinian are the most obvious examples of this. Some others may just have

[24] See e.g. the titles CT 3. 5, 4. 6; and Gaudemet (1965) 23–33.
[25] D. 22. 5. 3. 3 (Hadrian), 28. 4. 3 (Marcus), 4. 4. 38, 32. 27. 1, 36. 1. 76. 1 (a Severan emperor); CI 7. 26. 6 (Philippus), 9. 47. 12, 10. 48. 2 (Diocletian and Maximian) 12. 46. 1; CT 8. 15. 1 (Constantine), 11. 39. 5 (Julian).
[26] Honoré, e.g. (1979; 1986; 1993); see also Millar (1977: 203–72, 507–46; 1986); and for the quaestor, Harries (1988).

followed their legal advisers when they had to deal with such matters or they may even have routinely subscribed laws which an influential official presented to them.[27] I have tried to avoid wordings like 'a law of Valentinian III', especially for periods when the emperor in question was, for example, under 12 years old. But even when such expressions are used it should be clear that we can never reliably identify the actual planner or designer behind an individual law.

Leaving now the problems of authenticity and authorship, we have to tackle a few other general questions. The first is the validity of the laws. After the death of Constantine in 337, the empire was unified for only short periods. When there were two or more emperors reigning simultaneously their edicts did not automatically apply to the whole empire. In the fourth century there may have been some attempts to co-ordinate eastern and western legislation but in the fifth century it became more and more difficult. It was a pure convention to begin each law with the names of all emperors: the place of issue usually reveals which chancellery was responsible for an individual edict. When the Theodosian Code was brought into use in 438 both in the east and in the west it contained many laws which had never been seen in the other half of the empire, a fact which evidently caused some confusion.[28]

The second problem is the efficiency of the laws. It ought to be clear from the very beginning that constitutions were only normative statements, not descriptions of actual behaviour. 'How, to what extent and to whom the content of the constantly evolving case-law of imperial rulings was known in the provinces is a question which—if there were any way of answering it—would be of fundamental importance for the nature of the empire.'[29] The Roman government had very insufficient means to ensure that the laws were obeyed. Even high officials might be unaware of previous legislation. Of course, legal texts can tell much about social reality if they can be properly interpreted. Whenever a particular regulation is frequently repeated, we may suspect that the government considered the problem somehow relevant.

---

[27] For a famous anecdote of Theodosius II and his sister Pulcheria, see Zonar. 13. 23, PG 134. 1193.   [28] See Levy (1959b) 2–5; Kaser (1975) 4–5, 55–6.
[29] Millar (1983) 77.

It is also likely that earlier rulings had proved ineffective.[30] On the other hand, we cannot deny that very often Roman law was known, at least among the upper and middle classes. Such knowledge is attested, for example, by the constant need for imperial dispensations and by the many ingenious ways which private citizens found around the law. The obscure relationship between law and reality will be a recurrent theme in this study.

The third question is the general development of the legal system. Justinian's great collection gives a picture which emphasizes continuity and downplays changes in Roman law. It is not only because obsolete texts were omitted but also because Justinian deliberately returned to classical models even where they were clearly anachronistic. It follows that many of the legal institutions which he had revived remained mere oddities and had only an antiquarian value in his society. But it also follows that, if we find an old third-century rule in the sixth-century *Corpus Iuris Civilis* it bears little evidence of legal or social conditions in the intervening period.[31]

This intervening period is the time of the vulgarization of Roman law. It is usually taken to have begun after the reign of Diocletian, in the early fourth century. Anyone who compares fourth- and fifth-century legal texts with earlier ones must instantly notice a clear change, at least a change of style. The edicts are verbose and highly rhetorical, exaggerating moral indignation and threatening terrible penalties. Sometimes these laws were drafted by people who were better versed in rhetoric than in the juridic tradition. But often there is nothing particularly vulgar in the legal content, and it is better not to confuse rhetorical expression with 'vulgar law'. The high style seems to have been used especially in general edicts, and it can be seen already in the tetrarchic period, for instance in a famous emotional marriage law. On the other hand, the few surviving short rescripts from the fourth century are surprisingly similar to their third-century predecessors. In all, it may be that the change in legislation was not quite as great as the extant evidence would lead us to think.[32]

---

[30] Cf. e.g. MacMullen (1964). For ignorance of existing law, see *Const. Sirm.* 1 (333); and for difficulties in maintaining law and order, Symm. *rel.* 23, 31.

[31] On Justinian, see e.g. Levy (1929: 240; 1959*b*; 1960); Kaser (1975) 32–9, 51, 463–4.

[32] See Coll. 6. 4 (295); cf. e.g. CT 3. 16. 1, 9. 9. 1, 9. 24. 1; and for a more sober style, Cons. 9. See also Wieacker (1983) 250–1; Turpin (1985); Honoré (1986) 140–56; Evans Grubbs (1989) 82–3.

It would take many pages to present all the possible definitions of vulgar law, and it might be meaningless because from now on I will avoid the term.[33] To choose only one definition: vulgarization can be described as a tendency to make law more easily comprehensible to all. After Roman law had been extended to cover the whole empire, it was impossible to uphold the old standards of juridic profession any more. The exact and logically beautiful terminology was too difficult to learn, so that it was frequently misunderstood and gradually abandoned. This tendency was strongest in the law of property and obligations and less pronounced in the law of persons and family, which by their nature were easier to perceive. Certainly the development led to a lower general level of legal culture. On the other hand, for the great majority of imperial subjects the urban upper-class jurisprudence had always remained a rather theoretical option.

Of course, the Roman world was changing all the time, economically, socially, and culturally. Law had to be adapted to the new circumstances, and this was not the same thing as vulgarization. Moreover, provincial practices had to be taken into consideration, especially after the universal grant of citizenship in 212. Roman law was, according to many scholars, 'Christianized', 'hellenized', or even 'orientalized'. All these tendencies coincided and crossed, but again they were not vulgarization in the strict sense. In practice, it is often a highly controversial question how a particular legal change should be classified. As our primary interest lies in women's history and not legal history, we need not discuss this vast topic here on a theoretical level. Change in concrete cases will be examined in individual chapters.

Thus there were strong but rather undefined forces which were changing Roman law in this period. The development was slower in the east: there juridic schools tried to preserve the classical tradition, paving the way for Justinian's classicizing legal policy. Although this was an admirable feat in theory, it was also anachronistic. In the west there was less restraint, and in the fifth century norms of a more archaic and primitive society gradually surfaced. From a juridic point of view this development can hardly be cherished, but it certainly reflects more faithfully the

---

[33] On vulgar law, see above all Levy (1951*a*) 1–17; and his articles listed in the Bibliography; Kaser (1967; 1975: 3–40); Wieacker (1972; 1983).

realities of its time. That is why a social historian may find the western evidence more valuable.

Law in the Germanic Kingdoms

In the course of the fifth century the western Roman provinces were one after another overrun by Germanic immigrants. However, the Germanic kings did not want to assume legislative power over the former provincials. Thus, as there was no 'Roman' legal authority, there could not be new 'Roman' legislation. What the native people could expect from their surviving jurisprudents was reworked compendia and explanations of existing law, especially of the Theodosian Code. Such activity seems to have been lively in the decades around 500 in the Visigothic and Burgundian territories in southern Gaul. One might think that unoriginal works of this kind are a rather arid source for social history. In actual fact, it is highly interesting to see what was included in the collections. Although the compilers occasionally allowed through details which were not relevant to their society, in general they wanted to avoid antiquated and useless institutions.

By far the largest and most influential of these compendia was the so-called *Breviarium Alaricianum* or *Lex Romana Visigothorum*.[34] The Visigothic king Alaric II had it prepared for his Roman subjects in 506. Its main part was an abridgement of the Theodosian Code. The original constitutions were accompanied by *interpretationes*, relatively short résumés which attempted to explain the legal substance in a simpler language, without rhetorical embroidery. The *interpretationes* cannot be dated more accurately than to the period between 438 and 506, but evidently they were not all written at the same time nor by the same persons. The *Breviarium* contained further some other abridged texts, among them the postclassical Sentences of Paul (original from *c.* AD 300) and an epitome of Gaius' Institutes. Although the Visigoths were soon driven out of Gaul, the *Breviarium* retained its position and became the most important source of Roman law in the Frankish dominions.

At about the same time as the Romans of Spain and southwestern Gaul received the *Breviarium*, the Burgundian king

---

[34] See Gaudemet (1965); Siems (1978); Nehlsen (1982).

issued another code, the *Lex Romana Burgundionum*, for his own Romans. It was a much shorter work and it, too, was a compendium of reworked Roman law as it was applied in the provinces. It is not known whether it had much practical importance after the rapid collapse of the Burgundian kingdom. This does not, however, affect its value as a historical source, especially as it can be compared with a contemporary code for the Burgundians themselves, the *Lex Burgundionum*.[35]

Somewhat more problematic is the third major 'vulgar Roman' collection, which is called the *Edictum Theoderici*. It was based on late Roman law but was aimed at both Romans and Germans. It has traditionally been ascribed to the Ostrogothic king Theoderic the Great (489–526). That is still the dominant view, although several other possibilities have been raised: an alternative is to place the edict in southern Gaul in the reign of the Visigothic Theoderic II (453–66).[36] From our viewpoint, the attribution does not make such a big difference. The *Edictum Theoderici* is in any case the work of late Roman jurists for a mixed population under a Germanic king.

Visigoths were the first Germans to codify laws for themselves. King Euric's Code from the 470s is known only through a short manuscript fragment and through later collections. Next came the Code of Leovigild (568–86), which incorporated a great number of Eurician laws but has not been directly transmitted either. Most of its provisions have been preserved in the *Lex Visigothorum* (654), where they were marked with the label '*antiqua*', to separate them from seventh-century laws. In contrast to Euric's and Leovigild's Codes, the *Lex Visigothorum* applied to both Germans and Romans. It was again reworked in 681.[37]

[35] See Amira and Eckhardt (1960) 33–4; Nehlsen (1978a and 1978b); Schott (1979) 35–6; Wood (1994) 115.
[36] See e.g. Amira and Eckhardt (1960) 20, 28; Becker (1971); Kaser (1975) 45 n. 43; Schott (1979) 34–5. Cf. Sidon. *ep.* 2. 1. 3; *carm.* 5. 562. For legal conditions in the Ostrogothic Kingdom, see Cass. *var.* 1. 27. 1, 7. 3; 8. 3. 4, 9. 14. 7–8.
[37] See Isid. *Goth.* 35, 51; Zeumer (1898) i. 423 ff.; Amira and Eckhardt (1960) 16–27; Levy (1962); Kaser (1975) 44–5; Schott (1979) 32–3. In the following the '*antiquae*' are abbreviated LV.Ant; Nehlsen (1978c) 1969–71, is somewhat more sceptical about their authenticity. He has also raised the possibility that the 'Code of Euric' actually dates from the reign of Euric's son Alaric II, see (1978c; 1982: 182–5).

The legislation of the Franks has posed almost insurmountable problems for modern editors and legal historians. The most important part of Merovingian legislation is the *Lex Salica*. Its earliest version, the so-called 'A' redaction, or *Pactus Legis Salicae*, seems to date back to the early sixth century, perhaps to the reign of king Clovis himself. There followed a number of successive redactions until the Carolingian period, all of which are so contaminated in the manuscripts that there is serious doubt whether the 'original' text can be reconstructed at all. It has nevertheless been attempted. The *Pactus* probably in some degree reflects Frankish society in its early stage, whereas the later redactions may have been literary more than juridic products. What practical effect this collection had in the Merovingian state, if any, remains an open question.[38]

The Ripuarian Franks had their own code, as did their neighbours the Alamans: both date from the seventh century. The laws of the Anglo-Saxons, from the seventh century onwards, were the only ones that were not written in Latin. But all these have only very limited relevance to our study.[39] More important is the legislation of the Langobards in Italy. Their first code, the *Edictus Rothari* (643), is a collection of archaic norms even if the authors outwardly knew both Roman law and earlier Germanic codes. The *Leges Liutprandi* (712–44) already display more Roman influences.[40]

Compared with classical Roman jurisprudence, the Germanic laws reflect an alien world. There is little discussion of commerce but much of agriculture, livestock, and damage caused by animals. In most Germanic societies, like the Merovingian, the central government was weak indeed. It could not safeguard complex obligations or private agreements. People easily resorted to violent self-help, which ended up in long blood feuds between families. The kings could only attempt to restrict such practices. For this reason the laws laid down exhaustive rules

---

[38] Wood (1994) 102–19, is a survey of Merovingian legislation. On the textual tradition, see Nehlsen (1972) 251–8, 356–7; Schmidt-Wiegand (1978*b*); Schott (1979) 36–8; Murray (1983) 119–27. On the relationship between Frankish law and social reality, Nehlsen (1977) 449–83; Schott (1979) 48–9; Murray (1983) 128–33.

[39] Amira and Eckhardt (1960) 57–68, 73–4; Schmidt-Wiegand (1978*a*); Schott (1978; 1979: 38–43).

[40] Amira and Eckhardt (1960) 69–72; Nehlsen (1972) 414–16; Dilcher (1978).

about how certain damages should be compensated: if you put out your neighbour's eye you had to pay him 100 *solidi* and hope that he was content with that; if you broke his thumb it was 50 *solidi*, or 36 for a forefinger, and so on. Production of evidence could be supplemented by a purification oath or a ritual duel. There were very concrete methods to measure the gravity of the damage:

Si quis in caput vel in quacumque libet membro placatus fuerit, et ossum inde exierit, qui super viam duodecim pedorum in scuto sonaverit, 30 et 6 solidos factore culpabilis iudicetur. (LRib 71. 1)

If someone has been hit in the head or in any part of the body and a [chip of] bone has come out which can elicit a sound from a shield placed across a road twelve feet wide, the offender shall pay a penalty of 36 *solidi*.

The archaic, 'barbarian' elements, both in language and in substance, are most conspicuous in Frankish and early Lango-bardic legislation, to say nothing of Anglo-Saxon. They are the best available sources if we are looking for ideas and customs which were originally Germanic (*urgermanisch*). But we have to remember that the Germanic codes did not form a closed system: it was not possible to find an unambiguous solution to each individual dispute. If a clear general statement is lacking, it does not automatically follow that those specific problems were absent from the given society. There may have existed some well-known broad norms whose application in individual cases was ill-defined. In the absence of strict legal rules several people were able to lay claims to a property. Any 'rights' might thus be debatable. Such situations could naturally arise in the Roman empire, too, but they were certainly much more common in the early medieval kingdoms.[41]

On the other hand, to produce written codifications at all, the Germans had to use the Latin language and to be aware of Roman legislation. The Visigoths and Burgundians had for decades been living in areas where the proportion of Roman population was great. They could avail themselves of the Roman administrative experience. The Visigothic government was sufficiently estab-lished and authoritative to enforce laws in an imperial Roman

---

[41] In connection with women's landholding, see esp. Stafford (1993).

manner, or at least to attempt it. Thus their legislation shows
Roman influences from the very beginning. They are so clear that
sometimes the Code of Euric seems to provide indirect evidence
for late fifth-century Roman legal custom.

The differentiation between 'Roman' and 'Germanic' law in
early medieval Europe is by no means a simple task. The decline
and collapse of the empire, with its economic, social, and administrative consequences, had levelled differences between the two
cultures. When Roman law was 'vulgarized', it could more easily
be understood by the Romans themselves but also by the Germanic immigrants. In many issues their views may not have been
radically different. The same primitive characteristics which have
been ascribed to the naïve rusticity of the first barbarian legislators could often equally well be interpreted as the logical end-
product of vulgarized Roman law. Influences could go in both
directions, and the possibility of parallel development is in many
cases very strong.[42]

In Spain Roman law retained its official position until the
middle of the seventh century, when the *Lex Visigothorum*
became common law for both population groups.[43] In Langobardic Italy people of Roman descent preserved their own legal
system at least to the eighth century, while some parts of the
peninsula were still under Byzantine and papal rule.[44] In Gaul
the Romans continued to use the old law in their mutual relations
under the Franks. This practice was confirmed by king Chlothar
II at the turn of the seventh century.[45] Roman law seems to have
survived as a theoretical concept well into the Carolingian period:
from the ninth century more manuscripts of the *Breviarium* have
been preserved than from any other period. In the preceding
century the *Breviarium* was further abbreviated in a number of
epitomes. They bear witness to a continuing interest in the old
legacy. On the other hand, the epitomizers sometimes misunder-

---

[42] See Levy (1942; 1950; 1951a: 14–17, 96–9); Nehlsen (1972) 38–51; Schott (1979)
45; Murray (1983) 116–18; Wood (1986; 1993); Geary (1988) 90–1.

[43] Zeumer (1898) i. 477–86; King (1972) 18; see also Wretschko, in the introduction to Mommsen's edition of the Theodosian Code, pp. cccviii–cccxiii.

[44] LL 91, 127; cf. also Frezza (1974); and generally for the Byzantine rule, Brown
(1984).

[45] *Praec. Chloth.* 4 (MGH Capit. i. p. 19); for the continuing knowledge of the
Theodosian Code, see Greg. Tur. *franc.* 4. 46; *Vita Desiderii* 1; *Vita Boniti* 2 (MGH
Scriptores rer. Merov. iv. 564; vi. 120); and Wood (1993).

stood their original so badly that it is difficult to speak of a living tradition.[46]

What about the practical influence of Roman law? Our main sources are the Formularies, or collections of so-called *formulae*, stereotyped pattern books which scribes used when they drafted actual documents. They date from the seventh and eighth centuries but probably represent much older models. Some types may go back to late Roman documentary practice, although the lack of comparison material makes it impossible to attest. In any case, the *formulae* display a bewildering mixture of 'Roman' and 'Germanic' elements. Often they seem to copy expressions of Roman law rather mechanically, and it is doubtful whether they testify to any real knowledge of its substance any more. The only thing which they certainly prove is some kind of confusion of the two legal systems. It is also remarkable that in 633/4 a Frankish woman in her will refers to the 'Theodosian law'. As late as in the tenth century scribes sometimes used Roman legal phraseology without really understanding it. And in some regions, like the Rhaetian Alps, customary law preserved strong Roman elements beyond the first millennium. We may suspect that the same happened in other parts of western Europe, too, wherever the people of Roman descent formed the vast majority.[47]

Other Sources

To bridge the gap between normative statements and real life we naturally have to use all other available evidence from the late ancient world. The most obvious sources are documents recording genuine transactions. We have just seen that the *formulae* in early medieval Gaul offer some help. On the other hand, being entirely stereotyped, their probative force has clear limits. There are some authentic charters from the sixth century, and a few more from the next. Use has been made of them whenever possible, but on the whole the documentary evidence increases

---

[46] Wretschko, (n. 43 above), pp. cccxiii ff.; Steinwenter (1951); Gaudemet (1955a) 149–77, 205–6. On the epitomes, see Gaudemet (1965) 41–57; and on the so-called *Lex Romana Curiensis*, Meyer-Marthaler (1978).

[47] Gaudemet (1955a) 177–206; Wretschko, (n. 43 above), pp. cccxiv, cccxxii–cccxxiii; and for the Alpine area, Meyer-Marthaler (1975). See also Classen (1977). For the will of Burgundofara, Pard. 257; Guerout (1965).

only in the eighth century, and for the most part falls outside the scope of this study.

An occasional find in the border mountains of modern Algeria and Tunisia has brought to light a number of wooden tablets, the so-called *Tablettes Albertini*. They are mostly deeds of sale written in the 490s in the area then under Vandalic kings. The sellers were very humble sorts of people, but the buyers were obviously better off, and the documents testify to a continuing Roman notarial tradition. In Italy the episcopal archives of Ravenna have preserved some fifty papyri from the sixth and seventh centuries (published in *P.Tjäder* i–ii). They are of varied nature but the greater part are either donations or sales. Many of them are highly relevant for the legal position of women. Unfortunately, their absolute number is still so small that few firm conclusions can be drawn.

Of course, the area best documented in the Mediterranean world is Egypt. Tens of thousands of papyri supply just the sort of evidence from everyday life which we lack for the west: letters, contracts, wills, petitions, official records, court proceedings, and so forth. In principle, they reveal what ordinary people thought of legal matters. In practice, however, a particular expression may often have gone back to the scribe rather than to the parties concerned: the latter were commonly illiterate. Many papyri leave further uncertainty because of their fragmentary condition. The material as such is plentiful for the whole of our period, with the exception of the fifth century, which for unknown reasons is more sparsely represented. The basic remaining question is the validity of all this evidence. As very few papyri survive from elsewhere, we cannot straight away generalize the individual phenomena which are found inside Egypt. So far there is no clear solution to this problem.[48]

A peculiar eastern source is the Syro–Roman Law Book. It is known through a number of Aramaic, Arabic, and Armenian manuscripts but its core probably goes back to a Greek original from the late fifth century. It seems to present mainly Roman imperial law, mixed with some local or 'vulgar' elements, perhaps for elementary legal training. It is very difficult to use because

---

[48] For women in late Roman Egypt, see now esp. the methodically rigorous treatment of Beaucamp (1992*a*) 3–267; and for Egypt in general, Bagnall (1993).

there is no general consensus on its nature and reliability, and even the translation of many details remains obscure.[49]

For the purely 'literary' sources, a very general introduction may suffice. In theory, any secular or ecclesiastical author writing within our period is a potential source. It is perhaps somewhat disappointing that where we find some information on women, marriage, or the family, the writers tend to avoid all legal terminology. In the vast majority of cases we cannot infer from the narrative anything about the juridic context. One might be tempted to conclude that law simply did not matter. And certainly such details in themselves did not interest the contemporary audience. However, we cannot automatically assume that they played no role in the train of events.

Literary sources for the third and early fourth century are not particularly abundant. The church fathers Tertullian, Cyprian and Lactantius are perhaps the best known names of this period, and they do provide some useful bits of information. It is only in the late fourth century that the situation improves dramatically. True, the last great Latin historian, Ammianus Marcellinus, is a relatively poor source for women's history. But we now have a number of very productive Christian writers, who were interested not only in consecrated virgins and widows but also wrote about marriage and everyday life. This group comprises Augustine in North Africa, Ambrose and Jerome in Italy, John Chrysostom in Antioch and Constantinople, Basil, Gregory of Nazianzus, and Gregory of Nyssa in Asia Minor, and many less famous personalities. Their sermons, letters, and moral treatises paint a vivid picture of the late Roman world and its inhabitants, both male and female. A few pagan writers, like the rhetorician Libanius in Antioch, supplement the overall view and suggest that religious differences should not be over-emphasized.

After the early fifth century, literary activity again decreased, especially in the west. The voluminous correspondence of Sidonius Apollinaris still describes Roman life in Gaul in the latter part of the century. Caesarius of Arles wrote sermons to admon-

---

[49] The standardized Latin rendering in FIRA ii. 751–98 is handy but not always accurate. See above all Selb (1964), with critical remarks by Yaron (1966); and Kaser (1975) 49–50, with further references.

ish his parishioners in the first half of the sixth. A few decades later Gregory of Tours composed a history of the Merovingian kingdom, which relates the names of a number of Roman potentates in the late sixth century but reveals little of their culture and customs. On the other hand, the official letters of pope Gregory the Great belong firmly to the Roman world. They show a solitary figure at the turn of the seventh century, trying to preserve law and order in a classical civilization which is crumbling around him as one Italian city after another is lost to the Langobards.

Numerous church councils, especially from Spain and Gaul, supply additional material. From our point of view, the most interesting topics in their canons are divorce, sexual offences, monastic discipline, and the consecration of virgins. Saints' lives are another new literary genre which deserves attention. It is worth noting that women's biographies had not been written in pagan antiquity. Their achievements were not sufficiently remarkable in the classical value system. This clearly changed in the Christian world. Female ascetics were able to display the same virtues as their male counterparts and were duly remembered for it. Many such biographies from the fourth and fifth centuries are valuable sources for women's life in general. In the early middle ages the hagiographic tradition continued, but the proportion of legendary material increased, and dramatic miracles became more important than the real-life story. Besides, female saints perhaps spent more of their lives inside a convent than in earlier periods. That is why Merovingian hagiographies lose some of their value as a historical source.[50]

In all, we cannot claim that there is no material from late antiquity. For some periods and some topics there is even an abundance of it. But, by and large, it is not abundant after the early fifth century nor very rich for our purposes. The sources for early Byzantine women have recently been examined in a thorough way. My present search seems to yield some western

---

[50] For women's biographies, see e.g. Hier. *ep.* 108 (Paula), 127 (Marcella); Geront. *vita Melaniae*, SC 90; *Vita Olympiadis*, SC 13bis; Greg. Nyss. *vita Macrinae*, SC 178; Pallad. *hist. laus. (passim)*. The most important Merovingian female hagiographies have been translated and discussed by McNamara (1992). Generally, on women's praise, cf. Trojesen (1992).

evidence which has hitherto escaped general attention. However, a careful reading of all the western sources from the fifth and sixth centuries would certainly bring forward many other passages to complement the picture given here.[51]

[51] For the east, see Beaucamp (1992a) 271–365; and for Gaul, cf. Krause (1991). I would not characterize the general evidence quite as optimistically as Cameron (1993b) 8–9.

2

Fathers and Children

One of the most peculiar features of Roman law was the father's dominant position. In theory, he exercised an almost absolute authority, *patria potestas*, over his descendants until his own death. This should not be confused with the power of the kin. In societies where central power is weak, kinship groups have often taken a key role in securing internal order and external security. It is true that the system of *patria potestas* fulfilled some of these functions, providing a means of social control within the family. There was thus less need for direct state involvement in many areas.[1] The Roman republic did not have a particularly strong central government, and even in the imperial era the machinery of the state was only slowly developing. However, the clans (*gentes*) had already lost all practical importance in Roman law.

The nearest paternal relatives linked through males formed a special group, called *agnati*, comprising brothers, sisters, paternal uncles, aunts, cousins, and second cousins. The agnates were well placed in the law of succession and would be legitimate guardians for orphaned minors (see Ch. 3, Sects. 2–3). Originally they were entitled to the guardianship over adult women, too (Ch. 4, Sect. 1). During the empire the agnatic kin no longer had any noteworthy control over its grown-up members. All power was centred on the individual *paterfamilias*, whose death made his children independent citizens (*sui iuris*).

This characteristic structure of the Roman family had far-reaching consequences for the position of women in Roman law. It did not show only in the relationship between fathers and children. The system of paternal power affected women also in their roles as mothers and wives. So the present chapter

[1] For *patria potestas*, see Gardner (1993) 32–84, cf. esp. 83, 179–80.

will in part serve as an introduction to the following two chapters, which look at the Roman family from the viewpoints of a mother and a wife.

This is not a book on Roman children. Very little could in fact be said about them on the basis of legal material. Thus we shall begin only at the moment when girls reached marriageable age, which happened when they were very young by modern standards. It is a useful starting-point because it also introduces us to the basic demographic facts underlying the Roman family.

I. GIVING A CHILD IN MARRIAGE

The Marriage of Sons

In the Roman empire, people were not expected to marry for love. The choice of spouse was ideally not an emotional but a rational decision, often financial and in the aristocracy sometimes political. According to common sense, what mattered was above all such things as the partner's wealth, rank, birth, and good character. But although most participants in the upper classes tried to apply these conventional criteria, there may occasionally have been room for romantic love. The few surviving Greek novels perhaps reflect the fantasy of premarital romance but other evidence for it is rare indeed in the Roman world. However, one thing is clear: in Roman law neither sons nor daughters could contract a valid marriage without the consent of their *paterfamilias*. [2]

These principles remained unchanged throughout late antiquity. There is no indication whatsoever that arranged marriages would have been less popular among Christian Romans.[3] Prudent parents might negotiate the marriage so that the bride and groom had not even seen each other before the ceremonies. Love was

---

[2] D. 23. 2. 2; UE 5. 2; PS 2. 29. 2; CI 5. 4. 7 (240), 5. 4. 12 (285), 5. 4. 25 (530); CT 3. 5. 2. pr (319) + int; CT 3. 7. 1 (371); Nov. 22. 19; Inst. 1. 10. pr; Apul. *met.* 6. 9; Tert. *uxor.* 2. 8. 6, CCL 1. 393; Plut. *mulier. virt.* 12 (249D); etc. Corbett (1930) 53–67, and Treggiari (1982), with further references. For the criteria of choice, and marriage-markets in the principate, Treggiari (1991a: 83–138, 259–60; 1991c). For the novels, see e.g. Egger (1994).

[3] Ideological changes are postulated e.g. by Musca (1988) 169–73. On the legislation, see Voci (1985) 1–21, and further below.

hoped for, but only from the day after wedding.[4] Matchmakers
were often used to conduct the first discreet enquiries and suggest
suitable candidates. In the eastern empire elderly women seem to
have worked as *promnestriai* on a professional basis. In the west
matchmaking was an amateur activity conducted by friends and
relatives, at least among the upper classes. To take a somewhat
surprising example, in Augustine's correspondence we find a
Christian bishop who is trying to find a spouse for a pagan
man. The lawgivers mentioned matchmakers perhaps with
some reserve, but the activity itself was not illegal.[5]

Before having a closer look at the situation of daughters we will
briefly review what chances a son may have had to choose his
marriage partner. In theory, children could not legally be married
against their own wishes. It was quite possible that a son found a
suitable bride and secured his father's consent afterwards.[6] In
practice, however, the father was considered the best person to
make a successful match. The sons often simply accepted his
decision, sometimes with indifference, sometimes grudgingly.
For example, Ambrose was once approached by a young man
in trouble. His father, a proconsul, was planning to marry him
to his own niece, that is, the old man's granddaughter. The
prospective groom did not like the idea at all but he was too
obedient to oppose his father openly. Ambrose reminded the
proconsul that such a marriage was impossible not only on
religious grounds but also because it had been forbidden by
imperial law. Evidently he was able to save the youth.[7]

Another time Ambrose pleaded leniency towards a son who
had already married on independent initiative (*ep.* 35, CSEL 82. 1.
238ff.). He naturally admitted that the son should have awaited

[4] Joh. Chrys. *virg.* 57. 1–2, SC 125. 308; *cat. bapt.* 1. 12, SC 50. 115; *in Matth.* 73.
4, PG 58. 678; *qual. duc. ux.* 3, PG 51. 230; Beaucamp (1992a) 295–6. Love letters are
not known from antiquity; one amusing piece is included in an 8th-c. Frankish
Formulary, F.Sal.Merk. 47; cf. also Bagnall (1993) 190–1.

[5] For the whole topic, Noy (1990). See e.g. Lib. *ep.* 1488. 1; Joh. Chrys. *in psalm.*
48. 7, PG 55. 509; Symm. *ep.* 6. 3, 9. 49; Aug. *ep.* 252–5, CSEL 57. 600ff. (this and the
following not discussed by Noy); CT 3. 7. 1 (371); CI 5. 1. 6 (472/534 east).

[6] D. 23. 1. 13, 23. 2. 2, 21, 22; CI 5. 4. 5, 12; see Treggiari (1991a) 170–80.

[7] Ambr. *ep.* 58–9, CSEL 82. 2. 112ff.; on marriage between close kin, cf. Coll. 6.
4. 5 (295); CT 3. 12. 1 (342), 3. 12. 3 (396 east); Symm. *ep.* 9. 133. See further Sen.
contr. 2. 3. 2; Gell. 2. 7. 18–20; Amm. 28. 1. 35; Aug. *ep.* 255, CSEL 57. 602; Joh.
Chrys. *in psalm.* 48. 7, PG 55. 509; *in I Thess.* 5. 3, PG 62. 426; *de inani glor.* 81, SC
188. 186; Paul. Pell. 176–81, CSEL 16. 298; Greg. Tur. *vit. patr.* 6. 1; 16. 1; 20. 1.

the father's superior judgement, but he was happy to hear that
the father had accepted the fact afterwards and was ready to
welcome his new daughter-in-law. This incident shows that
young men were sometimes able to conclude a marriage without
the knowledge of their *paterfamilias*. Sidonius Apollinaris illustrates the same thing in a little story from the 470s (*ep.* 7. 2). A
well-mannered young man had managed to make high connections in Marseilles. As it later turned out, he was of modest but
reputable background and had secretly left his home because his
father was too niggardly towards him. He was thus an almost
penniless stranger and a *filiusfamilias*, as Sidonius stressed. But
since this was not known, he was able to marry a rich girl, whose
widowed mother did not check his background. When the
mother started regretting, it was too late: she was already blessed
with grandchildren (though Sidonius may be dramatizing here),
and the brave fortune-hunter carried his wife back to his native
town. We can only guess at the father's reactions. Sidonius does
not give a hint that the marriage might have been claimed invalid.

Roman males usually entered their first marriage around their
late twenties or even early thirties. The sons of the aristocracy
married in their early twenties, possibly because it was easier to
separate a share of the family property for them.[8] These estimates
apply only to the principate. Nothing certain can be said of later
developments. The epigraphical evidence we have, mainly from
the fourth century, does not indicate any radical changes.[9] In
theory, if young Christian men or their fathers could be per-
suaded that premarital sex was morally wrong, they would have
been more eager to marry early. For example, the parents of
Paulinus of Pella stopped his affairs with slave girls and forced
him to marry when he was 20. But it is by no means clear that this
was a typical case. Augustine claims that when he was 15 his
parents paid no heed to his sexual experiments. As we will later
see, male attitudes to sexual life do not seem to have changed
much during late antiquity.[10]

[8] Saller (1986): 12–15; 1987: esp. 25–9; 1994: 36–41); cf. also Hopkins (1965) 321–5;
Parkin (1992) 125; and for Egypt, Bagnall and Frier (1994) 116.
[9] See Nordberg (1963) 67–9; Hopkins (1965) 325; and esp. Carletti (1977) 42–4.
Cf. also Herlihy (1985) 17–23, whose suggestions are based on a number of saints'
lives and a very small sample of inscriptions; and Krause (1991) 542–3.
[10] Paul. Pell. 176–81, CSEL 16. 289; Aug. *conf.* 2. 2. 4. See also Joh. Chrys. *de
inani glor.* 81, SC 188. 186; *in I Thess.* 5. 3, PG 62. 426; *in I Tim.* 9. 2, PG 62. 546;

Another important demographic point is that Roman fathers died relatively young. On this there is no reliable statistical evidence from antiquity. Instead, we have to use model life tables based on empirical data from known populations, especially those with high childhood mortality. This may seem dangerous, and the tables naturally cannot claim any accuracy. It is nevertheless widely accepted that they give a useful impression of the demographic conditions in the Roman world. For example, they suggest that of all Romans living at the age of 25, something in the order of one half would still have been alive thirty years later. Coming back to our present topic, this meant that well over half of the young men had already lost their father when they contemplated marriage.[11]

Thus it is no wonder that legal texts in late antiquity suppose bridegrooms to be independent subjects, without any mention of their fathers.[12] A young man who had lost his father was not legally bound to the opinion of anyone else.[13] Of course, this did not prevent a mother from arranging her 30-year-old son's marriage, as Monica did for Augustine (*conf.* 6. 13. 23, CCL 27. 89). In late Roman law such maternal influence was strictly unofficial. In Visigothic law a mother was openly entitled to supervise her children's marriage. If she had died or remarried, elder brothers or uncles undertook the task of marrying off young people.[14]

The Marriage of Daughters

Girls in the Roman empire were usually first married in their late teens. There was considerable variation within this pattern, and many girls married quite young, in their early teens. It is not clear whether these youngest brides belonged to a particular social class: the aristocracy at least probably tended to marry their

---

Conc. Hipp. (393) 2 CCL 149. 20; *Brev. Hipp.* 18, CCL 149. 38; and cf. Brown (1987) 265; Krause (1994*a*) 31. For male sexual morals, see below Ch. 6, Sects. 1–2.

[11] See Saller (1986: 14–15; 1987: 31–3; and 1994: 48–65, 121), for some attractive estimates. On the problems of ancient demographic evidence and on the use of model life-tables, see Parkin (1992), esp. 70–85, and tables 6–10; Saller (1994) 9–69; Bagnall and Frier (1994), esp. 75–110.

[12] CT 3. 5. 5. int, 3. 11. 1; CI 5. 17. 11. pr; etc.

[13] CI 5. 4. 8 (241); the same applied to an emancipated son (see below Ch. 2, Sect. 2), D. 23. 2. 25; 37. 4. 3. 5.

[14] LV.Ant 3. 1. 7; cf. King (1972) 230; Greg. Tur. *vit. patr.* 9. 1.

daughters at puberty or soon after.[15] Be this as it may, Roman wives in their first marriage were on an average almost ten years younger than their spouses.

When the pagan inscriptions of Rome (roughly first to third century) are compared with the Christian ones (mostly fourth century) the typical age at marriage for girls appears to have risen a few years although it was still under 20. The difference between the two samples has been explained either as a religious change, or a religiously neutral social development. Or it may simply indicate a change in the social distribution of funerary commemoration, since the lower classes are thought to have married later.[16] Interesting as these suggestions are, they offer little concrete help, given all the methodic problems. Because of the lack of inscriptional evidence, similar scrutiny cannot be extended further than the fourth century. Occasional anecdotes suggest that at least some girls were still married very young. The 'Mediterranean marriage pattern', with a low age of girls at marriage, may have continued in some areas throughout the middle ages. But we have to reckon with considerable regional differences.[17]

The early betrothal of Roman girls meant that their father was much more often able to arrange their marriage in his lifetime. In the wording of legal as well as literary sources, the father chose his son-in-law and gave his daughter in marriage (*in matrimonium* or *nuptui collocare*): she was a passive object, in all social classes.[18] The mother, too, was usually expected to have her say in the matter. In late antiquity, both literary and legal sources sometimes reflect this idea when they speak of marriage arranged by

[15] Shaw (1987a); Saller (1994) 36–41; see also Hopkins (1965); Parkin (1992) 123–4; Raepsaet-Charlier (1994) 167–9; Krause (1994a) 22–4; for Egypt, Bagnall and Frier (1994) 111–16.

[16] Cf. Nordberg (1963) 67; Hopkins (1965) 320; Carletti (1977) 43–4; Herlihy (1985) 19–23; Shaw (1987a) 41–2.

[17] Sidon. *ep.* 7. 2. 6–7; Ven. Fort. *carm.* 4. 26. 35; 10. 2. 9; LL 112; Evans Grubbs (1995) 154–5 Verdon (1990) 243–4; Beaucamp (1992a) 296–7; Krause (1994a) 25–34; and Étienne (1978) 141, with tables 14–16 (on imperial families). Wemple (1981) 32, mentions that in Merovingian society both girls and boys were married by their mid-teens; but she produces little evidence for girls and none for boys. See also Shaw (1987a) 30–1.

[18] e.g. CI 5. 14. 3 (239); CT 3. 5. 5 (332), 3. 5. 11 (380). Greg. Nyss. *vita Macr.* 4, SC 178. 152; Hier. *ep.* 54. 6; Aug. *conf.* 9. 9. 19, CCL 27. 145; Sidon. *ep.* 3. 11. 2, 5. 10. 2; and e.g. Beaucamp (1992a) 297–9, for more references.

'the parents', but it was always a social convention rather than a legal prerequisite. There was no need to say explicitly what happened if the parents disagreed. Everyone understood that it was the *paterfamilias* who had the last word.[19]

The marriage contract was usually signed by the bridegroom and the bride's father or mother (if they were alive), with just a mention of the bride's name. Her consent was assumed and not explicitly stated. This was in a way logical. The contract was not necessary for the marriage to be valid. It was mainly intended to record the dowry which was given by the bride's parents. The girl owned no property and was herself not involved in the financial bargain.[20] Almost all marriage contracts between Roman citizens come from Egypt. None from the western empire have been preserved but among those found in Egypt two are written in Latin. They suggest that at least in the principate the Roman custom was similar.[21]

Much later, in the early medieval *formulae*, we find another type of contract. They were addressed by the groom to the bride, while the parents' consent was only reported. It is possible that such *formulae* go back to western practice in late antiquity: they have preserved many Roman elements. However, they hardly show that girls were now given more say in their own marriage. Rather, they were drawn up in a different financial situation. At that time, only the groom gave gifts (*donatio nuptialis*) to the bride, and little property was transferred from the bride's side. Thus her parents were no longer direct participants in the transaction. In fact, a similar phenomenon is attested in one Byzantine marriage contract from Egypt.[22]

[19] See e.g. Liv. 38. 57. 7; Dixon (1988) 62–3; CT 3. 5. 2. pr (319) 9. 24. 1. pr (320/326), 3. 11. 1. pr (380 east), 3. 10. 1 (409 west); CI 5. 1. 5. 1 (472 east); Nov. 143 (563); Joh. Chrys. *in I Tim*. 9. 2, PG 62. 547; *in psalm*. 48. 7, PG 55. 509; *virg*. 57. 2, SC 125. 308; etc. Beaucamp (1990: 338; 1992a: 299–300).

[20] P.Oxy. vi. 905 (170), x. 1273 (260); P.Vind.Bosw. 5 (304); P.Ross.Georg. iii. 28 (343/358); P.Strasb. iii. 131 = SB v. 8013 (363); P.Ness. iii. 18 (Palestine, 537); CPR i. 30 II = MChr 290 (6th c.); P.Masp. i. 67006v (6th c.); cf. Montevecchi (1936) 32–5; Beaucamp (1992a) 105–27. For the validity of marriage, see CI 5. 4. 2, 9, and below, Ch. 6, Sect. 2.

[21] PSI vi. 730 (1st c.); P.Mich. vii. 434 = FIRA iii. 17 (early 2nd c.). Cf. also *Tabl. Alb.* 1 (493?).

[22] *F.Tur.* 14 (cf. CT 3. 5. 2. int); *F.Vis.* 14–20; cf. also *F.Marc.* 2. 15; and *F.Sal.Lind.* 7, containing a greater number of Germanic elements; from Egypt, P.Lond. v. 1711 = FIRA iii. 18 (566/573). On the marriage gifts, see below, Ch. 2, Sect. 3.

Of course, we cannot exclude the possibility that some girls were able to influence the decision. In theory, their consent was needed, at least in classical law. In late antiquity this requirement seems to have been thought superfluous or irrelevant: the possibility that the girl would have had any convincing reason to withhold her consent was hypothetical.[23] She had little chance to form an independent opinion. It was not proper for a tender virgin to have too detailed knowledge of the prospective suitors and, even if she had, she was not expected to show it publicly by meddling in the affair. The father was better suited to look after her interests. At the age of 12 or 15 the brides were mere children: they were simply considered too young to understand what was best for themselves. One is perhaps tempted to agree.[24]

In general, the leaders of the Christian church shared this view. They frequently stressed the importance of parental authority.[25] They made an exception only if a girl did not want to marry at all for religious reasons. In that case Ambrose went so far as to advise her to defy her parents, something which he would never have done in other circumstances. He indicated that she faced threats of disinheritance if she did not accept the parents' decision. Justinian officially removed this menace, but even after that a reluctant bride might still see her share of the inheritance diminished.[26]

If the father had died, the young woman was theoretically independent, *sui iuris*. However, she usually did not have to choose her spouse alone: she had her guardian, her mother, and other relatives to help her. Sometimes the father had explicitly charged the mother, a trusted friend, or a bishop with the task of marrying off the girl.[27] But if such instructions were lacking,

[23] D. 23. 1. 11, 23. 1. 12 (the second sentence of which is possibly interpolated), 23. 2. 2; CI 5. 4. 20 (409 west), 5. 17. 11. pr (533); Nov. 115. 3. 11; see Voci (1985) 19; Beaucamp (1990) 246–56.

[24] e.g. CT 3. 5. 12 (422 west), 9. 24. 1. pr (320); CI 5. 4. 20. 1 (409 west); Leo M. *ep.* 167. 4–5, PL 54. 1205. Cf. also D. 4. 4. 48. 2; Sen. *ben.* 4. 27. 5; Fronto *ep. ad amic.* 2. 11; LL 12; Treggiari (1985) 331–7; Gardner (1986) 41–3.

[25] Ambr. *Abr.* 1. 91, CSEL 32. 1. 561; Basil. *ep.* 199. 38, 42; *Conc. Aurel.* (541) 22, CCL 148A. 137; etc.

[26] Ambr. *virg.* 1. 62–6; CI 1. 3. 54. 5 (533/4); see also Geront. *vita Melan.* 12, SC 90. 150; Nov. 115. 3. 11. See further below, Ch. 2, Sect. 2 on disinheritance, and Ch. 5, Sect. 1 on the ascetic habit.

[27] D. 23. 2. 62. pr, 33. 4. 14, 35. 1. 28. pr; Greg. M. *ep.* 11. 25, 11. 59.

there were no established rules to say whose opinion should prevail.

Theoretically, it was always clear that an orphaned girl could not be married against her own wish. On the other hand, no sensible person could believe that a small child had much practical influence on the decision. It would have been frankly stupid to let her marry just because she had taken a passing fancy to someone. Moreover, she needed her guardian's financial authorization to provide a dowry for herself. We thus have a somewhat inconsistent array of sources, both legal and literary, some of which stress the rights of the bride herself while others take it for granted that her guardian and relatives in reality made the decision. The general impression is that a girl could only exceptionally choose her first husband.[28] Ideally, of course, all parties concerned were expected to agree on the matter. If they did not, the choice of the spouse could be referred to a court. It had to weigh the social standing and moral character of the candidates. It also had to ensure that the marriage was not unjustly impeded by relatives who stood to gain something if the girl died without issue.[29]

The most natural support for a young bride was her mother. After the father's death she was thought to have the greatest interest in her children's marriage. Her influence was always accepted as a social fact, so that it was usually the mother who was approached when someone wanted to marry a fatherless girl.[30] The same thing is clearly reflected in marriage contracts as well as other papyri from Egypt.[31] Augustine put it succinctly:

. . . *mater, cuius voluntatem in tradenda filia omnibus, ut arbitror, natura praeponit, nisi eadem puella in ea iam aetate fuerit, ut iure licentiore sibi eligat ipsa, quod velit.* (ep. 254, CSEL 57. 602)

[28] D. 23. 1. 6, 23. 2. 20, 57a; CI 3. 28. 20 (294), 5. 4. 1 (199), 5. 4. 20 (409), 5. 17. 11. pr (533); CT 3. 5. 5 (332), 3. 5. 11 (380), 3. 7. 1 (371); Syro-Roman Law Book L 88; Ambr. *virg.* 1. 58; *virginit.* 5. 26; Basil. *ep.* 199. 22; Greg. Nyss. *vita Macr.* 2, SC 178. 144; Theodoret. *ep.* 43, SC 40. 107; Sidon. *ep.* 2. 4, 7. 2. 6–7; Prisc. *frg.* 14–15. 3 (Blockley). For Egypt, see P.Oxy. xvii. 2133 (*c.*300); MChr 300 = P.Lips. 41 (late 4th c.); P.Masp. i. 67005 (567); Beaucamp (1992*a*) 121–7. Note that CI 5. 4. 8 (241) is addressed to a man.   [29] CI 5. 4. 1 (199); CT 3. 7. 1 (371); CI 5. 4.20 (409).
[30] e.g. Tac. *ann.* 4. 40; D. 32. 41. 7; 46. 3. 88; CI 3. 28. 20 (294); CT 3. 5. 11 (380); Amm. 28. 1. 35; Ambr. *virg.* 1. 58; Hier. *ep.* 127. 2; Theodoret. *ep.* 43, SC 40. 107; Sidon. *ep.* 2. 4, 7. 2. 6–8. Cf. Beaucamp (1990: 337–8; 1992*a*: 300).
[31] P.Oxy. x. 1273 (260); P.Vind.Bosw. 5 (304); P.Oxy. liv. 3770 (334); P.Cairo Preis. 2–3 (362); SB vi. 9239 (548); CPR i. 30 II = MChr 290 (6th c.); Taubenschlag (1929) 120–1; Beaucamp (1992*a*) 111–12, 119–20.

. . . the mother, whose choice in her daughter's marriage nature prefers, I think, to all others, unless the girl is already of such age that she can as of right choose herself what she wants.

As the context of the letter and the words *quod velit* show, Augustine did not exactly say that an older girl would choose her spouse but only that she could decide whether to marry or remain a virgin. But it is clear that the more mature the girl was the more say she had in her own betrothal, and especially if the marriage was not her first.[32]

As a rule, a marriageable woman past her teens was already a widow or divorcée. In such a case, if a father did not openly disapprove of his daughter's choice, his consent would be assumed. He had to know about it, though: otherwise the marriage was not legitimate in the eyes of the jurists.[33] A law of 371 ordered that widows who were under 25, even if they were *sui iuris*, could not marry without the consent of their relatives. On the other hand, Justinian decreed that, if the parents had not married off their daughter by that age, she could betroth herself independently, without risk of disinheritance. If a woman was over 25 and *sui iuris*, no one questioned her right to make up her own mind.[34]

Abduction Marriage

Without doubt, most marriages in the Roman empire were concluded in an orderly fashion, but occasionally things could turn out much worse for the parents. A youth who was romantically in love or just adventurous might take the initiative and

[32] See e.g. Diocletian's daughter Valeria, Lact. *mort. pers.* 39; further CT 3. 10. 1 (409 west) + int, 3. 11. 1 (380 east) + int, 9. 8. 1 (326); CI 5. 4. 20 (409 west), 5. 17. 11. pr (533). Similar thoughts seem to have lain behind Visigothic laws: LV.Ant 3. 1. 7–8, 3. 3. 4, 7, 3. 4. 2; LV 3. 1. 3, 4; cf. King (1972) 228–32; see also LB 52. 3, 66, 69; ER 182.

[33] D. 1. 5. 11, 23. 1. 7, 31. 45. 2 (an emancipated daughter may here be meant, or alternatively the marriage became valid on the father's death); CI 5. 4. 2. The third marriage of Cicero's daughter Tullia was announced before he had had time to consent, see e.g. Treggiari (1991a) 127–34.

[34] CT 3. 7. 1 (371); CI 5. 4. 20 (409 west); Nov. 115. 3. 11; Syro-Roman Law Book L 88; Ambr. *Abr.* 1. 91 CSEL 32. 1. 562; Ambrosiast. *in I Cor.* 7. 39. 2, CSEL 81. 2. 90; Basil. *ep.* 199. 30, 41; *Conc. Tolet.* III (589) 10; P.Oxy. xii. 1473 (201); P.Masp. i. 67005 (567), iii. 67340r (6th c.); Beaucamp (1992a) 113, 122, 302; Krause (1994a) 144–56. For earlier times, see e.g. Tac. *ann.* 4. 40; Plut. *amat.* 10 (754E); and Treggiari (1985) 338–43.

abduct the girl. Then he would try to persuade her parents to recognize the marriage, often successfully. Sometimes the girl was not totally unwilling: it could even be suspected that she had participated in the planning. This practice was certainly uncommon in the cities, not to speak of Rome itself, but it seems always to have been widespread in more rural areas of the Mediterranean world.[35] This is perhaps the nearest to premarital romance we hear of in antiquity.

If there was imperial legislation against abduction marriage prior to the fourth century it has not been preserved. In the 320s Constantine imposed harsh penalties on all those concerned. He threatened not only the abductor and the girl but also her parents if they reconciled themselves to the abduction. His successors had to mitigate the most cruel punishments and to set a time limit for accusation: otherwise the law would have been impossible to enforce. In practice, the legislators had to concede that a marriage by abduction often became a stable union with children. Precisely such a course of events is implied in a papyrus from late Roman Egypt. However, in this case the marriage did not turn out to be a happy one. Churchmen like Basil of Caesarea took a much more lenient attitude towards abduction than did secular law. If the parents agreed to the *de facto* marriage afterwards the church accepted its validity.[36]

From the point of view of the woman herself, it naturally made a big difference whether she had deliberately run away or whether she had been kidnapped and raped. Roman law never drew this distinction: abduction was a crime against the parents, and against organized society. The feelings of the object herself were irrelevant except that she could be punished, too, if the suspicions of her co-operation were strong enough. A jointly planned elopement had to be followed by a headlong flight and thus could be treated under the same heading as violent abduction. Admittedly, for an outsider it would often have been difficult to distinguish between the two: if the participants were caught, their testimony could not be depended upon.[37]

---

[35] For the whole topic, see now esp. Evans Grubbs (1989); for the legislation, also Beaucamp (1990) 107–21.

[36] CT 9. 24. 1–3; cf. D. 48. 6. 5. 2; Amm. 16. 5. 12; P.Oxy. 1. 3581 (4th/5th c.), with Beaucamp (1992*a*) 73–4; Basil. *ep.* 199. 22, 30; Evans Grubbs (1989) 64–77. Cf. also Lib. *ep.* 1168–9, 1237–8, with Beaucamp, 341–2.

[37] CT 9. 24. 1; CI 9. 13. 1. 2–3b; LRB 9. 1; ET 17. Evans Grubbs (1989) 62–5. Cf. also P.Sakaon 48 (343), with Beaucamp (1992*a*) 71–2.

In spite of the apparent difficulties in enforcement, Justinian only slightly modified the law in the east: an abducted girl escaped the affair without penalties while an ensuing marriage remained strictly forbidden and the man was punished by death as before.[38] In the western empire, there were no mitigations by the early sixth century. All the participants were to be executed and the girl's parents exiled if they did not prosecute the crime.[39]

It may be that internal disorder and constant warfare made the early medieval world especially dangerous for young girls. Violent capture of women was a real threat in all classes of Merovingian society. In those circumstances, law was not a particularly effective means to stop the habit or the vendettas which may often have followed a raid.[40] Nevertheless, all Germanic codes considered rape and violent abduction a serious crime. A captured girl could not consent afterwards, under penalty of death, but her parents evidently could, something which parents living under Roman law had not been allowed to do.[41]

On the other hand, it seems that legal precepts, whether Roman or Germanic, had an even smaller role in the matter than before. The abductor could escape imminent death by fleeing to a church.[42] Furthermore, the practice of conciliating the parents afterwards was as strong as ever. This is shown by numerous *formulae* in which the man confessed that he had seized his wife without her parents' consent.[43] He agreed that he had incurred the risk of his life, as had the woman, if she had consented. But priests or other 'good people' had intervened on their behalf. Now he confirmed a financial compensation, sometimes going to the parents, sometimes to the wife herself, and all was well again. It is not clear whether these *formulae* were originally derived from late Roman documents. By the time

[38] CI 9. 13. 1; Nov. 143 = 150; Evans Grubbs (1989) 77–9; Beaucamp (1990) 114–18.

[39] CT 9. 24. 1, 3 = LRV 9. 19. 1–2; LRB 9. 1–3; ET 17–20.

[40] Caes. Arel. *serm.* 43. 8, CCL 103. 194; Greg. Tur. *franc.* 3. 7, 9. 27, 10. 5, 10. 8; Ven. Fort. *vita Radeg.* 1. 2; *carm.* 10. 12; *Conc. Tur.* (567) 21, CCL 148A. 187; *Conc. Par.* (556/573) 6, CCL 148A. 208; see also Wemple (1981) 33–36.

[41] LV.Ant 3. 3. 1, 2, 3, 7; cf. Zeumer (1898) iii. 600–4; King (1972) 232. LB 12. 1–3; PLS 13; LRib 38; *Decr. Child.* (596) 4 (MGH Capit. i, p. 16).

[42] *Conc. Aurel.* (511) 2 CCL 148A. 5; LV.Ant. 3. 3. 2; Greg. Tur. *franc.* 6. 16; *Decr. Child.* (596) 4 (see last note). Although the practice of asylum is old, it is not earlier mentioned with abduction.

[43] *F.Andec.* 44; *F.Marc.* 2. 16; *F.Tur.* 16, 32; *F.Sal.Merk.* 19; *F.Sal.Lind.* 16; a slave, *F.Sal.Bign.* 11; *F.Sal.Lind.* 20.

their wording had been standardized, in the seventh and eighth
centuries, they included both Roman and Germanic elements and
were certainly used by all parts of the population.

We may ask what happened if a girl had intentionally eloped to
form a union with the man of her choice but could not persuade
her parents to consent. For the parents, the simplest solution
would have been to attack the prospective bridegroom and kill
him. Perhaps to prevent this, many Germanic codes had rulings
for such a situation. Contrary to Roman law, the young couple
got off with a fine paid to the girl's parents. In the worst case the
girl was disinherited but the parents could evidently not take her
back.[44] The legal status of such 'free' marriages is impossible to
estimate. Gregory of Tours (*franc.* 9. 33) reports how one mother
asserted that her daughter's marriage was void because it had
been concluded without permission from the relatives. Whether
the claim was justified or not, the couple had been living together
for thirty years.

There is some reason to think that in the end even Roman law
was interpreted in the same sense. The Sentences of Paul had
once explained: '*Eorum qui in potestate patris sunt sine voluntate
eius matrimonia iure non contrahuntur, sed contracta non solvuntur.*'
This must have meant that if the father had originally consented
to the marriage he could not later break it. In the Tours Formulary it is taken to indicate that the parents had to accept a
marriage concluded without their consent.[45]

Thus it seems that early medieval society had a somewhat
greater tolerance towards girls marrying independently. This
hardly demonstrates a higher value on girls' judgement but
simply that the state was too weak to return them to their
parents. Of course, that had often been true in the Roman
empire as well, but the absolute monarchs had not accepted the
shocking idea that their decrees were not observed. To uphold
state authority the imperial chancelleries prescribed dire penalties for all those who appeared to circumvent the law. The
Germanic kings no longer maintained such pretences. To avoid
private retribution and long blood feuds, it was better to establish

---

[44] LB 12. 4–5, 101; LRib 39. 3; LV.Ant 3. 1. 8, 3. 2. 8, 3. 4. 7; ER 188, 214; LL 114,
119. Note that LB 12. 5 concerns a Roman girl cohabiting with a Burgundian. For
a violent solution, cf. Greg. Tur. *franc.* 6. 36.

[45] PS 2. 19. 2 + int; *F.Tur.* 16; see Levy (1951*b*) 241–5 and Kaser (1975) 163.

a reasonable method of compensation and leave the young couple in peace.

2. PATERNAL POWER AND ADULT CHILDREN

Fathers and Married Daughters

The extensive powers of the Roman father over his young children were not exceptional in the ancient world. What made Roman *patria potestas* unique was the fact that the *pater* did not lose it when his descendants matured and established independent households. Even a grandfather and a senior magistrate of the Roman state could be in his own father's power.

In practice, however, this picture of the Roman family was less likely to reflect the real sitation. As was already noted, Roman men married relatively late and died early. Consequently, the number of adult Romans who actually were in their fathers' power was never great: less than half by the time they reached their full majority at 25, and only a small fraction at the age of 40. Thus, although *patria potestas* was 'lifelong', it did not usually mean a very long period.[46] John Chrysostom quite rightly remarked that sons grew annoyed if their fathers lived too long (*in Coloss.* 1. 3, PG 62. 303).

Moreover, Roman law had always contained a method to end *patria potestas* during the father's lifetime. This procedure, called *emancipatio*, severed most legal ties between children and their agnatic relatives, making them immediately *sui iuris* just as if their father had died. We do not know how often it was used during the republic or the early principate, and for what specific purposes. Emancipation was certainly common in the third century: it is frequently attested in imperial rescripts.[47] On the other hand, there was no way to compel a father to do it: he could always decide himself whether to emancipate his descendants.[48] Sometimes all the children of a family were emancipated, sometimes only some of them, sometimes only the son but not the grand-

[46] See above all Saller (1986 and 1987).
[47] See Watson (1973: 23, and 1977: 24–5); but note also the criticism of Gardner (1993) 71–2.
[48] GI 1. 137a; D. 1. 7. 31, 30. 114. 8, 36. 1. 23. pr; CI 8. 48. 3 (293), 8. 48. 4 (Diocl.). One exception under Trajan is mentioned by Papinian, D. 37. 12. 5.

children. Their coming of age was not the only possible occasion, since minors, too, were emancipated.[49] We probably could not reconstruct a uniform pattern even if we knew the circumstances in every individual case. Daughters were emancipated throughout the period covered by our sources. It is impossible to say whether this was usually done at their marriage and whether there was any statistical difference between daughters and sons. But without any doubt, an emancipated woman was a perfectly normal phenomenon in the eyes of late Roman legislators.[50]

For these two reasons, the early death of many Roman fathers and the possibility of emancipation, *patria potestas* did not affect the lives of most adult Romans. On the other hand, there were always quite a number of those who really were affected by it. For them the system had far-reaching consequences.

Whatever problems of authority there may have been between a father and a son living in a common household, they became serious only when the son neared adulthood. The daughters rarely faced a similar situation. By their late teens they were usually already married. If the marriage was ended very soon the girl might return to her parental home.[51] But we can take it for granted that most adult women had passed outside their father's direct control. Augustine illustrates this by comparing the innately difficult relations between son and father to similar problems between daughter and mother-in-law.[52]

Thus, an adult daughter did not feel the power of her *paterfamilias* very often in her daily life. If the father was still living she was naturally expected to show continuing respect to him. There is no reason to doubt that the relations were normally warm and close.[53] However, our main subject here are conflicts, that is,

---

[49] See e.g. CI 3. 31. 6 (224), 4. 19. 16 (294), 5. 71. 7 (283), 6. 14. 1 (286), 6. 20. 6 (244), 6. 57. 2 (293), 6. 59. 1 (294), 10. 50. 2 (Diocl.); Cons. 6. 10 (293), CT 8. 12. 2 (316).

[50] D. 1. 7. 25, 23. 3. 44, 51, 31. 89. 3, 39. 5. 28; CPL 206 = FIRA iii. 14 (3rd c.); CI 6. 30. 1 (214), 4. 50. 2 (222), 4. 6. 2 (227), 2. 26. 2 (238), 4. 29. 8 (238), 8. 53. 2 (241), 1. 18. 3 (244), 7. 71. 3 (259), 2. 2. 3 (287), 6. 57. 2 (293), 4. 38. 10 (294), 6. 9. 4 (294); 6. 46. 5 (294), CT 3. 5. 2 (319), 3. 7. 1 (371), 5. 1. 3 (383 west), 8. 13. 6 (426 west); CI 6. 20. 17 (472 east), 6. 58. 11 (502 east), 6. 58. 15. 1b (534 east); Nov. 97. 5; Syro-Roman Law Book L 40; see also Symm. *ep.* 9. 150.

[51] Cf. e.g. D. 32. 41. 7; CT 3. 11. 1. pr; P.Panop. 28, with Beaucamp (1992a) 121; Krause (1994b) 6–13.

[52] Aug. *in psalm.* 44. 11, CCL 38. 502; for tension between father and son, see Shaw (1987b), with ample documentation, and much stress on violence inside the family.   [53] Cf. Eyben (1991); and, with caution, Hallett (1984).

those situations which could raise a legal issue. What if a married *filiafamilias* quarrelled with her father? There were at least three points that might concern her: (1) Could the father take some property away from her? (2) Could he separate her from her husband? (3) Could she be disinherited? We shall try to answer these questions in the same order.

Children who were *in potestate* had no independent ownership rights: everything they acquired belonged to their *paterfamilias* just as if they had been his slaves. The father could separate for them a *peculium*, a sum of money or other property which they could control more or less independently.[54] In theory, the father could take the *peculium* back at will. That may have been very rare in practice, though; perhaps social pressure prevented fathers from using this as a threat against disobedient children. Evidence on this is almost entirely lacking, which is probably significant.[55]

We do not know if all daughters received a *peculium*. They had less need for it than sons since they were given a dowry when they married.[56] Nevertheless, there are so many references to a daughter's *peculium* in the third century that it must have been a common phenomenon.[57] It secured a young wife some independence from her husband, who had control over the dowry. On the other hand, the father may sometimes have threatened to withdraw his daughter's *peculium*. According to the biographer of the rich heiress Melania, when she and her husband around the year 400 proposed to adopt an ascetic life her father wanted to take away their (*sic*) property. It is possible that the *peculium* was meant, but few details are given and we should perhaps reckon with some inaccuracy in the account.[58]

Although the father was certainly entitled to reclaim the *peculium*, the daughter was still somewhat better situated than

[54] D. 2. 14. 28. 2, 34. 4. 31. 3, 39. 5. 7, 41. 2. 14. pr, 42. 8. 12, 46. 2. 34. pr, etc. On the *peculium* and property relations between fathers and sons, see Kirschenbaum (1987); Gardner (1993) 55–62.
[55] D. 4. 4. 3. 4, 34. 4. 31. 3; CI 5. 18. 7 (294). Kaser (1938: 85–7; 1971: 344); Saller (1988) 396–7, 407–8; cf. also Crook (1967b) 119–20.
[56] Cf. Gardner (1986) 9–10. For the dowry, see next section.
[57] D. 6. 1. 65. 1, 13. 1. 19, 13. 6. 3. 4, 15. 1. 1, 27. pr, 23. 3. 9. 3, 24, 33. 8. 6. 4, 34. 4. 31. 3, 37. 7. 8, 39. 5. 31. 2 = FV 255; FV 294; CI 4. 12. 3 (293), 5. 18. 7 (294).
[58] Geront. *vita Melan.* 12, SC 90. 150. There is a short reference to a woman's *peculium* in Symm. *ep.* 6. 2.

her brothers: her dowry could not be taken back during marriage. In fact, the father could not reclaim the dowry even after divorce without her consent. All this Diocletian explained to a father who wanted to recover the property he had given.[59]

In most cases, if the daughter was living in harmony with her husband the father could not immediately ruin their finances. But could he ruin their marriage? Initially, a *paterfamilias* was certainly able to compel the divorce of his children. We do not know how common this actually was. Although the males of the republican ruling class arranged their daughters' marriages to highlight political alliances, political divorces are ascribed mostly to husbands, not to fathers. Lack of evidence does not prove that forced divorce did not exist. In the mid-second century, Apuleius gives the impression that a father could use it as a real threat against the young couple (*apol.* 77). In any case, actually forcing a divorce must have been regarded as on the verge of exceeding the bounds of decorum. A happy marriage (*bene concordans matrimonium*) seems to have received legal protection only from the reign of the last Antonine emperors, and there may still have remained some juristic doubt in the third century.[60]

But where we have some evidence of legal practice, in Roman Egypt, it is obvious that married daughters quite early obtained decisions favourable to them. Our main source is the famous case of Dionysia, a woman who resisted her father's claims in a series of lawsuits in 186. The father, Chaeremon, wanted to recover some property which he had promised Dionysia on her marriage. Dionysia had further claims to it on account of certain obligations which Chaeraemon had later assumed but which are no longer clear. She had already won her case concerning this monetary dispute when Chaeremon again approached the prefect. This time he wanted to separate his daughter from her husband and adduced a 'law' which enabled him to do that. He was probably referring to Greek law in Egypt; in any case a similar custom has been attested in classical Athens. Understandably, the prefect was reluctant to reopen the issue or hear anything more about their family problems. Nevertheless, the

[59] CI 5. 18. 7 (294). See also D. 24. 3. 2, 22. 5–6; UE 6. 6; Corbett (1930) 184–6.
[60] D. 24. 1. 32. 19, 43. 30. 1. 5, 2; PS 2. 19. 2, 5. 6. 15; FV 116; CI 5. 4. 11, 5. 17. 5. Corbett (1930) 122–5; Voci (1980) 41; Treggiari (1991a) 459–60, 476–82; and cf. below, Ch. 5, Sect. 3.

dispute continued. Dionysia evidently had an excellent lawyer: in her next statement she included a number of precedents from earlier lawsuits which supported her case. True, they seemed to prove that there really was a local custom which allowed the father to take his daughter back. But they also showed that Roman prefects had refused to separate spouses who wanted to live together. Now the persons concerned did not have citizenship, so that in all this Roman law was not directly involved, but it is certainly significant that Roman officials considered a foreign law so unjust that they overruled it in several individual cases.[61]

In late antiquity it must have been a more and more established practice that a Roman court would not allow a happy marriage to be broken up if this was proved to be against the woman's wish. In practice, many parents continued to interfere in their children's lives. Gregory of Nazianzus described how the parents of a young wife were suing for divorce. The girl obediently declared her consent before the officials although it was obvious that she actually wanted to stay with her husband.[62]

It is obscure as to how easy it was for children *in potestate* to divorce independently, without paternal consent. It may be that a tacit agreement with the *paterfamilias* was expected, at least in theory.[63] Open conflicts were hardly brought before Roman courts very often. Diocletian once stated that no legal precept had ever ordered a woman to return to her husband against her will (CI 5. 17. 5). But this rescript seems to have been addressed to a husband who wanted to keep his wife: thus the word '*invitam*' refers to her disagreement with him, not with her father. The next clause adds that a father had nothing to do with the divorce of an emancipated daughter, so obviously he had some say if the daughter was *in potestate*.

Thus there is no clear evidence on the legal standpoint in our extant sources. We may note, however, that when the state later began to control divorce, the laws were directed against the

---

[61] P.Oxy. ii. 237; on this process, see esp. Lewis (1970); and cf. Préaux (1959) 163–4; Anagnostou-Cañas (1984) 351–3; Modrzejewski (1988) 392–4.

[62] Greg. Naz. *ep*. 144; see also CI 3. 28. 18 (286), 3. 28. 20 (294), 5. 4. 11 (Diocl.), 5. 17. 4–5 (294); P.Sakaon 38 = MChr 64 = P.Flor. 36 (312); P.Oxy. i. 129 = MChr 296 = FIRA iii. 21 (6th c.); Beaucamp (1990: 256–9; 1992a: 145–6, 153–8, 305–6).

[63] As Gardner (1986) 11 n. 21 points out, the passages cited by Corbett (1930) 242, Kaser (1971) 327, and Treggiari (1991a) 445–6, 460–1, do not establish the question; see also D. 24. 3. 41.

spouses themselves and usually did not even mention their fathers. Deeds of divorce in Egypt were also regularly drawn up without reference to the parents.[64] In the sixth century Justinian heard that spouses who were *in potestate* were sometimes using divorce collusively to defraud their father of the *dos* or *donatio* which was technically his. The emperor wanted to stop this once and for all, subjecting divorce again to paternal approval, even in the case of emancipated children.[65]

To return to the initial question, we can conclude that, if the daughter was living in a happy marriage with her husband, the father may have found his immediate power over her to be rather limited. Given the trouble and loss of time which he could expect in a Roman court, he can rarely have considered a lawsuit an attractive alternative to uphold his *patria potestas*. The nightmarish process in which Dionysia's father got involved is a concrete example.[66] There remained for him one effective threat: he could disinherit his children.

This procedure had a weak point, too. A disinherited daughter could claim that the will was undutiful if her father had not left her at least a quarter of her intestate share (*querela inofficiosi testamenti*). This was a popular cause for litigation in Rome.[67] Sometimes a court might decide that the daughter's repute was bad enough to justify her father's action. Sometimes it found that the father had gone beyond the bounds of reason, as when the daughter had refused to divorce her husband. In late antiquity angry parents might try to disinherit their daughter because she wanted to remain a virgin against their wish. Paradoxically, she could sometimes face the same threat because she wanted to marry while they had decided to put her in a convent.[68]

Augustine sometimes refers to disinheritance (*exheredatio*) in his writings, presenting it as a realistic alternative. He does not give a hint that the heirs could appeal to any legal remedies, such

---

[64] e.g. CT 3. 16. 1–2; CI 5. 17. 10; Nov. 117. 13, 134. 11. 1; Beaucamp (1990) 259–60; cf. further below, Ch. 5, Sect. 3. On the papyri, see Beaucamp (1992a) 139–58.

[65] CI 5. 17. 12; Nov. 22. 19. Corbett (1930) 242–3.

[66] See above, P.Oxy. ii. 237; cf. also CI 8. 46. 1, 3, 5; BGU vii. 1578.

[67] CI 3. 28; D. 5. 2, esp. 5. 2. 1; Gardner (1986) 183–90. For later developments, Kaser (1975) 514–21.

[68] CI 3. 28. 18 (286) and 19 (293). Ambr. *virg.* 1. 62–4; NMaj 6. 3 (458 west); CI 1. 3. 54. 5 (533/4); Nov. 115. 3. 11; see below, Ch. 5, Sect. 1, for the diverse problems caused by Christian asceticism.

as the *querela inofficiosi testamenti*. In general, Augustine gives the impression that if there was a dispute about an inheritance it would be settled privately or before the bishop and not in an imperial court.[69]

In the east Justinian finally gave a long list of offences which justified disinheritance (Nov. 115. 3). Most of them were grave or rare misdemeanours, like manhandling or prosecuting the parents, trying to poison them, or failing to redeem them from captivity. A child who renounced the catholic faith or practised a shameful profession also gave just cause for disinheritance. And a girl who refused to be married by her parents, preferring an 'extravagant' life, certainly could only blame herself. In theory, by excluding all further causes this law diminished the parents' authority, at least in those cases which were brought before imperial justice. On the other hand, we may assume that the courts of the third century had already followed very similar principles when they had to decide cases of *querela inofficiosi testamenti* (cf. CI 3. 28; D. 5. 2).

In practice, outright disinheritance may not always have been a very convenient way to keep one's offspring disciplined. The father could enhance his authority most easily by reminding the children that he did not have to leave them more than their lawful portion, that is, one-quarter of their share on intestacy. Unequal division of the estate was much more common in Roman society than it is today. It certainly inspired children to keep on good terms with their parents.[70] For example, if the father had two children, he might bequeath seven-eighths of his estate to the favoured one and only one-eighth to the other. The children together did not need to receive more than one-quarter. Later in the east Justinian raised the legitimate share to one-third.[71]

In the west, Roman parents retained the right to discriminate among their heirs for as long as we can follow the legal sources,

[69] Aug. *serm.* 355. 3–5; 356. 5, 11, PL 39. 1570ff.; *in psalm.* 32. 2. 3, CCL 38. 248; 93. 17, CCL 39. 1318; *in Galat.* 39, PL 35. 2132. Cf. also Sidon. *ep.* 4. 23; Theodoret. *hist. eccl.* 3. 17; Ambr. *hex.* 6. 4. 22, CSEL 32. 1. 218; Greg. M. *ep.* 9. 48, 9. 90, 9. 198.
[70] Cf. Aug. *serm.* 21. 8, 45. 2, CCL 41. 283, 517; *in psalm.* 17. 32, CCL 38. 99; 102. 20, CCL 40. 1469; Shaw (1987*b*) 20–5; Ambr. *hex.* 5. 18. 58, CSEL 32. 1. 184.
[71] Nov. 18. 1 (536); the new quota is attested in P.Masp. iii. 67353 (569). See also P.Masp. i. 67097 = FIRA iii. 15; and the Syro-Roman Law Book L 9; cf. Selb (1964) 72–86; Beaucamp (1992*a*) 79–81.

until the early sixth century. And they could still transfer three-quarters of their property to a total outsider.[72] Among the Germanic peoples, testamentary freedom seems to have been more limited. The evidence is admittedly sparse and allows only glimpses of the different national usages.[73] We cannot tell how strictly the rules were observed nor how quickly the customs of Roman and Germanic populations were fused. The little we have indicates that in the early middle ages people's ability to use their wills to bring financial pressure on their adult children was diminishing.

The Survival of Patria Potestas

We have little evidence on provincial family life before the universal grant of Roman citizenship in 212. In the mid-second century Gaius remarked in his legal textbook that *patria potestas* was peculiar to Roman citizens and unknown to almost all other people.[74] Although his basic information has to be accepted with some confidence, the situation was not quite so simple. The newly discovered *Lex Irnitana*, a municipal law from the late first century, shows that inhabitants of a Spanish town who were not yet Roman citzens could recognize legal relationships which were modelled after Roman law, among them *patria potestas*. Thus it may be that Roman family patterns were being spread in the western provinces already in the early empire.[75]

In the east the situation was perhaps different. Unfortunately, even in Egypt the sources are less helpful than could be expected. In fact, there are only a handful of papyri which offer any explicit information about legal relations between fathers and their adult children. Among them the petition of Dionysia is the most important.[76] As we have seen, fathers in Egypt could assert an

---

[72] LRB 45. 4–5; PS 4. 5 + int, and CT 2. 19. 2, 4 + int, in the *Breviarium* (and its Epitomes).

[73] LB 1, 24. 5, 51, 75; ER 168–71; LL 113; cf. ER 158–60; LL 5, 65, 102. On LV 4. 5. 1, 3, cf. Zeumer (1898) iv. 138–46; King (1972) 246–7.

[74] GI 1. 55; cf. D. 1. 6. 3; Inst. 1. 9; Dion. Hal. 2. 26. And see Mitteis (1891) 209–12; Levy (1929: 257 n. 3; 1942: 24); Sachers (1953) 1057–8; Taubenschlag (1955) 130–1; Crook (1967b) 113; Watson (1977) 23–9

[75] *L.Irnit.* 21–2, 86; cf. GI 1. 93–5; Gonzales (1986) 148–9, 154, 176–7, 203–4, 231; Gardner (1993) 188–90.

[76] P.Oxy. ii. 237; P.Mil.Vogl. iv. 229; cf. Taubenschlag (1916: 177–207; and 1955: 130–1, 136–8), criticized by Lewis (1970) 251–4.

extensive authority (*eksousia*) over both the person and the property of their married daughters.[77] The exact nature of this authority is far from clear. But the sheer number of obligations,
contracts, claims, and counter-claims between Dionysia and her
father is enough to show that these people would not have
recognized *patria potestas* in the absolute form described by
Roman jurists.[78]

Most of the third-century evidence again comes from Egypt.
In principle, the papyri should now refer to Roman institutions.
Sometimes 'the law of the Romans' is explicitly mentioned. In
practice the situation was, of course, much more complicated: the
documents can present either local law, official Roman law, or any
popular interpretations of it. Moreover, it is usually impossible to
tell the actual circumstances in which the document was written.
It strikes the reader that very often the child who is said to be in
his/her father's power turns out to be a minor. This may reflect
the simple demographic fact that the younger the children were
the more likely they were to have a living father. On the other
hand, it might also support the view that in Egypt *patria potestas*
was understood as a kind of guardianship for under-age children.
There are cases where the father is specifically said to be the
guardian for a minor child or an adult daughter, or where his
children are otherwise indicated to own property independently
of him.[79] In Roman juridic terms this should mean that he had
emancipated them, but, as far as I know, emancipation is explicitly mentioned only in a few isolated instances.[80] In all, the
general impression is that different legal traditions coexisted.
The Roman concept of *patria potestas* had evidently been
embraced in Egypt at least to some extent. That many people

---

[77] See esp. P.Oxy. ii. 237, VI. 14, and VII. 41–2; in BGU vii. 1578 the veteran
father may be referring to Roman law.

[78] The whole affair is reconstructed in the introduction to P.Oxy. ii. 237; cf. D. 5.
1. 4: '*Lis nulla nobis esse potest cum eo quem in potestate habemus, nisi ex castrensi
peculio.*'

[79] P.Oxy. viii. 1114 = FIRA iii. 63, ix. 1208, x. 1268, xiv. 1642, 1703; BGU ii. 667,
vii. 1578; P.Gen. i. 44; PSI x. 1126, xv. 1546; P.Harr. i. 68 = P.Diog. 18 = FIRA iii. 28;
SB i. 1010 = FIRA iii. 61, 5692; vi. 9069; (these examples span the 3rd century); cf.
BGU iii. 907 (late 2nd c.). See Taubenschlag (1916: 207–30; 1955: 131–2, 143–9). On
the guardianship of adult women, see below, Ch. 4, Sect. 1.

[80] CPR vi. 12–30 (300/1), 78 (*c*.265); cf. CPR vi. p. 60.

were tempted to assimilate it with their inherited customs is hardly surprising.

Whatever problems the new provincial citizens may initially have had, *patria potestas* by no means disappeared from Roman society. It continued to be treated in both eastern and western laws. Its practical importance emerges very clearly from the trouble which was later taken to ensure that children *in potestate* were not deprived of their maternal inheritance (see next chapter). Many authors allude to the paternal power in more or less precise terms through the fourth and fifth centuries.[81] It is discussed as a living institution in the Syro-Roman Law Book (L 2–3, 18, 40, 42, 44). Moreover, there is no doubt that Justinian considered *patria potestas* an important and living part of the legal system which he tried to maintain in his empire. A few laws indicate that it had a real impact on the everyday life of his subjects, even in such a remote region as Osrhoene in Mesopotamia.[82] Papyri are here less helpful. Although children are occasionally said to be in their father's power (*hypokheirioi* and later *hypeksousioi*), the practical implications of this cannot really be inferred.[83]

We have every reason to believe that in late antiquity *patria potestas* was recognized as a fact of life throughout the empire. On the other hand, it was now clearly common to emancipate children when they married or reached adulthood. This is first explicitly attested in a law of Constantine (CT 8. 18. 2), and the habit seems to have won popularity in the later empire. However, it is by no means possible to speak of a rule, or even of a routine practice. Western laws in the early fifth century imply that a man could have adult children and successive generations *in potestate*. Emancipation around the age of 20 was popular, but the essential characteristic of *patria potestas* survived: the father himself could

---

[81] Greg. Naz. *or.* 37. 6; Joh. Chrys. *qual. duc. ux.* 2 PG 51. 226; *Conc. Hipp.* (393) 1, CCL 149. 20; Aug. *ep.* 262. 11, CSEL 57. 631; *serm.* 45. 2, CCL 41. 517; Sidon. *ep.* 7. 2. 7.

[82] See e.g. CI 5. 17. 12 (534); Nov. 74. praef. 2. The idea of *patria potestas* has permeated all of the *Corpus Iuris Civilis*: for a short statement, see Inst. 1. 9, 12.

[83] See SB x. 10728 (318); P.Oxy. liv. 3758. 156–80 (325); P.Panop. 28 = SB xii. 11221 (329); P.Lond. iii. 977 (330); P.Lips. i. 28 = MChr 363 (381); PSI xii. 1239 = SB v. 7996 (430); P.Ness. iii. 18 (Palestine, 537); P.Oxy. i. 129 = MChr 296 = FIRA iii. 21 (6th c.); P.Masp. i. 67006v. 14–15 (6th c.).

decide whether or not to release his descendants.[84] In this form
patria potestas was still known to Roman jurisprudents working
in the Visigothic territories in the late fifth and early sixth
centuries. It was clearly not excluded from the *Breviarium*. [85]
On the other hand, the Roman Law of Burgundy never mentions *patria potestas* nor *emancipatio*, although *filiusfamilias*
appears twice.[86]

Little is known about relations between parents and children
among the Germanic peoples. Only the Burgundian and Visigothic codes discuss them to any extent. Although the Visigoths
imitated some Roman solutions, the idea of a lifelong paternal
power as such seems to have been strange to all Germanic
nations.[87]

When did the former Roman provincials abandon the ancient
institution of *patria potestas*? There are too few pieces of evidence
to indicate the pace of the development or to disclose variations
in different regions. The definition of *'peculium'* in the etymolo-
gical compendium of Isidor of Seville, writing in Visigothic
Spain in the early seventh century, seems to imply that in his
time adult people were no longer *in potestate* (*orig.* 5. 25. 5). There
is an even more interesting contemporary document from the
Visigothic dominions, a *formula* of a deed of emancipation. It
begins:

*Prisca consuetudo et legum decreta sanxerunt, ut patres filios in potestate
habentes tempore, quo perfectos in eos praespexerint annos, postulata a
patribus absolutione, percipiant, quod tamen patres ipsi, si voluerint, con-
cedant.* (*F.Vis.* 34)

[84] See CT 9. 43. 1 (321); Hier. *ep.* 107. 6 (*'perfecta aetas et sui iuris'*); Symm. *ep.* 1.
6; 9. 150 (Symmachus probably and his wife certainly emancipated); *Conc. Hipp.*
(393) 1, CCL 149. 20; Aug. *serm.* 45. 2, CCL 41. 517; CT 8. 13. 6 + 8. 18. 9 + 8. 19. 1
(426 west); NVal 35. 10 (452) + int (not mentioning emancipation but perhaps
meaning it); cf. LRB 26; CE 321; and below, Ch. 3, Sect. 3.
[85] See e.g. GE 1. 5–6; CT 8. 13. 2. int, 8. 14. 1; 8. 19. 1, 9. 43. 1; CG 3. 10. 1; all
with their *interpretationes*. Cf. also Caes. Arel. *reg. virg.* 6, SC 345. 184; and
filiusfamilias in Sidon. *ep.* 7. 2. 7, 7. 9. 21.
[86] LRB 14. 4–5, cf. the inclusion of the mother; 22. 1–2, formally consonant with
Roman law, now somewhat ambiguous, when taken from the original context and
omitting any mention of paternal usufruct, cf. CT 8. 18–19, and below, Ch. 3, Sect.
3; see also LRB 26. 1.
[87] LB 1, 24. 5, 51. 1–2, 75, 78; CE 305, 321, 336; LV.Ant 4. 2. 2, 13, 4. 5. 5; LV 5. 2.
2; cf. Zeumer (1898) iv. 110–12, 146–8; Levy (1942: 24; 1950: 240); King (1972) 243–4;
Herlihy (1985) 48.

Ancient custom and the rulings of law have laid down that when children who are in their father's power reach their majority they should ask the father to set them free. This the father should grant, if he wishes.

The text, with its terribly garbled syntax, was certainly used by people who tried to continue Roman traditions. It shows that the last vestiges of the Roman family system may have lingered on among the old populations of western Europe for a much longer time than we would expect.

3. DOWRY AND INHERITANCE

Dos *and* Donatio ante Nuptias

In the previous section we saw how a Roman father could discriminate between his children in his last will. In extreme cases even outright disinheritance was possible. Now we shall return to the devolution of property in normal circumstances. How much wealth did women inherit in Roman society? When assessing the amount of property which women received from their father's estate, we should not forget their dowry (*dos*). Moreover, during late antiquity a totally new institution appeared in Roman law: the so-called nuptial donation, or a gift from the bridegroom to the bride (*donatio ante nuptias, sponsalicia largitas*). These subjects have to be considered before we examine the position of daughters in Roman succession.

Dowry was a normal though not compulsory part of Roman marriage. It was usually given by the bride's father (*dos profecticia*). If he was already dead she gave it from her own property (*dos adventicia*). Even other persons could occasionally provide dowries, notably the bride's mother, but that need not concern us here. If the wife died and her father was also dead, and unless something else had been agreed in the marriage contract, the dowry remained with the husband. In other cases *dos* or most of it returned to the wife or her father. During marriage it was the husband's property.[88]

A dowry could serve many purposes. First, it was a contribution to the expenses of the common household (*onera matrimonii*). Secondly, it provided capital for the wife after divorce or widow-

---

[88] For the basic rules, see e.g. UE 6; Kaser (1971) 332–41; Gardner (1986) 97–116.

hood; and thirdly, it might represent the daughter's share of the paternal estate, as in Athens and perhaps elsewhere in Greece. The classical Roman dowry could evidently have all these functions but the first one is predominant in our sources while the third is rarely attested. True, *dos* could be quite valuable and include real property. On intestacy it had to be taken into account if the daughter wanted to receive her share of the estate (*collatio dotis*). Sometimes a father actually thought that his daughter had received enough property at her marriage so that she could be disinherited subsequently. In theory, it should not have been possible: whatever the size of her dowry, as long as she did not receive one-quarter of her share in the remaining estate she was able to institute a suit of *querela inofficiosi testamenti*. But, even if her father's will was thus broken, the *collatio* eventually ensured that she could not acquire more than her siblings. Of course, most disputes over inheritance never came into the courts. The general impression is that in the third century it was exceptional for a woman to have all her property in the form of dowry, at least in those population groups which were covered by the legal sources. In the upper classes it may have been only a minor part of her total patrimony.[89] We shall return to this question later.

Egypt is the only region outside Rome where we have more than fragmentary evidence of actual dowries in the first centuries of the empire. There, too, dowry became essentially the husband's property during marriage. In contrast to the Roman upper-class dowry, it did not contain immovable property or slaves but only money and utensils, which were the wife's contribution to the common household. Moreover, its value seems to have decreased in the first centuries AD. It was overshadowed by another institution, *parapherna*, which mainly included the wife's personal everyday belongings and remained technically her property.[90] It is quite conceivable that the systems of matrimonial property differed in various parts of the Roman empire. The

[89] Saller (1984*b*); Gardner (1985; 1986: 97–116); Champlin (1991) 116–18; Treggiari (1991*a*) 361–4. See CI 2. 33. 1 + 5. 12. 4 (223/233), 6. 20; CG 2. 4. 1–2 (235/223); D. 4. 4. 9. 1, 6. 1. 65. 1, 19. 1. 52. 1, 28. 5. 62, 34. 1. 10. 2, 36. 1. 64. pr, 37. 7; FV 115.
[90] Matrimonial property in Roman Egypt has been examined in a number of exhaustive studies: see above all Montevecchi (1936) 38–54; Gerner (1954) 1–38; Wolff (1955); Häge (1968); Modrzejewski (1970).

evidence from Egypt will serve as a warning against generalizations. It reminds us about life in those classes and those regions which were not accounted for in juristic writings.

However, Graeco-Roman Egypt had one basic thing in common with classical Greece and Rome: they were all typically societies which practised dotal marriage. That is, they knew only the direct dowry (*dos*) described above. Most other cultures of Eurasia have recognized also (or only) gifts from the groom to the bride or her parents. Current names for such marital prestations are, among others, 'indirect dowry', 'dower', 'morning gift', 'bridegift', and 'brideprice'. The practical arrangements around them have naturally varied in different societies, and so has their value. In any case they should not be understood as an actual 'purchase' of a wife, any more than we can say that Roman fathers used the dowry to buy a son-in-law.

Like the dowry, a nuptial gift could have many purposes: it might form part of a joint family capital, or serve the wife after widowhood, or discourage divorce initiated by the husband (because he then lost it). Such functions may often have coexisted. Why this system was foreign to classical civilization remains unclear. Ancient authors casually attest it for Hispanic, Gallic, and Germanic peoples. Some kind of nuptial donation has also been found in many cultures of the eastern Mediterranean. However, the evidence is so meagre and comes from such distant periods that it can hardly prove the existence of substantial bridegift in any region of the early Roman empire. We can only cautiously assume that the practice was known in many provinces both in the east and in the west.[91]

As to the Romans themselves, it goes almost without saying that the bride and groom and their families often exchanged gifts, but it is clear that in the early third century such gifts did not yet have any special significance. They were mainly signs of affection, consisting of a few more or less precious articles, perhaps a slave, and only in exceptional circumstances more than that. Normally they did not have to be returned in case no marriage followed. However, there were special kinds of presents which

---

[91] See Strabo 3. 18; Caes. *Gall.* 6. 19; Tac. *Germ.* 18; Long. *Daphnis et Chloe* 3. 25; Ach. Tat. *Leuc. et Clit.* 5. 5. 4, 8. 17. 3–4; Heliod. *Aethiop.* 4. 15. 2; and for the Armenians in the 6th c., Nov. 21. Cf. Mitteis (1891) 256–89; Anné (1941) 395–439; Hughes (1978) 262–5; Katzoff (1985); Goody (1990) 13–16, 465–78; Cotton (1994) 82–4.

were given 'for the sake of marriage' (*adfinitatis contrahendae causa*) and which the groom could reclaim if he had not broken the engagement himself. The jurists already discussed this type of donation in the early principate but the extant passages do not reveal how in practice they could be distinguished from simple normal gifts. We may guess that the condition was usually mentioned in a written pact.[92]

From the end of the third century there are already many rescripts which deal with gifts between future spouses. For the first time we now hear of landed property being given to the bride. Unfortunately, we do not know whether this reflects just local customs or a more widespread habit. In Graeco-Roman papyri marriage gifts (*hedna*) from the groom appear at the beginning of the fourth century. Their emergence in Roman Egypt should probably be dated somewhat earlier: almost no marital documents from the late third century are extant.[93]

In 319 Constantine passed a law on the fate of engagement gifts when marriage did not take place. If either of the engaged couple died before marriage the gifts always had to be returned to the groom or his immediate family; the bride could keep them only if the groom had broken the engagement. This sounds very much like regularizing the private pacts of preceding centuries. A later text reveals that, although the bride could give gifts, too, this was in practice rare.[94]

The rule that everything should be returned in the event of premature death is natural if the gifts were more than mere tokens of affection. On the other hand, they had hardly yet taken on the value which they would later acquire. Otherwise their total forfeiture would have excessively penalized the groom for breaking the engagement. By the end of the fourth century a new system developed: only a part of the antenuptial gifts served to secure the betrothal. If the bride (or her father) broke her

---

[92] FV 96, 262; D. 3. 5. 31. 1, 6. 2. 12. pr, 16. 3. 25. pr, 24. 1. 32. 22, 39. 5. 1. 1; Inst. 2. 7. 3; CI 5. 3. 1–7 (early to late 3rd c.); CG 2. 2 (259); SHA *Maximin*. 27. 7; Anné (1941) 245–52, 294–6; Treggiari (1991a) 152–3.

[93] CI 2. 29. 1, 4. 6. 8, 5. 3. 8–14, 5. 71. 8, 7. 4. 13, 7. 14. 14 (all late 3rd c.). P.Grenf. ii. 76 = MChr 295 (305/6); P.Sakaon 38 = P.Flor. i. 36 = MChr 64 (312); Anné (1941) 413–14.

[94] CT 3. 5. 2 (319), 3. 5. 6 (336); the exact meaning of the phrase '*osculo interveniente*' is not known, so the interpretation of the latter law remains open; see Anné (1941) 296–313.

promise, she had to return these gifts (*sponsalia*) fourfold, later twofold. Such a pledge, or advance payment, was also called *arra*. This term of Semitic origin had been used by the Romans in commercial life for centuries. It was hardly perceived as a foreign word any longer, nor is there any direct evidence that its use in the law of marriage would have derived from oriental practice.[95]

In any case, *arra sponsalicia* was subsequently established both in the east and in the west. It survived in Byzantium and is mentioned by writers in Italy, Gaul, and Spain at least to the end of the sixth century. However, when *arra* had been separated from the rest of the nuptial donation its economic significance was quite limited. It seems to have included mainly small items, often a ring, sometimes gold objects or modest amounts of money. Of course, rich people always gave more precious gifts than the poor, and the arrangements certainly varied from case to case.[96]

Both legal and literary sources suggest that until the end of the fourth century *donatio ante nuptias* was not a clearly defined concept. All kinds of presents from the groom to the bride could be called *sponsalia*. For a long time their economic value was not comparable to the old dowry. It was only after *arra* had received a legal regime of its own that the other forms of *donatio* acquired utmost importance. In the early fifth century *dos* and *donatio* often appear together as counterparts.[97] Two western laws from the middle of the century reveal that *donatio* had swelled to equal or exceed *dos*: the emperors strove to reach at least an approximative equality between them. The *Edictum Theoderici* suggests that the groom's gifts could amount to about one-fifth of his

[95] CT 3. 5. 10–11, 3. 6. 1 (all 380 east), 3. 10. 1 (409 west); CI 5. 1. 5 (472 east); Corbett (1930) 18–23; Anné (1941) 87–135; Kaser (1971: 547–8; 1975: 160–2); Evans Grubbs (1995) 172–83; Anné's interpretation of the difficult CT 3. 5. 6 (336), p. 123 n., seems to conflict with his views on pp. 299–303. On the Syro-Roman Law Book, see Anné (1941) 101 n. 1 and 108 n. 3; Selb (1964) 98–104; Yaron (1966) 130–2.

[96] CT 3. 5. 11, 3. 6. 1, 3. 10. 1, all with their *interpretationes* in the *Breviarium*; LRB 27; Greg. M. *ep.* 1. 69; Greg. Tur. *franc.* 1. 47, 4. 46 (a special case with an enormous *arra*), 10. 16; Isid. *orig.* 9. 7. 5–6; Anné (1941) 94–102, with more references. For Egypt, CPR i. 30 II = MChr 290 (6th c.). For the objects, Anné (1941) 108 n. 3. For LV 3. 1. 3, see Zeumer (1898) iii. 578–82; and cf. Greg. Tur. *vit. patr.* 20. 1.

[97] CT 3. 5. 8 (363), 3. 5. 9 (c.370 west); 3. 7. 3 (428 east), 3. 16. 2 (421 west; contrast with 3. 16. 1); Joh. Chrys. *cat. bapt.* 1. 16, SC 50. 116; Aug. *in psalm.* 55. 17, CCL 39. 690; *in evang. Ioh.* 8. 4, CCL 36. 83; cf. Lib. *or.* 47. 28. Anné (1941) 239–68.

property. Eastern practice in the fifth and sixth centuries does not seem to have been uniform. *Donatio* could be greater or smaller than *dos*, or it could be omitted altogether. Local differences survived but the general trend was probably towards a balance between the two. Finally Justinian ordered that both property masses should be equal.[98]

In two centuries, Roman law moved from a purely dotal marriage to a system in which both bride and groom made a substantial contribution to the common household. It is not easy to explain this drastic development. For example, we can hardly maintain that the shift from *dos* to *donatio* represented a better position of women in the marriage market.[99] Undoubtedly both *dos* and *donatio* were sometimes used competitively, for example when either of the families wanted to improve its social position. There is evidence for that in late antiquity (Lib. *or.* 1. 12; Sidon. *ep.* 1. 11. 5; NMaj. 6. 10), and similar trends have been attested in other societies. But it was probably incidental rather than a general phenomenon. If anything, a broad Eurasian comparison suggests that dowry is preferred to brideprice in those cultures and social classes where the standard of living is higher. Possibly also dotal marriage is better consonant with a patrilineal structure of family economics while bridegift in Europe has been associated with bilateral principles. But this is only a very crude model, helping little to account for the change in Roman society.[100]

It is a reasonable guess that nuptial gifts were known in the national practice of many eastern and western provinces. In some places they perhaps transferred substantial wealth while in other places they had a limited value and an arraic function. That would explain why *donatio ante nuptias* had to be gradually recognized in Roman law after 212 and why it was so difficult to define in legal terms. It is quite possible that the gifts had

[98] NVal 35. 9 (452); NMaj 6. 9–10 (458); ET 59; CI 5. 14. 9. 1 (468 east), 5. 3. 19. 1 (527), 4. 29. 25 (531), 5. 3. 20. 5 (531/3); Nov. 21, 97. 1; P.Ness. 18 (Palestine, 537); CPR i. 30 II = MChr 290; SB xvi. 12230 (both 6th c.); cf. Beaucamp (1992*a*) 101 n. 102. For the Syro-Roman Law Book, see Mitteis (1891) 290–6; Anné (1941) 284–5; Selb (1964) 131–2. [99] For such a suggestion, see Herlihy (1985) 14–23.
[100] On broader perspectives, see Hughes (1978) 285–91; Goody (1990) 176–7, 195–6, 367–8, 445–6, 459–64, 477; cf. also Saller (1984*b*; 1994: 205–7); Treggiari (1991*a*) 95–100, 409–10; Krause (1994*a*: 133–8; 1994*b*: 73).

various origins and various functions, although the imperial legislation tried to treat them under a uniform concept.[101]

Thus we should not be surprised to see that the usages linked with nuptial presents varied, too. For example, a couple of papyri from the early fourth century indicate that it was the girl's parents who actually kept the *hedna* given by the groom. On the other hand, almost all imperial rescripts from the third century simply speak of gifts given 'to the bride'. If the girl was still *in potestate* she could obviously have the donation in her *peculium* although that is nowhere explicitly stated before the fifth century.[102] Sometimes women included *donatio* in their dowry, in which case it was possessed by the husband during marriage. An eastern law in 439 claims that this was what usually happened (*'ut adsolet fieri'*). It was even possible that no actual property was transferred at all. The bride might offer a dowry of, say, a hundred gold pieces but in the marital documents it was valued at two hundred. At the end of the marriage the woman could thus recover twice the amount that she had brought with her: the increase was the husband's nuptial donation. In whatever way the donation was specified, in reality the man often governed it during marriage. Such practices are attested from the early third century to the sixth but we cannot really say how widespread they were nor whether changes took place over time.[103] Moreover, two sixth-century papyri illustrate well the enormous difference between the marital assets of the rich and the poor: in one case (SB xvi. 12230) the nuptial donation and the dowry both consisted of fifty pounds of gold and five hundred pounds of silver, in the other (P.Lond. v. 1708) the husband had only managed to pay a single *solidus*.

From the end of the fourth century, *donatio ante nuptias*

[101] The best overview of the problem and available material is still Anné (1941) 395–471; cf. also Kaser (1975) 193–5.

[102] P.Sakaon 38 = P.Flor. i. 36 = MChr 64 (312); P.Oxy. liv. 3770 (334); similarly CI 5. 3. 2 (Alex.); but for the usual language of the laws, see e.g. CI 5. 3; CG 2. 2; CT 3. 5. For the *peculium*, NTh 14. 8 (439 east); and generally for the problem of paternal power, CT 8. 19. 1 (426 west), with Ch. 3, Sect. 3 below.

[103] CI 5. 3. 1 (Sev. and Carac.), 5. 15. 1 (204), 5. 15. 2 (229), 5. 3. 14 (Diocl.); CT 9. 42. 15 (396 east); 3. 5. 13 (428 east), NTh 14. 3 (439); Nov. 22. 24, 61. 1, 97. 6; Joh. Chrys. *qual. duc. ux.* 4, PG 51. 232; *Form. Andec.* 54; Anné (1941) 270–6, 287–92; cf. also Katzoff (1985); Cotton (1994) 82–4; P.Ness. iii. 33 (Palestine, 6th c.), with Beaucamp (1992a) 144–5.

gradually developed into a legal counterpart of *dos*. Many rules which concerned the dowry were by analogy applied to the nuptial donation as well. For example, if the wife died first, the donation had to be returned by her heirs.[104] At the same time, the destiny of *dos* itself underwent changes. The details of these developments are not totally clear. For example, the difference between the dowry of a girl *in potestate* (usually *dos profecticia*) and that of a woman *sui iuris* (in practice *dos adventicia*) had in classical law important consequences for its recovery after her death. Later legal sources no longer make this distinction. We cannot know whether they omitted it consciously or only because they thought that it was evident from the context. To make matters even more complicated, it was obviously common to include in the marriage contract provisions for the subsequent fate of *dos* and *donatio*. In this way the flow of wealth could be redirected almost at will. Although there were some legal regulations it is not certain that they were observed.[105]

In spite of such difficulties, we can discern some unmistakable trends of development which affected the functions of dowry and later of the nuptial donation as well. First, in case of unilateral divorce the party who was thought responsible forfeited them to the other. Secondly, both property masses were increasingly thought to form a common family fund which had to be preserved for the descendants. Thus, when either of the spouses died, the surviving partner acquired only the usufruct of the deceased's *dos* or *donatio*, ultimately to be inherited by their children. These developments will be examined in more detail in a later chapter on widowhood and divorce. If no children survived the situation was more complicated. It was clearly difficult to decide who had the best right to the marital assets: the surviving spouse or the decedent's blood relatives. Here legal rules wavered back and forth, and private pacts evidently took account of personal circumstances.

[104] CT 3. 5. 9 (*c*.370 west), undoubtedly adopted in the east, too, already before 438; cf. CI 6. 61. 2 (428 east); Anné (1941) 314–18. See also CI 6. 20. 17 (472 east), for *collatio ante nuptias donationis*.
[105] CT 3. 13. 3 (422 west); NTh 14 (439 east); NVal 35. 8–10 (452 west); CI 3. 38. 12. pr (530), 5. 3. 20. 7 (531/533), 5. 12. 29. 1 (528), 5. 13. 1. 6+16 (530), 5. 14. 9 (468 east); Joh. Chrys. *qual. duc. ux.* 2, PG 51. 226; *in Gen.* 48. 6 and 56. 3, PG 54. 442, 489. See Anné (1941) 276–83, 320–86; Selb (1964) 105–34; and Kaser (1975) 188–201, also for the following.

It was Justinian's special concern to stress that the dowry morally belonged to the wife although it was 'owned' by the husband during marriage.[106] To ensure this in practice, he in many ways improved the wife's rights. She could now more easily recover her property, and it was secured by a general hypothec. If the husband was becoming insolvent the wife could reclaim her *dos* even during marriage.[107]

When Justinian was legislating in the east the old dowry was losing or had already lost importance in the west. This development is not documented in any detail. Imperial laws in the 450s tried to ensure that *dos* and *donatio* were equal in value, and Sidonius Apollinaris mentions dowries in Gaul in the 460s and 470s. A fragmentary marital document from the North African hinterland in 493 also seems to enumerate the old type of *dos.* [108] Moreover, the *Breviarium* with its *interpretationes* still incorporates many laws on the dowry, obviously regarding it as a normal phenomenon (e.g. book 3 throughout). The same applies to the *Edictum Theoderici* (ET 54).

On the other hand, the Roman Law of Burgundy pays attention only to gifts from the man and uses the word *dos* in this sense.[109] The new situation is reflected also in Merovingian and Visigothic *formulae*, many of which probably go back to the sixth century. They give numerous examples of marital documents where a groom assigns gifts ('*dos*') to his bride.[110] There is not a single document with property coming from the bride. We may guess that in the west, too, brides had habitually included the nuptial donation in their dowry, although there is no direct evidence for that. If the groom's contribution gradually dwarfed the 'real' dowry, it was natural that the word *dos* underwent a

---

[106] CI 5. 12. 30. pr (529); this contradiction had been recognized already by classical jurists, e.g. D. 21. 2. 71, 23. 3. 75; PS 4. 1. 1.

[107] CI 5. 12. 29–30, 5. 13. 1, 8. 17. 12; Inst. 4. 6. 29; Corbett (1930) 190–2; Kaser (1975) 190–3.

[108] NVal 35. 9 (452); NMaj 6. 9–10 (458); Sidon. *ep.* 1. 11. 5, 7. 2. 7–8; cf. 2. 2. 3; *Tabl. Alb.* 1.

[109] LRB 21 (misunderstanding CT 3. 16. 1. int), 37. 1–2; evidently also 22. 2. However, it is possible that *nuptiales donationes* in 22. 2 and 26. 2 might refer to property coming from the bride; see Anné (1941) 392 n. 1.

[110] *F.Andec.* 1, 34, 40, 54; *F.Marc.* 2. 9, 2. 15–16; *F.Tur.* 14–15; *F.Tur.App.* 2–3; *F.Vis.* 14–20; etc.

semantic change. In the literary sources of the sixth century it often means the bridegift.[111]

Thus somehow the new bridegift replaced the ancient dowry in western Europe. The change cannot have been caused by the Germans as it had begun before the collapse of the empire, but it was certainly in line with their practice. All the immigrant peoples knew marital conveyances from the groom to the bride or her family. In their written codes these are called *dos, pretium uxoris, wittimon, meta,* or *morgengabe.* They may partly have had different origins and different functions: some were just token payments while most of them transferred real wealth, though not necessarily before the end of the marriage. Sometimes the kings tried to limit their size to a fixed share of the groom's property, between one-tenth and one-third in the known cases. Where absolute values are given they are not very high compared to Roman marital assets, perhaps due to general poverty.[112]

In the early middle ages women could and probably often did receive property from their own family at the time of their marriage. Among the Germans this may basically have been just a trousseau, although it could include valuable items in the upper echelons of the society. The typical dearth of sources prevents us from knowing if the dowry was something more among families of Roman descent. A Visigothic statute from the year 645 referred to it as a specific feature of Roman law. Unfortunately the passage does not reveal whether it was still a living institution anywhere in Spain. Italy may have remained a stronghold of dotal marriage. But in most areas the time-honoured Mediterranean dowry waned into insignificance.[113] At the end of the first millennium *morgengabe* and similar gifts prevailed in western societies. It was only in the eleventh century that the

---

[111] From Gaul, Caes. Arel. *serm.* 87. 3, CCL 103. 359; 168. 2, CCL 104. 688, taken from late 5th-c. Ps.Euseb. Gall. *serm.* 5 (*epiph.* 2), PL Suppl. 3. 561; Greg. Tur. *franc.* 1. 47, 9. 20; from Spain, Leander *reg.* praef., PL 72. 876C; and, somewhat ambiguously, Isid. *orig.* 5. 24. 25–6; from Britain, *Syn. Patr.* (456) 22 (Bruns ii. 303). For earlier instances, see Anné (1941) 263–7; and *Thesaurus Linguae Latinae* s.v. 'dos', p. 2044 ll. 19–28, and 45–72.

[112] LV 3. 1. 5–6; LB 14. 3–4, 42. 2, 52. 3, 66, 69, 86. 2; PLS 100–1, 110; LRib 41; ER 167, 178, 182–3, 192; LL 7, 89; King (1972) 225–6; Hughes (1978) 266–72; Wemple (1981) 32, 44–5; Herlihy (1985) 49–50, 73–4; Heidrich (1991) 122–7.

[113] LV 3. 1. 5; *Form. Marc.* 2. 10; *F.Tur.* 22; Greg. Tur. *franc.* 4. 28, 6. 45, 7. 40; PLS Capit. 1. 67; ER 181–2; 199; LL 102; Vismara (1977) 637–73; Hughes (1978) 272–5; Wemple (1981) 47.

dowry re-emerged in southern Europe, again assuming paramount importance in the cities of the high middle ages.[114]

Daughters in Late Roman Succession

It is a universal sentiment that property should be handed down
from parents to children.[115] But if all descendants receive an
equal share the patrimony may be broken up into such small
pieces that the new households are worse off than the old one.
This diverging devolution of property is a dilemma in all human
societies. In most of them, sons are somehow favoured at the
expense of daughters. For example, sons often inherit the land
while daughters receive only moveable property and in any case
less than their brothers. On the other hand, in the absence of
sons, daughters are mostly preferred to other relatives. This
seems to have been a common phenomenon in all major Eurasian cultures.[116]

One method of preserving the family property intact is primogeniture. Especially small farmers must often have faced the fact
that their estate could not maintain more than one heir. They
may have been tempted to leave their farm to one son, marry
their daughters as best they could, and send the other sons off, to
find employment in the army, for example. But such smallholders
are never discussed by Roman jurists, and their family behaviour
must remain highly conjectural. Propertied people had more
freedom to divide their estates, yet they knew perfectly well
that if they had too many children their wealth would be split
up. To avoid this they tried, if anything, first and foremost to
limit the family size. Some fathers certainly discriminated among
their sons, leaving them unequal shares and being censured for
this by Christian bishops. We should not expect to find a uniform
pattern: individual families tried to cope with their problems in
different ways. But primogeniture as a general family strategy is
not attested in the Roman empire, whether in the principate or in
late antiquity.[117]

---

[114] Hughes (1978) 276–85.
[115] Aug. *util. ieiun.* 10. 12, CCL 46. 240; Greg. Tur. *vit. patr.* 20. 1; see further
Ch. 5, Sect. 2.   [116] Goody (1990) 1–7.
[117] Aug. *in evang. Joh.* 2. 13, CCL 36. 17; *in psalm.* 49. 2, CCL 38. 576; *util. ieiun.*
12–13, CCL 46. 240; *nupt. et concup.* 1. 15. 17 CSEL 42. 229; *serm.* 57. 2, PL 38. 387;
Ambr. *hex.* 5. 18. 58, CSEL 32. 1. 184; *Iac.* 2. 2. 5, CSEL 32. 2. 34; *Noe* 26. 95, CSEL

According to Roman law, if the father did not leave a will, or if it was for some reason invalid, all his sons and daughters *in potestate* inherited an equal share. If there were no children the brothers and sisters of the deceased divided the estate, again equally, irrespective of sex. These principles dated back to the Twelve Tables, and they were never seriously questioned in Roman history. A few rescripts in the third century are addressed to people who obviously did not know the law, but that is nothing exceptional. During all of late antiquity, the Roman law of inheritance remained very favourable towards daughters and sisters.[118]

However, intestate succession was not the rule in Roman society. People usually wanted to draw up a will, to give all kinds of instructions for posterity. As we have seen, Roman law allowed the parents much flexibility in dividing their estate. Although few Roman wills have survived outside Egypt, literary and legal sources help to reconstruct some general patterns of testation in the upper classes. There is no doubt that people often divided their property equally among all sons and daughters, but it seems also to have been common to favour the sons. For example, if you had a son and a daughter you could leave the former two-thirds and the latter only one-third. Or a son might receive a half and two daughters the remaining half. In short, daughters often inherited somewhat less than their brothers but still a very substantial portion of their father's property. If no sons survived, the daughters usually received the bulk of the estate.[119]

We shall now return to the position of dowry in Roman succession. The size of the upper classes' dowries in the principate is in some cases known but the figures can rarely be compared with people's total property. The wealthy provincial widow

---

32. 1. 481; *Ioseph* 2. 5, CSEL 32. 2. 74; Bas. *hex*. 8. 6, PG 29. 178; Caes. Arel. *serm*. 52. 4, CCL 103. 231. On family size, cf. below, Ch. 3, Sect. 1. See also Kaser (1971) 668–70; Hopkins (1983) 76–8; Garnsey and Saller (1987) 142–4; Shaw (1987a) 25–6, 43–7; Corbier (1991c) 185–6; Saller (1994) 161–80.

[118] GI 3. 14; Coll. 16. 2. 2; CI 3. 36. 11 (Phil.), 6. 58. 1 (223), 3 (250), 9 (294); GE 2. 8; cf. D. 45. 3. 20. 1. See also CI 6. 58. 14 (531); and below, Ch. 3, Sect. 3, for a daughter's children.

[119] Champlin (1991) 107–20; see also Crook (1986a); and, with some caution, Woess (1911) 65–106; e.g. D. 23. 3. 85, 26. 7. 58. 3, 28. 2. 18, 28. 5. 48. 1, 31. 34. 6, 31. 77. 30, 32. 27. 1, 33. 4. 14; CI 2. 3. 15 (259), 3. 28. 12 (229), 6. 21. 6 (225). On Roman heirship strategies in general, see Saller (1991b).

Pudentilla gave Apuleius a dowry of 300,000 sesterces out of her capital of four million. Terentia brought Cicero 400,000 HS, and it seems that in the early principate one million was a very large dowry by any standards. This figure may have been exceeded, but in general the dowries of the very rich probably did not increase in proportion to their wealth. Among the affluent provincials and the moderately well-off senators something in the order of one year's annual income (about 5–10 per cent of the father's property) appears to have been considered normal. In any case, it was not normal in these circles in the first three centuries of the empire that a woman's dowry included all her inherited property or even most of it.[120]

In the mid-fourth century two laws established that a widow could not give more than three-quarters of her estate as dowry to a new husband; otherwise her children could claim that the dowry was 'undutiful' towards them (CT 2. 21. 1–2). Unfortunately, the laws do not reveal whether such excessive (*'inmodica'*) dowries were becoming common. On the other hand, unlike in classical law, in the late fifth century a daughter's dowry and a son's nuptial donation were taken into account when their legitimate portion was calculated.[121] This would have made it easier to disinherit a daughter who had already been dowered. Of course, it does not prove that such things happened more often than before. But in 531 Justinian made a surprising remark:

. . . *cum paene mulieribus tota substantia in dote constituta est.* (CI 8. 17. 12. 2)

. . . as women have almost all their property in their dowry.

This is puzzling. Had dowries grown bigger so that women now received a greater proportion of their inheritance at their marriage and less at their father's death? In other words, did Roman fathers sacrifice a larger share of their property already in their own lifetime to endow their daughters? Another alternative is that the daughters' 'residual' inheritance was simply diminishing. In that case the total amount which devolved on them

---

[120] See Saller (1984*b*; 1994: 212–24); Treggiari (1991*a*) 340–8; Krause (1994*b*) 49–55; and above in this section. The *SC Pisonianum* (so far unpublished) shows a daughter with a dowry of one million plus a *peculium* of four million; I thank Werner Eck for information on this text.

[121] CI 3. 28. 29 (479 east); cf. CG 2. 4. 1–2 (235/223), and above.

decreased as well. Perhaps, if women in late antiquity acquired a sizable donation from their husband, they were no longer thought to need a further contribution from their own family.

This interpretation would seem to be supported by a passage of the Syro-Roman Law Book (L 1). It discussed Roman succession and confirmed that on intestacy sons and daughters inherited equally. Then it proceeded to testaments and explained that a man had to leave every daughter at least a dowry consisting of a quarter of her intestate share although he could bequeath more if he wanted to. All this was perfectly consonant with Roman law. What is remarkable is the implicit suggestion that daughters often had to content themselves with their dowries. According to some scholars, this custom was not only ancient and common in the Mediterranean world but was also becoming prevalent in the later Roman empire.[122]

The first problem with this theory is that we actually do not know much about inheritance systems in other ancient Mediterranean societies. In Greece only the city of Athens is fairly well documented. There daughters really had to content themselves with their dowry, which did not include real property. A daughter inherited the estate only if her father had no sons. Nevertheless, at least in some Greek cities, such as Sparta and Gortyn, women seem to have had good chances to inherit. Aristotle complained that women possessed two-fifths of all Spartan land (*pol.* 1270[a]). After *c.*300 BC little evidence is available for inheritance practices anywhere in the area which was later covered by the Roman empire. But in Graeco-Roman Egypt daughters clearly inherited landed property, sometimes sharing equally with their brothers, sometimes receiving a smaller portion than the eldest son. Moreover, as was noted earlier, their dowries represented rather modest capital values.[123]

To confirm or disprove Justinian's statement, we would need statistics on the relative size of dowries, something which we will naturally never have. As far as I know the best information available is another law of Justinian himself (Nov. 22. 18), dis-

[122] See Mitteis (1891) 244–7, 327–30, 348–9; Selb (1964) 27–8; and esp. Woess (1911) 107–21.
[123] Schaps (1979); Just (1989) 95–104; Sealey (1990) 29–31, 63–9, 75 (but his interpretation of the Law of Gortyn iv. 31–43 is not clear), 82–95; Préaux (1959) 165–6; Hobson (1983) 318–21; Goody (1990) 390–6; Egger (1994) 268.

cussing penalties for unjustified divorce (see further below, Ch. 5,
Sect. 3). Usually the innocent party obtained all the marital
assets. The emperor was worried about those marriages in which
no dowry and nuptial donation had been given: the husband lost
nothing when he rejected his spouse. That is why he was ordered
to forfeit one-quarter of his property to the innocent wife.
Justinian said that this used to be the maximal amount of
dowries. The quota applied up to properties worth 400 pounds
of gold. Above that, the fine did not increase, indicating that even
for very rich people dowries did not normally exceed 100 pounds
of gold.

I would regard this information as basically reliable even if it is
not totally free of ambiguity. For example, the law refers to the
size of dowries although it would have been more logical to speak
of *donatio*, which originally derived from the husband's own
property. It might be possible that the quota of one-quarter
referred to the totality of marital assets, assuming that the bride
usually included the groom's contribution in her dowry. But it is
more likely that *dos* and *donatio* were here confused simply
because they were thought to be of equal value.

Most papyri from late Roman Egypt record very small dowries,
reflecting the humble life of the majority of people. But one
sixth-century document comes from totally different circles,
perhaps from the absolute top of Egyptian society: it mentions
a man titled *endoksotatos* (*illustris*). Here we encounter a substantial dowry of at least 50 pounds of gold and 500 pounds of silver,
making together the equivalent value of about 80 pounds of gold.
Moreover, the dowry was accompanied by a nuptial gift of
precisely the same value. Coming back to Constantinople, we
hear that in 512 the antiquarian writer John Lydus received
from his bride a dowry of, as it happens, 100 pounds of gold.
He evidently considered this a good match. Although he probably came from a well-off provincial family and was at the
beginning of a successful career in the imperial administration,
he was by no means part of the ruling aristocracy. He does not
mention whether he gave a nuptial gift himself.[124]

---

[124] SB xvi. 12230 (6th c.), with Migliardi Zingale (1990); Joh. Lyd. *mag.* 3. 28.
See also CI 5. 14. 9. 1 (468 east) and Nov. 97. 5 (539), mentioning dowries of 1,000
solidi (*c.*14 gold pounds) and 30 pounds respectively.

It appears that in the early sixth-century eastern empire large dowries were often valued and paid in gold. They could alternatively include land, silver, jewellery, clothes, or whatever had been agreed upon. But about 100 gold pounds seems to have been a common value in affluent provincial and metropolitan families. It would have equalled 400,000 sesterces in the early principate: this was roughly the level of the largest dowries reported (see above). The richest Constantinopolitan landowners may occasionally have provided even more. However, these figures cannot be compared with people's net wealth. They would have been trivial sums for western senators; in the early fifth century the wealthiest among them drew annual incomes worth over 5,000 pounds of gold, and many of the others between 1,000 and 2,000. Alas, we do not know the value of dowries in these circles. The eastern aristocracy does not seem to have been as rich.[125]

In any case, it is a reasonable conclusion that a typical dowry in the eastern upper classes was not more than one-quarter of male property, and was often much less, especially in the highest echelons of society. What proportion it was of female properties is unclear: they might have been smaller on average (and this is precisely the point at issue). However, the same law of Justinian that fined the husband one-quarter of *his* property subsequently applied the same quota to the wife in case she occasioned the divorce. The implication is that the hypothetical dowry would have constituted approximately the same share in both estates.

Thus it is hard to believe that in the eastern empire 'women had almost all their property in their dowry'. It held true first and foremost during the time before their father had died. Perhaps it was just a rhetorical exaggeration. Women in the upper and middle classes certainly continued to have large extradotal properties. Admittedly, we cannot exclude the possiblity that dowries were now somewhat bigger than in the principate, and many women of the lower classes may truly have inherited little over and above their dowry.

In the west the development was in any case different. As we

---

[125] On the typical contents of dowries, see CI 5. 12. 31. 5–8 (530). On senatorial properties, Olympiod. *frg.* 41. 2 (Blockley); Geront. *vita Mel.* 15, SC 90. 156; Jones (1964) 554–7; cf. Demandt (1989) 284–6; Clark (1990) 262–3.

have seen, the traditional dowry was overshadowed and later replaced by the nuptial gift from the groom. Whatever the early medieval women received from their own family, it did not come in the form of dowry.

In general, it is very difficult to estimate the influence of *donatio nuptialis* on late Roman succession. If a woman was dowered with a quarter of her father's property and if she obtained an equal sum from her husband, she already had almost as much as her brother could inherit. But it is very unlikely that a daughter with one or more siblings could really have such dowry. Playing with averages would lead us astray because family size and other circumstances varied. On the other hand, her brothers would in their turn have received dowries from their wives. Who was actually thought to own the marital assets? If the spouses separated amicably they could both take what they had brought. If they were widowed the surviving partner obtained everything, but in practice only to preserve it for their common children (see below, Ch. 5). Individual contracts, which were common, made the matter even more complicated. There was hardly a general pattern. The dowry and nuptial gift would certainly often have sufficed to maintain a daughter during her marriage and possible widowhood. But if a father wanted to treat all his children (and grandchildren) equally in his will he may have ignored what they received from their spouses (cf. Nov. 97. 5).

Literary sources seldom describe concrete decisions made in individual families. We are told that in the early fifth century the Athenian sophist Leontius bequeathed his property to his two sons, leaving his daughter Athenais only the trifling amount of a hundred gold coins (allegedly because he foresaw that she would become the eastern empress Eudocia). This story has sometimes been used to prove that it was customary to disinherit daughters in favour of sons.[126] But apart from problems of legendary elaboration, the narrative suggests just the opposite: Athenais is said to have been totally surprised at such an unusual and inequitable act.

It seems that in late antiquity the general opinion of the propertied classes still favoured roughly equal treatment for all

---

[126] Malalas 14, PG 97. 528; Zonaras 13. 22, PG 134. 1185; cf. Mitteis (1891) 329; Woess (1911) 115.

sons, and at least a fair provision for daughters. For example, Gregory of Nyssa tells that his parents' property in late fourth-century Cappadocia was divided equally among nine surviving children, including daughters.[127] The numerous rich Roman and Constantinopolitan heiresses in the late fourth and early fifth centuries are a further proof that property kept devolving on women, and it was clearly common that only females survived to inherit.[128] Of course, they might sometimes waive an onerous inheritance (Symm. *ep.* 9. 150; *rel.* 34. 8–13).

Evidence from late Roman Egypt is concentrated on the lower levels of the society. The few wills and other documents which record the division of a given estate are just enough to show the variety of arrangements. It emerges quite clearly that if only daughters survived they took the estate. In one family of five daughters, the two elder were left their dowries while the three younger divided the rest. Which of them fared better is not revealed. In fact, it may not even have been exactly known. The people in question were probably often thinking of particular items like houses, vineyards, and fields, which did not need to be assessed. In another family one daughter had already been dowered. Her unmarried sister seems to have received a special monetary bequest for that purpose. Together they inherited equal shares of specified plots. Their three brothers divided among themselves other farms and the town house, one of them obtaining also an additional farm. It is quite possible that this division favoured the sons although it cannot be established. But certainly the daughters always expected to be well treated, and there are cases in which brothers and sisters shared equally. When an adulterous daughter received only her legitimate portion it was a grave punishment.[129]

[127] Greg. Nyss. *vita Macr.* 20, SC 178. 206; cf. also Aug. *civ.* 3. 21, CCL 47. 90 (commenting on the republican *Lex Voconia*); *serm.* 355. 3, 356. 11, PL 39. 1570ff. On the *Lex Voconia*, see Dixon (1985); Gardner (1986) 170–8.
[128] See e.g. Symm. *rel.* 19, 30, 34. 12, 39; and below, Ch. 5, Sect. 1, for Christian aristocratic heiresses.
[129] See P.Oxy. vi. 907 = MChr 317 = FIRA iii. 51 (276); P.Cair.Isid. 62–4 (296–8), 77 (320); P.Oxy. liv. 3756 (325); P.Rainer Cent. 85 (364/366), with Bagnall (1993) 95; P.Lips. i. 33 = MChr 55 = FIRA iii. 175 (368); P.Masp. ii. 67156 (570); P.Monac. i. 1 = FIRA iii. 184 (574); P.Lond. v. 1727. 42 = FIRA iii. 67 (583/4); and for the adulterous daughter, P.Masp. i. 67097 = FIRA iii. 15 (6th c.), with Beaucamp (1992a) 79–81.

Legal sources themselves attest that the strong position of women in Roman succession had not radically changed. The rules on intestacy did not represent just a theoretical scenario or an obsolete relic of the past. Many estates were for some reason or another divided without a testament. In the late fourth century the children of a deceased daughter for the first time acquired rights of inheritance after their grandparents. Such a change is difficult to explain if a widespread custom increasingly discriminated against daughters themselves. In 458 a western law claimed that it was an impious act to punish a daughter by leaving her less than other children. And finally there is a law which Justinian in 536 addressed to the governor of Armenia. He demanded that the inhabitants of that province give up their barbarous habit of excluding women from inheritances. He ordered them to adopt the Roman custom that sons and daughters inherit equally. Even allowing for some over-simplification on the emperor's part, his claim suggests that in most of the eastern empire the practice had to be relatively uniform.[130]

How much then did women inherit? Given the nature of ancient economy, this is almost the same as asking: how much wealth did women possess in Roman society? The question is quite important, and it is a pity that we cannot answer it with any reasonable accuracy. In fact, it may be doubted whether we can answer it at all. But at least in those cases where there was no will, or where it was broken, female children inherited precisely as much as males. Moreover, when only one child survived, the father probably left him or her the bulk of his property. Thus property was again equally divided. Two children created more possibilities, but even then it was 25 per cent probable that both heirs were girls. When the estate had to be divided between a son and a daughter, there was certainly no universal rule: I would argue that on average girls did not receive less than a third. On that assumption, daughters would have inherited over 40 per cent of property in families with two surviving children.[131] If three

[130] CT 5. 1. 4 (389), and further below, Ch. 3, Sect. 3, for the succession of grandchildren; NMaj 6. 3 (458); Nov. 21 (536); see also CI 6. 28. 4 (531); Inst. 2. 13. 5.
[131] This total is made up from those cases where two daughters inherited all (25 % of families) plus those where a daughter and a son divided the estate (50 % of families, women taking a third, i.e. 17 % of the property). An uneven sex ratio would naturally affect the calculation (cf. below, Ch. 3, Sect. 1).

children survived the proportion would have dropped a little below 40 per cent, and further in larger families. Although these figures may seem to have been plucked out of the air, I believe that they suggest the right order of magnitude. There were also those fathers who did not manage to produce a single child. In such cases the estate would probably have been bequeathed to an adopted son or to a male relative, say a nephew, rather than to a female.[132]

All in all, this sketch suggests that women in the Roman empire could own a very great proportion of private property. Somewhere between 30 and 45 per cent of the total is possible and any figure under 25 per cent seems unlikely. The estimate holds only for the upper classes and thus for larger properties. Surviving land lists from Roman Egypt indicate a female ownership between one-quarter and one-sixth in the villages.[133] Of course, the distribution of wealth may have varied greatly in different provinces.

After the Germanic immigration, Roman law in the west continued to grant daughters equal rights of intestate succession.[134] Visigothic law seems to have followed this already in the Code of Euric, and at any rate from the sixth century onwards. Other Germanic laws are more difficult to interpret: they use ambiguous terminology, their textual tradition is sometimes insecure, and they seem to omit important things, presupposing knowledge which we do not have. It is no wonder that all details of Germanic inheritance are highly controversial. For example, the difference among moveables, ancestral land, and real property in general appears potentially relevant but is hopelessly confused in the existing sources. A thorough presentation of the many problems would lead to nothing. In short, it seems that all Germanic codes preferred men in the inheritance of land, or at least ancestral land. If there were sons they excluded the daughters, but in the absence of sons daughters usually excluded all others. This was the broad pattern. Within it, the different historical situation of individual societies certainly caused much variation.[135]

[132] I was reminded of this by Judith Evans Grubbs. Cf. e.g. Greg. M. *ep.* 9. 75.
[133] Bagnall (1992: 138; 1993: 130–1, cf. also 92 ff.).
[134] GE 2. 8; LRB 10, 45. 4; and the *Breviarium* throughout.
[135] CE 320; 327; LV.Ant 4. 2. 1, 10; LV 4. 2. 5, 9; LB 14, 51, 75, 78; PLS 59; LRib 56; *Edict. Chilp.* 3 (MGH Capit. i, p. 8); ER 158–60, 181, 199; LL 1–5, 65, 102. See Ganshof (1962) 33–40; Wemple (1981) 46–8; Kroeschell (1982); Murray (1983) 177–212; Arvizu (1984).

Did the written codes really reflect a customary 'law of succession' as the Germanic population perceived it? A few Merovingian *formulae* for a will indeed suggest that. However, they show also that people were not always happy to follow the general norm:

Dulcissima filia mea illa illi. Diuturna sed impia inter nos consuetudo tenetur, ut de terra paterna sorores cum fratribus porcionem non habeant; sed ego perpendens hanc impietate, sicut mihi a Deo aequales donati estis filii, ita et a me setis aequaliter diligendi et de res meas post meum discessum aequaliter gratuletis. (F.Marc. 2. 12)

My most sweet daughter. An ancient but impious custom prevails among us that sisters do not have a share of the paternal land along with their brothers. But I have pondered this impiety (and decided that), as God has given you to be equally my children, in the same manner I have to love you equally, and after my death you shall equally enjoy my property.

Another *formula* (*C.Senon.* 45) puts this in slightly different words and explicitly attributes the rule to the *'lex Salica'*. Then both *formulae* continue to make the daughter an equal heir to the whole estate.[136]

We have every reason to think that such testamentary practices were widespread. No actual will in favour of a daughter survives from the Merovingian period. However, one is indirectly attested in the famous testament of Burgundofara, in the year 633/4.[137] This noble lady had two brothers and a sister. Among her holdings she mentions half of a *villa* which her father had left her 'in his will' and the portion of another which she had received 'in a legitimate division with her siblings'. Several other deeds and some literary sources show that women possessed real property, often specifying that they had inherited it from their parents. A few papyri similarly attest the inheritance of land by Gothic and Roman women in sixth-century Italy.[138]

---

[136] Cf. also *F.Sal.Merk.* 23; *F.Marc.* 2. 10, 2. 17; *F.Tur.* 22; *F.Sal.Lind.* 12; Murray (1983) 183–91; Heidrich (1991) 124–5; and below, Ch. 3, Sect. 3.

[137] Pard. 257; a new edition with extensive commentary in Guerout (1965).

[138] Pard. 245 (628), 256 (632), 369 (673), 394 (680), 429 (692), 448–9 (698), 452 (*c.*700), 476 (710), 480 (711), 491 (715), Add. 82 (746), etc. Greg. Tur. *franc.* 8. 32, 9. 20, 9. 35, 10. 8, 10. 22, 10. 31. 14; *Vita Rusticulae* 5; *Vita Sadalbergae* 12; *Vita Rictrudis* 9 (in McNamara 1992: 125, 185, 203). From Italy, P.Tjäder i. 13 (553), 20 (*c.*600); ii. 33. 9 (541), all Goths; in ii. 30 (539) and 31 I. 1 (540) the names suggest a Roman origin. For later charters, see Herlihy (1976) 27–32; Wemple (1981) 113–20.

We do not know how long Germanic and Roman inheritance were perceived to be separate systems. We may surmise that the difference between them was not as great in practice as it was in theory. In all population groups, wills could be used to achieve a desired division of the estate. We cannot reconstruct a 'typical' devolution of property. Nor do the sources allow us to confirm any positive developments between the great migrations and the Carolingian empire. Thus it is nearly impossible to speculate about why Germanic fathers wanted to ignore the 'ancient' custom. Perhaps changes in their society affected the role of inherited property or maybe they were simply influenced by their numerically superior Roman neighbours. Or perhaps no real changes took place at all.

4. SUMMARY AND CONCLUSIONS

In the Mediterranean marriage pattern, girls left their childhood behind them when they entered into marriage in their teens. Quite conceivably, they were not thought capable of choosing their mate by themselves. Usually they were married off by the father. Of course, he could take the girl's opinion into account if it was reasonable and not based on such trivialities as romantic fancy. If the father was dead, the mother and other relatives took care that the girl was not guided by blind love. No one questioned these principles in late antiquity. It was only in the Germanic kingdoms that the lawgivers grudgingly accepted marriage without parental consent, and this was only because they wanted to avoid bloodshed between parents and prospective grooms. On the other hand, the Romans did not exercise such strict parental control over brides because they were women but because they were so young. If a woman married at a later age, when she had in most cases lost not only her first husband but also her father, no one could legally interfere in her decision.

In theory, *patria potestas* gave the Roman father very extensive powers over his daughters. In practice they may not often have felt its weight. Girls moved away from home very early with their dowry and often with an additional *peculium*. If the father was alive, he was a figure which balanced the husband's power. We shall return to this question in Chapter 4. In the opposite case, if there was a conflict between father and daughter, he could not exert financial pressure on her as easily as on his sons: she had her dowry and could be supported by her husband. What most enhanced the father's authority was his ability to divide the estate unequally among his descendants.

As *patria potestas* was a peculiarly Roman concept, it must have initially perplexed the peoples of the large empire when they came into contact with Roman law. We have very little evidence on these problems, but there is no doubt that in late antiquity *patria potestas* was still a living institution. It suggests that provincial citizens had managed to adopt the Roman family system. There may have been several reasons for this. First, most children did not acquire much property from other sources than their father. Thus the system of inheritance advance (*peculium*) did not conflict too harshly with economic realities. One major exception was maternal inheritance, and we will see in the next chapter that this actually caused some changes in Roman law. Secondly, fathers usually died so young that their children were not *in potestate* very long. Thirdly, it was clearly advantageous to older males to have their descendants in their economic power. It is no wonder that Roman law proved conservative about changing this matter.

There was one more factor which made *patria potestas* easier to accept for all late Roman citizens. It was the possibility of emancipating children from paternal power. How frequently it was used in the principate we do not know. In late antiquity it was certainly common to end *potestas* when children became adult or married, but it was still voluntary. A father who wanted to keep his descendants *in potestate* could do so for as long as we can follow the sources both in the east and in the west.

After many centuries of purely dotal marriage, nuptial gifts from the bridegroom's side emerged in Roman law in the third century. The reasons are unknown but they may have been connected with the new, wider circle of citizenship. In any case the husband's contribution grew in the fourth and fifth centuries, finally to eclipse the old dowry in the western kingdoms. This development may have had important consequences for the economic position of women. In practice, the woman often gave the gifts back as dowry, or they were otherwise administered by the husband. In most cases she probably came to control the property only after the end of the marriage. Thus it had the same function as a testamentary bequest from the husband. It was only more secure because it had been guaranteed in the marriage contract.

On the other hand, a sizable *donatio* from the husband may have affected the devolution of property more generally. If the dowry and bridegift sufficed to maintain a woman in her widowhood, she had less need for an inheritance from her natal family. Such considerations were perhaps relevant among the lower classes but they are nowhere recorded in our sources. The marital assets of the rich were smaller in relation to their total holdings. Probably these assets did not weigh too heavily in the behaviour of the late Roman aristocracy.

By historical comparison, daughters had a strong position in Roman succession. In late antiquity the generally accepted ideology was that, if possible, daughters should receive as much as sons or only slightly less. Real life may not have been that simple. After all, personal situations varied and Roman testators had an almost perfect freedom to bequeath their estate. Sometimes daughters received more, sometimes less. If any more general patterns can be found, they were probably based on social differences. The more wealth a family had the easier it was to divide it among all descendants. Besides, small families in the Roman nobility increased the possibility that there were no sons and that daughters inherited the whole estate. It is very probable that heiresses in the later Roman empire possessed more land than their counterparts in the successor kingdoms. But this is only a conjecture as we really do not know how much wealth the new early medieval upper classes transferred to their daughters and wives.

3

Mothers and Children

According to the Roman family system, a citizen of legitimate free origin belonged only to the paternal *gens* and *familia*. The mother was a member of another family. Theoretically, she had no rights to her children although she had not a few duties to them. Furthermore, there was between them no automatic right of succession.

Thus the legal ties between a child and his/her maternal family were relatively weak. But we should not conclude that the same automatically held true for social and emotional expectations. Literary sources of the imperial era show that the Romans loved their daughters' children, counting them as their true descendants, and took no less pride in their maternal ascendants than in the paternal ones.[1] In the later principate, the increasingly polyonymous aristocrats often inherited names from their maternal line. Demographic conditions, too, favoured the mother's family. Because of the age difference between spouses the maternal grandmother was on an average twenty years younger than the paternal grandfather, the maternal grandfather and paternal grandmother being in the middle. Of course, this pattern was often broken owing to remarriage or other individual deviations, but it is evident that the mother's parents survived much more often to see their grandchildren.

It seems that the old legal system preserved a rather artificial family structure, which did not correspond to the feelings of most Romans. In practice they accepted the intimate relation between mothers and children, not only emotionally but also financially. In the following sections we shall see how that was gradually

[1] e.g. Hier. *ep.* 107. 1, 4; Sidon. *ep.* 3. 1. 1, 4. 21. 1–2; on Fronto, see Corbier (1991*c*) 190–1, and on Ausonius' *Parentalia*, Herlihy (1985) 6–7. See also D. 50. 12. 15, 50. 16. 220. 3; Saller (1984*a*); Dixon (1988) 41 ff.

recognized in late Roman law. However, initially we will adopt a slightly different viewpoint, discussing fertility along with the official encouragement of maternity.

I. MOTHERHOOD AND POPULATION POLICY

The Marriage Laws

Roman population policy as we know it began with Augustus. He wanted the citizens to live in marriage and produce legitimate children. His famous marriage laws, the *Lex Julia de maritandis ordinibus* and the *Lex Papia Poppaea*, enjoined all Roman females between 20 and 50 years, and males between 25 and 60 years, to marry if they did not already have children. A widow between these ages had to remarry within two years while a *divorcée* was allowed only eighteen months. Unmarried people did not face criminal penalties, but their capacity to receive inheritances and legacies was limited to their own family. That could be quite uncomfortable in a society where propertied people habitually made bequests to distant relatives and friends.

The marriage also had to be fecund. Childless couples were allowed to receive only one-half of the bequests left to them, and the spouses could bequeath each other only one-tenth of their estate. On the other hand, fecundity was rewarded with a number of advantages. Men and women who had children reaped benefits from the so-called right of children (*ius liberorum*). This was a collective term for a number of different rules. For example, just one child surviving to puberty entitled married people to make mutual wills, perhaps also to receive external bequests. Two children exempted a freedman from certain obligations to his patron. Three children were needed in Rome to avoid the duty of being guardian, four children in Italy, and five in the provinces. For some public offices, the candidate who had more children might be preferred. Many other privileges are known, and the whole system seems to have been quite complicated. It was also modified during the principate.[2]

[2] See e.g. UE 14–18, 29; GI 2. 286, 3. 42–52; FV 191–2, 247; CI 5. 66. 1–2; D. 50. 6. 6. 2; *Gnom. Id.* (BGU v. 1210 = FIRA i. 99) 24–32; Tert. *apol.* 4. 8, CCL 1. 93. For more sources and the whole complex issue of marriage laws, Brunt (1971) 558–66; Kaser (1971) 318–21, 724; Humbert (1972) 138–78; Wallace-Hadrill (1981); Treggiari (1991a) 60–80.

Most details remain obscure because they were no longer recorded in later legal sources, nor do they directly concern us here. Women were first and foremost affected by one important rule: freeborn mothers who had given three live births earned the *ius trium liberorum*. Freedwomen needed four children to obtain the same privilege. It gave mothers certain rights of inheritance after their intestate children. Even more importantly, it freed them from the lifelong legal guardianship (*tutela mulierum*).[3] We shall return to this question shortly, and again in later sections.

The practical operation of the Augustan laws is not particularly well documented, and their success is debatable. They may have had an effect on nuptiality if not on fertility. In any case they continued to be enforced up to the early fourth century. The restrictions on inheritance undoubtedly caused inconvenience among the upper classes. On the other hand, they were soon evaded by imperial dispensations. The *ius liberorum* could be granted as a mere favour, irrespective of the actual number of children. Of course, the privilege was easiest to achieve if one had direct access to the emperor, either personally or through friends. Trajan claimed that he did not give it lavishly. However, it was not limited to the aristocracy: at least one freedwoman with the *ius liberorum 'beneficio Caesaris'* is inscriptionally attested already in the late first century.[4]

On the occasion of Constantine's wedding in 307 a panegyrist characterized the marriage laws as the 'foundations of the state' (*Paneg.* 7. 2). Few contemporaries may have shared such a positive view: Constantine himself did not. In 320 he abolished these time-honoured rules, claiming to remove the 'threatening terrors of the laws' and to liberate women from the commands 'placed on their necks like yokes' (CT 8. 16. 1). From then on, unmarried and childless Romans were to have no legal disadvantages.

Subsequent church historians, writing in retrospect, thought

[3] Usually *living* children were required for the *ius liberorum*, and this might originally have been the rule for women too. If it was, the rule was later modified, since in the late 3rd c. three live births clearly sufficed. GI 1. 145, 1. 194, 3. 44; UE 26. 8, 29. 3; D. 50. 16. 137; PS 4. 9; see also Kübler (1909) 156–64; Parkin (1992) 115–19.

[4] UE 16. 1a; PS 4. 9. 9; FV 170; Dio 55. 2. 5–6; Plin. *ep.* 2. 13, 10. 2, 10. 94–5; CIL vi. 1877; see also CIL v. 1768; 4392 (cf. add. p. 1079). Generally on the laws' effects, see Humbert (1972) 170–8; Treggiari (1991a) 77–80.

that the emperor was motivated by his sympathy for Christian asceticism.[5] Modern scholars have usually agreed with them. That is natural because there was an intimate connection between the new religion and the ideal of single life. The Christian church was developing into a powerful proponent of celibacy, and it certainly had nothing against Constantine's measure. Probably the emperor had some idea of this, however vague, in 320. On the other hand, the law itself (in its surviving form) does not refer to religious connections. Nor was celibacy yet such a fashion among Christians as a few decades later, and especially not in the upper classes, where the financial penalties had real significance.

It was the senatorial aristocracy which had always most strongly resented the marriage laws and which benefited from their abolishment. In fact, Constantine's enactment was originally part of a more extensive law. Its other surviving fragments deal with economic matters and especially inheritance. Obviously, CT 8. 16. 1 had more to do with inheritance legislation than family legislation, let alone church policy. It was perhaps connected with Constantine's strivings to improve his relations with the senate. Of course, it was only an advantage if it could at the same time be seen as a friendly gesture towards his Christian supporters.[6]

Moreover, it should be noted that, although Constantine removed the penalties for the unmarried and childless, he preserved the rewards for fertility. The number of children exempted people from various civic duties.[7] The *ius liberorum* did not disappear either in 320. A married couple needed it to be able to inherit from each other, and it still enhanced the inheritance rights of mothers.[8] On the other hand, the right

---

[5] Euseb. *vita Const.* 4. 26; Sozom. *hist. eccl.* 1. 9. 1–4; Cassiod. *hist.* 1. 9, PL 69. 893.

[6] The fragments to be connected are: CT 3. 2. 1, 11. 7. 3; CI 6. 9. 9, 6. 23. 15, 6. 37. 21. For an exhaustive treatment, see now esp. Evans Grubbs (1993*b*: 122–6; and 1995: 103–39), which I am essentially following; and cf. also Spagnuolo Vigorita (1988). On Christian asceticism, see further below, Ch. 5, Sect. 1.

[7] Such exemptions were still recognized by Justinian: D. 50. 6. 6. 2; CI 5. 66, 10. 52; see also CT 12. 1. 55 (363), 12. 17. 1 (324); Symm. *ep.* 1. 77; LRB 36. 6.

[8] e.g. CT 8. 16. 1. 2 (320), 13. 5. 7 (334), 9. 42. 8–9 (380 east); see also CT 5. 1. 3 (383 west). The *ius liberorum* is absent from 12. 1. 124 (392 east), perhaps a special case due to curial demands. On the succession rights of mothers, see further below, Ch. 3, Sect. 3; on the guardianship of women, Ch. 4, Sect. 1; on the inheritance between spouses, Ch. 4, Sect. 2.

continued to be given as a benefaction to supplicants. If we can deduce anything from the general development of Roman social privileges, the grants must have become more and more common:

Sancimus, ut sit in petendo iure liberorum sine definitione temporis licentia supplicandi, nec implorantum preces aetas vel tempus impediat, sed sola miseris ad poscendum auxilium sufficiat desperatio liberorum. (CT 8. 17. 1 (396 east))[9]

We sanction that there shall be the unrestrained freedom of supplication to the Emperor in petitioning for the *ius liberorum*, without any limits of time, and neither age nor time shall debar the prayers of those persons who implore the Emperor, but despair alone of having children shall suffice unhappy parents for demanding such aid.

In 410 the eastern government abandoned altogether the requirement of children and enabled all spouses to make mutual wills. Yet in connection with the succession of mothers the *ius liberorum* lingered on and was abolished only by Justinian.[10] In the west, childless spouses were still petitioning the emperor for it in 446 (NVal 21. 1. 3). By now it was no longer a real means of population policy but just a legal relic. At most, it preserved a vague idea that fertility was something which should be rewarded. But when the western government in 458 again briefly resorted to active encouragement of maternity, trying to make remarriage compulsory for widows, it did not even mention the *ius liberorum*.[11] The concept itself still appeared in the *Breviarium* (though it was suppressed in the contemporary Roman Law of Burgundy 10. 5). It was properly explained in the *interpretationes* to CT 5. 1, whereas the *interpretatio* to NVal 21. 1 had clearly misunderstood it. This incidentally shows that the interpretations were not written at the same time, or at least not by the same person. In the sixth century there cannot have been many people left in western Europe who understood the strange term (see below Ch. 4, Sect. 2). In the east it disappeared, as already noted, under Justinian.

---

[9] See also CT 15. 14. 9 (395 west), 8. 17. 3 (410 east), 8. 17. 4 (412 west).

[10] CT 8. 17. 2–3 (410 east); CI 8. 58. 2 (528); Nov. 22. 47. 2 and Inst. 3. 3. 4; cf. also the Syro-Roman Law Book L 10.

[11] NMaj 6; see further below, Ch. 5, Sect. 1.

Nuptiality and Fertility

The real social and demographic background of the Augustan population policy remains somewhat obscure. The main source is the historian Cassius Dio, who lived in the early third century. Dio (54. 16. 2) maintained that there were far fewer marriageable females than males in the freeborn Roman population. This presupposes that female mortality was much higher. On the model life-tables, there should actually have been a surplus of marriageable women, because the sexes were nearly in balance at birth and girls married earlier. It is indeed possible that fewer women survived to early adulthood and through the reproductive years. Maternal mortality was undoubtedly high, although its effects may have been exaggerated and anyway are impossible to measure. The same holds true for differences in childhood mortality. Exposure and infanticide seem to have been common in the ancient world, and there is some evidence that girls were more likely to be exposed. The practice continued unabated during late antiquity and the early middle ages, despite some unsuccessful and often half-hearted attempts to forbid it. Besides, when food is scarce even unconscious selection may favour the survival of male children.[12] However, although Ambrose complained that poor people exposed their offspring, he expressly said that the wealthy preferred abortion (*hex.* 5. 58, CSEL 32. 1. 184). Whether it was frequent or not, this method could not affect the sex ratio.

All in all, it is not easy to believe that the mortality of well-born women was so much higher that it caused a considerable imbalance of the sexes. A further uncertain factor is the frequency of female and male remarriage respectively. In any case, it is fairly certain that in the upper classes practically all girls married at least once. Whatever the number of well-born men who refused ever to marry, their sisters during the principate did not have such an option, nor did spinsterhood yet constitute a part of

[12] On exposure and infanticide, see e.g. P.Oxy. iv. 744; Apul. *met.* 10. 23. 3; Tert. *apol.* 9; CI 5. 4. 16, 8. 51; CT 5. 9–10, 11. 27; LB.extrav. 20; *Conc. Vasense* (442) 9–10, CCL 148. 100; etc. For more references, and discussions of the whole topic, e.g. Brunt (1971) 148–54; Coleman (1976); Boswell (1984; 1988); Kammeier-Nebel (1986); Grupe (1990); Treggiari (1991a) 398–410; Parkin (1992) 92–105; Bagnall and Frier (1994) 75–110, 151–3, 159–65; Harris (1994); Krause (1994a) 34–52.

upper-class family strategy. Developments in the Christian empire will be treated in a later chapter.[13]

We next turn to fertility. Theoretically, in a stable and stationary population, with average life expectancy at birth between twenty and thirty years, the gross reproduction rate is about two to three. In other words, on average each woman should bear four to six children, half of whom would die before adulthood. That the expectation of life in the Roman empire lay within the said limits is more than likely. On the other hand, the citizen population need by no means have been stable or stationary. Slaves were manumitted in great numbers and peregrines enfranchised (mainly before 212). Apart from this, the population as a whole may have been declining or increasing; no reliable evidence exists. Moreover, there were movements inside the population. Urban centres were likely to draw immigrants from the surrounding countryside. It is generally believed that the upper orders failed to reproduce themselves naturally: they were constantly replenished from below. Adding to these problems, family size need not have been constant over a longer period of time. Changing social conditions and sentiments, or heightened mortality due to recurrent epidemics, may have affected fertility on any level of society.[14]

Clearly no direct conclusions can be drawn from this theoretical scenario, especially not for the senatorial aristocracy. But it implies that, unless the Roman population was declining very sharply, large parts of the population had to reach a high level of fertility. Obviously, these people were most likely to be found outside cities and among the less propertied classes. The evidence on their families is necessarily thin. Asia Minor is an area where Christian grave inscriptions offer some information about family size. The relevant sample comprises seventy-nine families of 'provincial middle class'. Yet, although the epitaphs seem to record an unusually high proportion of children, females are

[13] Cf. Dio 56. 1–10; Hopkins (1965) 325; Brunt (1971) 136–55, 560–1; Dixon (1988) 91–3; Treggiari (1991a) 83–4; Krause (1994a) 34–73. For single life and remarriage in late antiquity, see below, Ch. 5, Sects. 1–2.

[14] Note that a 'stable' population means constant death and birth rates and no external factors (like migration) while 'stationary' also supposes that the birth rate equals the death rate, i.e. the rate of growth is zero. On all this, see Parkin (1992), esp. 72–5, 84–90, 111–33; Bagnall and Frier (1994) 135–47. For the reproduction of the republican and early imperial élite, see Hopkins (1983) 69–107, 194–8.

clearly under-represented and infant deaths are probably missing. Still other children may for various reasons have been
omitted, so that the sample just gives the minimum size of the
attested families. The average number of children born was
certainly above four and probably at least six.[15]

As to the upper classes, the situation was surely different. The
literary evidence suggests that the early imperial aristocracy
normally had only a few adult children, often just one or none.
In the early sixth century bishop Caesarius of Arles complained
that some 'rich' women might, after they had borne two or three
children, be tempted to kill or abort the subsequent ones. There
is no doubt that propertied people often wished to limit the
number of their offspring and were able to do so. On the other
hand, there were certainly always aristocrats who craved for
children but could not have any.[16]

A study of the most famous senatorial *gentes* in the fourth
century has revealed that for a clear majority of known unions
only one or two children are attested. However, this cannot be the
whole truth. First, the relevant family trees display sixty-one
male and twenty-seven female children (and two unspecified),
which is clearly an impossible sex ratio. Second, it is important
to bear in mind the difference between children born and children surviving. Even among the aristocracy infant mortality must
have been high. Yet the aforesaid *stemmata* include few children
who died before adulthood: again demographically a very unlikely situation. If we simply double the number of recorded male
progeny we arrive at *c*.120 children, or an average of 2.4 for the
fifty unions in question. Of course, this represents only the
absolute minimum. How many infant deaths and other unrecorded offspring should be added remains unclear. The true figure
may well have been above four.[17]

The purpose of these examples is not to postulate estimates of

[15] See Patlagean (1978), esp. 180–2; and cf. Parkin (1992) 111–13.

[16] Caes. Arel. *serm.* 52. 4, CCL 103. 231; cf. Ambr. *hex.* 5. 58, CSEL 32. 1. 184;
Aug. *nupt. et concup.* 1. 15. 17, CSEL 42. 229; *serm.* 57. 2, PL 38. 387; Amm. 16. 10.
18. On the economic motives, see above, Ch. 2, Sect. 3; on inability to have
children, e.g. Plin. *nat.* 7.57; Plin. *ep.* 10. 2; Aug. *in evang. Joh.* 2. 13, CCL 36.
17; and generally, Eyben (1980/1); Treggiari (1991a) 403–9.

[17] See Étienne (1978); I have used his tables 3–7, not counting unions in the first
generation. Children are attested for 46 of the recorded 50 marriages. Cf. also
Krause (1994a) 15. Similar calculations for the principate are not known to me.

fertility for any social class. There is not enough data to show chronological developments either. The main implication for our study is that the general level of fertility in the Roman empire had to be relatively high. It was probably so high that most ordinary women would have attained the *ius liberorum* (three live births) without difficulty. Among the propertied classes, the chances were probably somewhat less. Nevertheless, I would suggest that the majority of senatorial women who survived through their childbearing years achieved the required births. A number, of course, did not. Some of them at least could seek the privilege from the emperor. These assumptions will underlie further discussion in Chapter 4, Section 1.

2. MOTHERS' RIGHTS AND DUTIES

Mother and Father

Roman law did not recognize any maternal power which would have resembled *patria potestas*. The Romans never forsook this principle. On the other hand, they always realized that this was only part of the truth. In practice, both parents took care of their children and were entitled to similar reverence:

Pietas enim parentibus, etsi inaequalis est eorum potestas, aequa debebitur. (Ulp. D. 27. 10. 4)

For piety is owed equally to both parents, although their power is not equal.

In late antiquity literary sources often recorded the important role which mothers had in their children's life. If both parents were alive and living together their personal influence naturally varied. Gregory of Nazianzus criticized the inequality of secular law which gave only fathers a power (*eksousia*) over their children. However, the *paterfamilias* would hardly have passed his wife totally over when he was making major decisions on their common children. For example, she was likely to be consulted when daughters were married. The father's pre-eminence became important only if the parents disagreed, and then his view would probably have prevailed in any culture.[18]

---

[18] Greg. Naz. *or.* 37. 6; cf. Aug. *ep.* 262. 11, CSEL 57. 631; Beaucamp (1992a) 324–9; on the marriage of children, cf. above, Ch. 2, Sect. 1.

If the father died early, the mother's role was inevitably enhanced. As we have already noted, Roman law strictly observed did not recognize a special link between a mother and her children at all. Local practice often gave widows a more extensive authority. Thus a few papyri from late Roman Egypt show women giving their children in adoption: once a man and wife are acting together, once a widow is acting alone, once a grandmother. In Roman law, children *sui iuris* should have been arrogated, which was a quite difficult juridic process for an ordinary provincial. It is no wonder that in their own communities people resorted to private arrangements.[19] It is not known how strongly Roman officials actually objected to such practices. At least they did not accept the idea that widows sold their children into slavery—but it could still happen.[20] Taken together, the evidence from Egypt, supported by occasional legal fragments, indicates that in popular consciousness mothers had a *de facto* power over their children. When the father was living it was subsidiary to his authority, but after his death the widow had to shoulder the responsibility alone. How far the people themselves thought of this practical situation as a '*materna potestas*' remains uncertain.[21]

The relationship between a widowed mother and her children could not always be harmonious. She had the possibility of taking the children to court, whether for invectives or more serious offences. To be sure the emperors Valerian and Gallienus advised a certain Galla to settle the quarrels with her sons preferably at home, but if that were to prove impossible they promised severe punishments for the disobedient children.[22] However, the mother's authority is not likely to have often turned into a legal issue. From the mid-fourth century mothers were entitled to recover their gifts if it could be proved that the children had not shown proper *pietas* towards them. Fathers of

---

[19] P.Oxy. ix. 1206 = FIRA iii. 16 (335), xvi. 1895 (554); MChr 363 = P.Lips. i. 28 (381); Beaucamp (1992a) 163–71, 276; cf. Kaser (1971: 347–8; 1975: 208–11).

[20] CI 7. 16. 1 (Carac.), 2. 4. 26 (294); cf. Zos. 2. 38. 3 (for the time of Constantine).

[21] See Beaucamp (1992a) 158–71, 179–85, for Egypt; and cf. e.g. Taubenschlag (1929; 1955: 149–53); On the guardianship over children, see below.

[22] CI 8. 46. 4 (259); see also CI 9. 1. 14 (294); D. 37. 15. 1. On the relations between mothers and adult children during the republic and the principate, see Dixon (1988) 168–228. Cf. also e.g. Hier. *ep.* 117; Greg. M. *ep.* 9. 36, 9. 87; a paragon of obedience was Marcella, Hier. *ep.* 127. 4.

emancipated children achieved this right at about the same time. Fathers who retained their children *in potestate* had always been able to reclaim the *peculium*, at least in theory without any special justification. In a sense, the position of all parents was now less unequal.[23]

Still, this may not have been a very convenient method for upholding maternal authority: to recover a donation the mother had to win her case in the court. Disinheritance was slightly better. If the children found themselves disinherited they could recover their lawful portion only by bringing an action of *querela inofficiosi testamenti* and proving that their behaviour towards the mother had been beyond reproach. Again, the last word was left to the court. Sometimes it was concluded that the mother had excessively meddled in her children's affairs. Once a mother had included in her testament a condition that her daughter had to divorce. The daughter had obeyed but was later returning to her husband and asked the emperor if she could keep the property. She was reproached for her conduct and was told that the condition had been *contra bonos mores* anyway. In practice, the mother may have brought her children under control most easily in the same way as the father: she could threaten to leave them only their lawful portion. This was less dramatic than total disinherision but almost as efficient, and it could not be contested.[24]

Because of the patrilineal system, in divorce children normally went to the father. He was also responsible for their maintenance.[25] His death did not, in theory, affect their livelihood, as they inherited his property and were maintained from it by their guardian. However, in need the mother and her family were expected to contribute to their care. If the children were illegitimate it was the only alternative (D. 25. 3. 5. 2–5; CI 2. 18. 11). On the other hand, children were required to support a destitute mother.[26]

---

[23] CT 8. 13; see also FV 248 (330). D. 39. 5. 31. 1 is probably interpolated, cf. FV 254.

[24] CT 2. 19. 2 (321); CI 6. 25. 5 (257); cf. CI 6. 25. 2 (213), 3. 28. 20, and 5. 17. 4 (both 294); and see above, Ch. 2, Sect. 2, on paternal disinheritance.

[25] Cic. *top.* 4. 20; D. 25. 3; CI 5. 25. 3–4. For the mother's role, see Dixon (1986) 108–10; Treggiari (1991a) 467–70.

[26] D. 25. 3. 5. 2, 27. 3. 1. 2–5; CI 5. 25. 1; *Gloss.* iii. 36. 49 ff.

We cannot know how effectively this system worked in practice. In the lower classes small children were not so precious that the husband always wanted to keep them following a divorce. If he did not bother to rear his offspring the mother had to take them whether she could afford it or not. Even in the upper classes, where children were a more valuable asset, they sometimes remained with their mother.[27]

If there were special reasons even a Roman court could adjudge a child to the mother instead of the father. The earliest imperial rescripts to this effect that were known to Ulpian came from Antoninus Pius. They continued at least down to Diocletian.[28] However, the basic legal and social norm does not seem to have changed by the age of Augustine: he said that a mother could not question the father's rights to their child (*ep.* 262. 11, CSEL 57. 631). According to Ambrose, after the divorce children could be under the care of either parent, but he apparently assumed that it was the husband who determined whether he drove them off with their mother or not (*in Luc.* 8. 4, 6, CCL 14. 299). This view was certainly realistic, whatever the law exactly said at that moment.

It was left for Justinian to revise the legal norms systematically. If the father had occasioned the divorce and the mother did not remarry, she would keep the children but the father had to carry the expenses. Otherwise he kept them. However, if the father was clearly of lesser means the mother had to take full responsibility (Nov. 117. 7). This still left much room for negotiation, especially when the divorce was consensual, as most undoubtedly were. Not surprisingly, in contemporary papyri all sorts of arrangements appear. Sometimes the father, sometimes the mother took the children, sometimes a kind of joint custody seems to be meant. Once a girl had been living first with her mother and then with her father, after the mother had remarried and driven her off.[29] In the west, no further legislation is known to us.[30]

[27] See CI 5. 25. 3 (162); D. 25. 3. 5. 14; P.Panop. 28 (329); P.Oxy. liv. 3770 (334); l. 3581 (4/5th c.); and cf. Cic. *Cluent.* 27.

[28] D. 25. 3. 5. 14, 43. 30. 1. 3, 43. 30. 3. 5–6; CI 5. 24. 1 (294).

[29] P.Flor. i. 93. 19 = P.Lond. v. 1713 = MChr 297 = FIRA iii. 22 (569); P.Lond. v. 1712. 26 (569), v. 1731 = FIRA iii. 23 (585); P.Masp. ii. 67154r. 25 (6th c.), ii. 67155. 24 (6th c.). Beaucamp (1992a) 160–2.

[30] Only the Anglo-Saxon laws of the 7th c. give some short rulings on the children's fate in divorce: the mother could take them with her and was entitled to an alimony from the father, Aeth. 79–80; Ine 38.

To return to the question of adoption, it was clearly impossible in classical Roman law to be adopted by a woman. Women could not have their children in their own *familia*, not even children who had no legal father. Moreover, adoption created *patria potestas*, which no woman could have.[31] Women were nevertheless able to bequeath their property to someone on condition that he take her name. In the principate this was not regarded as a real adoption though in the republic the situation is less clear. The Romans themselves were not too meticulous about this: they called it a testamentary adoption, and Suetonius expressly stated that the emperor Galba had been adopted by his stepmother.[32]

There is evidence that throughout the empire women actually did adopt already in their lifetime. Roman authorities did their best to explain that such acts were not valid in imperial law. We may assume that their task was not easy. Diocletian had to answer a petition from a woman who had lost her own children and wanted to adopt (*arrogare*) her stepson. The emperor did not actually promise to sanction an adoption; he only stated that she could keep the boy as if he were her legitimate offspring. However, just a little later Lactantius saw fit to say that the emperor Galerius' wife Valeria had adopted his illegitimate son because she was herself barren. It was perhaps especially common that women tried to establish a link with their stepchildren. As there could be no question of *potestas* and hardly of the agnatic *familia* either, the main purpose, apart from emotional values, was certainly to ensure mutual support and rights of inheritance. It is unfortunate that we do not know how imperial law later reacted to such attempts. After Diocletian, the issue next appears only in Justinian's Institutes. Women were still said to be unable to adopt, but if they had lost their own children they might receive a special permission from the emperor. Nothing similar is attested in the west.[33]

---

[31] GI 1. 104; UE 8. 8a; D. 50. 16. 195. 5, 196. 1.

[32] Suet. *Galba* 4; Galba's new name appears in *Fast. Ost.* 33; see also Cic. *Att.* 7. 8. 3; Suet. *Tib.* 6; Salomies (1992) 6–10, 15, 32–3.

[33] See P.Oxy. iii. 504 (2nd c.), 583 (119/20); xvi. 1895 (554); Euseb. *hist. eccl.* 6. 2. 13, SC 41. 85; D. 5. 2. 29. 3 ('*sine iussu principis*' is probably interpolated); CI 7. 33. 8 (294), 8. 47. 5 (291); Lact. *mort. pers.* 50. 2; Inst. 1. 11. 10; GE 1. 5. 2; Beaucamp (1990: 48–52; 1992a: 167–71, 327).

Mother and Guardianship

All people agreed that after the father had died the children's best and most natural support was their mother: no laws were needed to say it.[34] Roman fathers often expressed in their will the hope that their widow and children would continue to live together. In late antiquity, widows who realized this ideal were sometimes praised in grave inscriptions.[35] But the widow's personal power over her children was not, according to Roman legal thinking, supposed to extend over their property. For that, they needed a guardian. Often the father had appointed him in his will (*tutor testamentarius*). Otherwise the nearest paternal male relative (brother, uncle, or cousin) automatically assumed the office (*tutor legitimus*); if these were unavailable, someone had to ask a magistrate to appoint a guardian. This was first and foremost the mother's duty.[36]

In classical law, the mother herself could not be tutor. Originally she was always under guardianship herself. Although later it was usually admitted that women could administer their own property, they were still forbidden to represent others (see below, Ch. 7, Sect. 1). Thus it was in some sense logical to think that guardianship was exclusively a male duty. Two second-century passages in the Digest appear to suggest that in special circumstances even women could be accepted:

Tutela plerumque virile officium est. (Gaius D. 26. 1. 16)

Tutelage is, for the most part, a masculine office.

Feminae tutores dari non possunt, quia id munus masculorum est, nisi a principe filiorum tutelam specialiter postulent. (Neratius D. 26. 1. 18)

Women cannot be appointed as tutors, because this is a duty for males, unless they petition the emperor especially for the tutelage of their children.

---

[34] Joh. Chrys. *vidua elig.* 7, PG 51. 327; Sidon. *ep.* 2. 8. 1; see also LV 4. 3. 1.

[35] D. 7. 2. 8, 7. 9. 11, 35. 1. 72. pr, 32. 30. 5, 33. 1. 21. 5, 35. 1. 8, 35. 1. 62. 2. For inscriptions, Humbert (1972) 356–8; CIL v. 6266, xi. 312; ICLV 2142; ICUR[1] ii. 447; ICUR[2] ii. 5492. From earlier times there is only one comparable inscription, CIL xiii. 2056, Humbert (1972) 68.

[36] D. 26. 6. 1–4 (cf. 26. 2–5); CI 5. 31. 6 (224), 8–10 (291/294), 11 (479 east); 6. 56. 3 (315); CT 3. 18. 1 (357); 3. 18. 2, probably western, because repealed by NTh 11 (439); LRB 36. 4; Pall. *hist. laus.* 46. 2 (cf. Paul. Nol. *ep.* 29. 9, CSEL 29. 256). Beaucamp (1990) 315–20.

However, a Byzantine scholiast reveals that the first excerpt has been interpolated, and the same certainly holds true for the second. In several other passages, throughout the third century, it is clearly stated that mothers cannot assume the office. Nevertheless the jurists imply that occasionally even imperial officials might be unaware of the ban and appoint female guardians.[37]

Ignorance or negligence of the law seems to have been common among lay people. It is clear that mothers very often failed to have a *tutor* appointed. Sometimes it was pardonable when the children did not own anything. Sometimes it happened in accordance with the late husband's expressed wish.[38] Some fathers evaded the law by bequeathing their property to the mother on condition that she transfer it to their common children at a specified age. Another alternative was to bequeath a usufruct to the mother until the children reached majority.[39] These were perfectly legal methods. The evidence from Roman Egypt suggests a more confused situation. For example, the Latin testament of a Roman cavalryman leaves little doubt that the mother of his minor son was *de facto* intended to be the guardian.[40] Other papyri show mothers (and grandmothers) appearing on behalf of their children under various designations either with or without male help. Many citizen fathers evidently tried to comply with Roman law by appointing a more or less nominal guardian while they expressly stated that they wanted the widow to participate in the administration.[41] Both within and outside Egypt, she often at least supervised the guardians. Normally guardianship was not a coveted privilege but merely a burden. If the mother was willing to take a more active role she was unlikely to meet strong

[37] *Basilica* 38. 1. 46 *sch.* 1 (Scheltema B vi. 2184); see Simon (1969) 374–5; Kaser (1971: 353 n. 3; 1975: 227 n. 30); Beaucamp (1990) 325–30. Interpolated is also Ulp. D. 38. 17. 2. 25. See further D. 26. 2. 26. pr, 26. 5. 21. pr; CI 2. 12. 18 (294), 5. 35. 1 (224).

[38] D. 26. 6. 2, 38. 17. 2, esp. 25–6; CI 2. 34. 2 (294), 5. 31. 10 (294), 5. 34. 6 (293), 6. 56. 3 (315); P.Harr. i. 68 = P.Diog. 18 = FIRA iii. 28 (225).

[39] D. 28. 2. 18, 33. 2. 37, 36. 1. 76. 1, 36. 2. 26. 2, 38. 17. 2. 46; CI 3. 33. 5 (226); Humbert (1972) 220 n. 1, 237, 297; Gardner (1986) 152–4; Saller (1991b) 40–1. For a lifelong usufruct and the widow's maintenance, see below, Ch. 5, Sect. 2.

[40] CPL 221 = FIRA iii. 47 (142); cf. D. 26. 2. 26. pr.

[41] e.g. P.Oxy. vi. 898 (123); FIRA iii. 30 = SB v. 7558 (172/3); 51 = P.Oxy. vi. 907 (276); 59 = PSI ix. 1027 (151); P.Sakaon 37 = P.Thead. 18 (284). Cf. D. 3. 5. 30. 6, 26. 7. 5. 8. See further Kübler (1910) 184–94; Taubenschlag (1929: 123–6; 1955: 153–9); Préaux (1959) 143–5; Gardner (1986) 147–9; Markus (1989) 70–105; Beaucamp (1992a) 172–5.

resistance: occasionally she could manage the affairs totally by herself. Only if things went wrong did the question of her authority create a legal problem.[42]

In sum, there were a great number of mothers all over the empire who were ready to act as virtual guardians for their children. Many men were also inclined to entrust them with this task. Of course, we should not think that all widows longed for the trouble and responsibility, but obviously most people found it difficult to understand why mothers were not allowed to take on the guardianship if they so wished. We do not know when Roman law finally accepted the widely practised custom. It had probably not happened by Diocletian's reign (CI 2. 12. 18). Fourth-century legislation on this topic has largely disappeared because the title 3. 17 of the Theodosian Code (*De tutoribus et curatoribus creandis*) was not preserved in manuscript T. The existing version derives from the *Breviarium* and includes only one law on the guardianship of mothers. Presumably it was the latest still in force:

Matres, quae amissis viris tutelam administrandorum negotiorum in liberos postulant, priusquam confirmatio officii talis in iure veniat, fateantur actis ad alias se nubtias non venire. . . . His illud adiungimus, ut mulier, si aetate maior est, tum demum petendae tutelae ius habeat, cum tutor legitimus defuerit. (CT 3. 17. 4)

Mothers who have lost their husbands and demand tutelage over their children to administer their affairs, before confirmation of such an office can legally come to them, shall state in the public records that they will not proceed to another marriage. . . . To the aforesaid provisions We add the following: that a woman who has attained her majority shall have the right to petition for a guardianship only when a statutory tutor is lacking.

This law was passed in 390 when Theodosius I was in Milan together with the young western emperor Valentinian II. It appears to modify an existing institution rather than establishing a new one. Although the preamble is missing, it is unlikely that the law's main innovation had been cut out. Be that as it may, even if the maternal guardianship had already been accepted

---

[42] e.g. D. 3. 5. 33, 16. 1. 8. 1, 46. 3. 88; PS 1. 4. 4; CI 2. 18. 1, 4. 29. 6, 4. 51. 4, 5. 31. 6, 5. 43. 1, 3, 5. 45. 1, 5. 46. 2, 5. 51. 9 (all 3rd c.); CT 3. 30. 3 (329). Cf. Beaucamp (1990) 323–5. For the remarkable archive of Babatha from the early 2nd-c. Arabia, see Cotton (1993).

some time previously, the interval must have been relatively short. The Romans always viewed the influence of stepfathers with suspicion: their wish to exclude remarried widows from the guardianship was natural from this viewpoint. It was probably a mere slip that such a restriction had not been recorded earlier. We should also remember that until 320 widows had been legally enjoined to remarry. Whether they actually observed this provision or not, this possibility may have been one reason why the lawgivers had been so reluctant to accept them as guardians.[43]

Thus the precise legal context of this solitary fragment from the *Breviarium* is not quite clear, still less its practical consequences. According to the text, agnatic relatives as *tutores legitimi* still took precedence over the mother, but it does not say what happened if the father had appointed the widow guardian in his will. In view of the evidence from the third century, we would expect that such a question was raised quite often. Once the male duty had in principle been opened for women, it is hard to see why the father's decision could not have been accepted. However, a passage denying it was taken into the Digest, so obviously Justinian's lawyers did not sanction the practice. On the other hand, mothers were by no means compelled to act as guardians. Some did not officially take on the guardianship but did not apply to the magistrate for someone else to be appointed either.[44]

Literary sources do not tell much about the practices in real life. Many writers, mostly before 390, allude to the strong influence which widows had on the finances of their children. However, their language is so imprecise that they shed no light on the legal subtleties of such arrangements. In the early sixth century, the widow of a high Byzantine official had assumed the guardianship of their daughter until her own remarriage, quite in accordance with the law. But in this particular case the maternal guardianship had proved far from beneficial: and that is just the reason why we hear of it in a contemporary law.[45] Among

---

[43] Saller (1991*b*) 46; for remarriage and stepparents, see below, Ch. 5, Sect. 2. Cf. also Beaucamp (1990) 325–7.   [44] See D. 26. 2. 26. pr; NTh 11 (439 east).
[45] Nov. 155. pr. Literary references e.g. Hier. *ep.* 108. 26, 125. 6, 130. 14; Ambr. *vid.* 2. 7, PL 16. 250; Symm. *or.* 8; Pall. *hist. laus.* 46. 2; Paul. Nol. *ep.* 29. 9, CSEL 29. 256; Aug. *conf.* 3. 4. 7, CCL 27. 30; Basil. *ep.* 107–9; Greg. Naz. *ep.* 207; Lib. *or.* 1. 4; Joh. Chrys. *in II Tim.* 7. 4, PG 62. 642; *non iter. conjug.* 6, SC 138. 192. See Beaucamp (1992*a*) 329–35, for discussion and further eastern evidence.

the propertied classes, the management of a minor heir's affairs might sometimes have had its attractions. Among the others, it had little relevance. Thus in many cases the current legislation hardly aroused any interest.

In late Roman Egypt mothers did not appear with the title of guardian. Only once, in 284, is the mother called *kedestria* (a general term comprising both *tutores* and *curatores*). At that time any kind of maternal guardianship was almost certainly in conflict with Roman law. On the other hand, in late third century Egypt even other female relatives are occasionally recorded as guardians. In the following centuries, when children have male guardians it is often possible to establish that their mother is dead. She is definitely alive only in a handful of such cases. Widows for their part frequently appear on behalf of their children, especially in the sixth century; only they are not called guardians. These observations suggest that relatives were appointed guardians mainly when both parents were dead. Widows later did not need the title of guardian because their position as such defined their authority. At that time, the terminology of guardianship in general was becoming rare in the papyri. Unfortunately, relevant documents for the whole period are so few that these conclusions are only tentative at best.[46]

In the North African *Tablettes Albertini* of the 490s a few widows appear selling land together with their sons but it is impossible to tell if that is in the capacity of a 'guardian', a co-heir, or a usufructuary possessor of the estate.[47] The two latter alternatives seem more probable, as also in an Italian sales contract of 539. In 557 a Gothic woman of some standing applied to the *curia* of an Italian town for a guardian to be appointed for her two minor sons as she did not feel herself capable of that task.[48]

Roman law had sacrificed its old principles when it legalized maternal guardianship in the fourth century. At first it was only a cautious step because the agnatic relatives were still preferred to the mother. As the evidence from Egypt shows, it remains open

[46] Beaucamp (1992a) 172–90, with documentation and a thorough discussion; see e.g. P.Sakaon 37 = P.Thead. 18 (284); P.Tebt. ii. 378 (265); P.Oxy. vi. 888 (late 3rd/early 4th c.).

[47] *Tabl. Alb.* 11, 15, 18; cf. also 24 and 27, in which the widow appears alone.

[48] P.Tjäder ii. 30; i. 7; cf. also i. 8.

how far this was observed in practice. In the east the agnates' preferential claim was expressly removed by Justinian, while in the west it was evidently forgotten by the late fifth century, at least where we have any sources (southern Gaul).[49] This system was adopted by the Visigoths and Burgundians without difficulties. It indicates that in their society the power of the paternal kin could not be decisive any longer (if it ever had been).[50] Thus in the sixth century all over the Mediterranean area widows could act as guardians for their own children if they wished to do so and did not remarry. What the situation was to the north, in the less established societies of the Franks and other Germans, is in the lack of evidence impossible to tell.[51]

3. MATERNAL KIN AND INHERITANCE

Inheritance from the Mother

Originally the Roman woman had been married into her husband's power (*in manum*). She thus joined his family and was in the same position in regard to succession as her own children (*filiae loco*). However, as marriage *sine manu* came to dominate during the republic, the mother ended up in a strange situation: she remained legally part of her father's family while her children belonged to another family governed by their father or grandfather. Intestate succession between mothers and children or children and mothers was ruled out, not to speak of the more distant maternal relatives.[52] This division was at the heart of the system of *patria potestas*.

The origins and purpose of marriage *sine manu* are a vexed

---

[49] Nov. 118. 5; LRB 36. 1; the *interpretatio* to CT 3. 17. 4 is inconclusive. The old rule is mentioned in the late 5th c. by the Syro-Roman Law Book L 8. Cf. also Beaucamp (1990) 330–7.

[50] LV.Ant 4. 3. 3, 4. 5. 5; LV 4. 3. 1; LB 59, 85. 1; see also Zeumer (1898) iv. 135–6; Levy (1942) 24. Cf. Conrad (1954) 58–9, 215–16, whose view is marked by a belief in the agnatic clan's paramount importance: it is certainly incorrect to see in the Burgundian and Visigothic laws only a '*Mitbestimmungsrecht*' of the mother. On the Germanic kinship system, see further below.

[51] See Greg. Tur. *franc.* 9. 19; and the Anglo-Saxon Hloth. 6, which indicates some sort of control by the paternal kin. Cf. Wemple (1981) 31, 61, with little documentation.

[52] GI 3. 24; Inst. 3. 1. 15, 3. 3. pr. On marriage *cum manu*, see below, Ch. 4, Sect. 2, with literature.

question which must remain outside the scope of this study. It is often assumed to have been introduced as a method to prevent property from moving from one family to another through women. It may have been connected with the Roman habit of letting daughters inherit equally with their brothers (see above Ch. 2, Sect. 3). Within this system, the woman's property would have reverted after her death to her nearest agnates, that is, brothers and their descendants.

If this was the rationale behind marriage *sine manu*, we must accept that it was later given up or forgotten. A first step was the possibility of drawing up a will. This was permitted to women quite early, first through certain legal tricks and then routinely from the reign of Hadrian (GI 1. 115a; 2. 112–13). There is no doubt that a mother often, if not always, wanted to benefit her own offspring. For some time, the nearest agnatic heir retained some control over this by being her legal guardian. However, for unknown reasons the Roman upper-class males surrendered their control through gradually increasing loopholes until the legitimate guardianship of the agnates was totally abolished under Claudius. By this time Roman women were very strongly expected to bequeath their property to their children.[53]

Thus, whether or not there had originally been an attempt to prevent succession through women, by the early principate the testamentary practice of the upper classes had effectively undermined this principle. The inevitable legislative change came only in 178 when the *senatusconsultum Orfitianum* was passed: in the case of intestacy a woman's property was to be inherited by her own children before any other.[54] A will in conflict with this could now, if not earlier, officially be claimed to be unduteous and broken (*querela inofficiosi testamenti*).[55] The connection between a woman and her children had thus been re-established.

However, these rules were not yet extended so as to cover the maternal grandparents. For two more centuries, their estate could

[53] e.g. Val. Max. 7. 7. 4, 7. 8. 2; Quint. *inst.* 4. 2. 5; D. 5. 2. 28; Gardner (1986) 13–20, 165–8, 185–7; Humbert (1972) 191–5; Dixon (1988: 51–60; 1992: 74–7). On the guardianship (*tutela mulieris*), see further below, Ch. 4, Sect. 1.

[54] UE 26. 7; D. 38. 17. 1; CI 6. 57. For a detailed treatment, see Meinhart (1967).

[55] D. 5. 2. 5, 5. 2. 27. 4; CI 3. 28. 1, 3, 15, 3. 29. 1, 7, 8; CT 2. 21. 1 (358). See Gardner (1986) 185–7; Humbert (1972) 191–5. Of course, there was no necessity to contest the will: cf. the behaviour of Marcella, Hier. *ep.* 127. 4.

come directly to the grandchildren merely through a will, or if they lacked all agnatic relations, in which case the inheritance could be claimed in the more distant class *unde cognati*.[56] This was changed only in the late fourth century. Then the grandchildren were allowed to represent their mother after her death. In other words, even a deceased daughter would automatically transmit property away from the agnatic family. However, her children got only two-thirds of the share which their mother would have received had she been alive: their uncles and aunts divided the rest. The quota was increased to three-quarters if they had only more distant agnatic relatives.[57]

As far as we know, this remained the official position in the east until Justinian revised the whole system of Roman intestate succession. In his *novellae* he rejected the agnatic principle altogether. After that, there was an absolute equality between the sexes in all inheritance classes as well as among relatives through masculine and feminine lines.[58]

In the west, it is evident that around the year 500 the Roman population still lived according to the predominantly agnatic principle, as it was left by the imperial legislation of the late fourth century. Daughters inherited like sons, of course, and their children received two-thirds of the maternal share. In the absence of children, the relatives of the father took precedence over those of the mother.[59] The Visigoths adopted the former principle (i.e. the reduced portion of the grandchildren from a daughter) directly from Roman law into the Code of Euric. By the seventh century, and probably already in the sixth, they had equalized the position of all grandchildren, thus achieving the same result as Justinian in the east.[60] We may assume that during

---

[56] D. 38. 8. 8, 44. 4. 17. 1; CI 6. 15. 3 (293), 6. 25. 1 (199), 6. 46. 1 (197); CT 8. 18. 5 (349 east). Cf. already Catull. 68. 119 ff.

[57] CT 5. 1. 4 (389 west) and 5 (395 east); this chapter was not preserved in the manuscripts of the Code: some laws may be missing. See already CT 8. 18. 6 (379 west) and 9. 42. 9 (380 east), which suggest that the children of daughters somehow took priority over other relatives on intestacy.

[58] CI 6. 55. 12 (528); Inst. 3. 1. 16; Nov. 118 (543); Kaser (1975) 497–512. For the Syro-Roman Law Book, which possibly here reflects Roman law before 389, see esp. Selb (1964) 19–20, 43–4, 60–6.

[59] LRB 10, 22. 9, 36. 4; GE 2. 8; PS 4. 8. 3. int; LRV CT 5. 1; see also Sidon. *ep.* 5. 1. 3.

[60] CE 327; LV 4. 2. 18, 4. 5. 4; cf. LV.Ant 4. 2. 8. See Zeumer (1898) iv. 124–33.

this time the Roman population living within Gothic territory had finally abandoned the agnatic system as well.

The importance of the patrilineal clan in early Germanic, and especially Frankish, society is a poorly documented and highly controversial question. Whatever was the social role of kin groups in the immediate post-migration period, it is now widely believed that the kinship structure was essentially bilateral: ties of kinship were traced through both the paternal and the maternal line.[61] The inference to be drawn from this assumption is that the system of inheritance was not markedly agnatic.[62] Rather, it may have followed the principle that ancestral property should revert to the family from which it had been inherited (*ius recadentiae*).[63]

As the Visigothic legislation from the very beginning adopted Roman models and the Frankish sources are so deficient, the reconstruction of an original 'Germanic' inheritance is a difficult task. Perhaps there was no common system in the first place. This problem need not immediately concern us here. However, it would be interesting to know if there were differences between 'Frankish' and 'Roman' succession in early medieval Gaul. In both systems children certainly inherited from their mother.[64] Moreover, daughters could inherit both moveable and immoveable property although the Frankish heiresses were in theory excluded by their brothers in regard to ancestral land (see above, Ch. 2, Sect. 3). On the other hand, it seems that in the Frankish system grandchildren could not replace their deceased parents but were excluded from the inheritance by their uncles and aunts. This applied to the children of both sons and daughters. In 596 the king, Childebert, tried to change the rule but with uncertain success: several *formulae* show that people felt they had to make a will to enable their grandchildren to inherit.[65]

It is against this background that we have to examine two

---

[61] Esp. Murray (1983) 11–32, 109–11, 217–24, etc. See also e.g. Kroeschell (1960); Herlihy (1985) 44–8; Kaufmann (1989); and more generally, Goody (1983) 222–39.

[62] On the obscure PLS 59, see Murray (1983) 201–12; cf. also PLS 58. 3–4, 62. 1, 68; Murray, 135–49; PLS 44; Murray, 163–75.

[63] Murray (1983) 212–15; see LV 4. 2. 6, and cf. already CT 8. 18. 4; LV 4. 2. 18.

[64] Cf. Pard. 245, 369, 394, 404, 448, 576–8; Pard. Add. 7, 11, 18, 20, 28, 36, 58, 71. The earliest of these documents is from the year 628.

[65] *Decr. Child.* 1 (MGH Capit. i, p. 15); *F.Marc.* 2. 10; *F.Sal.Merk.* 24; *F.Sal.Lind.* 12; see Murray (1983) 193–5. For the Burgundians, cf. LB 75.

slightly different forms of testament in favour of a daughter's children:

> . . . *dum et per legem cum filiis meis, avunculis vestris, in alode meo ad integrum minime succedere poteratis* . . . (*F.Tur.* 22)

> . . . as by law you could not wholly succeed to my inheritance together with my children, your uncles . . .

> . . . *dum et per lege cum ceteris filiis meis, abuncolis vestris, in alode mea accedere minime potueratis* . . . (*F.Marc.* 2.10)

> . . . as by law you could not at all succeed to my inheritance together with my other children, your uncles . . .

The crucial words in the first text are *ad integrum*. It seems to have been used by people who wanted to circumvent the old Roman rule that the children of a daughter inherited only two-thirds of their mother's share. The second formula, on the other hand, was intended to offset the precepts of the Frankish law which excluded them altogether.[66] This conclusion is made even more tempting by the fact that the first text in another clause expressly refers to the *Lex Romana*, a recurring habit in the *formulae* of Tours. There is at least a strong possibility that the *formulae* were originally born in two different legal traditions. They do not necessarily prove that the clerks who collected and copied them in the late seventh and eighth centuries perceived a marked difference in them any longer, still less those people who used them.

Maternal Inheritance and Patria Potestas

After the *SC Orfitianum* children in the third century could easily succeed to their mother's property. Furthermore, legal sources often discuss dowries and gifts from mothers to children.[67] However, the system of *patria potestas* presented serious difficulties: as children *in potestate* could not own anything, a bestowal on them actually accrued to their father. This could be quite inconvenient. If her husband was living and had not emancipated the children the mother could not give anything to them. Such a gift was void because all transfers of property

---

[66] Murray (1983) 194 n. 4.

[67] e.g. D. 17. 1. 60. 1, 23. 3. 5. 9; FV 254; CI 3. 28. 29, 4. 29. 12, 4. 50. 5, 5. 12. 2, 6, 8, 14, 5. 14. 9. 3–4, 6. 23. 6, 6. 50. 5, 7. 60. 2, 8. 55. 3, 6; CT 2. 24. 2.

between living spouses were forbidden.[68] A dowry from the mother did not cause similar problems: it enriched the daughter (and her father) only indirectly since technically it went to the groom.

Unlike gifts *inter vivos*, testamentary bequests between the spouses were valid.[69] Thus, if the mother left something to a child *in potestate*, her husband was the actual beneficiary. The problem must have been quite embarrassing for the Romans, who were so meticulous in the financial relations between the spouses. We know very little about practical arrangements in such situations. They were no longer relevant in the time of Justinian. The most natural assumption is that although the father was the legal owner there was strong social pressure on him to safeguard the children's interests. *Bona materna* seem to have been recognized as a special item within the paternal property. The inheritance was perhaps often included in the child's *peculium* and later assigned to him/her as *praelegatum* in the father's testament.[70]

Ultimately, these solutions depended on the goodwill of the father. Those who thought they could not count on it had other alternatives. Some mothers tried to assure by *fideicommissa* that the children really received the property after the father's death.[71] But there was an even more drastic method: many testators (and not only mothers) included in the will a condition that the children had to be emancipated before they could receive the inheritance.[72] The emperors and their jurists generally approved of such a precaution.[73] The practice was obviously not rare but not regular either, and, after all, most women could expect to outlive their husbands.

[68] FV 269; D. 23. 3. 34; 24. 1. 3. 4, 19, 49, 58; on the separation of the spouses' property, see further below, Ch. 4, Sect. 3.
[69] GI 2. 87; D. 29. 2. 6, 92, 29. 4. 21, 30. 11, 34. 2. 16, 35. 1. 42, 35. 2. 25. pr, 36. 2. 5. 7, 38. 17. 6, 9, 42. 8. 19, 49. 17. 3; CI 3. 31. 10, 6. 46.5 (both 294); CG 13. 14 (218). Cf. also Volterra (1966) 567–73; Meinhart (1967) 142–51.
[70] Cf. Tac. *ann.* 13. 43; Suet. *Tib.* 15; SHA *Marc.* 7. 4; Philostr. *vitae soph.* 558; D. 15. 1. 7. 5, 31. 77. 19, 31. 88. pr, 33. 7. 2; Humbert (1972) 246–52; Dixon (1988) 57; Champlin (1991) 125–6.
[71] D. 36. 1. 23. pr, 36. 1. 80. 10, 42. 8. 19, etc.; see further Humbert (1972) 214–24; Gardner (1987).
[72] Plin. *ep.* 4. 2, 8. 18; Suet. *Vit.* 6; D. 5. 3. 58, 29. 7. 6. pr, 32. 50. pr, 35. 1. 70, 77. pr, 92, 93, 45. 1. 107; CI 6. 25. 3 (216), 6. 42. 15 (256), 8. 54. 5 (294); PS 4. 13. 1; Humbert (1972) 224–32; Gardner (1986) 190.
[73] D. 26. 5. 21. 1 (Severus); CI 3. 28. 25 (Diocl.); 3. 28. 33. 1 (Just.).

The legal sources thus show that many Romans disliked the idea of the maternal inheritance falling under *patria potestas*. Obviously, as they were not willing to dismantle the system of *potestas* itself, they just had to accept the inconvenience in individual cases. Often they may have counted upon honesty and social pressure to ensure that justice prevailed. Otherwise they could resort to the legal expedients just described.

Of course, this applied to people who were reasonably well informed about Roman law. We have such a case in a papyrus from the 260s: the mother had instituted her children heirs on the condition of emancipation (CPR vi. 78). But there must have been many citizens around the empire who found it hard to understand how an inheritance left to a child would end up as the father's property. Alas, we have little evidence of their reactions. Another papyrus may illustrate the difficulty. Aurelius Thonios, son of another Aurelius Thonios, was selling land which he had inherited from his mother. In the document he (or rather the scribe) stated that he was acting together with his father who had him 'in his power according to Roman law', but later on he clearly presented himself as the owner by right of inheritance. Such a wording would hardly have been recommended by a Roman jurist. It preserved the popular idea that the child, not his father, was the real beneficiary. However, the disagreement with Roman law does not appear too serious since the father was present and sanctioned the sale. This fact may have been sufficient to satisfy an official who was more familiar with imperial law. Besides, the question did not arise at all unless there were someone who wanted to contest the sale's validity.[74]

In the course of time, it must have seemed desirable to establish more definite rules for the fate of maternal inheritance. This was done early in the reign of Constantine. Thenceforth the father was forbidden to alienate anything from the estate but had to preserve it for the children. He retained what was called both '*dominium*' and '*ius fruendi*' of the property. Constantine's chancellery seems to have meant that the father was still a kind of owner, though only with limited rights. In terms of classical law,

---

[74] P.Oxy. ix. 1208 (291); Volterra (1966) 576–85. Cf. also FIRA iii. 61 = SB 1010 (249); 63 = P.Oxy. viii. 1114 (237); in these cases it is quite obscure how the parties interpreted the legal situation.

this was very inaccurate language. The arrangement was essentially a lifelong usufruct, and was so called in later laws. In practice, it officially enjoined Roman fathers to do what they had earlier been expected to do voluntarily or by force of *fideicommissa*.[75]

Roman law did not go further than that. If the father wanted to exploit the *bona materna* during his lifetime, he was not prevented from doing it any more than during the principate. This is an important point because it shows how resistant the concept of *patria potestas* remained through late antiquity. Although Constantine and later emperors clearly wanted to protect the children's long-term interests, they could not put more restrictions on the father's power. It was simply considered too unjust to take the enjoyment of his children's goods away from him.

It is quite natural that the conflict of interests between the father and his children was most apparent in the case of maternal inheritance. After the Romans had taken the first legislative steps to solve this conflict, they gradually became aware of a number of other situations where the same problem existed. Consequently, the same solution (the father's lifelong usufruct) was applied to these cases: in 379 to any property inherited from the maternal grandparents;[76] in 426 to property received from the spouse;[77] and finally, from the reign of Justinian, to any funds acquired outside the family. The last step cannot be attested in the west.[78]

Constantine's rulings did not by any means remove the possibility of unease and conflict in individual cases. One obvious source of trouble was remarriage and stepparenthood (see below Ch. 5, Sect. 2). An enigmatic law from the last years of Constantine's reign discussed this situation. Some fathers, it said, were after remarriage causing damage to their children:

qui quoniam in his usufructuarii remansisse videntur, usurpare ea ac pervertere confidunt, ut per hoc his, qui in orbitate remanserunt, nulla nec possidendi nec litigandi tribuatur occasio. Ideoque placet, ne quis pater

[75] CT 8. 18. 1 (319 [315]). See esp. Humbert (1972) 397–401; also Levy (1951a) 34–40; Kaser (1975) 216–18, 248–51; Voci (1985) 52–9.

[76] CT 8. 18. 6 (379 west) and 7 (395 west); not yet in CT 8. 18. 5 (349 east).

[77] CT 8. 19. 1 (426 west); CI 6. 61. 2 (428 east); NTh 14. 8 (439 east); CI 6. 61. 4, 5 (472/3 east).

[78] CI 6. 61. 6 (529); Inst. 2. 9. 1. Cf. in the *Breviarium* CT 8. 18–19 (= LRV 8. 9–10); LRB 22. 1–2.

receptis deinceps matrimoniis earum rerum, quae prioris coniugis fuerunt,
sibi ius defendendum existimet nisi tutelae vice, donec minores probata aetate
esse videantur. His autem moderatio nostra cuncta iubet servari atque
restitui. (CT 8. 18. 3 (334)

Since such fathers appear to have remained as usufructuaries in the
goods of their children, they trust that they can appropriate these goods
and convert them to their own use [or: alienate them], so that by these
means the children who remain in bereavement may be given no
opportunity to obtain possession or to institute suit. Therefore, it is
Our pleasure that no father, after contracting a subsequent marriage,
shall consider that he may defend any right to the property of his former
wife, except as a guardian until the minors appear to be of fit [or: proved,
legal] age. This Our regulation orders everything to be preserved and
restored to the said children.

Perhaps, if we had the missing beginning and end of the law,
we would understand it better. Now it remains uncertain what
kind of malpractice exactly is meant, and what the solution
purports to be. The mention of guardianship and fit age are
surprising because, if the children were *in potestate*, their age
should have made no difference. We might think that the father
was compelled to emancipate them when they reached majority:
but that is not explicitly said, nor is such a detail likely to have
been suppressed. Constantine's decision evidently cannot be
explained by help from classical law. As we have it, the text
implies that if the father remarried the maternal estate was
isolated from his property. The children were otherwise still *in
patria potestate* but their *bona materna* remained outside it. This
may have resembled the regular arrangement by which soldiers
and civil servants could freely govern their salaries (called *peculium [quasi] castrense*).[79]

Assuming that this interpretation is correct, the rule did not fit
very elegantly into the Roman legal system. We cannot even be
certain that it was generally enforced: a western law in 426 does
not seem to know about it (CT 8. 18. 10. 1). However, it was
brought to general attention when the Theodosian Code was
published. Whether or not it was observed after that, it was not
included in the *Breviarium* in the west. In the east it was claimed

---

[79] On *peculium castrense* and *quasi castrense*, see Kaser (1971) 344; (1975) 215–16.

to be 'confusingly ambiguous' and was repealed in 468. Fathers were not to lose their usufruct even if they remarried.[80]

Thus, despite tendences which favoured children, in general the fathers retained their position in imperial law. What the paternal usufruct in practice meant is not so clear. The evidence is meagre and comes almost all from the east. For example, in 430 an Egyptian monk and his dead sister's three children were selling property which they had inherited from his mother, their maternal grandmother (SB v. 7996 = PSI xii. 1239). The children, whose age was not specified, were acting through their father. He had them in his power (*hypeksousioi*) and declared to sanction and guarantee their decision. How much did the scribe know about imperial law on maternal inheritance? Did his language reflect only popular ideas and local usage? Or was he using phrases which were officially accepted and current throughout the empire? We cannot exclude either possibility. The document may have been written in due form: the participants were acting jointly to transfer a property to which both the father (as usufructuary) and the children (as 'real' proprietors) had certain rights.

Most of our information comes through the laws of Justinian. One of them recalled a man who had wanted to legitimize his children. Their mother happened to possess some property, and the children tried to stop the process because they knew that after her death the father would have the use and enjoyment of their maternal inheritance. In this and many other cases the usufruct appears as a privilege which the father was entitled to. On the other hand, some laws envisage the possibility that he actually permitted the children to keep their *bona materna* as a *peculium*. Finally, it could be claimed that the whole system was to the children's own benefit. It enabled the father to restrict their youthful fire and prevent them from dissipating their fortunes. Since he was compelled to maintain them, why should they wish to sell anything? The general impression deriving from these texts is that situations varied. There was a wide choice between different arrangements, depending on the circumstances. A good

---

[80] CI 6. 60. 4. Although CT 8. 18. 3 was not taken into the *Breviarium* it seems to have influenced an early Visigothic law, CE 321 = LV.Ant 4. 2. 13; see further below, Ch. 5, Sect. 2.

father looked after his children's interests, a bad father might not, but the decision remained his. That was how the Romans had always wanted it to be.[81]

However, in 542 Justinian again introduced a major innovation into the regime of the *bona materna* (Nov. 117. 1). Now the mother or in fact anyone else who made a bequest or donation to children *in potestate* could prescribe that the father have no right to it, not even the normal usufruct. If the children were of legal age, they were free to control and alienate the property. If they were minors the donor might choose a curator to govern these particular goods. In other respects the father naturally continued to have the children in his power. It is remarkable that the task of *gubernatio* could be assigned even to the children's mother or grandmother. In theory, Justinian's ruling implied a very long step away from the system based on paternal authority: the father himself could not prevent this encroachment upon his sphere of power. In a way, however, it was less dramatic than the condition of emancipation which had been used since time immemorial.

Of course, emancipation always remained a viable alternative. The habit seems to have become increasingly popular in late antiquity, although the development cannot be precisely traced, let alone statistically measured (see above, Ch. 2, Sect. 2). The existence of *bona materna* and an impending remarriage may sometimes have contributed to the decision. Whatever the motivation, Constantine recognized the strong possibility that the children would be emancipated when they attained majority. In that event they would receive their maternal inheritance but the father could keep a third of it as compensation for his liberality. In theory he acquired full ownership rights to this portion. In practice he was nevertheless expected to preserve it for the children. In the east Justinian increased the father's share to one-half but reduced his ownership officially to a usufruct.[82]

In the west similar changes were already taking place in the mid-fifth century. Evidently most children were now emancipated when they married or reached the age of 20. The traces of

[81] See Nov. 74. praef. 2 (538); CI 6. 22. 11 (531), 6. 61. 6 (529), 6. 61. 8. 5a (531); CT 8. 18. 9 (426 west); cf. also '*ius peculii*', NTh 14. 8 (439 east).

[82] CT 8. 18. 1–2 (315/319), 8. 18. 9 (426 west); CI 6. 61. 6. 3 (529 east); Inst. 2. 9. 2.

patria potestas in later western sources are so slight and obscure that we cannot reasonably expect them to shed much light on the problem of maternal inheritance. We may assume that as time went on the question lost its relevance in the Germanic kingdoms. However, a letter of Gregory the Great from the year 594 presents a Sicilian man whose *res maternae* had remained with his father until the latter's death. Although no further details are given, it is quite likely that Roman law here continued to be observed.[83]

The Mother's Right of Succession

It remains to consider briefly how far the mother herself could inherit anything from her children. Generally, in all hereditary systems the children of the deceased are the first to succeed. In particular, in Roman law no one could inherit from children *in potestate* as they owned nothing. After emancipation, the father still took precedence. Thus the mother's rights became a question only when her children had no children of their own nor a living father.

In a marriage with *manus* the mother inherited the same portion as her own surviving children, the brothers and sisters of the deceased. Later, marriage without *manus* having become the norm, the mother was preceded not only by the siblings but also by other agnatic relatives. It was in the reign of Hadrian that the *SC Tertullianum* changed the situation. It applied only to mothers who had the *ius liberorum*: women with fewer than three live births did not qualify. Those who had borne enough children could inherit together with their own daughters (sisters of the deceased). If there were surviving sons who had been *in potestate* at the time of their father's death they excluded their mother altogether. These conditions meant that, while only mothers with the required fertility stood any chance of inheriting, they were also more likely to be either totally excluded or at least to share with their daughters. Of course, it was not impossible to bear three children and outlive them all. Anyway, these rules ensured that it was very difficult to anticipate where the property would

---

[83] NVal 35. 10 (452) + int; LRB 22. 1–2, 26. 1; CE 321 = LV.Ant 4. 2. 13; *Form. Marc.* 2. 9; PLS Capit. III. 101. 1; Greg. M. *ep.* 4. 36. On the survival of *patria potestas*, see above, Ch. 2, Sect. 2.

eventually remain. It would be interesting to know the number of women who were actually able to benefit from the law.[84]

We may ask why the *SC Tertullianum* was passed so much earlier than the *SC Orfitianum* which in 178 regulated the succession the other way round, from mothers to children. The answer probably lies in the fact that both affected intestate succession: mothers could always be expected to make a will in favour of their children whereas the children were more likely to die young and intestate. Later, a will which passed the mother over could also be broken with the *querela inofficiosi*.[85]

The imperial legislation made several changes to this system in the fourth century. Their main purpose may have been to decrease the differences between those women who had the *ius liberorum* and those who had not and between those brothers who had been emancipated and those who had not. This certainly reflected the diminishing importance of both distinctions. However, it again led to a very complicated set of rules, especially as the Romans were not prepared to reject totally the claims of the agnates. It is also difficult to assess the consequences of these changes because we really do not know how frequently children were emancipated and how easy it was to obtain the *ius liberorum*.

In short, in the fifth century a Roman mother could inherit from her children if she had no surviving unemancipated sons; sisters and emancipated brothers did not exclude their mother but inherited together with her. If there were no siblings the mother had to divide the inheritance with her brothers-in-law (paternal uncles) as the nearest agnates. Her precise share depended on the circumstances. All the more distant relatives were excluded by the mother.[86]

It is important to notice why it was not thought self-evident that the mother should succeed to her children's estate. Property being essentially static in Roman society, it could be assumed with some certainty that the bulk of the children's assets had been

---

[84] UE 26. 8; D. 38. 17; CI 6. 26. 2, 8, 6. 55. 8, 6. 56. 1–2. For details, see Meinhart (1967). Cf. also Gardner (1986) 196–8. On the *ius liberorum*, see above. In P.Oxy. xviii. 2187 (304) the mother evidently precedes a paternal uncle, but whether she actually has the *ius liberorum* is unclear.

[85] CI 3. 28. 17 (284); 3. 29. 4 (286, cf. FV 282); CT 2. 19. 2 (321); cf. Gardner (1986) 187–9. [86] CT 5. 1. 1 (317/321), 5. 1. 2 (369 east), 5. 1. 7–8 (426 west).

inherited from their paternal family.[87] It was not considered fair that they would devolve upon the mother and through her pass outside the direct line. The problem was closely analogous with the case of the *bona materna* discussed above. If there were other surviving children, the risk was less serious as they would eventually inherit everything from the mother.[88] Otherwise the ownership was bound to pass to her blood relatives. That is why the paternal uncles were brought in, to rescue at least a portion for the original family. It is symptomatic of the total ruin of the agnatic principle that Justinian decisively improved the mother's position. He removed all remaining obstacles (abolishing also the *ius liberorum*) and enabled her to inherit equally with the dead child's brothers and sisters, before any agnates.[89]

In western Europe the tension between conflicting sentiments continued: both the mother and the paternal relatives were somehow felt to have a just claim to the children's estate. In Gaul the Roman provincial jurists applied the solution developed by late imperial legislation. According to it the mother had to divide the inheritance with her child's siblings, uncles, or cousins.[90] The Germans, on the other hand, tended to give the mother precedence over all others but to consider it only a usufruct. Thus on her death (or remarriage) the property reverted to the siblings or paternal relatives. The details and possible variations of this system are poorly documented. It seems to have been followed by the Visigoths and Franks whereas the Burgundians wavered between it and the Roman system.[91] It is questionable what importance the intestate rules had in the turbulent times that ensued. When the children had grown they no doubt often drew up a will to determine the mother's position.[92]

---

[87] Cf. Lib. *ep.* 1511–12 (Foerster 11. 535–6), with Beaucamp (1992a) 343–4.

[88] In case the widow remarried she was legally prevented from alienating the property, CT 3. 8. 2. 1 (382 east), 5. 1. 8 (426 west); see further below, Ch. 5, Sect. 2.

[89] CI 6. 56. 7; Inst. 3. 3; Nov. 22. 47. 2. On the Syro-Roman Law Book L 1, 102–3 (already neglecting the *ius liberorum*), cf. Selb (1964) 54–60.

[90] LRV CT 5. 1; LRB 10. 5 (the *ius liberorum* is here suppressed), 28.

[91] CE 327, 336 = LV.Ant 4. 2. 2; PLS 59. 1–2; LRib 57. 1–2; Greg. Tur. *franc.* 9. 33, 10. 12; LB 24. 3–4, 53. This interpretation is based on Murray (1983) 197–200, 211, 235–42. Note that CE 327 has now a new reading, cf. Murray, 236 n. 5.

[92] Cf. LRB 45. 7; Pard. 179 (572?); Pard. Add. 39 (717), 45 (723).

4. SUMMARY AND CONCLUSIONS

In a society where almost all property is inherited its devolution certainly is a crucial question. It may be that at some early stage of their history the Romans had tried to prevent family wealth from passing away through women. If such property movements are to be stopped, a barrier has to be placed either between fathers and daughters or between mothers and children. In the distant past, when women entered their husband's family through marriage *cum manu*, they were legally as close to their own children as possible while their links with the natal family were severed. When the Romans began to prefer marriage *sine manu* the emphasis shifted: the connection between fathers and daughters was restored while that between mothers and children was broken. This system, too, was gradually eroded. During the empire children acquired inheritance rights in their maternal family. In the end of antiquity male and female lines inherited equally both in the empire of Justinian and probably also in the western kingdoms. Perhaps we would not be surprised to see the tide again turning. For example, we might expect a tendency to leave less property to daughters, but as we noted in the previous chapter, there is no such evidence for the late Roman upper classes.

Thus there was in late antiquity no legal barrier to the diverging devolution of property. It is only natural to ask if this was connected with some more profound structural change in Roman society. The preservation of family possessions has usually been thought more important in economies based on agriculture and in those classes where land is the principal form of wealth. This certainly held true for the nobility of early Rome. The interest in landed wealth and its stability should be less clear in cities and generally in economies based on a more developed exchange of commodities. We might speculate that the control of senatorial landowners over legislation retarded the inevitable developments in the late republic and early empire. The traditional attitude would thus only later have given way to the more 'modern' approach of the equestrian service aristocracy. Moreover, we might suspect that the emperors wished to weaken the richest families so they would have supported any changes which favoured the dispersal of large estates.

However, there are serious problems in this scheme. First, it is debatable how far the economy of the Roman empire ever rose from its original underdeveloped level.[93] Commerce and small-scale handicraft industries existed but agriculture always remained the primary means of production. No influential merchant class emerged. Neither the senatorial nor the equestrian order was homogeneous, and there may have been no sharp distinction between them after all. At least the turnover seems to have been rapid. Nor is there much evidence, I think, that the emperors tried to use family legislation in that way for their long-term political interests.[94] All this would, of course, need a much more comprehensive examination than is possible here. However, the most decisive objection is the chronology of the change. The agnatic property system was first broken when women were allowed to draw up wills in favour of their descendants. It was the senatorial males themselves who had surrendered their control over this already before the end of the republic.

Thus, although the wider explanations are in some sense attractive, they do not seem to fit in with the known facts. Instead, we should perhaps ask whether males had any common interests at all. The law attempted to regulate everyday life with a more or less consistent set of principles. Families and individuals had goals which might be mutually contradictory. A father wanted to benefit his daughter and her husband would naturally approve—but neither of the males would like his own sisters to inherit too much. What people lost as members of the paternal family they may have gained in the maternal one.

The Romans did not have anything against mothers as such. The main problem was their predilection for the agnatic family and for *patria potestas*. In a legal system where the father's role is so extraordinarily dominant it is no wonder that the mother's position is difficult to define. Agnation slowly waned, but *potestas* proved more resistant. It is characteristic of Roman legal thinking that they were so reluctant to readjust their law. They used testaments to leave their property where they wished. They also resorted to every sort of legal tricks to let their widows administer

---

[93] For an overview, see Garnsey and Saller (1987) 43 ff.

[94] Wallace-Hadrill (1981) 70–1 argues for opposite motives in the Augustan legislation.

their children's estate. New citizens in the provinces did the same, in so far as they did not simply continue their own local traditions.

Eventually the law of inheritance was reformed, and mothers were accepted as guardians. In divorce they could sometimes take their children with them, and they gained a limited right to adopt. The dilemma of maternal inheritance and paternal power was partially solved by the father's usufruct. It is unlikely that family feelings in themselves changed much during the empire. All these developments had precursors in the principate. In many respects the new legislation in late antiquity only officially required or enabled people to do what they had always wanted to do.

One point in this should perhaps be noticed. As we have seen, the Romans had always recognized a moral obligation to preserve a specified property for an eventual 'rightful' heir. But even if someone (usually the *paterfamilias*) neglected this duty, his acts were not revocable. Although it may have resulted in situations which were felt to be unjust, the system nevertheless made property relations very clear and simple. After the changes in late antiquity this was no longer so. Someone buying a property could not be certain that the seller was a full owner: the possession might often have been burdened by some restrictions on alienation. This would have been very inconvenient in an economic system with developed trade and free movements of property, but in late antiquity and the early middle ages it was evidently not felt to be a nuisance.

4

Married Women

There should be no doubt that marriage was a very important institution in Roman society. The state encouraged it because it produced new citizens. Individual people, too, had many reasons to crave for a family. In the lower classes it provided social security: it was not good to grow old without children. Well-born people wanted legitimate offspring to inherit their property and to continue their line, that is, to ensure their immortality after death. Males did not usually need marriage for sex, although many females did. In Chapter 6 we will discuss other sexual relations, and the definition of marriage. The present chapter is devoted to the role of the housewife and to her economic independence.

Conflicting ideals for the conjugal relationship existed in the Roman upper classes. First, the husband was considered to be the leading figure in the family, being responsible for its external contacts and for major decisions. On the other hand, the wife had property of her own, which was kept strictly separate and was on no account meant to enrich her husband. How were these ideas combined in Roman law and in real life? It has also been claimed that religious changes in late antiquity affected the legal relationship between spouses.[1] Does such a view correspond with reality?

We have to start with a topic which may initially look strange: the guardianship of women. In classical law guardianship was in no way tied to marriage. However, it will prove a necessary introduction to the economic position of married women at the very end of antiquity.

---

[1] Thus e.g. Biondi (1952–4) iii. 105–6; Kaser (1975) 171–2; Vismara (1977) 633–7.

1. GUARDIANSHIP OF WOMEN

Tutela Mulierum *in Roman Law*

All those Romans who were no longer in their father's power
were in principle independent citizens. However, not only under-
age children (*impuberes* or *pupilli*) but also adult women were
required to have a guardian (*tutor*):

*Veteres enim voluerunt feminas, etiamsi perfectae aetatis sint, propter animi
levitatem in tutela esse.* (GI 1. 144)

For it was the wish of the old lawyers that women, even those of full age,
should be in guardianship as being scatterbrained.

*Tutores constituuntur tam masculis quam feminis. Sed masculis quidem
impuberibus dumtaxat propter aetatis infirmitatem, feminis autem tam
impuberibus quam puberibus, et propter sexus infirmitatem et propter foren-
sium rerum ignorantiam.* (UE 11. 1)

Guardians are appointed both for males and for females. But for males
only before puberty, because of the weakness of their age, while for
females both before and after puberty, because of the weakness of their
sex and because of their ignorance about judicial matters.

Undoubtedly women were often unfamiliar with financial and
legal affairs, like many men, of course, but this was not the crux
of the matter. Originally *tutela mulierum* was connected with the
Roman system of succession. As a daughter could inherit a
considerable estate, it was in her brothers', uncles', and cousins' personal interest to see that she did not alienate property
which would after her death revert to the family. That is why the
nearest agnatic male relative automatically became the guardian
(*tutor legitimus*), unless the father had appointed someone else in
his will. This system was already eroded in the late republic, and
Claudius finally abolished the agnatic guardianship. Thus in the
imperial period guardians were appointed either through a will or
by a magistrate.[2]

Although the *tutor impuberis* and the *tutor mulieris* had a similar
name, their functions were totally different. The guardian of an
adult woman did not administer her property, nor could he
compel her to do anything. In theory she needed his consent to

---

[2] See GI 1. 144–92; UE 11; D. 26. 4. 1. pr; Kaser (1971) 367–9; Dixon (1984) 345–
56; Gardner (1986) 14–22; (1993) 89–97.

certain legal acts, like selling Italian landed property, cattle, or slaves. These items traditionally constituted the most important productive resources of a family and were called *res mancipi* in Roman law. Consent was further required for making a will, giving a dowry, manumitting a slave, or assuming an obligation.[3] There was much logic in this as long as the property of most citizens was situated in Italy. There was less logic after 212. Land outside Italy was not *res mancipi*. Women who lived in the provinces could freely sell farms and houses but not slaves and animals (as they were *res mancipi* everywhere). They could donate the family estate without their guardian but needed him to bequeath it. Clearly *tutela mulierum* must have appeared a strange institution in the third century but, as far as we know, the Romans did nothing to remove the anomaly.[4]

After the agnatic guardianship had disappeared in the mid-first century, only the *patronus* of a freedwoman and the father of an emancipated daughter retained any real tutelary power. All other guardians could be changed, and they could be compelled in a court to give their consent (GI 1. 114–15; 1. 190–2). The post was no longer a privilege but a burden (GI 1. 168; FV 202). When the guardian's consent was only nominal, some jurists began to wonder whether it was necessary at all. For example, if a woman sold a property which was *res mancipi* and the buyer possessed it for a year, he became the lawful owner by *usucapio* (FV 1). It was also suggested that a will might be valid even without authorization (GI 2. 118–22).

We know that jurists in the early third century discussed *tutela* as an existing phenomenon.[5] But the little *de facto* power which the guardians had is probably the reason why they are hardly ever mentioned in literary sources. They figure in a few Latin papyri from the second century and in at least one inscription.[6] It thus seems that inserting the guardian's name remained a fixed part of

[3] GI 1. 178, 1. 190–2; 2. 80–5, 2. 112–13, 2. 118–22, 3. 176; UE 1. 17, 11. 25–7; FV 1, 45, 110, 259; *Lex Irnit.* 28; *Frg. Dosith.* 15 (FIRA ii. 620); Kaser (1971) 277–8.

[4] See esp. FV 259. Cf. GI 2. 14a–21; UE 19. 1. Some provincial localities could be equated with *fundus Italicus*, D. 50. 15. 1, 6–8; CI 11. 21. 1 (421 east). The difference between *res mancipi* and *nec mancipi* was finally abolished only by Justinian, CI 7. 31. 1.   [5] FV 1, 45, 110, 229, 259, 264.

[6] FIRA iii. 4 = P. Mich. iii. 169 (145), 20 = P.Mich. vii. 442 (2nd c.), 59 = PSI ix. 1027 (151), 93 = CIL vi. 10231 (Rome, 2nd/3rd c.). Cf. Gardner (1986) 22; and Apul. *apol.* 101.

Latin documentary usage, whatever his role in practice. Moreover, Greek papyri supply much evidence on this question. They
are discussed separately a little later, to examine the interrelation
between imperial law and local institutions.

In any case, in the late second century Gaius considered the
whole idea of *tutela* out of place. This is perhaps the most famous
contemporary statement about Roman women:

*Feminas vero perfectae aetatis in tutela esse fere nulla pretiosa ratio suasisse
videtur; nam quae vulgo creditur, quia levitate animi plerumque decipiuntur
et aequum erat eas tutorum auctoritate regi, magis speciosa videtur quam
vera; mulieres enim quae perfectae aetatis sunt, ipsae sibi negotia tractant et
in quibusdam causis dicis gratia tutor interponit auctoritatem suam, saepe
etiam invitus auctor fieri a praetore cogitur.* (GI 1. 190)

There seems, on the other hand, to have been no very worthwhile reason
why women who have reached the age of maturity should be in guardianship; for the argument which is commonly believed, that because they
are scatterbrained they are frequently subject to deception and that it was
proper for them to be under guardians' authority, seems to be specious
rather than true. For women of full age deal with their own affairs for
themselves, and while in certain instances the guardian interposes his
authorisation for form's sake, he is often compelled by the praetor to give
authorisation, even against his wishes.

The purpose of guardianship was certainly the more difficult to
explain since many women were legally entitled not to have a
guardian. The Augustan marriage laws had allowed a freeborn
woman with three live births and a freedwoman with four (*ius
trium/quattuor liberorum*) to escape from tutelage altogether. Such
a measure would have been strange if *tutela* had been regarded as
a generally useful institution for women. It seems that women
who lived long enough could easily attain the required number of
births (see above, Ch. 3, Sect. 1). Furthermore, the *ius liberorum*
was often given as a mere favour. Thus it may have turned out
that only a minority of women were actually under guardianship.[7]

Why then did *tutela mulierum* not disappear? Although it was
in many ways an anachronistic custom, it was perhaps not totally
useless. Gaius was right that many independent women could

---

[7] See GI 1. 145, 1. 194, 3. 44; UE 29. 3; CIL vi. 10247 = FIRA iii. 95 (Rome, 252);
P.Oxy. xii. 1467 = FIRA iii. 27 (263); Kübler (1909) 154–73; and further below for
evidence from Egypt.

manage their own affairs without male help. However, some others were not so self-confident. They were quite happy to be supported by an adviser. In Egypt women who expressly asserted that they possessed the *ius liberorum* and did not need a guardian nevertheless often mentioned that they had a man by their side, their husband or someone else.[8] The protection of women may not have been the primary motive behind the republican *tutela mulierum*, but it could be applied for that purpose by those who so wished.

Even this explanation may seem strange if we are right in concluding that the great majority of women gave three births and qualified for exemption. We have to ask who actually were under guardianship. Freedwomen are an obvious answer. They had to give four births after their manumission, something which many of them certainly found difficult. *Tutela legitima* over them continued to benefit their *patroni*. What about freeborn women? There was in fact one sizeable homogeneous group of women who were not exempted from *tutela*: young girls. And I think that this is the very reason why the guardianship still had general value during the principate. *Tutela impuberis* over girls ended at the age of 12. It is no wonder that their competence was distrusted. *Tutela mulieris* was a useful safeguard which continued as long as the young wives had not given three births, perhaps usually until their mid-twenties.

However, in the early third century the general system of wardship was changed. It had to be admitted that 12 years for girls and 14 years for boys was an excessively low age to reach one's majority. The contemporary tendency was to stress 25 years as the real threshold of adulthood. Now girls between 12 and 25 regularly had a *curator minoris*, who by and by assumed the same powers as a *tutor impuberis*. It meant that before the age of 25 *tutela mulierum* proper was of little consequence. A rescript of the emperor Gordian in 241 reminded that fecundity (that is, the *ius trium liberorum*) did not give freedom of administration to someone who had not reached her full majority (CI 5. 37. 12). Thus, essentially, *cura* now covered that age in which the guardianship was really needed and was not yet removed by the *ius liberorum*.

[8] See below; and cf. Kutzner (1989) 98–9; Beaucamp (1992a) 45–9. See also CI 2. 3. 8 (222), 2. 12. 13 (239), 2. 18. 16 (252), 4. 44. 8 (293), 8. 55. 6 (294).

By the time *cura* ended most women would have had three children and be independent.[9]

After these developments in the third century, any real significance of *tutela mulierum* certainly waned. Its later history in imperial law is shrouded in mystery; as it had definitely disappeared by Justinian's time, it did not have any place in his legal compilation. In the 290s *tutoris auctoritas* was still a fact to be reckoned with in imperial rescripts.[10] Moreover, *tutela mulierum* was frequently discussed in the vast legal collection whose remains are now called the *Fragmenta Vaticana*. The work was compiled from earlier sources around the year 320 for practical use in the legal profession. It is hard to see why the collectors should have wanted to include in it totally antiquated material.[11]

On the other hand, the guardianship of women does not figure in the Theodosian Code. Private law was treated mainly in the first books, notoriously defective in manuscript T. Especially titles 3. 17–18, which were devoted to guardianship, are missing. If there were laws which mentioned *tutela mulierum*, they were not taken into the Visigothic *Breviarium*. Only one ambiguous passage from the year 326 has survived:

In feminis tutelam legitimam consanguineus patruus non recuset. (CT 3. 17. 2)

A consanguineous paternal uncle shall not refuse the statutory guardianship over a woman.

The interpretation of this sentence depends on another, much later law. In 472 the eastern emperor Leo promulgated a statute which dealt extensively with the legal capacity and guardianship of women, especially if they were minors. It is a pity that this law has survived only as fragments in the Justinian Code.[12] However, one clause referred directly back to Constantine's law:

Constitutione divae memoriae Constantini lege Claudia sublata, pro antiqui iuris auctoritate salvo manente agnationis iure tam consanguineus (id est

---

[9] Curators of women appear frequently in legal sources: D. 26. 5. 13. 2, 26. 7. 32. 6, 59; FV 110, 201–2; CI 2. 4. 3, 2. 12. 14, 2. 18. 17, 2. 24. 1, 2. 43. 2, 3. 28. 12, 4. 53. 1, 5. 31. 7, 5. 34. 2, 5. 37. 9–10, 5. 62. 4, 17, 8. 37. 7, 9. 9. 7; Symm. *rel.* 19, 39. Generally for *tutor impuberis* and *curator minoris*, see Dupont (1937) 201–20; Kaser (1971: 352–72; 1975: 222–37).

[10] FV 325 (293/4), cf. 326–7; Beaucamp (1992a) 260 n. 11; I would not agree with Kaser (1975) 222 n. 3.			[11] See FV 1, 45, 110, 229, 259, 264, 325–7.

[12] CI 1. 4. 16, 1. 18. 13, 5. 1. 5. pr, 5. 6. 8, 5. 30. 3.

frater) quam patruus ceterique legitimi ad pupillarum feminarum tutelam vocantur. (CI 5. 30. 3)

Since the constitution of Constantine of divine memory has revoked the *Lex Claudia*, now, according to the authority of ancient law, if the nexus of agnation has not been broken [sc. by emancipation or adoption], a *consanguineus* (i.e. brother) as well as an uncle and other legitimate persons are called to be guardians over under-age women.

According to this, Constantine re-established the agnatic guardianship over women but only for girls below 12 years (*pupillae*). The problem is that the crucial word '*pupillarum*' may have been added later, in Justinian's time. And even if it is authentic, it may have been only an inference; we do not know if the writer of CI 5. 30. 3 had seen Constantine's law in its entirety or only as the short fragment in the Theodosian Code. In any case, the interpretation may have been correct. When Claudius had abolished the *tutela legitima* of agnates it had meant that they could not automatically assume the guardianship of female children (GI 1. 157). And, if they were appointed by a magistrate, they might try to decline, appealing to the law. How far this was observed in practice is of course difficult to say. In any case it would have been natural to clarify the situation, and this provides a plausible explanation for Constantine's law. On the basis of CT 3. 17. 2 we simply cannot decide what Constantine thought about guardianship of adult women.[13]

The age of majority was again debated in the fourth century. Admittedly, if 12–14 years had been too low a limit, 25 was in many cases too high. After 324 boys aged 20 and girls of 18 were allowed to request *venia aetatis*, that is, a personally granted majority (CT 2. 17. 1). If successful, the girls received 'in all contracts the same rights as men'. There is not a word about *tutela mulierum*, nor is it ever mentioned in the literary sources of the fourth century. When rich, ascetic women scandalously gave away a large part of their family property, the church fathers did not record any conflicts with guardians (see below, Ch. 5, Sect. 1). From 390 at the latest mothers could assume the guardianship of their own children (CT 3. 17. 4, and above Ch. 3, Sect. 2), yet this does not prove that they might not sometimes have been subject to *tutela* themselves. Nevertheless we would expect to find some

[13] Cf. Dupont (1937) 197–200; Beaucamp (1992a) 261.

mention of it here or elsewhere in the Theodosian Code if it still existed. It does not appear in any later western or eastern sources.[14]

Thus before the sixth century there is no secure *terminus ante quem* for the disappearance of the guardianship. But it should be noted that the connection between *tutela* and the *ius liberorum* was very frequently recorded in Greek papyri up to the third decade of the fourth century. After that, the cases become much more sporadic, perhaps mere notarial relics (see below). This suggests that the Roman guardianship survived at least as a theoretical concept up to that time. We may connect this with the evidence of the *Fragmenta Vaticana* and with the general absence of *tutela* from the Theodosian Code. If there was a single law which abolished the guardianship of women, it should probably be placed in the first half of the fourth century. A likely date would seem to be in the early 320s. However, certainty is impossible to attain: *tutela* might have survived even to the fifth century.

Guardianship in Roman Egypt

Guardianship of women had been an established institution in hellenistic Egypt and it continued unchanged after the Roman occupation. We do not exactly know the powers of a Graeco-Egyptian guardian. His consent seems to have been required in all major private transactions which were publicly recorded. His name was also often mentioned in petitions to authorities, but in such cases it was probably superfluous. In any case, it appears that Greek usage in Egypt expected the co-operation of the guardian in many cases where Roman law did not.[15]

The standard term for a guardian in Greek law was *kyrios*. The same word was used to denote a Roman guardian (*tutor*), a fact which may have caused some confusion. To avoid this, Greek-speaking Roman citizens in Egypt, both before and after the *Constitutio Antoniniana*, sometimes specified that they had a

[14] *Tutela* is definitely absent from the *Breviarium* (see e.g. GE 1. 7–8) and from Justinian's law. Cf. also Boeth. *in top. Cic.* 2 (4. 18), PL 64. 1074. The universal grant of the *ius liberorum*, CT 8. 17. 2–3 (410 east), was not necessarily relevant since it seems to have applied only to the succession between spouses, see above, Ch. 3, Sect. 1 and below, Ch. 4, Sect. 2; Beaucamp (1992a) 260–3.
[15] See Weiss (1908); Taubenschlag (1938; 1955: 170–8); Préaux (1959) 139–43; Rupprecht (1986); Kutzner (1989) 79–99. For the absence of guardians in the Greek novels, Egger (1994) 268.

kyrios 'according to Roman law'.[16] This shows that the concept of the Roman *tutela mulierum* had gained a foothold in Egypt. Moreover, in the middle of the third century several papyri show women approaching the prefect of Egypt and requesting for a guardian to be named 'according to the Julian and Titian law and the decree of the senate', as the proper Roman formula went.[17] The last of these, from the year 261, is also the last indubitable proof anywhere in the Roman empire that guardians were officially appointed for women.

Of course, all this does not prove that the Roman *tutela* as such had been adopted in the east, at least not in a juridically correct form. Probably *tutela mulierum* and the local guardianship of women were sufficiently similar that they could be assimilated. Roman officials operated with Roman terminology and the new citizens embraced it to the best of their ability. Thus, while people tried to employ Roman legal terms the precise nature of the guardianship may have varied from case to case.

However, not only *tutela mulierum* was known in the provinces but also the exemption from it by virtue of the *ius liberorum*. In 263 a certain Aurelia Thaisus asked the prefect to record her rights because 'there are laws which permit women with three children to administer their own property and to act without a guardian' (P.Oxy. xii. 1467 = FIRA iii. 27). She is borne out by dozens of papyri where women are said to act 'without a guardian by the right of children', in Greek '*khoris kyriou khrematizousai dikaio teknon*'. The expression had been used by Roman citizens in Egypt already in the second century, mostly with explicit reference to Roman law. It became very common after the universal grant of citizenship.[18] It can also be attested elsewhere: local women in third century Pisidia, Asia Minor, frequently recorded in inscriptions that they were 'exempt from guardianship by the right of children' (*auteksousioi teknon dikaio*).[19]

[16] SB iii. 6291 (143), xvi. 12950 (230/1); P. Hamb. i. 101 (Elag.); P.Harr. ii. 227 (221); P.Oxy. x. 1274 (3rd c.); xxxiv. 2723 (3rd c.); PSI xii. 1238 (244).

[17] P. Mich. iii. 165 (236); P. Oxy. xii. 1466 (245); P. Oxy. iv. 720 = FIRA iii. 24 = MChr 324 (247); P. Oxy. xxxiv. 2710 (261); all reprinted and discussed by Modrzejewski (1974).

[18] See Sijpesteijn (1965); and an updated list of 114 papyri in P. Mich. xv (1982), p. 158–71. For further updates, corrections, and a thorough discussion, see now Beaucamp (1992a) 197 ff.

[19] TAM iii. 383, 482, 669, 705, 714; SEG xli. 1270; see also Kübler (1910) 194.

Women who act without a guardian '*dikaio teknon*' are commonly found in Egypt to the 320s.[20] In the fourth century the phrase appeared sometimes in a slightly different form: '*dikaion teknon ekhousa*'. This was clearly modelled after the normal Latin '*ius liberorum habens*'.[21] It is impossible to say why the new formula was adopted. Certainly it was not used in Egypt before the early fourth century. This is noteworthy because it then becomes difficult to believe that the expression was only a frozen relic from an earlier time. Rather, it indicates that the connection between the *ius liberorum* and *tutela mulierum* was still known outside Egypt, too, since otherwise the formula could not have been imported to Egypt at such a late time.

The papyri thus suggest that the guardianship was a recognized institution in the Roman empire at the beginning of the fourth century. After 325 there is a clear decline in documents mentioning the *ius liberorum*. However, a few isolated instances appear even up to 389.[22] They certainly cause some confusion, making it more difficult to establish when exactly *tutela* vanished. In my opinion, the clauses were now most likely mere obsolete survivals, preserved by ignorant people or conservative scribes.

Returning to the third century, there is one notable problem with all this evidence. Literally taken it does not show that women were in *tutela* but rather the opposite. The difference becomes clear when we look at such papyri where women actually appear with a guardian (*meta kyriou*). They are very frequent in the period before the *Constitutio Antoniniana* and continue for some two decades after it, but in the 230s the evidence dries up. In the latter half of the third century few women are accompanied by a *kyrios*.[23] This is a striking phenomenon, contrasting sharply

[20] See also P. Oxy. liv. 3758. 39–77 (325), the proceedings of a lawsuit in which a woman was said to enjoy the *ius liberorum*; but the context is regrettably unclear, Beaucamp (1992a) 193 n. 5.

[21] The Latin phrase appears e.g. in CIL vi. 10246, vi. 10247 = FIRA iii. 95 (AD 252), iii. 755 (Christian); Kübler (1909) 171–3.

[22] P. Charite 33 (331/347); P. Matrit. 5 (336/7); P. Charite 8 = SP xx. 98 (348); P. Coll. Youtie ii. 83 (353); P.Abinn. 63 and 64 (mid-4th c.); PSI viii. 951 (388); BGU iii. 943 (389); the four last say only 'having the right of children', and omit 'acting without guardian'. For the decade 315–25 there are in all eight cases, Beaucamp (1992a) 198–202.

[23] PSI xii. 1238 (244); P. Oxy. xlii. 3049 (247); P. Grenf. ii. 69 (265); P. Oxy. xlix. 3499 (end 3rd c.?); P. Princ. ii. 38 (c.264) is especially interesting as the woman has both a *kyrios* (her husband) and a *curator*; for the 4th c., see below, Ch. 4, Sect. 3.

with the great number of women who at the same time boasted that the *ius liberorum* exempted them from guardianship. Was the phrase totally superfluous? Or did all women in practice possess the *ius liberorum*?

It is difficult to say on which occasions the Roman *tutela* was called into action in practice. Alienation of landed property would have been a likely case but, as provincial soil was not included in the category of *res mancipi*, it did not fall under the restrictions. The making of a will was another case in which Roman law required the guardian's authorization. Two papyri in the third century display a woman's will: in the first one she really has a guardian and in the other she appeals to the *ius liberorum*.[24] Perhaps imperial law was here observed, but the two cases are not enough to base any firm conclusions on. Some affairs incidentally entailed an obligation because the seller or the buyer offered a security. But the general impression is that the phrase 'acting without guardian' was often used in documents and transactions where the guardian according to Roman law would not have been necessary anyway.[25]

It is quite possible that some women referred to their *ius liberorum* needlessly, just because it had status value. It is also possible and indeed likely that people in Roman Egypt tended to confuse *tutela mulierum* with their own inherited guardianship. The Graeco-Egyptian *kyrios* had had wider functions than his Roman counterpart. Besides, his presence had depended not only on the nature of the affair but also on the form of the document.[26] Certainly it was difficult to believe that land could be freely alienated while some other items could not. If someone felt herself unsure, she may have wished to mention the *ius liberorum*, just to be on the safe side. A case from 330 illustrates the point.[27] Aurelia Demetria was selling land to another woman. The buyer wanted to cancel the deal on the grounds that Demetria's son had not co-operated in the transaction. Demetria

The list should be nearly exhaustive, cf. Taubenschlag (1938); Préaux (1959) 142; Kutzner (1989) 94; Beaucamp (1992a) 194–7; Krause (1994a) 226–38.

[24] P. Princ. ii. 38 (c.264); P. Lips. 29 = MChr 318 (295); cf. also P. Oxy. vi. 990 (331); P. Coll. Youtie ii. 83 (353).
[25] Cf. Kübler (1909) 173–83; Sijpesteijn (1965) 179–88; Beaucamp (1992a) 227–47.
[26] See Taubenschlag (1938); Beaucamp (1992a) 216–18.
[27] CPR 19 = MChr 69, with Beaucamp (1992a) 221–2.

replied that the whole reasoning was contrary to law in the first place. We do not know more details so we cannot say on which legal principles the women based their respective arguments, but clearly all kinds of claims and counter-claims were possible. It was wise to list early enough any corroborating facts which might help in an eventual dispute.

Such legal and psychological factors may account for the great number of papyri recording the *ius liberorum*. They do not explain why from the middle of the third century there are only a handful of women who actually have a *kyrios*. The reason is to be sought elsewhere, and it must be, I think, fairly simple. I have suggested that most women over the age of 25 had given three births and qualified for exemption. The evidence from Egypt seems to support the view that few adult freeborn women in the Roman empire were under guardianship.

However, in the middle of the third century another word, *synestos*, became frequent in the papyri. It was not a technical term and may loosely be translated as 'a man who is present and supports the woman'. It can be found in the phrase 'woman so-and-so with *synestos* so-and-so', thus simply replacing the old expression 'with *kyrios*'. But the most remarkable aspect is that it is often connected with the *ius liberorum*: 'woman so-and-so acting without a guardian by the right of children, with the support of so-and-so'.[28] This shows that when people in the late third century referred to the *kyrios* they really had the *tutor* of Roman law in mind. It also appears that they did not fail to mention *kyrioi* in the documents because they themselves deemed male support superfluous but just because it did not tally with the prevailing legal order.

In sum, for some two decades after the year 212 the new citizens in Egypt preserved their old habits. After that, they got increasingly acquainted with the Roman guardianship. Whether this was due to some deliberate public effort remains an open question. Of course, few people had more than a very vague idea of legal rules. What they grasped was probably only the main point: imperial law expected women to have guardians but in practice it required their presence on rare occasions, and women

---

[28] See Sijpesteijn (1965) 176, with his updated list in P. Mich. xv (1982); Kutzner (1989) 93–5; Beaucamp (1992a) 247–57.

with three children were always exempt. This new awareness led to a decrease of documents where *kyrioi* were named. On the other hand, the use of *synestos* was a voluntary and unofficial means of covering situations where the legal guardianship did not apply. I suspect that similar devices spread in many provinces during the third century. We shall return to this point later, after we have examined the relationship between man and wife in Roman law.

2. HUSBANDS AND WIVES

The Conjugal Relationship

During the republic there were two alternative ways to conclude a Roman marriage (see above, Ch. 3, Sect. 3). If wives were married *cum manu*, they and their property were in the husband's power, in very much the same way as children were *in potestate*. In contrast, if marriage was contracted *sine manu*, the wife was not legally transferred to the new family. Whatever the reasons, by the end of the republic this alternative had become more common. It is impossible to say why some people continued to marry *cum manu*. The alternatives had certainly more to do with traditions or the devolution of property than with wifely subordination. Gaius spoke of marriage *cum manu* as a living institution, and it seems to have existed in the third century. Little evidence is available since *manus* has consistently been interpolated away from the Digest. It does not appear in the Theodosian Code either, so it must in practice have disappeared by the fourth century. At most it could have survived as a religious curiosity of a few ancient priesthoods.[29] This might explain why in the late fourth century the cultured senator Symmachus used the words '*in manum optat accipere*' to say that a friend of his wanted to marry a certain woman. On the other hand, it may have been just a deliberately antiquarian expression. When some Christian writers say that the wife will pass to an alien *potestas* or change

---

[29] GI 1. 108–13, 1. 136; UE 9, 26. 7; Coll. 4. 2. 3, 4. 7. 1; *Frg. Berol.* 3 (FIRA ii. 427); Tac. *ann.* 4. 16; Apul. *met.* 10. 29; CIL 10. 6662; Serv. *Georg.* 1. 31. See e.g. Corbett (1930) 68–90; Kunkel (1930) 2269–71; Kaser (1971) 76–81, 323–5; Gardner (1986) 11–14; Noy (1988) 299–304; Goody (1990) 400–4; Treggiari (1991a) 16–36.

over from one *familia* to another, they are not thinking in legal terms but reflect the factual event.[30]

Thus, in the period which we are examining, the spouses always belonged to different families. The wife was often in her father's power, and after his death she was *sui iuris*. Her husband had no legal power over her, and their properties remained separate. These principles were closely guarded by Roman jurists in the classical period and even later, as will be seen below. However, they could not totally disregard the intimate relationship between the spouses:

Nuptiae sunt coniunctio maris et feminae et consortium omnis vitae, divini et humani iuris communicatio. (Modest. D. 23. 2. 1)

Marriage is the union of a man and a woman, a partnership for life involving divine as well as human law.

This idea surfaced in a number of legal rules. The wife's social status and legal domicile followed those of her husband. If a woman of low rank married a senator, she received the noble title of *clarissima femina*, and her status was further heightened when her husband became consul. On the other hand, if a senator's daughter married downwards, her rank suffered the corresponding loss. These rules were formulated in the late second and early third centuries. They seem to have been relaxed by the reign of Diocletian, so that a *clarissima* would lose her title only if she had acquired it from a previous husband and later remarried. It is difficult to know how rigorously the details were observed in practice. As a general rule wives continued to share their husband's rank in late antiquity both in the west and in the east.[31]

When all kinds of privileges and immunities assumed importance in the fourth and fifth centuries, they were often extended so as to cover wives, too.[32] Domicile was important because it

---

[30] Symm. *ep.* 6. 3; Ambr. *virg.* 1. 33; Sidon. *ep.* 7. 9. 24; Arnob. *nat.* 4. 20; cf. Saller (1994) 76.

[31] D. 1. 9. 1, 8, 12; FV 104; CI 12. 1. 1 (Alex.), 5. 4. 10 (Diocl.); CT 2. 1. 7 (392 east) + int; Nov. 22. 36; Sidon. *ep.* 5. 16. 3; Chastagnol (1979: 12–23; 1983); Raepsaet-Charlier (1981) 198–212; Beaucamp (1990: 271–4; 1992a: 129–39, 309–14); and cf. Arjava (1991). For the widow of a *comes*, Greg. M. *ep.* 1. 13 (590), see below, Ch. 7, Sect. 2.

[32] CT 13. 3. 3 (333), 16. 2. 10 (346?), 16. 2. 14 (356), 13. 3. 10 (370?), 13. 3. 16 (414 east); CI 12. 16. 4 (Zeno), 12. 10. 2, 12. 20. 6. 2 (Anast.); etc. Beaucamp (1990) 274–8. But cf. CT 11. 16. 18 (390 west).

decided the court before which the wife had to appear. Moreover, it determined the city where she mainly had to fulfil her civic duties (although some financial obligations remained for the city of her origin). Of course, the spouses could sometimes actually choose her native place as their common residence.[33] Clearly all these precepts reflected the sentiment that a married couple formed one social entity.

As the spouses did not rank among near relatives in Roman law, they had only slight hopes of succession on intestacy. There was a curious short-lived eastern statute which, for unknown reasons, tried to improve their position in 427 or 428, but it was promptly repealed.[34] Intestate succession between the spouses thus remained an exception, but this was hardly a major nuisance as people preferred to make wills anyway. The surviving spouse was likely to receive a reasonable bequest, either permanently or as a usufruct. It was especially important if the widow did not have enough property of her own to support herself. Of course, if the couple had children they obtained the bulk of the estate. In their absence the spouse was usually preferred to any other relatives. This broad pattern allowed for much flexibility in individual cases.[35] Testaments bequeathing property to spouses are recorded in different parts of the empire to the end of antiquity and beyond.[36]

For most of the imperial period, the Augustan marriage laws posed problems for childless couples: they could inherit only one-tenth from each other's estate (see above, Ch. 3, Sect. 1). This restriction was part and parcel of the grand imperial popu-

---

[33] D. 2. 1. 19, 5. 1. 65, 50. 1. 22. 1, 32, 37, 38. 3; CI 10. 64. 1 (Phil.), 10. 40. 5 (Diocl.); CT 13. 5. 12 (369 west), 2. 1. 7 (392 east) + int; Beaucamp (1990) 270–1. For civic obligations, cf. Neesen (1981) 207, and below, Ch. 7, Sect. 2.

[34] See CT 5. 1. 1 (428 east); cf. also 4. 21. 1 (395 west).

[35] See Humbert (1972) 207–45, and esp. Champlin (1991) 120–6; Treggiari (1991a) 379–96; and Krause (1994b) 75–104, citing ample evidence from literature and from the Digest. See also CI 2. 3. 24, 3. 28. 12, 22, 3. 33. 1, 5. 62. 18, 6. 21. 3, 6. 24. 5, 6, 6. 26. 4, 6. 34. 3, 6. 35. 10, 6. 37. 19, 6. 49. 5, 7. 4. 8, 13 (all 3rd c.); and for Egypt, Préaux (1959) 168–9; Hobson (1985) 320; Rupprecht (1985; 1987); Krause (1994b) 97–100, 264–73.

[36] Amm. 28. 4. 26; Hier. *ep.* 79. 6; Aug. *serm.* 356. 3, PL 39. 1576; Joh. Chrys. *qual. duc. ux.* 2, PG 51. 226; CT 5. 10. 1 (392 east); CI 6. 25. 10 (531); Nov. 18. 3; FIRA iii. 52 = P.Ant. 1 (c.460), 67 = P. Lond. v. 1727 (583/4); P. Tjäder ii. 30. 20 (539), 37. 28 (591), 55 (mid-6th c.); Greg. M. *ep.* 4. 10, 9. 75, 9. 165; etc. For widows, see further below, Ch. 5, Sect. 2.

lation policy which tried to raise fertility. Initially it may not have had any deeper motives. True, the existence of common children made it more likely that the inheritance eventually reverted to the direct line. Otherwise it almost certainly passed outside the original family. But such motives cannot initially have underlain the law because even dead children sufficed to remove the restrictions.

After Constantine had abolished other penalties for childlessness in 320, the inheritance of spouses and that of mothers continued to depend on the *ius liberorum*. Why this was so is somewhat mysterious. Perhaps the family sentiments mentioned above now played some role. But I would suspect that there was no well-thought-out scheme: the laws just continued to operate with their own logic. Although the restrictions remained in force until the beginning of the fifth century, exemptions were willingly granted. Whether or not any petitions were actually rejected, their sheer number must have been a problem. In 410 the eastern government admitted this and finally gave the *ius communium liberorum* to all childless couples.[37]

In theory, this should have been adopted in the west in 439. Nevertheless a senator and his wife asked Valentinian III to confirm their mutual will in 446 (NVal 21. 1). If the emperor knew that their request was superfluous he did not say it. Later the whole rule was forgotten in the west. The appearance of the law must have seemed anomalous: the spouses were required to have children to be able to inherit while in practice it was precisely the childless couples who had a special need to benefit each other. Thus an amusing semantic change took place: in the sixth century the term *ius liberorum* was used to denote the mutual will of a couple without children.[38]

Merovingian and Visigothic *formulae* show that such mutual wills were very popular. A clear majority relates to the succession of childless couples. In some of them the widow(er) obtains the whole estate or the greatest part of it and is entitled to dispose of it freely. Interestingly, these examples mostly belong to those collections which are closer to Roman traditions. Other *formulae* reflect a different custom: even when no children existed, the

---

[37] CT 8. 16–17, 13. 5. 7, 15. 14. 9.
[38] NVal 21. 1. int; Isid. *orig.* 5. 24; *Form. Andec.* 41; *F. Vis.* 24.

surviving spouses could enjoy the property only during their own lifetime. After that, it reverted to the blood relatives. This observation seems to support the view that testamentary freedom was more restricted and the family interests better guarded among the Germans. Alas, we cannot trace the development any further.[39]

Love and Subjection

Few Romans questioned the ideal model of a married couple united by mutual love and partnership. It appears as well in literary sources as in the inscriptions of the early empire. Matrimonial bliss was undoubtedly often attained, though not always, of course.[40] Similar ideals of deep affection and co-operation were current among Christian writers in late antiquity.[41] There is no sign of any change, during the principate or later, in the way the marital bond was perceived.[42] If there were significant variations at all, they may have been greater between different areas and social classes. It goes without saying that some marriages were happy and some were not, and it would be useless to attempt any statistics.

It was true that the Christian proponents of ascetic celibacy sometimes could not resist the temptation to defame the married state. Their arguments had long roots: ancient writers had always found enough evidence of unhappy unions to suggest that a wise man should not marry. In pagan society this advice had been given only to males. In the Christian period women were reminded of the vexations of married life perhaps even more

[39] *Form. Vis.* 23–4; *F. Andec.* 41; *F. Tur.* 17–18; *F. Marc.* 1. 12, 2. 7–8, 2. 17; *F. Sal. Merk.* 16; *F. Sal. Lind.* 13; Pard. 412 (690); see also LRib 50. For inheritance in the early middle ages, cf. above, Ch. 2, Sect. 3, and Ch. 3, Sect. 3.
[40] For a wide selection of evidence, see now esp. Treggiari (1991a) 205–61; cf. also Dixon (1991; 1992: 83–90).
[41] Ambr. *hex.* 5. 7. 18, CSEL 32. 1. 153; Hier. *ep.* 117. 5; Paul. Nol. *ep.* 44. 3–4, CSEL 29. 372.; Aug. *bon. conjug.* 1. 1, CSEL 41. 187; Aster. Amas. *hom.* 5; Greg. Naz. *carm.* 2. 2. 6, PG 37. 1543; Joh. Chrys. *qual. duc. ux.* 3–4, PG 51. 230; *cat. bapt.* 1. 11–13, SC 50. 114; Caes. Arel. (= Aug.?) *serm.* 21. 6, CCL 103. 97; etc. See also Reinsberg (1983); Schouler (1985); and CIL vi. 1779, the funeral monument of a pagan senatorial couple from the late 4th c.
[42] Cf. Goody (1990) 420–4, 485–6; Beaucamp (1992a) 317–19; Saller (1994) 4–8. For supposed changes during the principate, see e.g. Veyne (1987) 36–45; Brown (1987) 247–8.

frequently than men, so that on this question a change had really taken place.[43]

When a marriage had been concluded, however, the division of tasks in a Christian family did not stand out in any way. The roles of husband and wife were expressed in the same terms as always before, and thereafter. He spent most of his time away from home and represented the family to outsiders, or perhaps became absorbed in philosophical or religious meditation. She was responsible for the working of the family unit itself: purchases for common needs, storing of supplies, supervision and discipline of the slave staff, education of children, and all the other tasks which kept a smaller or larger household running. These were extremely traditional duties in Greek and Roman culture: there was little new in the ideal of a virtuous Christian housewife.[44]

Co-operation, love, and mutual respect did not mean that the spouses were thought to be equal. Male domination appeared the more natural as the wife in her first marriage was much younger than the husband, on an average perhaps by almost ten years and in extreme cases even more. The age difference had its greatest effect in the early years of marriage when the girl was in her teens. If she survived childbirth, the age-gap gradually lost its importance. The pattern was further confused by frequent remarriage: in subsequent unions the spouses might be closer in age. A man who married a widow had to accept the fact that she was not as obedient as a young virgin would have been.[45]

It is clear that the husband was expected to be the dominant partner in marriage, in Roman as in all later societies. At the turn of the second century, Plutarch, a man who straddled Greek and

[43] Hier. *adv. Jovin.* 1. 47, PL 23. 288 (quoting Theophrastus); cf. Joh. Chrys. *lib. rep.* 1, PG 51. 217; for earlier authors, see Treggiari (1991a) 205–7. Such arguments were refuted by other writers, e.g. Lib. *thes.* 1 (Foerster 8. 550–61); see also Stob. 4. 22. 1–3. See further below, Ch. 5, Sect. 1.

[44] Tert. *castit.* 12. 1, CCL 2. 1031; Ambr. *parad.* 11. 50, CSEL 32. 1. 307; Hier. *in Eph.* 3. 5. 33, PL 26. 570; *in Tit.* 2. 3–5, PL 26. 617; Greg. Naz. *or.* 8. 9, 18. 8, PG 35. 797, 993; Joh. Chrys. *qual. duc. ux.* 4, PG 51. 230; *virg. subintr.* 9, PG 47. 507; Paul. Nol. *ep.* 44. 4, CSEL 29. 373. Cf. e.g. Xen. *oec.* 7; Colum. 12. praef. 1–6; Philo Alex. *leg. spec.* 3. 169–71; Lib. *thes.* 1. 13–18 (Foerster 8. 554); Thraede (1972) 248–9, 253–4; Dassmann (1986) 823–5; Treggiari (1991a) 183–203; Beaucamp (1992a) 289–91; Krause (1994b) 123–9.

[45] Apul. *apol.* 92; cf. Treggiari (1991a) 400–2. In Egypt, it seems that the age-gap was greatest when the husband had married in later life: widowers tended to marry young girls; see Bagnall and Frier (1994) 118–21.

Roman culture, put it in a particularly amiable way. I doubt that anyone anywhere within the empire would have disagreed with his advice to young brides and grooms:

Whenever two notes are sounded in accord the tune is carried by the bass; and in like manner every activity in a virtuous household is carried on by both parties in agreement, but discloses the husband's leadership and preferences. (*conjug. praec.* 11, tr. Babbitt, in Loeb)[46]

On the other hand, not too much weight should be put on ideals, especially in such delicate and highly personal matters as the conjugal relationship. Most Roman men would certainly have liked to hold sway over their wives and they obviously believed that their forefathers had done so. In their own lives, however, they did not always find it easy.[47] Especially in the upper classes women had considerable properties of their own and were able to divorce at will, so the husband was in danger of losing the dowry. Thus Greek and Roman males often feared that a rich wife could defy or even dominate them.[48]

The same phobia survived in late antiquity. John Chrysostom in particular warned his audience about propertied women who overturned traditional hierarchy in the family. That is why he cautioned men not to marry a woman who was richer than themselves. On the other hand, he remarked that a rich husband and a penniless wife were not a good match either: she would be like a slave because she was not supported by any property of her own. Moreover, in another context the bishop addressed fathers who were marrying off their daughters. Now he shamelessly reversed the situation and advised them to choose a husband of equal or lesser means. In that way the daughter would be happier in her marriage. This well demonstrates how flexible the ideology was. The same man would adopt a different viewpoint depending on the role in which he was acting. We do not know how far the women themselves took such factors into consideration. They

[46] The whole little treatise is written in the same spirit, cf. e.g. 33–4; and Treggiari (1991a) 224–6.

[47] Cf. e.g. Liv. 34. 7. 12–15, 34. 3. 1; Sen. *benef.* 1. 9. 3; Juv. 6. 212–24, 281–84; from Roman Egypt, see e.g. P. Mich. iii. 217 = SB iii. 7249 (296).

[48] e.g. Sen. *contr.* 1. 6. 5; Mart. 8. 12; Juv. 6. 136–41; for further evidence, see Treggiari (1991a) 196, 199, 210, 329–31; and Schaps (1979) 76, for Greece. On divorce, cf. below, Ch. 5, Sect. 3.

were in any case able to make an independent decision only for a subsequent marriage.[49]

Sometimes the church fathers stressed wifely subordination in such excessive terms that it is hard to find exact parallels in the principate. Augustine even claimed that in her marriage contract the bride literally pledged herself to be a slave to her husband. That may have been a slight exaggeration. In the papyri of the sixth century brides usually promised to be submissive and to love and obey the husband.[50] The marriage contracts of the early empire regulated only financial matters and hardly took any notice of the couple's expected behaviour. However, it is interesting to note that in the hellenistic period their mutual obligations had often been recorded. When exactly such clauses reappeared in late antiquity is difficult to determine because so few marital documents survive from the fourth and fifth centuries.[51] As almost none are extant outside Egypt, local differences are equally difficult to demonstrate. Late western practice may be reflected in some early medieval *formulae*. They list only property items, neglecting all other aspects of married life. The bridegroom always addresses his bride in very respectful terms. The wife for her part calls herself his 'slave' in one model mutual will.[52]

Some husbands could maintain their authority at home only by very brutal means. Augustine claims that his own father had been particularly violent and that his mother was able to avoid angry outbursts only by her prudent behaviour. Other married women in his North African home town had often displayed their

---

[49] Joh. Chrys. *virg.* 53–5, SC 125. 299 ff.; *qual. duc. ux.* 4, PG 51. 231; *in Matth.* 73. 4, PG 58. 678; *in acta* 49. 4, PG 60. 344; *in Col.* 12. 7, PG 62. 390; Hier. *ep.* 127. 3; *adv. Jovin.* 1. 28, PL 23. 261; Auson. *technop.* 7. 1. For the conclusion of marriage, see above, Ch. 2, Sect. 1.

[50] Aug. *serm.* 332. 4, PL 38. 1463; *conf.* 9. 9. 19, CCL 27. 145; *c. Faust.* 22. 31, CSEL 25. 625; *serm.* 37. 7, CCL 41. 454; 392. 4, PL 39. 1711; see also Hier. *in Eph.* 3. 5. 21–3, PL 26. 563; Didym. *gen.* 7. 5, SC 233. 238; Ps. Basil. *virg.* 23, PG 30. 717; and further Gaudemet (1969) 348–9.

[51] See e.g. P. Eleph. 1 = MChr 283 (311/310 BC); P. Tebt. i. 104 = MChr 285 (92 BC); P. Dura 30 (Syria, 232); P. Oxy. x. 1273 (260); P. Ross. Georg. iii. 28 (343/358); P. Strasb. iii. 131 = SB v. 8013 (363); P. Ness. 18 (Palestine, 537); CPR i. 30 II = MChr 290 (6th c.); P. Masp. iii. 67340r (527/565); P. Lond. v. 1711 = FIRA iii. 18 (566/573); PSI viii. 889 (6/7th c.); Montevecchi (1936) 69–75; Beaucamp (1992a) 127–9.

[52] *Form. Marc.* 2. 17 ('*ego ancilla tua*'); see also Isid. *orig.* 5. 24. 26. For the contracts, see e.g. F. Andec. 1, 34, 40, 54; F. Tur. 14–15; F. Tur. App. 2–3; F. Vis. 14–19.

bruises.[53] In contemporary Spain a church council allowed priests to use home arrest and famishing (though not lethal) to discipline their peccant wives. In Justinian's law, rough handling of the wife was punished by a fine. Such legislation obviously became necessary because Justinian no longer regarded maltreatment as a permissible ground for divorce. Earlier, the wife had been free to leave whenever she was beaten.[54]

The bishops did not approve of physical abuse, of course. They affirmed that a wife could not be treated like a slave and should definitely not be beaten. All agreed that the husband's leadership was not to be used for tyranny but for tender care.[55] Such texts balanced the more authoritarian view which they presented elsewhere. But it may still be asked whether the Christian writers as a group reflected new attitudes towards the conjugal relationship. Was there an increasing concern for male dominance in late antiquity?

There is no doubt that Greeks and Romans, both men and women, had always accepted wifely subordination as an integral part of a well-ordered family. I would not exclude the possibility that this ideal was expressed with slightly more force in late antiquity. It was not a very prominent theme in classical Roman literature. In this sense the Christian writings are more reminiscent of earlier Greek prescriptive treatises than of Roman works in the late republic and the early principate.[56] In fact, if the bishops had been writing a few hundred years earlier, their views would have been classed as moral philosophy. Moreover, they and their audience had a predominantly middle-class background whereas the politicians, historians, erotic poets, and satirists of the principate essentially reflected attitudes in the upper classes. These differences in literary genre and social class make it

---

[53] Aug. *conf.* 9. 9. 19, CCL 27. 145; *util. ieiun.* 4. 5, CCL 46. 235; *ep.* 246. 2, CSEL 57. 584; a good survey is Shaw (1987a) 28–32, although I would not stress conflicts, domination, and fear in the evidence of Augustine quite as much as he does.

[54] *Conc. Tolet.* I (398) 7. Basil. *ep.* 188. 9; Joh. Chrys. *in I Cor.* 26. 7, PG 61. 222; Greg. Tur. *franc.* 8. 36, 10. 8; P. Lips. 39 (390); P. Oxy. vi. 903 (4th c.); l. 3581 (4/5th c.); CI 5. 17. 8. 2 (449 east); Nov. 22. 15. 1, 117. 14; and further below, Ch. 5, Sect. 3. Cf. Treggiari (1991a) 430–1; Beaucamp (1992a) 321–2.

[55] Ambr. *hex.* 5. 7. 19, CSEL 32. 1. 154; Ambrosiast. *in Eph.* 5. 25–9, CSEL 81. 3. 118; Joh. Chrys. *virg.* 54–5, SC 125. 302; *in I Cor.* 26. 2, 6–8, PG 61. 214, 221 ff.; Hier. *in Eph.* 3. 5. 28, PL 26. 566; Aug. *contin.* 9. 23, CSEL 41. 168; *mor. eccl.* 1. 63, PL 32. 1336. [56] Cf. Treggiari (1991a) 202–3, 209–10, 238–61.

difficult to compare evidence from the late empire with testimony from earlier periods.

For example, physical violence had hardly become any more common in senatorial families, however often it appeared in pastoral writings. Women in the upper classes had in general more personal property, which gave them independence. On the other hand, the property rights of married women were exceptionally well guarded in Roman law (see next section). That typically Roman attitude was perhaps not easily embraced by all new citizens. Such factors may explain the shift of emphasis when the social and geographic perspective of our sources is widened during late antiquity.

In any case, Christianity as such made little difference. The church fathers certainly thought that male domination was an important constituent of the Christian family. But, although they often cited the Bible for the submissive role of the wife, they never claimed that it would have been a particularly Christian idea. On the contrary, they believed that it was a commonly accepted part of the natural order. Contemporary pagan writers bear them out, and there is no indication that Christian wives in practice were more submissive than the pagan ones had been.[57]

All in all, the available evidence does not suffice to show any significant developments over the course of time. Two passages from Jerome illustrate the difficulty. In the first one he described how young widows justified seeking a new husband:

Solent adulescentulae viduae . . . subantes dicere: 'Patrimoniolum meum cottidie perit, maiorum hereditas dissipatur, servus contumeliose locutus est, imperium ancilla neglexit. Quis procedet in publicum? Quis respondebit pro agrorum tributis? Parvulos meos quis erudiet? Vernulas quis educabit?' (ep. 54. 15)

Young widows . . . in their lustful moments are wont to say: 'My little estate is wasting every day, the property I have inherited is being scattered, my footman has spoken insultingly to me, my maid pays no attention to my orders. Who will appear for me in public? Who will be

[57] e.g. Aug. *bon. conjug.* 1. 1, CSEL 41. 188; *nupt. et concup.* 1. 9. 10, CSEL 42. 222; *quaest. hept.* 1. 153, CCL 33. 59; *in evang. Ioh.* 2. 14, CCL 36. 18; Hier. *in Eph.* 3. 5. 22–3, PL 26. 564; *in Tit.* 2. 3–5, PL 26. 617; Ambrosiast. *in Eph.* 5. 22–33, CSEL 81. 3. 117; Joh. Chrys. *reg. fem.* 6, PG 47. 524; cf. Jul. *misop.* 356B; Lib. *or.* 16. 47–8; Procop. *hist. arc.* 3. 3, 4. 30; and notes above. See also Thraede (1972) 248–9; Beaucamp (1992a) 322–4.

responsible for my land-tax? Who will educate my little children and bring up my house-slaves?' (tr. Wright, in Loeb)

Jerome considered this only a pretext, but he did not say that the claim as such was false, and it was likely to sound credible among his audience. Are we to believe that wives in the late fourth century were unable to run a household without a husband? Had the old Roman independent matron disappeared? Before making a hasty judgement, we should read another passage of Jerome. This time he was absorbed in a biblical exegesis. He found it difficult to understand why wives should always revere or fear (*timere* in the Latin translation) their husbands:

. . . *cum frequenter multo meliores maritis inveniantur uxores et eis imperent, et domum regnent, et educent liberos, et familiae teneant disciplinam: illis luxuriantibus et per scorta currentibus. Hae viros suos utrum regnare debeant an timere, lectoris arbitrio derelinquo.* (in Eph. 3. 5. 33, PL 26. 570)

. . . as wives are often found to be much better than their husbands: they govern the husband, they rule over the house and bring up the children and keep the slaves under discipline. At the same time the men lead a dissolute life and run from one harlot to another. Whether these women should rule over their husbands or fear them, I leave to the reader's discretion.

Two passages from the same author, two totally different pictures of the late Roman family. We could hardly hope for better evidence against sweeping generalizations. It is not only that all writers chose their examples to suit some specific purposes: there simply was no such thing as 'a typical married couple'. Age, financial position and personal qualities affected the marital relationship so profoundly that the endless variety in real life would have masked any shifts on the ideological level. This is important to bear in mind when we next turn to the economic aspects of conjugal life.

3. ECONOMIC INDEPENDENCE

Separation of Property in Classical Law

The intimate relationship between the spouses was not a legal issue as such. Roman jurists were mainly interested in property, not in emotions, whether the owners were married or not. They rarely discussed the affection which the husband and wife were supposed to feel for each other—perhaps a wise course. Once a husband had used money for his sick wife, who died afterwards. He was reminded that he had been moved by conjugal love and could not recover anything afterwards from her father. He had not realized this himself. However, he did not have to bear the cost of the funeral: it was always paid by the person who received the dead woman's dowry.[58]

In the system of separate properties, dowry occupied a special place. It stemmed from the wife's part, and she was considered to have a continuing right to it although it was normally administered by the husband during marriage. He was expected to use its fruits to maintain her and to bear the costs of their common living, *onera matrimonii*.[59] Sometimes the wife received a monthly or annual allowance for her personal expenses.[60] It was also possible to let her keep the yield from the dowry on condition that she or her father maintained her and her servants.[61] Clearly such arrangements were sensible only in those social classes whose income came from inherited capital. We cannot expect to find much information about life in poor families. In most households of the empire the spouses probably shared their poverty alike unconcerned by any juridical considerations.

As we have seen above (Ch. 2, Sect. 3), the wife rarely gave all her possessions as dowry. Thus she usually brought additional property with her, either her inheritance or, if she was *in potestate*, her *peculium*. It was these assets which had to be kept separate from her husband's wealth. The spouses could lend and borrow and conduct transactions between them like any strangers, and they were not liable for each other's debts or civic obligations. In brief, they were treated like two totally unrelated persons, as far as property was concerned. But, since this rule had

[58] CI 2. 18. 13 (230); cf. D. 11. 7. 16–32, 24. 3. 60.
[59] D. 2. 8. 15. 3, 4. 4. 3. 5, 10. 2. 20. 2, 46, 17. 1. 47. pr, 17. 2. 65. 16, 23. 3. 7. pr, 56. 1–2, 69. 8, 75, 76, 23. 4. 11, 28, 24. 1. 53. 1, 54, 24. 3. 20, 21, 51; CI 5. 12. 20 (294); see Corbett (1930) 147–202; Gardner (1986) 68–71; Treggiari (1991a) 324–40; cf. also Inst. 2. 8. pr; CI 5. 12. 30 (529), 8. 17. 12. 3 (531); and generally on dowry, above, Ch. 2, Sect. 3. [60] D. 23. 4. 22. pr, 24. 1. 15, 28. 6–7, 33; CI 5. 16. 11 (241).
[61] D. 15. 3. 20. pr, 21; 17. 1. 60. 3, 23. 3. 73. 1, 23. 4. 12. 1, 24. 1. 21. 1, 24. 3. 42. 2, 29. 2. 98, 44. 4. 17. pr; CI 5. 14. 2 (213), 5. 16. 8 (233); see also Treggiari (1991a) 336–8.

to be confirmed in numerous statutes over the course of time, it was perhaps not self-evident for everyone.[62]

Protection of separate property went so far that the spouses faced more restrictions than outsiders: gifts between them (and between their *patresfamilias*) were invalid. This ban certainly existed by the end of the republic. In the imperial period even the jurists did not really know why it had been imposed, not to speak of lay people. Various explanations appear in the legal sources. Some claimed that if the spouses were too fond of each other their judgement was impaired. Others hinted that their affections might be simulated out of greed. Still others feared that either of the partners could use divorce as a threat to extort favours. These suspicions, though perhaps not always groundless, do not sound like the real motive. By modern analogies, we might rather suspect that married people wished to defraud their creditors by transferring their property to the spouse, but Roman jurists never connect the ban with such considerations. It may have been just one more aspect of the Roman system which tried to prevent mixing of property from different families.[63]

Of course, the jurists had to accept the fact that when two people lived in a common household they used each other's property. The house where they lived was owned either by the man or by the wife. Their individual slaves belonged to either one but were used and often maintained together. Their clothes were perhaps made from the same raw material. They could give each other presents on birthdays and other normal occasions. As was noted earlier, the husband was expected to maintain his wife's standard of living according to the size of her dowry. These normal and necessary transactions received due attention and careful interpretation from the jurists. They were not counted as invalid gifts as long as they kept within reasonable limits and did not make the other partner permanently richer. We could

[62] See e.g. Gell. 17. 6; D. 15. 1. 19. 1, 19. 5. 12, 20. 6. 11, 23. 3. 82, 24. 1. 7. 4, 14, 31. 2; CI 3. 28. 22 (294), 4. 12. 1–3 (287–93), 4. 50. 6 (293), 4. 65. 24 (293), 6. 3. 6 (222), 6. 24. 6 (246), 7. 1. 3 (Diocl.), 7. 8. 1 (205), 7. 73. 3 (213), 9. 12. 1 (205), 10. 32. 11 (294); CT 9. 42. 1 (321), 15 (396 east); Cass. *var.* 4. 10. 2 (507/511); for the dowry, cf. D. 50. 1. 21. 4; CI 8. 14. 4 (283).

[63] D. 24. 1. 1, 2, 3, 31. 7; CI 5. 16. 2 (213); CT 8. 16. 1 (320); 5. 1. 9 (428 east); Nov. 74. 4. pr; cf. Plut. *quaest. rom.* 7–8; *conjug. praec.* 34. See Kaser (1971) 331–2; Gardner (1986) 74; Treggiari (1991a) 366–74. For the creditors, cf. D. 23. 3. 72. pr; CI 5. 3. 13, 5. 16. 12, 13; Nov. 97. 2.

even say that in their everyday life Roman spouses held their property in common. It was only after marriage had been ended by death or divorce that problems arose. As a precaution, the husband often bequeathed to his wife everything he had purchased for her use.[64]

However, legal sources record also major financial arrangements which clearly transferred considerable property from one spouse to the other. Sometimes people may simply not have known that such gifts were invalid. Sometimes they knew it very well and tried to evade the ban by an imaginary sale.[65] In practice, anything could happen when the members of a family were conducting business with each other or with outsiders. To take an example, a man could write his wife's name in a document of purchase and pay the price himself, so that you needed a jurist (or the emperor himself) to tell who had actually acquired the ownership. Often everything had taken place openly and bona fide but occasionally that had not been the case, or at least it was so suspected.[66] Again, these transactions were mostly discovered afterwards when the spouses quarrelled over divorce or heirs demanded their rights.

Certainly the ban on gifts was one of the most difficult rules to interpret and enforce. In 206 the law was so modified that a gift during marriage became valid if the donor died first and had not reclaimed it. This may have settled some problems but it did not remove them altogether, as the relevant title in the Justinian Code attests.[67] How carefully the ban was observed by ordinary people remains another question. In any case, it was well known to Roman jurists in late antiquity: it was firmly entrenched in Justinian's law and seems to have been preserved in the west at least to the end of the fifth century.[68] We do not know what

[64] See esp. D. 24. 1 *passim*; also D. 7. 4. 22; 7. 8. 4. 1; 10. 4. 3. 14; 24. 3. 22. 8, 66. 1; 29. 5. 1. 15; 31. 35; 32. 45–9, 58, 60. 2, 100. 2; 34. 2. 2–4, 10, 13, 30, 32. 6, 34, 39. pr; 35. 2. 81. 2; CI 6. 2. 17 (294). Gardner (1986) 68–75; Crook (1990); Treggiari (1991a) 374–8, 388–90.

[65] D. 16. 1. 17. pr, 18. 1. 38, 24. 1. 5. 5, 32. 25–6; PS 2. 23. 4; CI 5. 16. 15 (291), 20 (294); FV 273 (315). See also P. Catt. r. VI (136), with Anagnostou-Cañas (1984) 351.

[66] CI 3. 29. 8. 1, 4. 22. 2, 4. 29. 4. 1, 5, 10, 13, 15, 17; 4. 38. 7, 4. 50. 1–6, 5. 16. 6, 9, 12, 13, 16; 7. 73. 3, 8. 27. 19, 8. 44. 11; CG 3. 7; D. 16. 1. 27. 2, 28. 1, 20. 1. 1. 4, 42. 8. 10. 14, 18. These cases span the 3rd c.

[67] D. 24. 1. 32; CI 5. 16; FV 273 (315); 276 (290); etc. Treggiari (1991a) 371–4.

[68] CT 3. 8. 2 (382 east), 3. 13. 3 (422 west) + int, 5. 1. 9 (428 east); these were included in the *Breviarium*. See also the late 5th-c. *interpretationes* to PS 2. 23 (= LRV PS 2. 24), which were then cited much later in *Form. Tur.* 17. In the east, e.g. the Syro-Roman Law Book L 14.

importance it may have had in the early middle ages. If the spouses normally held their property in common during marriage, they rarely needed to make gifts to each other except in anticipation of their death (*mortis causa*). That is in fact what numerous *formulae* show: all the deeds of gift between the spouses are in practice mutual wills. Only one *formula* adds that the couple will share the properties already during marriage (*F.Marc.* 1. 12). It is unlikely that the Roman ban on gifts had much force any longer. At least it was not adopted by Germanic lawgivers.[69]

We can now return to the third century and to a strange passage of Ulpian. He had dealt with the dowry and then proceeded to other property which was transferred at marriage:

Ceterum si res dentur in ea, quae Graeci parapherna dicunt quaeque Galli peculium appellant, videamus, an statim efficiuntur mariti. Et putem, si sic dentur, ut fiant, effici mariti, et cum distractum fuerit matrimonium, non vindicari oportet, sed condici, nec dotis actione peti, ut divus Marcus et imperator noster cum patre rescripserunt. (D. 23. 3. 9. 3)

When property is given as what the Greeks call *parapherna* and the Gauls *peculium*, let us see whether it becomes the husband's straight away. I think that if it is given with this intention it passes to him at once and, if the marriage is dissolved, the woman should not claim it as hers, but bring a *condictio*, not an action for dowry, as the deified Marcus and our emperor stated in a rescript.

Ulpian speaks here of a particular mass of property which the wife brought with her when she married. He does not specify what kind of belongings came into question. Personal utensils, clothes, jewellery, and perhaps slaves, are the most obvious conjectures. Ulpian thought that their ownership could be transferred to the husband although they had to be returned if the marriage was broken. They would have passed as a valid gift if they were delivered before marriage or if they derived from someone other than the wife and her *paterfamilias*. But the arrangement still sounds strange: it runs counter to the whole Roman idea of separate properties. Nowhere else do we hear that

---

[69] For *donationes mortis causa*, see e.g. *F.Andec.* 41; *F.Tur.* 17–18; *F.Vis.* 23–4; *F.Marc.* 2. 7–8. For legislation, see LV 3. 1. 5 (AD 645); LV. Ant 5. 2. 4, 5. 2. 5 (= CE 319), 5. 2. 7 (= CE 307); Kaser (1975) 172 n. 38. On the community of property, see further below.

the husband might 'own' anything which the wife had brought with her or received from her relatives.

In fact, Ulpian gives the impression that the practice was not common in Italy at all: it was more familiar to citizens of Greek and Celtic origin. True, the *parapherna* which figures in contemporary papyri and in some later imperial laws did not become the husband's property during marriage although it could in practice be administered by him. Possibly Ulpian did not know provincial customs very well, nor need they have been uniform everywhere. In any case he did his best to reconcile them with imperial law. These customs could not be a mere curiosity because the emperors had been confronted with them already since the reign of Marcus Aurelius.[70]

The above interpretation is tentative at best. One complicating factor is that such use of the word *peculium* may not have been confined to the Gauls alone. There are a couple of other classical juridic fragments which imply that some items of property brought by the wife could be called *peculium* to separate them from her dowry, even if she was no longer *in potestate* and they were not *peculium* in the normal sense.[71] It has been suggested that Ulpian did not write *'Galli'* in the first place but *'alii'* ('others').[72] Be that as it may, the whole topic remains regrettably unclear.

However, immediately after this, in the same passage (D. 23. 3. 9. 3), Ulpian returns to Rome itself and purports to record a common habit there. This description is much easier to combine with other sources and with the general principles of Roman marriage *sine manu*. According to Ulpian, the wife brought to her new home many tangible items which were not included in her dowry. She retained full ownership and often tried to secure

[70] Cf. CI 5. 14. 8, 11; Wolff (1955); García Garrido (1958) 31–50; Häge (1968) 238, 246–7, 270–7; Kaser (1971: 329–30; 1975: 201); and further below. As to the authenticity of D. 23. 3. 9. 3, it seems to derive essentially from Ulpian himself. For example, the reference to *parapherna* can hardly be taken just as a Byzantine gloss. Radical interpolations are no longer suspected. Admittedly, no proof is possible one way or the other.

[71] FV 112, 254 = D. 39. 5. 31. 1; PS 5. 11. 1; cf. Goody (1990) 431, for the survival of the word *peculium* in rural Albania.

[72] *Galli* is in the manuscript: Mommsen amended it to *alii*, and he has been followed by some scholars. But *Galli* is certainly *lectio difficillior*, and it is supported by the Byzantine *Basilica* 29. 1. 5 (Scheltema A iv. 1446).

it by preparing an inventory, which the husband had to sign. This very practice shows that it was not easy to keep the properties separate once they had been united in a common household. Ulpian remarked that 'the husband often assumes responsibility for the custody of this property unless the wife is left in charge of it'.

Total separation may have been difficult to achieve not only in utility articles but in the case of landed property as well. Even without any explicit decision, it was natural to expect that the wife allowed her possessions to be administered by the husband. On the other hand, her role as household manager presupposed financial responsibilities, too. Journeys were long in the Roman empire and communications often cut off: in her husband's absence a dutiful wife managed his property as any trusted friend would have done. It was perfectly normal for either of the spouses to do each other this service as *negotiorum gestio* (as a jurist would have defined it) or simply on account of their marriage. None of the jurists seems to have taken offence at these habits.[73]

Thus legal theory did not prevent a Roman married woman from sharing common goods with her husband and from accepting his leadership. In so doing she realized the common ideal which was discussed earlier.[74] As a brief reminder, let us take Plutarch again to represent the views of many others:

Such a copartnership in property as well is especially befitting married people, who should pour all their resources into a common fund, and combine them, and each should not regard one part as his own and another part as the other's, but all as his own and nothing as the other's. As we call a mixture 'wine', although the larger of the component parts is water, so the property and the estate ought to be said to belong to the husband, even though the wife contribute the larger share. (*conjug. praec.* 20, tr. Babbitt, in Loeb)

[73] D. 3. 5. 32, 34. pr, 15. 3. 21, 24. 1. 47, 25. 2. 1, 29. 2. 87, 34. 1. 16. 3, 35. 2. 95. pr, 36. 1. 80. 8, 42. 1. 52, 46. 3. 48; CI 2. 18. 14 (234), 4. 50. 5 (290), 6 (293), 7. 73. 1 (Carac.), 9. 32. 4 (242). See Treggiari (1991a) 374–9.
[74] Above, Ch. 4, Sect. 2. See further Plut. *conjug. praec.* 34; Cic. *off.* 1. 54; Colum. 12. praef. 8; Mart. 4. 75; Treggiari (1991a) 249–51. A very famous presentation of the same ideal is *Laudatio Turiae*, CIL vi. 1527 + 37053 = FIRA iii. 69, in sects. I. 13 ff., 37 ff., and II. 46 ff.

It appears that if all went well people were rather reluctant to live up to the principle of separate properties, which was (and still is) so prominent in theoretical treatises on Roman law. It was usually realized only after a marriage had been ended. That was why the jurists were so interested to record how property had been transferred during marriage: when a divorced couple started to quarrel or a group of interested heirs appeared, they needed firm rules and hard facts to divide the estate. As long as the marriage lasted and all parties were in agreement it was not important to know how individual decisions were taken inside the family.

However, the case was different if the parties were not in agreement. It is not difficult to imagine situations of that kind. Perhaps the wife refused to accomplish what the husband advised her to do, or the husband administered their common property in a way which the wife thought was to her disadvantage. In the third century the emperors often received petitions from women who wanted to assert their property rights against their husbands. The emperors' answer was absolutely clear: the wife retained full control over her property. All unauthorized acts by her husband were null and void.[75]

Could the husband wield some power as a *tutor*? Usually in ancient cultures the husband automatically became his wife's guardian. This practice is well attested for Roman Egypt and for other parts of the Greek east, and it can with some reason be conjectured for the west, where no sources are available.[76] Roman law was different. Originally, a woman who was married *sine manu* had an agnatic relative as her *tutor legitimus*. According to this reasoning, the guardian was someone who looked after the family interests and balanced the husband's power. But after the mid-first century there were no more *tutores legitimi*. It is quite certain that a father could name the husband as guardian in his will. On the other hand, we do not know whether the husband might be appointed by a magistrate. Any hypothesis is difficult to verify since *tutela mulierum* appears so rarely in literary sources

[75] CI 3. 32. 3 (222), 3. 42. 1 (222), 4. 29. 5 (224), 4. 51. 2 (Gord.), 5. 16. 17 (293), 7. 8. 1 (205), 8. 42. 11 (293); Cons. 1, esp. 1. 9 (290/293); CG 3. 6. 5 (287).
[76] GI 1. 193; Mitteis (1891) 218–21; Taubenschlag (1955) 171–5; Kaser (1975) 222; Rupprecht (1986) 97; Kutzner (1989) 87–9; Just (1989) 26–7; Sealey (1990) 154. Cf. also Caes. *Gall.* 6. 19.

and does not figure in the *Corpus Iuris Civilis* at all. In Egypt, female citizens often had their husband as guardian both before and after 212.[77] Local tradition may naturally have played some role here, but at least we can infer that the practice was not forbidden by provincial authorities. It seems probable that there was no general ban in Roman law. The woman could choose as her *tutor* whomever she wished. Husbands may often have been called upon but we really cannot say how often. It was obviously not an automatic choice.[78]

In any case, *tutela mulieris* had already been weakened so much in the imperial period that it brought the husband little authority over his wife. The Romans were obviously more worried about *tutela impuberis* and the office of the *curator*. These persons actually administered the property of their ward. It might be feared that an ensuing marriage would conceal some malpractice. Thus, a *senatusconsultum* in the late 170s banned unions between a girl and her former *tutor*. Nor could a husband be made his wife's *curator*:

Maritus etsi rebus uxoris suae debeat affectionem, tamen curator ei creari non potest.[79]

Even if the husband ought to be favourably disposed towards his wife's property, he still cannot be made her curator.

This was the general tenor of Roman law: husbands had to be prevented from misusing their influence. Another protective measure was the *senatusconsultum Velleianum*, a decree from the first century, which stated that women could not stand surety for anyone's debts. Although it applied to all women and all obligations, it was initially meant to protect the property of wives from

---

[77] BGU ii. 472 (141); i. 301 (157); P. Ryl. ii. 172 (208); P. Oxy. xii. 1463 (215); SB i. 5831 (226); SP xx. 28 (227); SB i. 4370 (228/9); P.Fay. 94 (222/235); P. Princ. ii. 38 (c.264); Weiss (1908) 84; Taubenschlag (1955) 175 n. 23.

[78] See Apul. *apol.* 101; FV 110. Although *Laudatio Turiae*, CIL vi. 1527 = FIRA iii. 69. I. 37 ff., need not be technical language, the husband may well have been appointed in the will. In P.Lond. ii. 470 = FIRA iii. 26 = MChr 328 (168) the wife and her *tutor* are citizens while the husband is not. Cf. also García Garrido (1958) 141–9; Gardner (1986) 16; Treggiari (1991a) 377.

[79] CI 5. 34. 2 (225). See also D. 23. 1. 15, 23. 2. 36, 64. 1, 66. pr, 67. 3, 27. 1. 1. 5, 27. 10. 14, 48. 5. 7; FV 110, 117, 201–2; CI 2. 12. 14 (241), 2. 43. 2 (226), 4. 16. 6 = 7. 72. 7 (294), which has been tampered with; 5. 6. 7 (Diocl.), 5. 62. 4 (216), 17 (265); P. Princ. ii. 38 (c.264); Inst. 1. 25. 19.

their husbands, and it clearly worked that way in the third century.[80]

It is important to note that Roman law did not enjoin the husband not to help his spouse in financial or legal matters. The Justinian Code records numerous instances where a man acted on behalf of his wife, appearing in court or asking for a rescript.[81] There was nothing objectionable in this, but for some reason or another, the Romans did not want to give the husband any legal power which the wife could not hold back if she so wished. The unanimity of third-century emperors and legal experts in this question was remarkable. It is extraordinary in the light of later legal history as well.[82]

Originally it must have been thought that the protection of separate properties worked favourably for the woman's father and her other blood relatives. The feeling that wealth should stay in the family where it has originated is certainly widespread, perhaps universal. It was especially problematic in Roman society, where daughters inherited substantial properties. The attempts to restrict the husband's influence are thus another aspect of the same general idea which we have encountered earlier in connection with *patria potestas* and the position of mothers. But, as fathers died early and the agnatic family had little practical power, it seems that Roman women were able to utilize the situation for their own benefit.

Of course, one can ask whether wives really could assert themselves, with or without imperial rescripts, which may not have had much practical effect. The Justinian Code shows women acting independently in a multitude of affairs but it is rarely known whether they are married or widowed. That is why we have to look at an imperial rescript to a certain Diogenes from the end of the third century:

Si praedium uxor tua dotale venumdedit, sponte necne contractum habuerit, nihil interest, cum rei tibi quaesitae dominium auferre nolenti minime potuerit. (CI 5. 12. 23)

---

[80] See D. 16. 1, esp. 16. 1. 2; CI 4. 29, 8. 27. 11; Nov. 134. 8; Gardner (1986) 75–6; Crook (1986b) 90–1; and further below, Ch. 7, Sect. 1.
[81] e.g. CI 2. 12. 2 (161), 9. 1. 4 (222), 8. 29. 3 (223), 8. 32. 2 (Alex.), 4. 32. 14 (234), 10. 3. 3 (239), 2. 12. 14 (241), 4. 32. 15 (242), 7. 72. 7 (294), 8. 55. 6 (294); D. 46. 7. 3. 3.
[82] See e.g. Robinson (1988) 54–5.

If your wife sold her dotal farm, it does not matter whether she made the contract of free will or not because if you did not agree she could not deprive you of the ownership of the property which you had acquired.

The wife of Diogenes had sold landed property which was part of her dowry, something that was clearly illegal because the dowry was owned by the husband during marriage. This should have been self-evident, and the rescript is not interesting for its legal contents. What makes it significant is the fact that the wife had actually been able to sell the plot in question. If she could make money out of her husband's property without his consent, she had certainly no difficulties in managing her own.

The Property of Married Women in Late Antiquity

Private rescripts dry up in the beginning of the fourth century, and it is no longer possible to follow what happened inside private families. We have to content ourselves with a few general laws. Without their original context, they are quite difficult to interpret.

Constantine had decreed that no property belonging to minors could be sold without special permission from a court (CT 3. 32. 1; 3. 30. 3). But we also learn that he had exempted married women from this rule: a wife who was under 25 could freely dispose of her estate if her husband gave his consent and signed the documents. In this respect the husband now had more authority than an ordinary *curator*. The whole arrangement is known only because Julian repealed it in 362 (CT 3. 1. 3). It is hazardous to guess at either emperor's motives. Julian was evidently not so much interested in defending wifely independence: he indicated that Constantine's rule imposed an excessive financial burden on men since they were liable for possible losses.

The role which Constantine gave to the husband was in any case conspicuous, whether he was thought of as a kind of *curator* or not. Many people in the empire certainly reasoned that while a young boy had to receive a *curator*, his sister mainly needed a husband. If we had the first books of the Theodosian Code in their entirety we might know better how Roman law reacted to this idea. Constantine's law appears to have been the only imperial constitution where it clearly surfaced.[83]

In another law Constantine stated that a husband could represent his spouse in court without an explicit mandate. This was no innovation as it had probably been possible in classical law, too, but it is interesting to see that even this modest concession made Justinian's compilers wary. When they included the edict in their Corpus they added to it another constitution which came from the end of the fourth century and is found also in the Theodosian Code:

Procurator, licet maritus sit, id solum exequi debet, quod procuratio emissa praescripserit.[84]

A procurator, even though he be the husband of the principal, must execute only that which has been prescribed by the procuracy issued to him.

There is no doubt that late Roman law continued to uphold the old principle of separate properties during marriage.[85] One notable exception was connected with the problem of decurions. Women were not liable for service in a city council themselves. However, several eastern laws in the fifth and sixth centuries took it for granted that if they married a councillor their inherited property was used for municipal obligations through the husband. Exactly how it was meant to happen remains obscure.[86]

Otherwise, the eastern government did not forsake the traditional attitude towards matrimonial property. In the mid-fifth century it firmly defended an opinion which Ulpian would certainly have shared:

---

[83] Cf. CT 13. 10. 4, 6 (370); FIRA iii. 51 = P. Oxy. vi. 907. 18–20 (276); Sidon. *ep.* 4. 24. 8. But see also P. Princ. ii. 38 (*c*.264), in which the husband is called *kyrios* and another man *kourator*.

[84] CT 2. 12. 4 (393 east); CI 2. 12. 21. pr (315), cited below in Ch. 7, Sect. 2; cf. D. 46. 7. 3. 3; Kaser (1975) 172 n. 33; Beaucamp (1990) 137–8.

[85] e.g. CT 9. 42. 1 (321), 9. 7. 4 (385 east), 9. 42. 15 (396 east); Nov. 134. 8. See also the Syro-Roman Law Book, L 13, 31, and 43, the implications of which are not quite clear, cf. Selb (1964) 149–53, with Yaron (1966) 141.

[86] NTh 22. 2. 11 (443); CI 10. 35. 3. 1 (528); Nov. 38 5, 101. 4; cf. CI 10. 32. 11 (294); CT 12. 1. 124, 137 (392/3 east); Lib. *or.* 2 36; Beaucamp (1990) 29–31; on the guild of bakers, cf. Sirks (1988) 481 ff.; and generally on the compulsory services of women, below, Ch. 7, Sect. 2.

Hac lege decernimus, ut vir in his rebus, quas extra dotem mulier habet, quas Graeci parapherna dicunt, nullam uxore prohibente habeat communionem nec aliquam ei necessitatem imponat. Quamvis enim bonum erat mulierem, quae se ipsam marito committit, res etiam eiusdem pati arbitrio gubernari, attamen quoniam conditores legum aequitatis convenit esse fautores, nullo modo, ut dictum est, muliere prohibente virum in paraphernis se volumus immiscere.[87]

By this law we decree that the husband shall have nothing to do with that property which the woman has outside her dowry and which the Greeks call *parapherna*, nor shall he exert any pressure on her concerning it. For although it would be good if the woman, who entrusts herself to her husband, would also allow him to administer her property, nevertheless, since it is fit that the legislators favour equity, in no way, as said, do we want the husband to meddle with the *parapherna* against the woman's wish.

The husband's beneficial influence on his wife's affairs was recognized but not at the cost of her independence. Similar ideas were still current among western jurists at the turn of the sixth century.[88] On the other hand, in 444 Valentinian III confronted the following problem:

Conperimus enim quasdam post maritorum obitum filios suos proposita indecora actione nudasse, cum ab his patrimonii sui fructus quaererent, quos utique stante matrimonio in illa aequalitate vivendi in commune consumptos convenit aestimari quorumque ratiocinium perplexum atque confusum ad veritatis fidem discuti posse non credimus. Cumque illud frequentius noverimus accidere, ut maiores expensas flagitet matronalis ornatus, et cum numquam viri post uxorum obitum huiusmodi aliquid credant communibus filiis opponendum, durum est muliebri tantum licentiae ista permitti. (NVal 14. 1)

For we learn that certain women after the death of their husbands have despoiled their own children by bringing a disgraceful action when they sought from them the income from their patrimony which certainly must be estimated as having been consumed in common while the marriage existed, in that well known equality of living. We do not believe that the account of such income, since it is involved and confused, can be investigated according to truthful reliability. Since We know that it

---

[87] CI 5. 14. 8 (450); the law must come from the east because western laws were not included in the Justinian Code after 438. See also CI 5. 14. 11 (530).

[88] CT 2. 12. 4 + int, 3. 1. 3 + int; CG 3. 6. 5; all included in the *Breviarium*; Cass. *var.* 4. 10. 2 (507/511) See also Cons. 1, 2. 1–5, 8. 1–3 (this western treatise is dated to the late 5th c.). The statement of Wemple (1981) 31, is clearly mistaken.

happens rather frequently that the adornment of a matron requires greater expenditures, and since men, after the death of their wives, never suppose that they should bring any such claim against their common children, it is hard that such things should be granted only to the license of women.

We may doubt whether feminine adornment really surpassed all other expenses. But Valentinian, or whoever wrote the law, was certainly right that it was very difficult to divide the costs of a common household afterwards. This was the very problem which the classical jurisprudents faced so often. They might have been more scrupulous, analysing the marital property up to the last hairpin, to find out whether the other party had been enriched at the other's expense.[89] Valentinian's attitude was simpler, and perhaps the only feasible one in his time, but clearly women sometimes felt that they had not been able to exert sufficient control over their property during marriage.

The church fathers occasionally offered advice on the control of matrimonial property. Mostly they reflected the common sentiment that women needed a man to manage their property and sometimes they complained that wives were too independent. Here we again see how the variety in real life and different pastoral motives produced apparently conflicting statements. Augustine was perhaps too extreme when he demanded that the wife should ask permission even for the smallest everyday transactions. That would have made the housewife's task really cumbersome. On the other hand, he also urged the man to secure his wife's approval on almsgiving. As a whole, the bishops clearly recommended a community of property under the husband's responsible leadership.[90] This is no surprise: we have seen that similar ideals prevailed already in the early empire.

Christian authors did not discuss the legal side of the conjugal relationship. Surviving documents throw somewhat more light on this issue. They suggest that in practice the questions of marriage and guardianship were more closely interrelated than

[89] Cf. e.g. D. 24. 1, and further above, on donations during marriage.
[90] Hier. *ep.* 54. 15 (cited above, Ch. 4, Sect. 2); 123. 13; Greg. Naz. *carm.* 2. 2. 6. 23, PG 37. 1544; Joh. Chrys. *in acta* 49. 4, PG 60. 344; *in Eph.* 20. 9, PG 62. 147; Aug. *serm.* 392. 4, PL 39. 1711; *ep.* 262. 4–9, CSEL 57. 624; *de serm. dom.* 2. 2. 7, CCL 35. 97; and further Beaucamp (1992a) 319–21.

Roman law would lead us to expect. By the end of antiquity they cannot be discussed separately.

It is natural to start again with Egypt. We have noted earlier that in the Graeco-Egyptian system the husband was normally his wife's guardian. This custom seems to have continued after 212, but in the late third century the guardians were replaced in documents by other male advisers. Their presence was common but unofficial, at least in the eyes of Roman law. It is no surprise that the man who was called *synestos* was mostly the woman's husband. He was still regarded as the best support for his wife.[91]

The old phrase 'with *kyrios*' was hardly ever used after the end of the third century. Men who are named *kyrioi* appear four times in later documents: twice in the mid-fourth century, once in the early fifth, and once in the late sixth. Strikingly, they are all husbands. It might be argued that these papyri prove the survival of *tutela mulierum* in imperial law, not otherwise attested after the early fourth century (see above). We cannot totally exclude this possibility for the three first documents. On the other hand, such interpretation does not suit the fourth case since it is absolutely certain that *tutela* was absent from late sixth-century Byzantine law. It is perhaps safer to assume that all the four papyri reflect local practice rather than anything explicitly sanctioned by imperial law.[92]

With this phenomenon we have to connect another curious fact. In the sixth century women often recorded that they acted 'without their husband as guardian' (*khoris kyriou andros khrematizousai*). Formally this phrase resembles the one which was current up to the fourth century but the logic is entirely different. Now the *ius liberorum* plays no part: it is the lack of husband which is crucial. Most of the women who mention that they are acting without a husband can be shown to be widows while none are securely married. Sometimes the word 'widow' actually appears as an equivalent to the phrase 'without husband'.[93] On

---

[91] e.g. P.Vindob.Bosw. 6 (250); P.Strasb. vi. 555 (289); SB iv. 7338 (300); P.Oxy.Hels. 44 (324); Sijpesteijn (1965) 180ff.; P.Mich. xv, p. 158ff.; Beaucamp (1992a) 251–7.

[92] BGU iv. 1049 (342); MChr 361 = P.Oxy. iv, p. 202 (355); SP xx. 117 (411); P.Lond. v. 1724 (578/582); Beaucamp (1992a) 194–7, 262–3.

[93] e.g. P.Lond. v. 1855 (493); SB xvi. 12864 (505); P.Flor. iii. 323 (525); P.Masp. ii. 67156 (570); P.Monac. i. 11 (586); PSI vii. 773 (611). The basic treatment is Beaucamp (1992a) 193–266, esp. 198–212, which I am essentially following.

the other hand, it seems that if the husband was alive he was present in all major agreements signed by his wife. He might then be called a guardian (in the four cases mentioned above), or alternatively he was said to consent to the act, or the contract was concluded jointly by both spouses.[94]

Thus in Byzantine Egypt married women were regularly assisted by their husbands. Only widows were effectively free from male supervision. We may also include divorced women in this category, although that is not clearly attested. Unmarried girls, on the other hand, were usually so young that they still had a *curator*. The position of adult women not yet married became a question only after the spread of Christian asceticism. It is possible that consecrated virgins past their majority were in practice treated like widows.[95] In any case, all this depended solely on local custom since nothing similar existed in imperial law.

The historical development cannot be traced with any accuracy. The new system is clearly documented only from the turn of the sixth century, but its roots are perhaps visible already in the fourth, while the fifth notoriously lacks surviving papyri. I would suggest that the change was first and foremost brought about by the influence of Roman law in Egypt. In the third century Roman *tutela* disrupted the old tradition of Graeco-Egyptian guardianship. There may well have ensued a lengthy period of confusion during which the official and unofficial types coexisted and perhaps intermingled. But when *tutela* finally disappeared in the fourth century it left a vacuum which was again filled by local adaptations. Whatever the details and possible variations, the result was what we see in the sixth century.

Although the husband clearly had great authority in Byzantine Egypt the married couple did not form one financial entity. The spouses might of course possess something in common if they had acquired it together. It was especially frequent that a house was purchased jointly by husband and wife, but their inherited assets did not merge. During marriage nothing prevented them from enjoying the properties together. If they divorced they both took with them what they had brought. The two estates became

---

[94] Beaucamp (1992*a*) 212–47.
[95] Cf. for a nun (*monakhe*), P.Lond. v. 1731 (585), with Beaucamp (1992*a*) 209–10.

united only when they were inherited by the couple's common descendants. Whether or not there were children, the spouses could draw up a mutual will, leaving each other at least the usufruct of their property. In this way there may sometimes have developed an idea that all family members in a sense shared the property rights.[96]

What has been said above applies only to Egypt. Documentary evidence from other regions is much more scattered. There is just enough to suggest that similar or related habits existed elsewhere. For example, the notion of a communal family property was strong among peasants in formerly Roman North Africa. When married couples sold or bought land they always acted together. Widowed fathers and mothers acted with their children. There is no trace of a guardianship of women.[97]

Papyri from Gothic and Byzantine Italy show the same tendencies but with more variation. Often married people and even their children were named together as sellers, donors, or tenants, but it never emerges in what way they were regarded as co-owners.[98] On the other hand, in some documents the wife was said to be disposing of her personal assets, which she had received from her father or a previous husband. In such cases her husband's consent was expressly recorded.[99] There were also a few women who transferred their landed property without any male assistance. We may presume that they were unmarried. Once a widow and her two children were jointly selling land inherited from her late husband.[100] Sometimes people in these charters have Gothic names, sometimes Roman, and occasionally they belong to the Byzantine garrison. It might be added that the letters of Gregory the Great often mention women who possess and donate property or build monasteries in their own name.[101]

---

[96] On all this, see Beaucamp (1992b), with documentation. The property relations of married people in hellenistic and early Roman Egypt are a moot question as well, cf. Wolff (1939) 52; Häge (1968) 65–72, 148–59.

[97] *Tablettes Albertini*, throughout the collection.

[98] P.Tjäder i. 12 (491), 14–15 (572), 23 (c.700), 25 (early 7th c.?), ii. 35. 25 (572), 43 (542?), 44 (c.650), 49. 17 (557); cf. Greg. M. *ep.* 9. 73 (598).

[99] P.Tjäder i. 13 (553), ii. 37 (591), 46 (c.600); P.Rainer Cent. 166 (c.600).

[100] P.Tjäder i. 17 (early 7th c.?), 20 (c.600), 28 (613–41), ii. 30 (539).

[101] Greg. M. *ep.* 1. 42, 1. 46, 1. 50, 1. 53, 2. 11, 4. 8, 4. 36 (*bona materna*), 5. 2, 6. 35 (husband appealing for his wife), 9. 171, 9. 181, 9. 233.

From sixth-century Gaul we have a *formula* in which the wife gives a mandate to her husband:

Dum et humana prodidit utilitas, et lex Romana exposcit, ut, quicumque uxoris suae negotium fuerit prosecutus, quamvis maritus sit, nihil aliud agat, nisi quod ei agendum per mandatum illa conmiserit. Igitur ego in Dei nomine illa, filia illius, te dulcissime iugali meo illo. Dum me simplicitas dominatur, quod minime rebus vel causas meas valeo exercere, te in omnibus rebus vel causis meis instituo dominum procuratoremve et auctorem, ita ut, quicquid exinde egeris gesserisve, ratam vel diffinitam me in omnibus esse cognoscas . . . Et adhuc mihi inserere placuit, ut hoc mandatum civitate illa cum curia publica, ut mos est, gestis municipalibus facias alligari. (F.Tur. 20)

Both the public interest requires and Roman law demands that whoever deals with a matter of his wife should not carry out anything else than what she has committed to him through a mandate. Thus, I so-and-so, the daughter of so-and-so, to you my sweetest spouse so-and-so: since I am so simple that I cannot manage my property or stand on my rights, I appoint you as a lord, procurator, and guardian over all my property and my lawsuits, so that whatever you hereafter carry out or accomplish you know that I will perfectly approve and ratify. . . Moreover, I want to add that you should have this mandate confirmed in the official records of the council of the city named so-and-so, as the custom is.

This remarkable piece of evidence shows that very late in Merovingian Gaul scribes tried to preserve formalities which had their origins in a distant past and in an alien culture.[102] Whether they always really understood the old legal texts which they cited is obscure. Still less is known about actual behaviour among the Gallo-Roman population. In numerous other *formulae* the man and wife together dispose of their estates. They sell or donate land and free slaves, without bothering to specify whose property was in question. The same happens in the actual charters where members of the Frankish ruling class transfer their wealth to monasteries.[103] On the other hand, in many

---

[102] Similar *formulae* are *F.Tur.App.* 4 and *F.Andec.* 1b; the legal rule is directly quoted from CT 2. 12. 4. int. See also *F.Arvern.* 2, in which a widow gives the general mandate to her son.

[103] *F.Andec.* 25, 27, 37, 46, 59; *F.Arvern.* 4, 6; *F.Marc.* 2. 3–5, 2. 32, 2. 39; *F.Sal.Bign.* 18; *F.Sal.Lind.* 1, 4, 11, etc. Pard. 140 (543), 196 (587), 256 (632), 364 (670), 384 (677), 393 (680), 408 (687), 412 (690), 414 (691), 442 (697), etc. See also husbands representing their wives, Pard. 253 (631); and a document in which 'nos' first implies a joint action but in the end confusingly refers to the husband alone, Pard. 490 (714). Wemple (1981) 112; Heidrich (1991) 127–30.

documents widows and nuns alienate landed property with no mention of guardians and usually without consenting relatives.[104]

This leads us back to discuss the general legal capacity of women in the early medieval west. It emerges that there were marked differences between the various cultures. Late imperial law did not recognize any guardianship of adult women. Even the independence of wives was preserved, at least in theory. It may be, though, that the husband's strong position often eclipsed the letter of the law. The Visigothic legal system was strikingly similar. No guardianship of women is recorded in their codes, and although the man was certainly the leading figure in the common household, he did not have unlimited powers over his wife's property.[105] It is tempting to think that the Visigoths here as in so many other questions followed Roman models.

At the other end of the continuum we have the archaic law of the Langobards. In their warlike society women always fell under male domination (*mundium*). They were subjected either to the husband or to a blood relative or in the last place to the king. A female could never alienate anything without permission from the man who held her *mundium*.[106] Other Germanic laws hardly ever touch this topic. The Burgundian Code is often taken to represent their original views:

Quaecumque mulier Burgundia vel Romana voluntate sua ad maritum ambulaverit, iubemus, ut maritus ipse facultatem ipsius mulieris, sicut in ea habet potestatem, ita et de omnes res suas habeat. (LB 100)

We prescribe that if a Burgundian or Roman woman of her own free will joins a husband he will have power not only over the wife herself but in a like manner over all her property, too.

It is exceptional that a decree which was included in a purely Germanic code contained provisions for people of Roman descent as well. It may have been intended for cases of intermarriage. In any case, it suggests that there was some dispute about this topic in the Burgundian territory. The position of widows is not

---

[104] Pard. 241 (627), 450 (699), 452 (*c.*700), 457 (703), 459 (704), 480 (711), 491 (715), Add. 15 (702), Add. 31 (714, son consenting); etc.

[105] LV 2. 3. 6, 3. 1. 4, 4. 2. 15 = CE 323, 4. 2. 16, 20, 5. 2. 3, 7; cf. Zeumer (1898) ii. 96–7, iv. 122–4; King (1972) 236–8.

[106] ER 186, 195–7, 204; LL 22. But in 8th-c. documents especially nuns occasionally appear alone, see Heidrich (1991) 135–6.

clearly laid down, but since they were permitted to act as guardians for their own children it is unlikely that Burgundian law considered them incompetent. Frankish codes are even more reticent about women's legal capacity. The *formulae* and charters mentioned above indicate that there, too, married women were somehow dependent while widows and nuns had much more freedom.[107]

To summarize, then, all the documentary evidence which we have from the end of antiquity, from Gaul, Italy, North Africa, and Egypt points to a similar conclusion: a wife needed her husband's consent for major transactions. Unmarried adult women, on the other hand, could dispose of their property without male supervision. Clearly a change had taken place.

How should we explain the husband's new conspicuous position? Was this a new type of guardianship? Maybe some people understood it to be so. For most purposes the technical definition was irrelevant, and no theoretical treatises have been preserved. Women, however, were hardly considered incapable as such. Why should a wife in her fifties have needed protection when a 30-year-old widow or nun did not require it? It seems more likely that the husband's role was enhanced because the conjugal relationship was perceived differently.

Could this have something to do with the new system of marital assets? Did the bridegift, by whatever name it was called, make the wife more dependent on her husband? Perhaps, though it is difficult to prove. Numerous *formulae* state that the bride will have free and total control over the nuptial donation.[108] There is only one which declares that during marriage both spouses will hold it in common (*F.Andec.* 54). But this may have been nearer to the truth. For example, it was frequently specified that if the couple had descendants the bridegift had to be preserved for them. Obviously, the prospect of offspring prevented the wife from alienating anything before the marriage had been ended. It is natural to think that the donation was first and foremost meant to support her in widowhood. Before that, it belonged to her only in theory. We should, of course, reckon with

[107] Cf. LB 24. 4, 59, 85. 1; LRib 84; Ganshof (1962) 10–17, 29–31; Heidrich (1991) 131–5.
[108] *F.Vis.* 15, 20; *F.Andec.* 1, 34, 40; *F.Marc.* 2. 9, 2. 15–16; *F.Tur.* 14–15; *F.Tur.App.* 2–3; *F.Bit.* 15a; etc.

a wide range of practices which may be concealed behind the stereotyped phrases of the *formulae*.

Among those people who preserved the old Mediterranean dowry the situation was even more complicated. In the eastern empire a bride often gave the *donatio* back as part of her *dos*. If she did not, she may sometimes have administered it herself. Eastern laws seem to assume that usually (though not always) the husband had control over both property masses.[109] If the wife had more of her property in the form of dowry it inevitably affected their mutual economic situation. The dowry might well have been thought of as a common pool of property. Unfortunately, such considerations cannot be attested in practice. The documents hardly ever specify the provenance of the assets which were going to be alienated.[110] If it had been relevant, it certainly would have been mentioned. We have to conclude that the same phrases were used, from whatever source the property stemmed. On the other hand, the estates were hardly thought to have been fused together. They remained distinct in theory and were ultimately separated if the couple died without children.[111]

What we see in the charters is by no means always a wife who needs her husband's consent to a transaction. As was just noted, it is usually not possible to say whose property was in question, but sometimes it emerges that it was *his* hereditament whose transfer *she* accepted. The spouses seem to have managed together a kind of joint family enterprise. Although the man was naturally the dominant partner, all family members had claims on the wealth of the common household. It was not only children who were waiting for an inheritance which their parents held in usufruct, but Germanic widows, too, were often entitled to a fixed portion of their husband's property as dower. In any transaction, it was safest to record that the spouse had consented, just to make sure that no problems arose later.[112] This may

---

[109] CI 5. 3. 1, 14, 5. 15. 1–2 (all 3rd c.); CT 9. 42. 15 (396 east) + int, 3. 5. 13 (428 east) + int; NTh 14. 3 (439); Nov. 61. 1, 97. 6. 1. Cf. above, Ch. 2, Sect. 3.

[110] For Egypt, see Beaucamp (1992*b*) 62, 75–6. And when Sidonius Apollinaris calls a particular piece of property '*uxorius*' we cannot know if it belongs to his wife's dowry or is just otherwise used by him, Sidon. *ep*. 1. 4. 1, 2. 2. 3.

[111] Cf. e.g. LB 14, 96; PLS 101; ER 167; LV.Ant 5. 2. 3–5.

[112] See Wemple (1981) 112; Heidrich (1991) 128–9; for Egypt, Beaucamp (1992*a*), esp. 247, 266.

explain why the spouses preferred to speak of their properties as if they were held in common.

Roman jurists from the classical period would have abhorred the whole idea. In their world only individuals had ownership rights: family members could base their claims solely on moral arguments. If a couple had jointly disposed of a piece of property, the lawyers would have used all their talent to specify who had actually owned the item. However, we have to remember that we do not have any documentary evidence from the west before the late fifth century. Although we may guess that upper-class couples had the erudition and incentive to keep their properties separate, it was less likely in the middle and lower classes. For them the idea of communal matrimonial property would perhaps not have been so strange after all.

4. SUMMARY AND CONCLUSIONS

Married couples in the Roman empire faced ideals which were difficult to attain: to love each other, for example. Many of them tried and some succeeded; others did not. There is nothing historically unique in this. Somewhat more interesting is the question of authority. The evidence discussed has suggested that neither the ideal nor the practice of family hierarchy changed very much in the upper classes. Men were commonly expected to take the leading role although they could not always achieve it. In Roman law, the wife had considerable independence, but, if she chose to rely on her husband and allowed him to administer her property, no one blamed her for that. On the contrary, even juridically trained Romans considered it to be the wisest course. Nothing indicates that anyone would have perceived this as an ideological question in late antiquity. The problems which were discussed in prescriptive literature were of a more practical nature. If the wife was too wealthy or if she was not as much younger than her husband as was usual, her independence could be embarrassing and attract unfortunate attention. A wise man avoided such situations.

Thus male predominance was always considered perfectly normal in the Roman family. But this 'natural' order of things was complicated by the Roman family system. Because both spouses were primarily members in their own families, and perhaps still *in potestate*, their assets could not merge. I have tried to stress that this separation was largely theoretical during marriage. If the estates were inherited only by the couple's common children, they finally became united. But divorce, remarriage, and childlessness were common phenomena in the Roman upper classes. All parties had to reckon with the possibility that they would divide their household already in their lifetimes or that their heirs would not be closely related. Thus it made some sense to uphold the proprietary rights, at least on paper. Where *patria potestas* was not a central institution, or emancipation was common, there was certainly less incentive to take such an approach. Similarly, where children were numerous and divorce less frequent, it was more likely that both estates would be fused in the next generation.

The strong position of married women in Roman society was certainly connected both with *patria potestas* and with their extensive rights of inheritance. Males had to look at the matter not only as husbands but also as fathers and brothers. In the latter role they shunned the idea that part of their family estate would slip into another man's hands. The principle of separate properties was preserved in Roman law for as long as we can follow, but there is little trace of it in late ancient and early medieval documents, at least in the west. Perhaps we ought to conclude that the partnership of a married couple was after all the more natural notion. The Romans themselves had accepted it in their ancient *manus*-marriage. The independence of married women seems to have been a peculiarly Roman interlude in legal history. To what extent it ever prevailed in the provinces must remain open. It is hard to believe that wives could preserve their autonomous position beyond the end of antiquity. Anyway, this was a relevant question only where women succeeded to major properties from their natal family. If they did not have any inherited wealth, they had little independence to lose.

There was no guardianship of women in the later Roman empire. Originally Roman *tutela* had been part of a system in which families tried to protect their members and their property. By the early empire it had in practice lost this function. One reason why it theoretically survived so long may have been that Augustus had linked it with official population policy. In any case, probably most adult freeborn women in the empire possessed the *ius liberorum* and were free from guardianship. Thus, when *tutela* formally vanished sometime in the fourth century, it did not mean a radical change.

It is quite possible that in some provincial societies women already had a strong position before 212. But I believe that in general the adoption of Roman legal concepts increased women's independence. Official *tutela* replaced or contaminated local systems, while the *ius liberorum* and the *tutor*'s feeble authority ensured that female freedom was not much curtailed. On the other hand, when the Roman guardianship finally fell into disuse, the local variations probably survived better. Young girls were supervised by their own family and married women by their husbands. It might be a mistake to seek a uniform concept behind such arrangements. Some people certainly thought that women in general were feeble and helpless—because some women really were. Others observed strong women and rejected the whole idea of incapacity. They may have stressed the idea of conjugal partnership instead. However, in those societies where we have any documentary evidence, widows always appear independent.

It is perhaps surprising that in the early medieval kingdoms (except for the Langobards) there was no guardianship over unmarried women. We might think that in the very chaotic and physically dangerous period which followed the great migrations women needed support more than ever. This fact can hardly be denied. But the protection was not of the kind that a guardian could offer. In the ancient literary cultures, the guardian had been expected to see that the woman was not cheated or led astray in legal matters. He took care that she did not put her name to a contract which would risk her family property. He was not required to fight other men. The binding force of pacts was the threat against which women had to be protected.

In the early medieval world, the most imminent dangers lay elsewhere. A woman could lose much more because agreements were *not* respected and because legal claims did not suffice to establish factual control over a given property. The family interests in general were well guarded: neither males nor females could freely alienate property on which their relatives had any claims. Women certainly needed male physical help, either from their husband or from their own family. But this had nothing to do with guardianship.

5

Separation and Single Life

As we have seen, the young age of Roman girls at marriage was typical of the Mediterranean family pattern. Consequently, extended youth, so characteristic of modern western society, was virtually non-existent in Rome; the girl left her childhood as she married. On the other hand, as mortality in general was high and especially as husbands were so much older, wives were often, and relatively early, widowed.

The independence of married women may have varied in the course of history, and there were even more important differences between individual wives. The most essential distinction, however, has always been that between married and unmarried women. A wife has lived, at least to some extent, in the shadow of her husband. The end of the marriage—whether she wanted it or not—has usually led to a new autonomy and direct dealings with the rest of the society.

This is why many legal and social norms governing marriage are important to women, even if they are not themselves conscious of it. Is it usual to remain unmarried? If the husband's rule turns despotic is it possible to divorce? If the union is terminated by divorce or widowhood, is the woman supposed to remarry? Are there many solitary women in the society? We shall next examine how such issues affected women's lives. It is the more interesting because in all these aspects there were legal developments in which Christianity has been considered a major factor.

I. CHRISTIAN ASCETICISM

The Independence of Celibate Women

The Christian church embraced very early an ideal of unmarried celibate life. At first the characteristic of a small Jewish eschatological movement, it survived even after the new religion had become established and expanded all over the Roman empire. In the fourth century celibacy and asceticism won much popularity among recently converted people and gained surprising prominence in Christian teaching. Why that happened has so far not really been explained.[1]

In many places the number of Christian celibates must have been significant, although precise estimates are difficult to give. The new habit arrived in Rome and Constantinople as well and soon spread among a portion of aristocratic women. According to Jerome, Marcella, in the middle of the fourth century, was the first young widow in Rome to remain unmarried because of an ascetic Christian vocation. He did not claim, of course, that she was the first unmarried widow in general.[2] But widows could now more strongly than ever justify their decision not to remarry. We may guess that the religious fashion brought about more such decisions while it in part only channelled and organized an existing phenomenon.

Virgins were a different case. As far as we know, spinsters did not exist in pagan Rome. Ancient society provided employment for women in entertainment, retail trade, and services. This would have permitted some daughters of lower-class families to remain single although they perhaps had reason to regret their choice when they grew old. Ammianus claims that there were hosts of unmarried dancing girls in Rome who could, so far as age went, already have been mothers of three children (14. 6. 19–20). But for well-born women there had been no career outside marriage. Paradoxically, although their inherited wealth had allowed them a living without a husband, they yet always married. It would probably never have occured to them to remain single even if they had been given a say in the matter.

The Christian ideal of celibacy for the first time offered a meaningful alternative. When the ascetic movement was spreading in Rome, it was usually the girl herself who refused to marry. She could meet fierce opposition in her own family. The upper

---

[1] The most recent thorough description of the whole development is Brown (1988).

[2] Hier. *ep.* 54. 1, 127. 5; Aug. *c. Faust.* 30. 4, PL 42. 492; Joh. Chrys. *in Matth.* 66. 3, PG 58. 630; Pallad. *hist. laus.* 59. 1, 67. 1, etc. Brown (1988) 264–7. On aristocratic women, see Yarbrough (1976); Drijvers (1987); and cf. Salzman (1989).

classes were mostly pagan in the late fourth century, but Christian aristocrats did not care for their line to become extinct either. Often the children who contemplated celibacy were very young. If the father was alive he was usually able to assert his right to marry them off. Orphaned girls (and boys) probably had somewhat more freedom but they, too, could face strong pressure from the relatives.[3]

Most contemporaries, pagan and Christian, evidently did not view asceticism with such favour as the church fathers, or posterity. It was an alternative lifestyle ideology with all the arrogant and extremist features of such a movement, including unkempt personal appearance. It is no wonder that socially prominent families scorned ascetics and did not want to see their members associated with them.[4]

Independent virgins and widows might not only imperil the continuity and reputation of a family: they could also squander its inherited fortune. It seems that financial concerns lurked very often behind the conflicts between ascetic women and their kin. Many women took the advice of their spiritual teachers seriously and distributed their earthly wealth generously to the poor. They could also donate or bequeath large sums to the church or to the bishops and monks themselves. Especially the latter practice must have looked very suspicious to the women's relatives.[5]

So it was very probably the Roman senate that had a new law promulgated under Valentinian I in 370: it prohibited priests and monks from visiting widows and orphaned girls 'under the pretext of religion' and invalidated all transfers of property between them. Ambrose and Jerome regretted the law but even more the fact that it was needed. Neither of them denied that there were clergymen who used most unscrupulous methods to seek donations and bequests from elderly people. This may have

[3] e.g. Ambr. *virg.* 1. 33, 58, 62–6; 2. 22–4; Hier. *ep.* 54. 6, 55. 4; Greg. Nyss. *vita Macr.* 5, SC 178. 154; Paul. Nol. *ep.* 29. 10, CSEL 29. 257; Pallad. *hist. laus.* 66. 1; Geront. *vita Melan.* 12, SC 90. 150; Salv. *eccl.* 3. 21–39, CSEL 8. 275; Hil. Arel. *vita Honor.* 6, 8, SC 235. 84, 88. See Yarbrough (1976) 154–7; Clark (1981) 249–50; Harries (1984); Dassmann (1986) 884–5; Drijvers (1987) 252–62.

[4] See e.g. Hier. *ep.* 39. 6, 127. 5; Ambr. *ep.* 27. 3; Lib. *or.* 30. 8; Salv. *gub.* 4. 32–3; Zos. 5. 23. 4–5; Clark (1981) 241–2, with more references; and Hunter (1987; 1989).

[5] e.g. Hier. *ep.* 54. 14, 77. 6, 127. 4; Ambr. *ep.* 24. 7, 12, CSEL 82. 173, 175; *Vita Olymp.* 5–8, 13–14; Pallad. *dial.* 61; *hist. laus.* 54; cf. Aug. *ep.* 262. 5, CSEL 57. 624; Salv. *eccl.* 3. 26, CSEL 8. 276.

resembled the notorious inheritance-hunting of the early empire. Jerome also disclosed that the law could be evaded.[6]

It seems that even the most Christian emperors had strong suspicions about the ascetic habit of rich women and the role churchmen played in it. In Constantinople the immensely rich young widow Olympias was related to Theodosius I himself. The emperor is said to have pressed her to remarry against her ascetic conviction, though in vain.[7] On 21 June 390, while Theodosius was staying in Milan, a new law established that only widows over 60 years who had children could be ordained deaconesses. This was justified by a biblical passage (1 Tim. 5: 9–10). However, they were also forbidden to bequeath anything to a church or to individual clerics. Only two months later, on 23 August, this ban was again lifted. We may read between the lines that the legislator changed his policy somewhat reluctantly. It is tempting to suspect that bishop Ambrose was directly responsible for the turn the situation had taken.[8]

Theodosius did not explicitly repeal the older law of Valentinian. A letter of Jerome suggests that in 394 it remained in force. The next time we hear of it is in 455 when a particular will was discussed in the Constantinopolitan senate, again bringing the whole problem to the fore. It is certainly difficult to see why the issue had not been settled in the intervening period. In any case, this time the emperor Marcian removed all ambiguity and declared the restrictions abolished.[9] Later in the west, too, the *Breviarium* contained Marcian's law and not that of Valentinian.

Clearly the aristocratic families did not like to see the clergy encroaching upon their properties. In the late fourth century the imperial government still sided with the families. In the following century official opposition evidently declined as it became more and more common to confer private property on the

[6] CT 16. 2. 20; Ambr. *ep*. 18. 13–14 (dated 384), PL 16. 1017; *off*. 3. 9. 58; Hier. *ep*. 22. 28, 52. 6, 60. 11; Amm. 27. 3. 14; for the attitude of the senate, cf. Geront. *vita Melan*. 19, SC 90. 162. On *captatio*, see Champlin (1991) 87–102, 201–2.

[7] *Vita Olymp*. 3–5; Pallad. *dial*. 61.

[8] CT 16. 2. 27–8; cf. Sozom. *hist. eccl*. 7. 16. 11. See also the 5th-c. Miracles of Thecla 9 (*Vie et Miracles de Sainte Thecle*, ed. G. Dagron), which gives a fictitious account of the law but at least shows that clerics really were threatened by it.

[9] NMc 5. Hier. *ep*. 52. 6; in 394 Jerome had already spent ten years in the east; but through his correspondence he was probably informed about the legislation that was applied to his friends in the west.

church. The power of the church had grown, and perhaps it had learnt to bring the selfishness of individual clerics under control. When the most blatant malpractices had been removed, the whole custom became better organized and an accepted part of late Roman society. Justinian no longer disapproved of property moving through ascetics to churches and monasteries.[10]

However, as late as in 458 the western chancellery under the emperor Majorian promulgated a long edict which was clearly hostile to the female ascetic habit. Childless widows who did not want to remarry were ordered to surrender half of their property to their nearest kin. Moreover, the legislators claimed that often religion was only a pretext to increase the women's individual freedom:

Viduarum sane obstinationibus permovemur, quae nulla prole suscepta fecunditatem suam reparationemque familiae repudiata coniugii iteratione condemnant et solitariam vitam non eo eligunt, ut pudicitiae religionis amore famulentur, sed potentiae ambitum orbitatis suae casibus viduitatisque captantes lascivam vivendi eligunt libertatem. (NMaj 6. 5)

We are deeply disturbed by the obstinacy of widows who have borne no offspring and who condemn their own fecundity and the renewal of their family by repudiating a repetition of marriage. They do not choose a solitary life in order that they may cherish their chastity out of love for religion but, seeking after the courtship of power by the fortunes of their childlessness and widowhood, they choose a lascivious freedom of living.

This misgiving was not far-fetched at all. When a woman chose not to marry, the most obvious practical consequence was that she would live without a husband and often without children, too. The church fathers themselves frequently presented this prospect in a very favourable light: a single woman was not required to serve a husband, she could control her own life, and escape the dangers of childbirth and the troubles of motherhood.[11] To cite Ambrose:

---

[10] e.g. CI 1. 3. 54. 5–7; Nov. 123. 30, 38. Augustine clearly felt a need to dispel the suspicions of his congregation, *serm.* 355–6, PL 39. 1568ff. For continuing occasional dishonesty, see Greg. M. *ep.* 9. 205.

[11] e.g. Ambr. *virg.* 1. 25; *vid.* 8. 44, PL 16. 261; Hier. *ep.* 22. 16, 45. 4, 49. 14, 54. 4; Joh. Chrys. *virg.* 52. 8, 57, SC 125. 298, 306ff.; Ps.Basil. *virg.* 23, PG 30. 717; Aug. *virg.* 13. 13, 22. 22, CSEL 41. 245, 256; Ven. Fort. *carm.* 8. 3. 325–84; Leander *reg.* praef. PL 72. 879; etc.

Non ergo copula nuptialis quasi culpa vitanda, sed quasi necessitatis sarcina declinanda. Lex enim astrinxit uxorem, ut in laboribus et in tristitia filios generet, et conversio eius ad virum sit, quod ei ipse dominetur. Ergo laboribus et doloribus in generatione filiorum addicitur nupta, non vidua; et dominatui viri sola subditur copulata, non virgo. Omnium autem horum virgo libera est. (vid. 13. 81, PL 16. 273)

Thus the bond of marriage should not be avoided like a fault but like a burden imposed by nature. The law [of nature?] compels a wife to bring forth children with toil and sorrow, and her conversion is to her husband because he dominates her. That is why a married woman is destined to toil and pain in childbirth, but not a widow; and only a wife is subjected to a man's domination, not a virgin. But a virgin is free from all these.

This open praise of freedom was effective, sometimes more effective than its preachers would have wished. The number of celibate women increased, but the contemporary clerics worried about virgins and widows because their new free life included adornment, social activities, all kinds of entertainment, even contacts with new men and secret liaisons. Jerome especially extolled young Fabiola, who did not act as many others:

post mortem secundi viri in semet reversa, quo tempore solent viduae neglegentes, iugo servitutis excusso, agere se liberius, adire balneas, volitare per plateas, vultus circumferre meretricios, saccum indueret, errorem publice fateretur; (ep. 77. 4)

After the death of her second husband, at a time when widows, having shaken off the yoke of slavery, are wont to grow careless and indulge in licence, frequenting the public baths, flitting to and fro in the squares, showing their harlot faces everywhere . . . she came to herself, put on sackcloth and made public confession of error. (tr. Wright, in Loeb)

In some places it became common that celibate men and women lived as companions together in private houses. The bishops feared that such couples did not always preserve their chastity.[12] All in all, the life of unmarried Christian women took forms which would not seem unnatural to us but which did not harmonize with the aims of the contemporary church, or of most laymen, for that matter. The clerics were well aware that religious conviction could be just an ostensible motivation for single life.[13]

---

[12] On this phenomenon, see Clark (1977a).

[13] e.g. Hier. *ep.* 22. 13–14, 22. 29, 54. 13, 79. 8, 117. 5–8, 125. 6, 127. 3, 130. 18–19; Aug. *bon. coniug.* 23. 30, CSEL 41. 225; Joh. Chrys. *reg. fem.* 1–2; *subintr. virg.* 7–10; *non iter. coniug.* 3, SC 138. 176; *Conc. Gangr.* (*c*.345) esp. 9.

Majorian's policy did not outlive him by much (NSev 1). People could not be compelled to marry or to remarry. But the leaders of the church wished at least as fervently as the emperor to prevent unmarried women from 'abusing' their freedom. They advised that the virgins and widows should be kept strictly inside the walls of their homes, or the homes of their parents, or, best of all, in an ascetic community. And if necessary their door could be locked.[14]

Although I am stressing supervision over women, it should be noted that priests and monks were under similar surveillance. Their moral life was the concern of almost every council from the earliest ones down to the middle ages. It figures prominently in the correspondence of pope Gregory the Great as well. Sometimes it seems that male celibates constituted an even greater problem for the church than women. Perhaps the sexual and financial restrictions of a religious life really were more difficult for men than for women, who had always been taught submission.

Such strict control could not be exerted over the rich aristocratic widows who financed the church and conversed with both secular and ecclesiastical rulers. Even though the biographers of these women wanted to stress their piety and humility, we know that they travelled as they wished and disposed freely of their property. As a matter of course they used the power inherent in their wealth and social status.[15] Celibate women of lesser means enjoyed a limited freedom and esteem as well, either in their own households or in small informal groups.[16]

But, as we have seen, men were already seeking means to rein in this new female culture. It was not considered proper to have independent women going around in society. Ascetic communities were forming, no doubt often to protect the young women in a very insecure world but also to limit their individual freedom. These communities were developing into regular convents

[14] e.g. Ambr. *virg.* 2. 9; Hier. *ep.* 107. 7–13, 128. 4; *Brev. Hipp.* (397) 31, CCL 149. 42; *Stat. eccl. ant.* (*c.*475) 7, CCL 148. 167; on the lock, see Pallad. *hist. laus.* 59.

[15] e.g. Hier. *ep.* 22. 38, 77. 6, 9, 108. 5, 15, 127. 4, 130. 7; *Vita Olymp.* 5–10; Pallad. *hist. laus.* 46; see also Clark (1981: 251–7; 1985); Brown (1988) 279–84; Consolino (1989).

[16] Brown (1988) 263–73. See also Krause (1994c), who perhaps somewhat underrates the independence of widows, at least in comparison with married women.

and being transferred under episcopal control. Their separation from the rest of the world was considered vitally important.[17] However, although the monastic system absorbed most of the single women during the early middle ages, it could not completely solve the problem. Female celibates would still occasionally live outside the convents, arousing suspicions about their behaviour and motives.[18] Moreover, the rich heiresses who founded and supervised monastic communities could at times exercise considerable power.[19]

Asceticism as Family Strategy

From the evidence so far presented it might appear that for many women Christian asceticism was a great leap towards emancipation. This claim may not be totally unjustified, despite the fact that it is impossible to measure the subjective happiness of ascetic women. However, it is worth briefly examining the reverse side of this new religious culture.

First of all, women did not always have much real influence on the decisions taken over their lives. Pious parents might dedicate their children to virginity before they were even born (Hier. *ep.* 107. 3). When ascetic vocation gradually became a respectable phenomenon, many people learnt to use it for their own purposes. If there were too many children, it was expensive to raise and marry them all. A clever *paterfamilias* or a widowed mother might try to direct them into the lap of the church, to save the cost of a dowry, for example. Ambrose himself did not shrink from offering it as an argument for a daughter's consecration (*virg.* 1. 32). But a decision thus motivated could be against the girl's own wish. At least her lack of judgement at a tender age could be misused. The leaders of the church admitted that this practice was a problem, and the emperor Majorian was enraged

[17] CI 1. 3. 43 (529); Nov. 123. 36; Greg. M. *ep.* 4. 9 (593); Caes. Arel. *reg. virg.* SC 345.170ff.; *Conc. Agath.* (506) 28, CCL 148. 205; *Epaon.* (517) 38; *Arel.* (554) 5; *Latun.* (673/675) 12, CCL 148A. 34, 171, 316; *Hispal.* (618) 11. See e.g. Nolte (1986); Hochstetler (1992) 3–15.

[18] Hochstetler (1992) 63–104. See e.g. Nov. 6. 6, 123. 30; Avit. *ep.* 55; *Edict. Chloth.* (614) 18 (MGH Capit. i, p. 23); *Conc. Aurel.* (549) 19; *Paris.* (614) 15, CCL 148A. 155, 279; *Conc. Vern.* (755) 11 (MGH Capit. i, p. 35); LL 30 (723); and esp. the Langobardic late 8th-c. *Cap. Aregis* 12 (LL p. 209).

[19] On the Frankish kingdom, see Wemple (1981) 127–88; Schulenburg (1989); and cf. Nelson (1990b) 328–9.

by it. He decreed that a daughter could not be disinherited if she wanted to marry.[20]

Majorian also forbade the solemn consecration of virgins before the age of 40. The same precaution was often recommended by the bishops, though with differing minimum ages.[21] In principle they thought it desirable that the child was able to make a personal decision, but even here the practice does not seem to have been uniform. Parents continued to offer very young boys and girls to monasteries, and usually the church regarded their decision as binding upon the children. In the seventh century this custom can be seen most clearly in Spain, and it certainly later prevailed everywhere. In Gaul the rulings mention mainly girls, while the Spanish councils often discussed the problem of boys, too.[22]

In any case, when a girl had been consecrated, the choice was thought to be permanent. The councils and bishops declared with all their authority that after she had taken the veil she could no longer return to the world.[23] In the fourth and fifth centuries a virgin who married faced mainly ecclesiastical penalties. To be sure, secular laws took account of consecrated women from 354 onwards, but their main issue was rapists and seducers, not 'lapsed' women themselves. For a long time the state did not take a firm stand on Christian celibates who wished to renounce their vocation. Such clauses emerged in eastern legislation with Justinian. In the west, too, they appeared only after the collapse of the empire.[24] For many women this development did not cause

[20] NMaj 6. pr–3 (458); Basil. *ep.* 199. 18; Hier. *ep.* 130. 6; Aug. *ep.* *3, CSEL 88. 21; Leo M. *ep.* 167. 15, PL 54. 1208; cf. Brown (1988) 260–1; Beaucamp (1992a) 303–5; and further below.

[21] *Conc. Caesaraug.* (380) 8 and *Agath.* (506) 19, CCL 148. 202 (both 40 years); *Conc. Arel.* (442/506) 52, CCL 148. 124 (25 years); *Brev. Hipp.* (397) 1, CCL 149. 33 (25 years; cf. *Reg. Carth.* 126, CCL 149. 227); Basil. *ep.* 199. 18 (16–17 years).

[22] Aug. *ep.* 254, CSEL 57. 602; *Conc. Tolet.* II (531) 1; *Tolet.* III (589) 10; *Barcin.* (599) 4; *Tolet.* IV (633) 49, 55; *Tolet.* X (656) 6; *Aurel.* (538) 7; *Aurel.* (549) 19; *Matisc.* (581/583) 12; *Lugd.* (583) 3, CCL 148A. 117, 155, 226, 232. See Boswell (1984: 17–18, 25–7; 1988: 231–5, 243–9); Nolte (1986) 263; Hochstetler (1992) 31–43.

[23] e.g. *Conc. Ancyr.* (314) 19; *Chalc.* (451) 15–16; *Araus.* (441) 27; *Arel.* (442/506) 52; *Tur.* (461) 6, CCL 148. 85, 124, 145; *Tur.* (567) 21; *Paris.* (556/573) 5; *Paris.* (614) 14–15; *Clipp.* (626/7) 26, CCL 148A. 185, 207, 279, 296; *Tolet.* VI (638) 6; *Tolet.* X (656) 5–6; Greg. M. *ep.* 4. 24, 5. 19, 8. 8–9, 10. 3.

[24] CT 9. 25. 1–3; CI 1. 3. 53 (533); Nov. 6. 6 (535), 123. 30, 43 (546); Beaucamp (1990: 118–20, 183–4; 1992a: 353–5). For the west, see *Edict. Cloth.* (614) 18, CCL 148A. 285; LV 3. 5. 3 (642/653); LL 30 (723).

any problem; for some others it evidently turned out to be a tragedy.[25] It is largely for this reason that Christian asceticism can only be called a mixed blessing for women.

We may ask whether Christian asceticism was more a religious or a social phenomenon. Certainly most people themselves felt that they acted from pious motives. On the other hand, the fashion would never have spread so effectively if it had not responded to acute social needs as well. According to Ambrose, celibacy was more popular in the east in those regions where the birth rate was high. He was probably not thinking of any underlying demographic factors. But today the success of late ancient and early medieval asceticism is often linked with the need to control the family size. What had begun as a spontaneous religious movement became later a well-organized method of family strategy. It surpassed the old system of killing or exposing surplus children; it was more acceptable in moral terms and it could be used after the children had passed the first dangerous years of their life. In that way the parents could avoid a fatal mistake because it was as bad to have too few heirs as too many. These problems were more acute in poor families but they could not be neglected in the propertied classes either.[26]

Thus asceticism provided a sound method for disposing of extra children in a family, perhaps predominately daughters. It had always been much easier to locate unmarried men in the society, for instance in the army. Of course, many men became priests and monks, too. But in the aristocratic families voluntary asceticism seems to have been first and foremost a feminine habit, at least in the beginning. Apart from the fact that men had been able to remain unmarried even without such an explicit justification, marriage and childbirth obviously were a more onerous burden for women. It was something they often quite willingly avoided if they had a satisfying alternative. Upper-class males got interested in an ecclesiastical career on a large scale only later, after it had become a respectable route to power. It is important to remember that the social background of the ascetic movement was not uniform in all areas and all social classes, just as its outer

[25] See e.g. Boswell (1984) 25–7.

[26] Ambr. *virginit*. 7. 36; cf. also Caes. Arel. *serm*. 1. 12, CCL 103. 9. See Patlagean (1969; 1978: 183); Yarbrough (1976) 162; Stafford (1978) 97; Boswell (1984: 17–23; 1988: 228–66); Brown (1988) 260–1. For the problems of partible inheritance, cf. above, Ch. 2, Sect. 3.

nature was different among the rich senators of the west and the monks of the Egyptian desert.[27]

2. WIDOWHOOD AND REMARRIAGE

The Ideals of Widowhood

There was no clear ideology of widowhood in the early Roman empire. The Augustan marriage legislation openly urged widows to remarry. On the other hand, Latin sepulchral inscriptions sometimes recorded the concept of *univira*. She was a woman who had been married only once in her lifetime and had predeceased her husband. It did not mean that if the wife was left a widow herself she would have been expected to abstain from remarriage.[28]

It seems that especially young women remarried quite often. The older the widow was, the less likely she was to find a new spouse. Egyptian census records from the second century imply that already in their late thirties most widows did not remarry. A similar pattern in the other parts of the empire is probable but not verifiable. Clearly this had demographic and practical reasons rather than ideological.[29] For all we know, remarriage was a perfectly normal phenomenon in late republican and early imperial society. It is frequently attested in senatorial families, nor did ordinary people try to conceal it in epitaphs. Obviously this general approval did not conflict with the feeling that a certain reverence for the deceased would be appropriate.[30]

It is true that some husbands left a legacy to the wife on condition that she not remarry. The practice was well known to classical jurists, and in the sixth century it was common enough to attract Justinian's attention. Certainly many a husband would have liked his widow to remain faithful to his memory. They may also have thought that after remarriage she did not need so much material support.[31]

---

[27] See e.g. Jones (1964) 923–4; Yarbrough (1976) 157–60; Clark (1981) 244–7; and for a general overview, Brown (1988).

[28] Humbert (1972) 59–75; Lightman and Zeisel (1977); Treggiari (1991a) 233–6.

[29] Bagnall and Frier (1994) 126–7, 153–5; Saller (1994) 68; Krause (1994a) 34–132.

[30] Humbert (1972) 76–112; see also Bradley (1991) 156–76.

[31] Such a condition was difficult to reconcile with the Augustan legislation, and relevant passages in the Digest are partly contradictory: D. 32. 14. pr, 35. 1. 22, 62–4, 74, 96; CI 6. 40. 1–3; Nov. 22. 43–4; see Humbert (1972) 160–70; Beaucamp (1990) 236–7. See also a similar idea in the Merovingian *formula* of a last will, *F.Marc.* 2. 17.

Roman law knew a compulsory ten-month period of mourning (*tempus lugendi*), during which the widow was not allowed to remarry. This rule was traced as far back as to king Numa (Plut. *Numa* 12; D. 3. 2. 1). There was certainly a religious note in this custom, but during the principate many people tended to stress a practical reason: a wait of ten months guaranteed the filiation of posthumous children.[32] Divorced women could remarry without delay. There were other complicated rules to ascertain their possible pregnancy (D. 25. 3. 1–3; 25. 4. 1).

In 380 and 381 Theodosius I promulgated at least two laws on this issue. He prolonged the statutory period to one year and emphasized the financial and infamizing penalties which threatened.[33] In the fifth century the compulsory wait was also extended so as to cover divorced women. There could be no question of reverence here. The ban was frankly explained to ensure 'that none will have any doubt about the children'.[34]

Whoever wrote Theodosius' laws clearly had a more ethical or 'religious' view of the *tempus lugendi*. Their tone would suggest that a new moral emphasis was placed on the mourning period. It is difficult to analyse the mixture of motives behind this legislation. It had nothing in common with contemporary Christian ideals: the church fathers never advocated a mourning period. It could only very artificially have been justified by Christian teaching.[35] It was perhaps supported by a general tendency in later periods to see legal matters in moral terms. In practice, of course, the change from ten months to one year was little more than a symbolic gesture. It is very tenuous evidence for increasing hostility towards remarriage as such.

Are there other indications that attitudes were changing in late antiquity? The answer is far from simple. Of course, the Chris-

---

[32] D. 3. 2. 8–11, 23, 23. 2. 6; PS 1. 21. 13; Ov. *fast.* 1. 33; Apul. *met.* 8. 9; Dio 59. 7. 5; CI 2. 11. 15 (239); Lact. *mort. pers.* 39; Lib. *ep.* 1511–12 (Foerster 11. 535–6); Humbert (1972) 113–31; Gardner (1986) 51–4; Beaucamp (1990: 210–14; 1992a: 343–4).

[33] CT 3. 8. 1 (381) + int; CI 5. 9. 1 + 6. 56. 4 (380); Nov. 22. 22; Beaucamp (1990) 214–21. Syro-Roman Law Book, L 16 and 61, ignores the change. In the west these rules were preserved in LRB 16. 1; ET 37; LV.Ant 3. 2. 1.

[34] CT 3. 16. 2. 1 (421 west); CI 5. 17. 8. 4b (449 east), 5. 17. 9 (497), 1. 3. 52. 15 (531); Nov. 22. 16. pr, 18; Beaucamp (1990: 227–9—on legislation; 1992a: 62–6—on papyri which show that divorcing couples did not take any notice of the rules).

[35] Cf. Humbert (1972) 378–87.

tian ideal of sacred widowhood appealed to many people. Religious and secular motives combined to increase the voluntary single state of women, as we have just seen. A growing respect for widowhood without remarriage appears in Christian inscriptions. It is indeed conceivable that the hope of posthumous reunion would favour a tendency to maintain the marital bond even after the death of one of the spouses.[36] Moreover, there is sufficient evidence to show that even pagans praised prolonged widowhood in the fourth century. It was justified especially by the existence of children. We shall return to this particular topic in the next section.[37]

Thus, both literary and inscriptional sources suggest that perpetual widowhood was prized more openly in late antiquity. Christian teaching may have contributed to this although the idea was not totally confined to Christians. But even if the change was real (and not due to some bias in the available evidence) it should not be stressed too much. It did not lead to a general repulsion for remarriage. The attitude of the church itself has often been exaggerated. Not remarrying was certainly recommended but, although the fathers sometimes used very heavy language to highlight their opinion, they did not usually condemn weaker souls nor remarriage itself. Jerome wanted to refute this misconception so emphatically that he promised to accept an eighth marriage if that was needed (*ep.* 49. 8). He claimed that there were more remarried bishops than there were participants in the council of Rimini, the greatest of his time (*ep.* 69. 2). Many other bishops reassured their flock that remarriage was not forbidden.[38]

John Chrysostom once claimed that 'all people' reproached those who remarried (*virg.* 37. 1, SC 125. 218). Although this was clearly an overstatement, such feelings evidently existed. However, the bishop expressly stated that the legislators did not have anything against remarriage but even approved of it.

---

[36] Humbert (1972) 345–59, especially for the inscriptions. On the problem of having two spouses at the Last Judgement, see Tert. *castit.* 11. 1–2, CCL 2. 1030. Cf. also Bremmer (1995).

[37] Julian. *enc. Euseb.* 6; Lib. *ep.* 285 (Foerster 10. 270); Joh. Chrys. *vid. iun.* 2, SC 138. 120; Beaucamp (1992*a*) 334–5, 349–50.

[38] e.g. Ambr. *vid.* 2. 10, 11. 68, PL 16. 251, 267; Joh. Chrys. *lib. rep.* 1; *vidua elig.* 5, PG 51. 219, 325; Aug. *bon. viduit.* 4. 6, 12. 15, CSEL 41. 309, 320; Hier. *ep.* 41. 3, 49. 6–18; Greg. M. *ep.* 4. 34. Basil took a more reserved view, *ep.* 188. 4, 199. 50, 217. 80. See also Humbert (1972) 314–26; Kötting (1988); Krause (1994*a*) 157–71.

In this he was demonstrably right. As we saw above, such an emperor as Theodosius I tried to force his young relative Olympias to remarry in Constantinople. In general, asceticism was an ideology which the state could accept but not highly recommend. Remarriage was a legal issue only as far as property and succession were concerned: they will be treated in the next section. But if these questions had been properly solved, eastern laws in the late fifth century did not object to even three or more successive marriages (CI 5. 9. 6. pr; 6. 60. 4; 6. 61. 4. pr). Justinian, too, although he praised widowhood, regarded remarriage as something quite natural:

concedimus . . . licere mulieribus . . . ad secundas migrare nuptias . . . sive habeat liberos, sive non . . . Cum enim mulieres ad hoc natura progenuit, ut partus ederent, et maxima eis cupiditas in hoc constituta est . . . Augeri . . . nostram rem publicam et multis hominibus progenitis frequentari . . . volumus. (CI 6. 40. 2; see also Nov. 2. 3)

We permit women to enter into a second marriage . . . whether she has children or not . . . Since nature has created women for the purpose of giving birth, and they feel a strong desire for it . . . we want our state to be increased and filled with people who are begotten in great numbers.

In the west the failure of the Augustan legislation had barely been forgotten when the emperor Majorian reverted to an active population policy. In his famous law of 458 he ordered all childless widows under the age of 40 to remarry within five years (NMaj 6. 5). The law must have been loathsome to all women, pagans and Christians alike. Five years later the emperor Severus repealed it (NSev 1). No aversion to remarriage emerged in the last years of the western empire. Nor did Germanic laws in the early middle ages make any objections against it.[39]

In the early 380s Jerome saw the wedding of two lower-class people in Rome: the bride attended it with a twenty-twofold experience while the groom had laid twenty previous wives in the grave (*ep.* 123. 9). Whether or not this anecdote is true, it does not help at all to estimate the real frequency of remarriage among common people. More than a century later bishop Caesarius of Arles indicated that in his parish both women and men could be

---

[39] See e.g. LV 3. 1. 4; LV.Ant 5. 2. 5; LB 24. 1; PLS 44; PLS Capit. III. 100. 1; ER 182; for *reipus* and *achasius*, a sum paid by the new suitor to compensate for the nuptial donation which the widow took with her, see Murray (1983) 163 ff.

expected to remarry before long (*serm.* 33. 3, CCL 103. 145).
Better statistics are lacking, of course. Thus we cannot know
what demographic consequences the ideal of widowhood had,
but at least there is no actual sign that people in late antiquity
found more fault with remarriage than before.[40]

Why then did women want to remarry? Perhaps sometimes
because they needed love and companionship, but certainly
there were often more practical reasons. The church fathers
recount those arguments which especially young widows might
use when they were going to remarry and turned down clerical
advice. According to Jerome they claimed that alone they could
not manage their property, keep their slaves under discipline, or
represent the household in public.[41] Jerome's information
inspires some confidence because it was against his own opinion. It is somewhat surprising that Christian writers in this
connection did not attach more importance to the alleged frailty
of the female sex. In their opinion a woman could very well
manage even a great property, with the aid of trusted servants
if necessary.[42]

The bishops naturally suited their arguments to underline the
attractions of widowhood. They were probably right if the household was sufficiently well off and the widow was a strong person-
ality. In such cases widowhood meant freedom and emancipation.
However, the general impression of widowhood in the ancient
world was very different. Destitute of male kin, widows would
often appeal to their fellow men for pity and support. In difficult
circumstances even a propertied woman could feel insecure.[43]
Poor people were in greater straits, of course. With few opportunities for earned income, they had to live off the little property
they had. In small holdings the pressure of work may often have

[40] Beaucamp (1992a) 61–70 (on papyri), 350–1; Krause (1994a) 181–91. Cf. also
Goody (1983) 188–9. On continuing remarriage after divorce, see below, Ch. 5,
Sect. 3.   [41] Hier. *ep.* 54. 15, cited above, Ch. 4, Sect. 2.
   [42] Hier. *ep.* 123. 13; Joh. Chrys. *reg. fem.* 7; *non iter. coniug.* 4, SC 138. 180ff. On
female frailty, see below, Ch. 7, Sect. 1.
   [43] e.g. Tert. *uxor.* 1. 4, CCL 1. 377; P.Oxy. i. 71. II (303); Greg. Naz. *or.* 43. 56, PG
36. 568; Basil. *ep.* 107–9; Ambr. *vid.* 9. 53, 58, PL 16. 263, 265; *ep.* 24. 7–8, CSEL 82.
173; Hier. *ep.* 127. 2; Joh. Chrys. *in acta* 49. 4, PG 60. 344; *vid. iun.* 2, SC 138. 118;
Sidon. *ep.* 6. 2; Nov. 22. 43; P.Tjäder i. 7 (557); Greg. M. *ep.* 1.13, 1. 60–3, 3. 5, 3. 43,
6. 37, 9. 36, 9. 75. See also Beaucamp (1985; 1992a: 33–5, 277–9); Krause (1994b) 224–
55.

proven too heavy: the sample of North African documents in the
490s includes many cases where widows sell off their land. If poor
women had not been blessed with children, or could not rely on
their help, remarriage was the only alternative.[44] It is no wonder
that needy widows were regularly supported by the church.[45]
They were also thought to deserve special attention from the
state, like orphans, invalids, and others buffeted by fate.[46] There
were, then, for many women enough reasons to remarry if they
did not want to enter an ascetic community for the rest of their
lives.

Remarriage and Family Finances

What most worried the Romans in multiple marriages was the
situation of children. Stepfathers and stepmothers had always
been a well-known menace in Roman literature.[47] Jerome
describes the feelings eloquently:

*Aut si evenerit ut et de secundo marito habeas filios, domestica pugna,
intestinum proelium. Non licebit tibi amare liberos, nec aequis aspicere oculis
quos genuisti. Clam porriges cibos, invidebit mortuo, et nisi oderis filios adhuc
eorum amare videberis patrem. Quodsi de priori uxore habens sobolem te
domum introduxeris, etiamsi clementissima fueris, omnes comoediae et mimo-
graphi et communes rhetorum loci in novercam saevissimam declamabunt. Si
privignus languerit et condoluerit caput, infamaberis ut venefica. Si non
dederis cibos crudelis, si dederis malefica diceris. (Hier. ep. 54. 15)*

Or if it should happen that you have sons by your second husband,
domestic warfare and intestine feuds will be the result. You will not be
allowed to love your own children, or to look kindly on those to whom
you gave birth. You will hand them their food secretly; for he will be

[44] Tabl. Alb. p. 208 with nos. 11, 15, 18, 24, and 27. See also e.g. D. 25. 3. 5. 2, 27.
3. 1. 2–5; CI 5. 25. 1 (Pius), 8. 54. 1 (258); *Gloss*. iii. 36. 49ff.; Aug. *serm*. 356. 3, PL
39. 1575; Salv. *ep*. 1. 5–6, CSEL 8. 202; Greg. Tur. *vit. patr*. 9. 1; Greg. M. *ep*. 9. 48;
LB 74. 1–2; and more evidence in Krause (1994a: 108–13; 1994b: 105–73).
[45] Eus. *hist. eccl*. 6. 43. 11, SC 41. 156; Hier. *ep*. 1. 13, 64. 2, 123. 5; Joh. Chrys. *in
Matth*. 66. 3, PG 58. 630; *Stat. eccl. ant*. (c.475) 7, 36, 102, CCL 148. 167, 172, 185;
Testam. Perpetui, Pard. 49 *in fine; Conc. Matisc*. (585) 12, CCL 148A. 244; Greg. M.
ep. 1. 37, 1. 57, 2. 50. 141; cf. also ICUR i. 1582 = ILCV 1581 adn. and ILCV 1581.
[46] CT 1. 22. 2, 9. 21. 4; *Form. Marc*. 1. 8; Lact. *inst*. 6. 12. 21, CSEL 19. 528; etc.
Krause (1994b) 244–51.
[47] e.g. Liv. 39. 9; Quint. *decl*. 338; Sen. *dial*. 11. 2. 4; Tac. *ann*. 1. 33; *SHA Marcus*
29. 10; Ambr. *in Luc*. 8. 6, CCL 14. 300; Aster. Amas. *hom*. 5, PG 40. 236D; Joh.
Chrys. *virg*. 37. 3, SC 125. 220; *vidua elig*. 4–6, PG 51. 325; Greg. Tur. *franc*. 3. 5, 4.
25. See also Humbert (1972) 195–204; Dixon (1988) 155–9; Gray-Fow (1988) 741–9;
Noy (1991).

jealous of your dead husband, and unless you hate your sons he will think you still in love with their father. If he, for his part, has issue by a former wife, when he brings you into his house, then, even though you have a heart of gold, you will be the cruel stepmother, against whom every comedy, every mime-writer, and every dealer in rhetorical commonplaces raises his voice. If your stepson falls sick or has a headache, you will be maligned as a poisoner. If you refuse him food, you will be cruel; if you give it, you will be said to have bewitched him. (tr. Wright, in Loeb)

Imperial rescripts in the third century record several cases in which stepparents were accused of misdemeanour.[48] Moreover, they were generally suspected of exerting undue influence on the surviving parent, whose affections were divided between two families. Remarried fathers and mothers could neglect the rights of their earlier offspring in succession and might even begin to hate them. It may well be that such suspicions were ill-founded in most cases but they nevertheless often recur in both literary and legal sources throughout the imperial period and beyond.[49]

Rules which were based on these fears appeared in Roman law in the fourth century. The first extant decree comes from Constantine. He wanted to restrict the father's usufructuary rights to his children's maternal inheritance if he remarried. The interpretation of this obscure law has already been discussed. Here it is just well to repeat that it was included in the Theodosian Code but not in the *Breviarium* in the west. In the east it was claimed to create confusion and repealed in 468.[50] Visigothic law put similar restrictions on remarried fathers: they could not even be guardians for their minor children. But these rules, too, were finally considered unjust and removed in the late seventh century.[51] Clearly it was difficult to solve the dilemma inherent in the remarriage of fathers.

Legislators did not have such scruples about supervising

[48] CI 6. 2. 3, 11, 7. 34. 1, 9. 22. 4, 9. 32. 2–3, 9. 33. 5.
[49] See e.g. *Laud. Murdiae* CIL vi. 10230 = FIRA iii. 70; Val. Max. 7. 7. 4; Plin. *ep.* 6. 33; Apul. *apol.* 71; Gaius D. 5. 2. 4; Diocl. CI 3. 28. 22; Const. CT 3. 30. 3. 5, 8. 18. 3; Lib. *ep.* 1169. 2 (Foerster 11. 256); Ambr. *hex.* 6. 4. 22, CSEL 32. 1. 218; *vid.* 15. 88, PL 16. 275; Joh. Chrys. *non iter. coniug.* 6, SC 138. 192; Leo CI 5. 9. 6; Cass. *var.* 4. 12; Just. CI 5. 9. 10. 5; Nov. 22. 35, 155; P.Lond. v. 1731 = FIRA iii. 23 (585); CE 321; LL 113 (729). See also Treggiari (1991a) 391–4; Beaucamp (1992a) 349–50.
[50] CT 8. 18. 3 (334); CI 6. 60. 4; see above, Ch. 3, Sect. 3.
[51] CE 321; LV.Ant 4. 2. 13; LV 4. 2. 13*; see Zeumer (1898) iv. 110–19.

mothers who remarried. They were obviously thought to be even less independent, and the presence of a stepfather a more imminent threat. Thus remarried women could not be guardians for their children from the first marriage. This rule was introduced into Roman law in 390, probably soon after the guardianship of mothers in general had been allowed. Before that the whole problem had, of course, not arisen at all.[52] In view of the prevailing attitudes the ban appears quite natural. The Visigoths and Burgundians knew it as well (LV.Ant 4. 3. 3; LB 59). Its absence from other Germanic laws does not prove that the question was thought irrelevant: especially the Frankish codes had little to say about guardianship anyway. Much was left to unwritten custom.

After Constantine's first law on remarriage and family property few other changes are known for several decades. When mothers were permitted to reclaim their gifts from undutiful children in 349, remarried women were excluded (CT 8. 13. 1, 4). The most important laws were passed only at the end of the century. If a woman had children and remarried she could no longer dispose of the property she had received from her late husband. These assets consisted mainly of the nuptial donation and possibly of testamentary bequests. She retained only a usufruct and had to preserve the property for her children from the first marriage. And if she inherited anything from these children, she held it likewise only in usufruct. This was logical because in practice the bulk of the children's property had come from their father.[53]

On the other hand, if the husband had left his wife only a legacy of usufruct, she lost it immediately to the benefit of her children. We cannot explain this solely by children's inheritance rights for the usufruct would have been enough to safeguard them. The answer lies in the purpose of such a legacy: it had been intended to maintain the widow. When she remarried, she did not need it any longer. The rule survived in the *Breviarium*. A similar arrangement is later attested in Merovingian Gaul by *Form. Marc.* 2. 17 though only as a private agreement between the spouses. In the east Justinian finally decided to remove it: he

---

[52] CT 3. 17. 4 (390) + int; NTh 11 (439 east); Just. CI 5. 35. 3; Nov. 22. 40, 94. 2, 155. Cf. Humbert (1972) 410–13; and above, Ch. 3, Sect. 2.

[53] CT 3. 8. 2 (382 east), 3. 8. 3 (412 west). For a more detailed description of this legislation, including Justinian's revisions, see Humbert (1972) 387–456; Beaucamp (1990) 229–37. Their explanation, however, sometimes differs from mine.

reaffirmed the widows' rights to any testamentary usufruct, as long as the children received at least one-third of the inheritance to support themselves.[54]

Originally the rules of 382 were legally binding only on women, but men were very emphatically advised to follow the example 'by the law of religion' (CT 3. 8. 2). In the second quarter of the fifth century the restrictions were formally extended so as to also cover men.[55] There may have been other laws which we do not know because the relevant titles 3. 8 and 3. 9 of the Theodosian Code were not preserved in the manuscripts and are transmitted only through the *Breviarium*. The missing pieces would hardly revolutionize the picture here given.

The memory of these rules was in the west later preserved not only by the *Breviarium* but also by the Roman Law of Burgundy (LRB 16. 2). They clearly served as a model for some Visigothic and Burgundian laws on the same questions. In other Germanic codes such provisions usually seem to be implicitly assumed rather than explicitly stated.[56]

Many scholars have wanted to see Christian influence behind these legal developments.[57] It is true that the church paid a great deal of attention to remarriage and its attitude was certainly recognized in the society at large, if not fully accepted. Ideological reasons could thus easily be used to justify the measures. But there is good reason to believe that secular legislation was not so much motivated by hostility towards remarriage *per se*. First, the rules did not apply to widows who were without children (CT 3. 8. 2. 2). Secondly, over the course of time the same restrictions were gradually extended to cover those widows and widowers who did *not* remarry. That happened independently both in the west and in the east.[58]

---

[54] CI 5. 10. 1 (392 east); CT 3. 9. 1 (398 east); Nov. 18. 3; 22. 32.

[55] CT 5. 1. 8 + 8. 18. 10 (426 west); NTh 14 (439 east) + int.

[56] Visigoths: CE 321–2, 327 (note a new reading); LV.Ant 4. 2. 13–14; LV 4. 5. 2; LV.Ant 5. 2. 4–5 (cf. CE 319); Burgundians: LB 1. 2, 24, 42, 62, 74; Franks: PLS Capit. III. 100–1; LRib 41; Alamans: *Lex Alamannorum* 54. Cf. Levy (1951a) 88–90.

[57] e.g. Humbert (1972) 387–94, 415–17, 427–9, 453–8; Kaser (1975) 180. For a more balanced view, see Fedele (1977) 829–31; Beaucamp (1992a) 349–50, 363–5; Krause (1994a) 171–81.

[58] CT 3. 13. 3 + CI 5. 9. 4 (422 west); NTh 14. 7 (439 east) + int; CI 5. 17. 8. 7 (449 east); NMaj 6. 7 (458 west); NSev 1. pr (463 west); LRB 26. 2; ET 54; Nov. 98; 127. 3; cf. Humbert (1972) 429–34, 439–41, 445, 450–53. Similarly in the Visigothic laws: CE 322 = LV.Ant 4. 2. 14; LV 4. 5. 2; LV.Ant 5. 2. 4. On Merovingian *formulae*, see note below.

The late Roman legislation on remarriage reflected the universal sentiment that property should be preserved and inherited in the direct line of descendants.[59] That principle was felt to be threatened first and foremost in the event of remarriage, when the conflicting loyalties of the surviving spouse could cause some assets to slip into another family. Classical Roman law did not yet regulate such things: a system of widespread usufruct and conditional ownership rights would have been regarded as too complicated. Citizens were expected to attain the same objectives by private pacts and voluntary measures.[60]

It is important to note that much of the later legislation would have been totally irrelevant in earlier times. One did not have to exclude remarried widows from guardianship as long as female guardians were not accepted anyway. Similarly, it was the fate of the nuptial donation which in late antiquity constituted the most acute problem in remarriage. This would not have been a problem at all for the classical jurists, who knew only modest gifts on betrothal (see above, Ch. 2, Sect. 3). At that time the only substantial transfer of property between the families was the dowry. The husband's rights to it were carefully defined, and in classical law it would have been difficult to restrict them further to the benefit of his children. But here private pacts could be useful, especially in the case of remarriage (Apul. *apol.* 91; D. 32. 37. 4). As we have seen, even in late antiquity the rules were more reluctantly applied to fathers.

Because in Roman law all gifts between living spouses were forbidden, testamentary bequests were, after the dowry, the only way to receive property from the other party. They might cause problems, too, but usually the testator could be assumed to be aware of the circumstances. Thus he would provide sufficiently for his children if he chose to leave something to their mother. Usually the widow received just a minor part of the estate. The essential task was, of course, to secure her maintenance. An ideal

---

[59] See above Ch. 2, Sect. 3. Such a wish is occasionally expressed in papyri, P.Oxy. iii. 489 (117), 493 (2nd c.); P.Lond. v. 1727 = FIRA iii. 67 (583–4); cf. Taubenschlag (1955) 209–10. It appears in early medieval *formulae* as well: *Form. Andec.* 54; *F.Vis.* 15, 20. 64; *F.Marc.* 2. 9, 2.17; *F.Tur.* 14, 18; *F.Sal.Merk.* 16; etc. See also the Merovingian document in which a son gives his consent to a donation from his mother's dower, Pard. Add. 31 (714).

[60] See the exhaustive treatment by Humbert (1972), 207–300, 422–7, with full documentation.

way to do so was to bequeath her a lifelong usufruct. Another method was the *fideicommissum restitutionis*: the mother was enjoined to pass on her share to the children after her death. Even if there was no obligation, many parents fulfilled this duty voluntarily.[61]

The laws of late Roman emperors were perfectly consistent with this pattern of thought. They tried to satisfy the expectations of widows who often had to remarry, whether they wanted or not. At the same time they tried to reassure the children that 'their' property was not being imperilled. In well-to-do families the question was about sentiments rather than survival. In poor families people may have shared the same feelings but in practice their choices were limited more by the estate's feeble resources than by legal rules.

3. DIVORCE

The Legal Regulation of Divorce

In classical Roman law, divorce was free. After Augustus' legislation it had to be formally announced, perhaps mainly for reasons of proof. The other party did not need to consent: in fact, the divorce could be valid even before the rejected spouse knew what had happened. Men and women were equally entitled to break their union. Originally the idea may have been that the all-powerful *paterfamilias* could take his daughter back if he wished, but in later times the advantage clearly accrued to the wives themselves, at least when their fathers were dead.[62]

Though permissible, unilateral divorce was not without financial consequences. In principle, the husband had to return the dowry—the real property at once and cash in three annual instalments. He could keep one-sixth or one-eighth of it if he showed that his wife had behaved immorally (*retentiones propter mores*). If his own behaviour had been immoral, he might be compelled to repay the cash in six months or immediately. When children existed, further deductions could be made *prop-*

---

[61] e.g. CIL vi. 10230 = FIRA iii. 70; D. 7. 8. 4. 1, 31. 88. 2, 36. 1. 59. 2, 83; CI 3. 28. 12, 3. 33. 9, 6. 53. 4, 6. 54. 4 (all 3rd c.); see further Humbert (1972) 207–24, 233–45; Dixon (1988) 47–51; Champlin (1991) 120–6.
[62] See Gardner (1986) 81–93; Treggiari (1991a) 435–61.

ter liberos: one-sixth for each, up to half the dowry, provided that the wife had either initiated the divorce or necessitated it by misbehaviour. Thus she could dismiss her husband without financial loss only if she did not have children. It is debatable how far *retentiones propter liberos* were meant to punish divorce and how far they only reflected what was thought a reasonable contribution to the children's maintenance.[63] In any case, when unilateral divorce is discussed in the Digest, the question of *culpa* is a recurrent topic. *Retentiones* were an obvious reason for this, of course, though evidently not the only one. Sometimes a private pact required that responsibility was determined, sometimes there may have been other considerations which we do not know. After all, the rules of divorce in the principate are only imperfectly documented because much of the legal material was obsolete when the Justinian *Corpus* was put together.[64]

It is probable that no drastic changes took place in this system before Constantine's reign. From the third century few imperial pronouncements on the topic have been preserved, for the reason just stated. Alexander Severus unequivocally declared divorce free, and some Diocletianic rescripts give the same impression.[65] Moreover, divorce is often discussed in the *Fragmenta Vaticana*. Around the year 320 the classical regime of divorce had evidently not yet been altered.

In any case, a very strict law was enacted under Constantine's name in 331 (CT 3. 16. 1). Now unilateral divorce was clearly penalized. A wife could be repudiated only for adultery, sorcery, or procuration; a man for homicide, sorcery, or destruction of tombs. All these were very severely punished crimes in late Roman law: in practice, to be convicted of them would have meant not only divorce but a 'capital' penalty, perhaps death. If

[63] See UE 6. 9–13; FV 107, 121; D. 24. 3. 39; Quint. 7. 4. 11; Cic. *top.* 4. 19; Boeth. *in top.* Cic. 2 (*ad loc.*); Corbett (1930) 182–97; Gardner (1986) 89–91, 112–14; Treggiari (1991a) 351–3.

[64] See e.g. FV 107; 120–1; D. 4. 4. 9. 3, 23. 4. 11, 24. 1. 57, 24. 2. 6, 24. 3. 38, 40, 44.1, 45; 35. 1. 101. 3, 48. 5. 12. 13, 49. 15. 8; CI 5. 12. 24 (294); Aug. *adult. coniug.* 2. 8. 7, CSEL 41. 389 (a quote from the Gregorian Code); a few of the texts could be interpolated, but not necessarily so. On private pacts, see further below.

[65] CI 8. 38. 2 (223); FV 284 (286); CI 5. 4. 14 (Diocl.) though devoid of context, 5. 17. 5 (294), 5. 12. 24 (294) seems to have been tampered with: Justinian's compilators may well have substituted the word '*hanc*' (i.e. *dotem*) for the original '*retentiones*' or similar, to harmonize it with 6th-c. law; more on this text below. A similar possible interpolation e.g. D. 24. 3. 38; cf. also 24. 2. 5.

the husband rejected his wife without any of the specified reasons, he lost her dowry. In fact, he had lost it anyway under classical law. Now there was the added penalty that he had to remain celibate. A wife, on the other hand, was punished much more harshly: she not only forfeited the dowry but was also exiled. Thus in financial terms the husband would not have been worse off than during the principate while the wife would have lost somewhat more. It is the threat of exile and celibacy which shows that the lawgiver really wanted to prevent divorce. As a whole, CT 3. 16. 1 is a strange piece of law-making. Not only did its substance deviate from classical law but it also contains unusual vocabulary which does not appear elsewhere in the Theodosian Code. The constitution was obviously not drafted by anyone well-versed in Roman legal tradition.[66]

This need not have been Constantine's only statute on divorce. The whole title *De repudiis* (3. 16) is missing from the manuscripts of the Theodosian Code. Thus only those two constitutions which were included in the *Breviarium* are preserved. We know for certain that there was at least one other law, from the reign of Julian. It is recorded by an unknown Christian author, the so-called Ambrosiaster:

Quantum autem possit timor legis, hinc advertamus. Ante Juliani edictum mulieres viros suos dimittere nequibant, accepta autem potestate coeperunt facere quod prius facere non poterant: coeperunt enim cottidie licenter viros suos dimittere. (quaest. de utr. test. 115. 12, CSEL 50. 322)[67]

But how much the fear of law can do, we will perceive from the following. Before Julian's edict women were not able to divorce their husbands, but when they had received the licence they began to do what they could not do before: they began to divorce their husbands daily without restraint.

Here are at least three interesting points. First, Ambrosiaster believed that Constantine's law had been effectively enforced. Secondly, it was particularly women who had caught his eye. And thirdly, it emerges that Julian, the defender of traditional Rome, was opposing Constantinian policy even in this detail.

Julian's view seems to have prevailed even after his sudden death. Ambrosiaster himself, who was writing around the 370s,

[66] See Evans Grubbs (1995) 257–9.
[67] CT 3. 13. 2 (363) was certainly part of this edict.

indicated that no change had taken place in the mean time (ibid. 115. 16). Between 385 and 420 several western bishops professed openly that secular law did not punish unilateral divorce nor subsequent remarriage.[68] On the other hand, we have a couple of reports from contemporary eastern bishops which suggest that divorce could result in financial penalties. An African council of 407 asked the emperor to prohibit remarriage of men and women who had been rejected by their spouses. It might indicate that a similar law already existed against those who had initiated the divorce: the wording is not quite clear about this. The general tenor of all these passages and several others is that secular laws, as far as there were any, were not sufficiently severe to prevent free divorce. On the contrary, men were rejecting their spouses for the slightest reason and 'changing wives like clothes', as one bishop put it.[69]

Of course, we cannot be sure that the bishops always knew the latest imperial law in force. On controversial issues, like divorce or illegitimate children, laws could waver back and forth, often independently in either part of the empire. Such vacillations were cut out in the *Breviarium*. Thus there may easily have been several different rulings on divorce between 363 and 421, but it is quite certain that Constantine's law as such was not re-enforced nor remarriage prohibited. If some restrictions existed, they had to be in a much milder form which we can no longer reconstruct.[70]

The next extant law in the Theodosian Code dates from the year 421 (CT 3. 16. 2). The official attitude to divorce was now clearly tightened. Equally clear is the very unequal treatment of the sexes. The law distinguished three grades of reasons for unilateral divorce. A woman who divorced without any justified

---

[68] Aug. *bon. coniug.* 8. 7, CSEL 41. 197; *nupt. et concup.* 1. 10, CSEL 42. 223; Ambr. *in Luc.* 8. 5, CCL 14. 300; Chromat. *in Matth.* 24. 1. 4, CCL 9A. 310; all quoted in Arjava (1988) 10.

[69] Joh. Chrys. *lib. rep.* 1, PG 51. 219; Aster. Amas. *hom.* 5. 5; *Reg. eccl. Carth. exc.* 102, CCL 149. 218. See also Greg. Naz. *ep.* 144–5; *or.* 37. 8, PG 36. 292; Joh. Chrys. *qual. duc. ux.* 1, PG 51. 226; *in Coloss.* 1. 3, PG 62. 303; *Const. apost.* 6. 14. 4, SC 329. 340; Hier. *ep.* 49. 6–7, 55. 4, 127. 3; Aug. *in psalm.* 149. 15, CCL 40. 2189; and Arjava (1988) 9–13, for quotations, further references and a more detailed treatment.

[70] For vacillating legislation, cf. CT 4. 6 and 4. 12, below, Ch. 6, Sects. 2–3. A law of Valentinian I permitting divorce and remarriage may lurk behind mistaken reports of his bigamy, Socr. *hist. eccl.* 4. 31; Jord. *Rom.* 310, MGH AA v. 1. 40; cf. Manfredini (1990) 522–8.

cause lost her dowry and nuptial donation and was deported. A man doing the same met the same financial consequences but was not deported: he only had to remain unmarried. If there were 'minor reasons' (*morum vitia ac mediocres culpae*) the divorcing wife lost her right to remarry, along with the dowry and donation. For the same conduct, the man lost only the dowry. He kept the donation which he had given and could remarry after two years. Only if the spouses adduced very grave reasons (*magna crimina* of the other party) were they treated less unequally, but even then the wives were forbidden to remarry for five years, to leave no doubt about their motives.

This law was promulgated in the western empire. It became known in the east probably only in 438 when the Theodosian Code was published. In the next year Theodosius II revoked it and again restored the classical freedom of divorce, with the old *retentiones* as sole punishment (NTh 12, 14. 4). Clearly no restrictions had been in force in the eastern empire immediately before 438: otherwise Theodosius' prompt measure would be difficult to explain. As for the Theodosian statute of 439, it was evidently published in the west only in 448 with his other *novellae* (cf. NTh 2; NVal 26). The next year saw a new emendation. An eastern law gave a long list of grounds which justified unilateral divorce. The lack of any grounds brought with it only a loss of the dowry and donation, and additionally five years' celibacy for the wife. It is possible that this compromise never reached the west. In any case, soon after Theodosius had died the western emperor Valentinian III in 452 re-enforced his father's more severe CT 3. 16. 2. To confuse the issue, the Syro-Roman Law Book recounts rulings allegedly derived from successive eastern laws of Theodosius and Leo. There are clear resemblances with known Theodosian precepts, but some details may reflect unofficial oriental usage.[71]

None of the extant imperial decisions could be applied when a couple divorced by mutual consent. It is unlikely that any fourth- or fifth-century emperor tried to tackle this practice. In 497 an eastern law explicitly mentioned that it was permitted (CI 5. 17.

---

[71] CI 5. 17. 8 (449 east); NVal 35. 11 (452); cf. 31. 5 (451). For the Syro-Roman Law Book, R II. 44, 51, 87–8, and L 114–15, see Selb (1964) 118–26, with Yaron (1966) 134–7.

9). On the whole, the liberal eastern tradition continued in the sixth century when Justinian introduced some new legal grounds for unilateral divorce and maintained the mainly financial penalties (CI 5. 17. 10–11; Nov. 22. 3–19). But later his attitude changed. Celibacy was again imposed on *divorcées*, and both sexes were for the first time treated in the same way. In 542 even divorce by consent was prohibited. However, this last restriction was again removed in 566 by Justinian's successor Justin II, who was softened by unfortunate couples flocking to him for help.[72]

Ever since 421, legal sources in the west preserved a more hostile attitude towards divorce. As has already been noted, the compilers of the *Breviarium* chose the strict constitutions CT 3. 16. 1–2 from the Theodosian Code. They ignored Julian's edict and perhaps other unknown laws of the same title. Of the Theodosian *novellae* they logically omitted NTh 12, which had proclaimed freedom of divorce. Both the *Edictum Theoderici* (ET 54) and the *Lex Romana Burgundionum* (LRB 21) closely follow Constantine's law in condemning unilateral divorce. They do not, however, state clearly what happened if the rules were broken. In the sixth century secular laws could not be particularly well enforced, even among the Roman population. Ecclesiastical authorities tried to cope with the cases that were brought to their attention. We may guess that their task was not easy. Men and women in all social classes could just leave their spouse behind and disappear. Apart from 'illegal' unilateral ruptures, the church had to put up with consensual divorce. A number of *formulae* attest that it was a licit and continuing practice well into the Carolingian period.[73]

There is little evidence on Germanic habits before contact with Roman law. According to the *Lex Burgundionum*, a woman who tried to dismiss her husband had to be drowned in mire. Men could apparently escape with financial penalties. The Burgundians and Visigoths later adopted Roman rules from the *Breviarium*: this new stratum partially obscures their original law. Many other Germanic codes did not regulate divorce at all. They show

---

[72] Nov. 117. 7–14, 127. 4, 134. 11, 140; Beaucamp (1990) 174–7, 222–6.
[73] Sidon. *ep.* 6. 9. 1; Greg. Tur. *franc.* 8. 27, 10. 8; Cass. *var.* 2. 11. 1, 5. 33, 9. 18. 4; Pel. I *ep.* 64 (559); *Conc. Andeg.* (453) 6; *Venet.* (461/491) 2; *Agath.* (506) 25, CCL 148. 138, 152, 204; *Aurel.* (533) 11, CCL 148A. 100; *Tolet.* XII (681) 8. For consensual divorce, see LRB 21. 1; *Form. Andec.* 57; *F.Marc.* 2. 30; *F.Tur.* 19; *F.Sal.Merk.* 18.

more concern for the validity of betrothal. The best conjecture seems to be that divorce by women had always been a serious and strongly censured matter. Divorce by men had been a pardonable and more lightly punished affair. Under Roman, and ecclesiastical, influence men also began to face increasing restrictions. What this meant in practice is poorly known. The Frankish and Anglo-Saxon nobilities continued to use divorce as an integral part of their family strategies. In Gaul it was only in the eighth and ninth centuries that both the Carolingian state and the church strove to get a firmer hold of their subjects' marital customs.[74]

Divorce in Theory and Practice

It remains to explain the general development of divorce legislation. To sum it up once more: Constantine's harsh law was repealed in 363. After that, there were in the west no serious obstacles to unilateral divorce for sixty years. Restrictions were again introduced in 421. They continued in force in the western empire and its successors, except for a brief interlude from 448 to 452. In the east, almost total freedom of divorce lasted until 449; since then unilateral divorce caused financial inconveniences but was otherwise not punished. It was over two hundred years after Constantine, in the latter part of Justinian's reign, that the eastern state placed a real ban on divorce.

There are two basic questions: what motivated this new legislation, and what effect did it have on the practice of divorce? These problems are at least indirectly linked. To put it another way: had the legislators adopted a new moral ideal which they tried to impose on a reluctant populace? Or, on the contrary, did they just embrace an attitude which had all the time been widespread among their subjects?

The most controversial issue, of course, is the influence of Christianity. The church fathers unanimously condemned divorce, whether unilateral or consensual. Because no other

---

[74] LB 34. 1–2, probably older than LB 34. 3–4; LV.Ant 3. 6. 1; LV 3. 6. 2; PA 3. 2–3; *L.Grimv.* 6 (LL p. 97); cf. Tac. *Germ.* 19; Ps.Aug. *quaest. de utr. test.* 115. 16, CSEL 50. 323; Greg. Tur. *franc.* 3. 27, 4. 25–6, 9. 13, 2. 12 (a very special case). On betrothal, LV 3. 1. 3, 3. 6. 3; LB 52; PLS 13. 12; ER 178–80, 190–2. See also Zeumer (1898) iii. 619–30; Ganshof (1962) 31–3; McNamara and Wemple (1976); Wemple (1981) 42–3, 76–88; Stafford (1983) 71–86; Heidrich (1991) 130–1.

group in the Roman empire is known to have opposed it so vehemently it is natural to suspect that the change was caused by ecclesiastical pressure. On the other hand, it has been noted long ago that imperial legislation on divorce realized Christian ideals only very imperfectly. For example, the two existing laws in the Theodosian Code discriminated openly between sexes, contrary to the church's teaching. In addition, remarriage remained possible in most cases, especially for men, and the spouses could break their union by mutual consent. For this reason, among others, many scholars have tried to explain away Christian influence or at least have sought additional factors.[75]

Lay opinions about divorce have been equally difficult to determine. Moralists and satirists in the principate claimed that contemporary women freely sought divorce whenever they wished. They criticized the practice vehemently. In general, literary sources give the impression that divorce was a common phenomenon among the upper classes, but how frequent it really was remains a matter of debate. Instead of statistics we have historical accounts of just a couple of dozen individual cases, many of them in the Julio-Claudian imperial house and politically motivated. This does not mean that divorce otherwise was rare. It was tolerated, occasionally scandalous, and always somewhat embarrassing for the individuals concerned. Often married couples terminated the union peacefully by mutual consent, but this was by no means always the case. Even unilateral divorce usually had some reason, although not always a good one.[76]

The incidence of divorce in the Roman lower classes is not verifiable at all.[77] It is true that poor people had fewer financial resources and no political motives to break their marriages. On the other hand, numerous marriage contracts, divorce agreements, and other documents from Egypt attest a continuing practice of divorce among all classes from hellenistic through

---

[75] To cite just some more recent discussions, see Castello (1983); Bagnall (1987); Arjava (1988); Barone-Adesi (1988); Caron (1988); De Robertis (1988); García Garrido (1988); Gaudemet (1988); Nocera (1988) 134–7; Clark (1993) 17–27; a balanced new treatment of Constantine's law is Evans Grubbs (1995) 242–60.

[76] See Sen. *benef.* 3. 16. 2; Mart. 6. 7, 10. 41; Juv. 6. 224–30; Tert. *apol.* 6. 6; *Laud. Turiae*, CIL vi. 37053 = FIRA iii. 69. I. 27; Plut. *quaest. rom.* 105; Verrius *apud* Fest. 281 (s.v. '*repudium*'); D. 24. 1. 32. 10, 60–2; Raepsaet-Charlier (1982; 1994: 169–74); Treggiari (1991a: 461–82, 518–19; 1991b); Corbier (1991c) 49–63.

[77] Cf. Kajanto (1969); Treggiari (1991a) 482.

Byzantine times. Both men and women could terminate the union. However, there is relatively little evidence of cases which we might call frivolous divorce by women. Wives certainly often did initiate the process but it happened because they had been abandoned or maltreated so badly that they had little choice. The wife had to take action if she wanted to recover her possessions: a husband could simply break the relations and continue holding the dowry. Certainly he often controlled her other property, too.[78]

Egypt thus had a long tradition of liberal attitudes towards divorce. It is possible that in other regions women customarily had less freedom. True, bishops writing in Asia Minor, North Africa, Spain, Gaul, and Italy used so much energy to fight divorce that it had to be a widespread phenomenon among their flock. They could not be addressing only the uppermost social strata. It is noteworthy that, although they mentioned both men and women, a clear majority of their reproaches were directed against husbands.[79] This may indicate that by and large wives did not have the habit of rejecting their spouses at will.

What can we say about the relation between late Roman divorce law and social practices? At least it is clear that a near total ban on divorce, with penalties such as exile and celibacy, would not have found support in Egypt nor among the old aristocracy. In many population groups a ban on women's unilateral divorce might have been accepted or even welcomed. The existing imperial laws display just this sexual bias. It is, of course, methodically dangerous to deduce hypothetical motives from the apparent results which we see. But we know that the double standard was not a part of classical Roman divorce law, nor did it originate in Christian teaching. Could it stem from anywhere else than lay morals?

Be that as it may, although Constantine's law favoured husbands, it still caused inconvenience to them. It is no accident that it was later forgotten. When restrictions were again introduced in the east in 449, they included only financial penalties: the loss of

---

[78] Montevecchi (1936) 20–1, 65–9, 75–8; Merklein (1967); Bagnall (1987); Bagnall and Frier (1994) 123–4; Beaucamp (1992a) 62–6, 82–103, 139–58, esp. 148–52. For marital problems, see e.g. PSI i. 41 (4th c.); P.Oxy. vi. 903 (4th c.); liv. 3770 (334); l. 3581 (4/5th c.); P.Lips. 39 (390); and for a consensual divorce, e.g. P.Flor. i. 93 = MChr 297 = FIRA iii. 22 (569).

[79] See notes above in this section, and in Arjava (1988) 10–12.

dowry and nuptial donation. This was certainly more in line with traditional attitudes. As we have seen, Roman women had lost part of their dowry already under classical law if they had children. It is true that aristocratic couples may often have separated amicably, whoever initiated the process. It had been common to work out a special agreement on the dowry (*pactum dotale*) in anticipation of divorce. In principle women were not allowed to make agreements which diminished their rights of recovery. However, if there were children, it was obviously possible to agree that the wife forfeited all her dowry. Otherwise it was maintained that contracts which tried to limit the freedom of divorce were invalid.[80]

Marriage contracts of the hellenistic period in Egypt attest similar arrangements. They often laid down that if the marriage was broken because the wife did not fulfil her marital duties, she forfeited her dowry. If the husband rejected her without reason, he had to repay the dowry with an additional penalty of half its value. There was considerable variation in these rules because they always depended on the individual contract. In any case, such clauses disappear from the contracts of the Roman period, only to re-emerge in a couple of Byzantine agreements.[81]

Could the eastern law of 449, or any other law, affect the divorce rate? Ambrosiaster obviously thought that Constantine's legislation had been effective. He may have been right, at least if he was thinking of those population groups whose behaviour could be monitored. On the other hand, contemporary evidence from Egypt shows that unilateral divorce continued from the fourth to the sixth centuries. Congruity with imperial law is a rare feature in these documents. In 458 a woman claimed that she had been unjustly repudiated and demanded her dowry along with the nuptial donation. This was consonant with the law in force at the time (CI 5. 17. 8): just a coincidence? In the sixth century two marriage contracts specified the husband's penalty for dismissing his wife. Remarkably, the sum in these private agreements seems to have been higher than the total of the

[80] See esp. FV 120; D. 23. 4. 2, 24. 1. 57, 24. 3. 48, 45. 1. 19, 134. pr; CI 8. 38. 2 (223); and cf. e.g. FV 106; D. 2. 14. 27. 2, 4. 4. 48. 2, 23. 4, 33. 4. 1. 1; Corbett (1930) 198–200; Treggiari (1991a) 357–61.
[81] Montevecchi (1936) 75–8; Häge (1968) 75–81, 160–7; Beaucamp (1992a) 100–2.

dowry and nuptial donation, which the husband had to pay under Theodosius' law.[82]

The importance of private pacts is further underlined by a certain passage in the Justinian Code. It derived originally from Diocletian and was probably changed a little to suit later developments:

Si dotem marito libertae vestrae dedistis nec eam reddi soluto matrimonio vobis in continenti pacto vel stipulatione prospexistis, hanc culpa uxoris dissoluto matrimonio penes maritum remansisse constitit, licet eam ingratam circa vos fuisse ostenderitis. (CI 5. 12. 24)

If you gave a dowry to the husband of your freedwoman and did not provide in a connected pact or *stipulatio* that it would be paid back to you in case the marriage were dissolved, it certainly remained with the husband when the marriage had been dissolved through the wife's fault, even if you have shown that she had been ungrateful towards you.

The passage is remarkable for what it tells of the sixth century. Justinian's compilers obviously accepted the idea that, if the patrons had made a special pact, they could have reclaimed the dowry. Thus a private agreement would have overruled the innocent party's legal rights. Would that have been possible even in the case that the wife had given the dowry herself? Perhaps not, in official law, but the above-mentioned documents from Egypt strongly suggest that often imperial pronouncements were just a secondary source of rulings, to be applied if no special agreement existed.

Even when the law was duly enforced, its consequences must have varied considerably from case to case. An impending celibacy would have been a very different thing for people in varying situations and at different ages. Under the western law of 421 the husband just had to show *morum vitia* in his wife (perhaps not too difficult) to escape with his own property intact and to remarry in two years. If the woman had brought a large dowry, both spouses

---

[82] PSI ix. 1075 (458); cf. P.Masp. iii. 67295. II. 8–12 (491/493), with Beaucamp (1992a) 100–1. It is a pity that just a few of the relevant papyri can be securely dated: P.Oxy. liv. 3770 (334), and P.Cair.Preis. 2 (362) are contemporary with CT 3. 16. 1 (331). Contractual penalties: P.Lond. v. 1711 = FIRA iii. 18. 44 (566/573); P.Masp. iii. 67340r. 37 (Just.); there is some uncertainty in both cases because the size of the dowry is not mentioned: probably it equalled the *donatio*; cf. Beaucamp (1992a) 101. For the whole, see Bagnall (1987) 54–61; Beaucamp (1992a) 85–103, 139–58.

had higher stakes in the business. Although the husband only lost something which had originally not been his, the inconvenience of repaying the dowry might still be considerable and deter him from divorce.[83] Much thus depended on the relative value of the spouses' marital assets in their total wealth. I have suggested earlier (Ch. 2, Sect. 3) that in the richest families the *dos* constituted a relatively small part of women's property. Those people would not have been greatly affected by rulings such as the eastern law of 449. On the other hand, when there were no dowry and nuptial gifts at all, there was absolutely no deterrent to divorce, as Justinian remarked. He ordered that in such cases the culpable party forfeited a quarter of his or her property: according to him this was the normal maximum of dowries (Nov. 22. 18).

It is quite possible that women who sought divorce were not only morally but also numerically a greater problem for upper-class society than men. Since the time of Seneca and Juvenal, male observers had paid special attention to wives, and Ambrosiaster agreed: the liberty of divorce was liberty for women. The reason may have been the same as today. When a marital conflict became acute, the weaker partner had fewer options. If only the dowry or even celibacy was at stake, it did not restrain a wealthy lady for long.

The possibility of divorce had an effect on firm marriages, too. It was based on the fact that the dowry and often perhaps the wife's other property were governed by the husband. Consequently, she had little to lose in divorce, while the husband had more reason to preserve the *status quo*. Thus the freedom of divorce limited the husband's power even if the actual threat was never uttered. When divorce was more or less restricted, it evidently weakened the position of propertied women, whose wealth would have offered them the opportunity to lead an independent life.

The situation was, if not exactly reversed, at least more complicated amongst other classes. Few women could manage totally by themselves. It might also be difficult in practice to reclaim the dowry, if she had any. The disadvantages of herself being aban-

[83] See for earlier times, Cic. *Scaur.* 8; Sen *contr.* 1. 6. 5; Apul. *apol.* 92; Treggiari (1991a) 328–31; Schaps (1979) 76; and cf. Joh. Chrys. *qual. duc. ux.* 4, PG 51. 232.

doned were greater. Augustine recounts some reasons men had for rejecting a wife: if she was poor, ugly, infertile or ill and unable to have intercourse (*adult. coniug.* 2. 16. 17, CSEL 41. 403). A little later he admits:

Incomparabiliter quippe numerus est amplior feminarum, quae cum pudice adhaereant maritis, tamen si dimissae fuerint a maritis, non differunt nubere. (2. 17. 18)

Incomparably greater is indeed the number of women who, although they would chastely stick to their husbands, yet if they are dismissed by the husbands do not delay marrying [again].

Thus, rejected wives were not outcasts and could remarry if they wished. This was essential, for it was not good for a woman to remain unmarried in the Mediterranean world—unless she was a rich heiress, or joined an ascetic Christian community. It would seem that in the lower classes women had less use for a freedom to divorce. A few might even have gained from an increased stability of marriage. Still, the violent scenes of married life in some papyri explain why many women preferred to divorce, despite the financial insecurity it might cause.[84]

4. SUMMARY AND CONCLUSIONS

Since the reign of Augustus, the Roman government had enjoined all citizens to marry. This policy was unpopular and hardly effective, and it was at last abandoned by Constantine. But even after that the legislators did not conceal that they were sympathetic towards fertile families. For this reason, and also because of the harm caused to upper-class properties, the state for a long time showed clear reserve towards Christian asceticism, although it was outwardly tolerated.

Remarriage is a natural and practically inevitable event in pre-industrial conditions with high mortality rates, so much that hardly any society could have afforded to prevent it. It is not surprising that the late Roman state's attitude was extremely tolerant. In fact, there was little change in the official position. Remarriage aroused some concern only as regarded the children's financial interests. During the principate this question was left to

[84] For the papyri, see above, n. 78.

the discretion of individuals. In late antiquity it was increasingly regulated by laws to ensure that inheritance was preserved for the direct heirs. It is revealing enough that in the course of time similar rules were applied even to widows and widowers who did not remarry. Of course, in practice the needs of a poor widow and the rights of equally poor children were always difficult to reconcile.

Many widows had to remarry to support themselves. That is probably the main reason why remarriage remained common. Otherwise, women had reasons enough not to marry, as the church fathers tried to assure them. They did not need much exhortation to realize it themselves. Not only older widows but also young girls began to aspire to an unmarried life, sometimes running up against strong opposition from their own family. Such things had been totally unheard of in pagan society, at least in the upper classes.

It may be that during a relatively short period in late antiquity males found it increasingly difficult to control wealthier women in the society. The church defended their independence from the traditional secular subordination, while it had not yet developed its own methods of control. Some ladies, like Paula, the two Melaniae, and Olympias, lived in accordance with the ascetic ideals but at the same time could not avoid exerting their influence on men. Others used the new religious practice, consciously or not, to gain new freedom and to enjoy a life without male oversight. They remained unnamed because they were not considered good examples for posterity.

On the other hand, celibacy could serve family interests as well. Early imperial aristocracy had not used spinsterhood as a family strategy. For whatever reason, the senatorial families seem to have had so few surviving children that the splitting up of properties was not their main problem. Besides, they could usually well afford to provide a dowry, which was moderate in proportion to their resources. Thus there was a generally accepted moral obligation to marry off all daughters. It is not known what poor couples did with their surplus daughters in the early empire. In late antiquity Christian celibacy provided them with a new acceptable method of family planning. When well-born fathers had overcome their scruples, they, too, learnt to use it. It would be very difficult, if not impossible, to prove that the fertility of the landowning aristocracy had risen in the later empire. The hypothesis can hardly be excluded either. In any case, during late antiquity and the early middle ages European nobility adopted a religious practice which enabled them to refrain from marrying off some of their children. Of course, there was always individual variation: some fathers had too many children, some too few. The particular solutions they planned might often conflict with the personal desires of their offspring.

We finally come back to the legislation on divorce and its motives. It seems that Christianity cannot be discarded as one factor behind the developments. Constantine's law had been a departure from Roman legal tradition. Even if restrictions for women could have been motivated by popular concerns, restrictions for men could not. However, Christian teaching as such was not embraced by the lawgivers nor by the populace at large. In practice they tended to adopt those aspects which they found the least difficult to accept. Not surprisingly, this meant that the heaviest burden fell on women.

Although Christianization in some way contributed to the Roman law on divorce, it is not a totally sufficient explanation. Legislation in the fifth century shows the incapacity of the eastern and western governments to agree on a uniform policy. Reasons may be sought in the cultural tradition. The eastern legal schools, and also apparently the eastern court, preserved a scholarly, respectful attitude towards classical jurisprudence with its old urban, upper-class values. In the west these were more easily forgotten. Thus what seems to have been crucial was not the extent of Christianization but the general cultural and juridical climate in the society. After all, hostility towards divorce, especially female divorce, is not a unique feature in human history. Aside from more distant cultures, similar legal conditions have been postulated for archaic republican Rome and the Germanic peoples.[85] Neither case can be explained by Christian influence.

On the whole, it may be that this legislation changed people's behaviour less than has often been assumed. First, for a long

[85] For early Rome, see Dion. Hal. *ant.* 2. 25; Plut. *Romul.* 22; Humbert (1972) 132; Treggiari (1991a) 441–3; Dixon (1992) 73. For the Germans, see above.

period the laws were actually not in force. Secondly, many people seem not to have complied with the law. Thirdly, even when the laws were enforced, the sanctions were ineffective in many cases, particularly in regard to men. And fourthly, although divorce by women became increasingly complicated, it may not have changed so much since women had not often initiated divorce anyway. The last point is conjectural and much less certain than the others because too little is known of regional and social variations. Among the upper classes and in Egypt, where some evidence exists, it did not hold true. On balance, those women whose capacity to divorce was limited undoubtedly suffered a setback. Yet, whatever the wider social implications, most individual women certainly regarded both divorce and widowhood as a human tragedy rather than an emancipatory victory.

6

Sexual Relations outside Marriage

Marriage is not the only way to satisfy sexual needs. However, for women it has usually been the only one which has been legally and morally accepted—except when they have been reserved for the common use of several men as prostitutes or slaves. In sexual morals the inequality of males and females appears most clearly. On this question the Christian church claimed to advocate a radically novel view. Its influence on late ancient society will be examined in the following sections.

It is important to remember that in this area, probably more than in any other, norms and ideals do not tell what actually happened. We cannot compile reliable statistics about adultery even today, still less in those times when it was threatened with the gravest sanctions.[1] On the other hand, in Roman society there existed a whole series of sexual relationships which were neither honourable matrimony nor criminal adultery: not only the act but also the partners' social status decided whether they were breaking the law.

1. MARITAL INFIDELITY

Punishments

In the Roman republic adultery could be repressed both privately and publicly. It seems that a woman could be tried by her relatives and that if her husband caught her in adultery he could kill her without fear of punishment. It is not clear how far this was sanctioned by any written law. The cultivated late republican senators evidently preferred tolerance or discreet divorce to any graver methods of vengeance.[2]

---

[1] Cf. Richlin (1981) 396–8; Treggiari (1991a) 294–5.
[2] See Cato *apud* Gell. 10. 23. 5, and on the whole question now esp. Treggiari (1991a) 264–77, 307–9. Cf. also Syme (1960) 325–7.

When Augustus promulgated his *Lex Julia de adulteris coercendis*, the state's role in the repression of adultery was strengthened. The law strictly regulated private violence and tried to ensure that the culprits really were prosecuted.[3] Traces of private punishment survived even after that: if a father caught his daughter in the very act of adultery in his own or his son-in-law's house, he could kill the daughter and the lover. He was expressly required to slay both or neither. The point was that he would have been more inclined to kill the man but now paternal love would restrain him from it.[4] There is much juristic speculation on this question but only one reference to an actual case in the 170s (D. 48. 5. 33. pr). The practice is not mentioned in the Theodosian or the Justinian Code either. Perhaps the prescribed situation was after all not very common in real life. We may wonder why Justinian with his high and rather civilized legal standards took such a relic of archaic law into the Digest at all.

At least in the heyday of classical jurisprudence, the right to kill an adulterous woman was said to belong to her father expressly because he was thought to be the most reluctant to use this right, while 'the heat and impetuosity of a husband . . . should be restrained' (D. 48. 5. 23. 4). Clearly it was not considered unnatural that an enraged husband harmed his wife and her lover in the heat of the moment.[5] Jurists of the principate were positive that he was not legally permitted to kill them, but they agreed with the emperors that in those mitigating circumstances he should be shown some leniency. Moreover, the husband was allowed to kill the lover out of hand if he was a freedman of the family or a slave or belonged to some despised groups of people, including, for example, pimps, dancers, and gladiators.[6] All in all, adultery was typically a crime which a husband would have been tempted to take revenge for in private, either more or less gravely than a court could have done. Few men would have totally condemned him for that.

[3] A more detailed account is given e.g. by Treggiari (1991*a*) 277–94; see also Cohen (1991); Cantarella (1991).

[4] Coll. 4. 2–12; D. 48. 5. 21–5, 33. Cf. Voci (1980) 61–4; Treggiari (1991*a*) 277–83.

[5] See also e.g. Apul. *met.* 9. 25–8; Richlin (1981) 389–91, 394, for earlier examples; and Cantarella (1991), for a longer historical perspective.

[6] Coll. 4. 3, 4. 10. 1, 4. 12. 3–6; CI 9. 9. 4 (Alex.); D. 29. 5. 3. 3, 48. 5. 25, 48. 5. 39. 8, 48. 8. 1. 5.

The penalty prescribed by the *Lex Julia* was exile without loss of citizenship (*relegatio*) and partial confiscation of property for both offenders. From time to time public prosecution was encouraged. After one such period in the reign of Septimius Severus, Dio reported 3,000 registered accusations. Such round-ups never lasted long, though. The emperors could mete out a more severe penalty than the statutory one at their own discretion. Even death sentences were passed, but it remained an exception, at least among the upper classes.[7]

The Sentences of Paul, which were edited around the year 300, refer to *relegatio* and confiscations as still being the norm (PS 2. 26. 14). But in a few laws, the first as early as the reign of Severus Alexander, adultery is said to be a crime punished by '*capitalis poena*', which could mean either death or exile with loss of citizenship (*deportatio, aquae et ignis interdictio*).[8] In theory, this is in conflict with the Sentences since *relegatio* was definitely not a *capitalis poena*. Yet interpolation can in this case be proved. A Byzantine commentator noted that he had read the Gregorian and Hermogenian Codes (thus seeing both CI 2. 4. 18 and 9. 9. 9 in their original form) and that adultery was considered a capital crime only from the reign of Constantine.[9] This confirms that *capitalis poena* in both rescripts was added by Justinian. It supports the view that there was no law to change the statutory penalties of the *Lex Julia* during the third century.

Nevertheless, it may be that punishments were in practice becoming harsher. As there is little evidence concerning adultery, conclusions can only be drawn from parallel developments in other crimes. Ever since the beginning of the principate, more and more people were judged not in the old jury courts but *extra ordinem* by urban prefects and provincial governors, who were not tied to the statutory penalties. This affected especially the lower classes. As it was not feasible to sentence humble people to exile or to monetary fines, they habitually received a more severe

---

[7] See PS 2. 26. 14; D. 34. 9. 13, 48. 18. 5; and e.g. Dio 67. 12. 1, 77. 16. 4, 78. 16. 4; Hartmann (1894) 434; Richlin (1981) 380–8; Treggiari (1991a) 295–6.

[8] CI 9. 9. 9 (224), 2. 4. 18 (293); CT 9. 40. 1 (314); on the word '*capitalis*', see e.g. Inst. 4. 18. 2; D. 48. 1. 2, 48. 19. 2, 28. pr; and further Levy (1930/1), esp. 39, 56–62.

[9] *Basilica* 11. .2. 35 *sch.* 3 (Scheltema B i. 409); Levy (1930/1) 59; Beaucamp (1990) 166. See also Bauman (1980) 191 n. 191, for those who have been less convinced (hardly with good reason). In fact, the scholiast is probably not a reliable witness to Constantine's legislation, see below.

punishment, not uncommonly death. It is no wonder that people tended to link adultery with the death penalty. Moreover, we know little or nothing about jurisdiction and penal measures in local provincial courts. In the late third century there was probably a wide range of punishments for adultery. The statutory *relegatio* mentioned in the Sentences of Paul was hardly considered sufficient in most cases, certainly not outside the uppermost classes.[10]

In the very beginning of the next century several sources indicate that adultery could be punished by death. Lactantius tells that in 311 Maximin Daia in an outburst of anger ordered even senatorial women executed on trumped-up charges. A Constantinian law of 313/15 listed adultery among the most serious crimes which received a capital penalty. A little earlier Arnobius made a similar claim. In these cases *capitalis poena* certainly meant death.[11]

Constantine may have stated even more explicitly that adultery brought a death sentence. There is no direct testimony since no such law appears in the Theodosian Code.[12] Only two years after Constantine's reign still more drastic punishments were pronounced: adulterers were to be drowned in a sack or burned alive like parricides. It is unlikely that this law was often (or ever) enforced in its extreme form. It was not included in the title 9. 7 (*Ad legem Juliam de adulteriis*) of the Theodosian Code but came in perhaps inadvertently in another title and was never referred to later.[13]

In the literary sources of this period, we encounter a bewilder-

---

[10] Directly on adultery only Apul. *met.* 9. 27; see also PS 5. 4. 14. Ach. Tat. *Leuc. et Clit.* 8. 8. 13 pictures a local court, cf. Millar (1981) 70–2. SHA *Aurel.* 7. 4 is a military punishment. But cf. e.g. PS 5. 23. 1, 5. 29. 1, 5. 30b. 1; D. 48. 1. 8, 48. 8. 3. 5, 48. 19. 1. 3, 2. 1, 13. See also Hartmann (1894) 434; Levy (1938), esp. 133–52; Garnsey (1967; 1970: esp. 111, 122); MacMullen (1986a) 147–57, 163–6. For the evidence of NMaj 9, see below.

[11] Lact. *mort. pers.* 39–40; Arnob. *nat.* 4. 23; CT 9. 40. 1 + 11. 36. 1 (313/315); see also CT 9. 38. 1 (322); CI 5. 17. 7 (337); Levy (1930/1) 56–7.

[12] The last clause of CI 9. 9. 29. 4 ('*Sacrilegos autem nuptiarum gladio puniri oportet.*') was added by Justinian: it does not appear in the original CT 9. 7. 2 (326). The Byzantine scholiast cited above did not notice this as he did not check the Theodosian Code; Nov. 134. 10. pr is to be explained similarly. See Beaucamp (1990) 166–8; Evans Grubbs (1995) 216–18.

[13] CT 11. 36. 4 (339); cf. execution by sword, Amm. 28. 1. 16 (371/2). It is worth noting that such cruel threats were not exceptional in the mid-4th c.: even counterfeiters faced the stake, CT 9. 21. 5 (343).

ing variety of allusions to the legal consequences of adultery. First, a senator in Constantine's reign was exiled for adultery.[14] Much later, around 370, an influential official of Valentinian I terrorized the senatorial nobility in Rome, having both men and women accused and executed for various crimes, including adultery (Amm. 28. 1. 16, 28, 48–56). Moreover, some Christian writers clearly indicated that death was the typical penalty for adultery.[15] On the other hand, many ecclesiastical sources discussed problems which would have been totally irrelevant if adulterers and adulteresses had regularly been put to death.[16]

It is illuminating to review a problem which Augustine had to face. The church insisted that men should not remarry while the first spouse was alive, even if she was repudiated for adultery. This led some men to wonder whether it would have been better to kill the adulterous wife. Augustine devoted a long passage to the question and his answer was firmly negative, of course. What strikes the reader is the fact that he clearly took this option for granted: a husband living under Roman law could decide whether to kill his adulterous wife or not. What did he mean? Only one short clause seems to hint at the right answer: '*Si autem accusando adulteram occiderit . . .*'. If the husband accused his wife in court it meant her death but if he did not make it public she was saved. And it was the latter thing which a good Christian was expected to do.[17]

This is clearly the right context of Augustine's pastoral problem. It is confirmed by Basil the Great. He mentions that adulteresses who were performing penance were not exposed in order to save them from the death penalty. The Roman state's old policy to ensure that sexual offences were publicly prosecuted had been practically abandoned by Constantine. He had abolished the general right to accuse an adulteress, reserving it only for her husband and nearest relatives. Although this may not have been too rigorously observed (no Roman laws were), normally

---

[14] Firm. *math.* 2. 29. 10–20; the incident is probably to be dated in the 320s, see Barnes (1975).
[15] Hier. *ep.* 1 with its horrible scene of torture (the story is probably invented); *ep.* 147. 4; Basil. *ep.* 46. 4; Joh. Chrys. *virg.* 1. 2, 52. 7, SC 125. 94, 296.
[16] *Conc. Eliber.* (295/314) 7, 14, 31, 64–70; *Conc. Ancyr.* (314) 20; *Conc. Arel.* (314) 11, CCL 148. 11; *Conc. Venet.* (461/491) 4, CCL 148. 152; *Const. Apost.* 6. 14. 4, SC 329. 340; Basil. *ep.* 199. 26, 217. 58–9.
[17] Aug. *adult. conjug.* 2. 14–17, CSEL 41. 398ff., esp. 401.

people seem to have been able to avoid legal proceedings if they
so wished.[18]

If someone was uncertain about the statutory penalty for
adultery, the promulgation of the Theodosian Code in 438 was
of little avail: the large title CT 9. 7 on adultery did not give a
specified punishment at all and, if the cruel CT 11. 36. 4 was
noticed, it was probably not taken seriously. When the emperor
Majorian in 459 heard that a governor had sent an adulterer only
into temporary exile (*relegatio*), he considered this attitude too
liberal. Wanting to establish the correct penalty, he stated:

*secundum legem divorum retro principum, qui in simili crimine talia cen-
suerunt, relegationem probrosi ac nefandissimi rei deportatio adiecta con-
tinuo sequatur et bonis eius omnibus fisci utilitatibus vindicatis eum a
congressu totius Italiae submovendum.* (NMaj 9)

according to the law of former divine emperors who have decreed such
regulations in similar cases, deportation shall be added and shall immediately follow the relegation of such opprobrious and nefarious criminals. All their goods shall be vindicated to the resources of the fisc, and
they shall be removed from the society of all Italy.

The law of former divine emperors could not be from the
Theodosian Code, as no such one existed there, and it is unlikely
to have been any of the *novellae* published since 438. Consequently, Majorian must have referred to some much earlier law
which could be found either in the Gregorian or the Hermogenian Code. It is certain that he had these codes before his eyes
since further on in the same law he uses the phrase '*ita nobis pudor
cordi est*', which has been taken from the Diocletianic CI 9. 9. 27.
It may have been this very same rescript which in its original
form named *deportatio* as a suitable penalty but was later shortened when it was taken into the Justinian Code.

Whatever the source of Majorian's penalty, it was clearly
difficult in the middle of the fifth century to find an established
rule to say how to deal with adulterers. Later, people in the west
had even less help from their law codes. Only the *Edictum
Theoderici* set down an unconditional death sentence.[19] In the

---

[18] CT 9. 7. 2 (326); Basil. *ep.* 199. 34; see also Aug. *ep.* 78. 6, CSEL 34. 2. 340;
Innoc. *ep.* 6. 10, PL 20. 500; Hier. *ep.* 147. 6–8 with CT 9. 25. 2; Pel. I *ep.* 54; Greg.
M. *ep.* 3. 40, 42; Evans Grubbs (1995) 208–12; cf. also Bauman (1980) 213–15, 231–3.
[19] ET 38–9; cf. also Cass. *var.* 5. 33 (523/526) and 9. 18. 5 (533/4), which do not
specify the penalty.

Breviarium, the title on adultery (9. 7) of the Theodosian Code was for the most part included but, as already noted, it did not give any penalty. The harsh rule in CT 11. 36. 4 was excluded as were also the ninth *novella* of Majorian and the relevant parts of Paul's Sentences (PS 2. 26). Equally silent was the Roman Law of Burgundy. One could almost believe that the compilers systematically avoided this topic. Adultery was certainly not a light matter in their society, so how is this negligence to be explained?

We have to go back in time and recall the beginning of this chapter. It had always been possible that an enraged husband took private vengeance on his wife and her lover. Although it had been legally prohibited for a long time, the practice had never been totally suppressed. In the later empire it was attested by Jerome and John Chrysostom among others. They evidently considered it natural and common although they do not explicitly say whether it was legal or illegal in their time.[20] But it seems that by the early sixth century governments in the west gave in, and Roman husbands regained their archaic right to retribution. It was permitted in Italy under the Ostrogothic government, and the Roman Law of Burgundy stated the same thing explicitly in the title '*De adulteriis*'.[21] It is found also in the *Breviarium*, in a rare case of textual alteration. The Sentences of Paul had originally stated the classical rule:

Inventa in adulterio uxore maritus ita demum adulterum occidere potest, si eum domi suae deprehendat. (PS 2. 26. 7 = Coll. 4. 12. 6)

When the husband detects his wife in adultery he can kill the adulterer only if he overtakes him in his own house [and if the man belongs to the ignoble categories].

In the *Breviarium*, the same sentence appears in a different form, now permitting the husband to kill his wife:

Inventam in adulterio uxorem maritus ita demum occidere potest, si adulterum domi suae deprehendat. (LRV PS 2. 27. 1)

When the husband detects his wife in adultery he can kill her only if he overtakes the adulterer in his own house.

---

[20] Hier. *ep.* 147. 11; Joh. Chrys. *virg.* 52. 3, SC 125. 292; see also Lib. *or.* 1. 147; BGU iv. 1024, with Keenan (1989).   [21] Cass. *var.* 1. 37 (507/511); LRB 25.

The unknown compiler may have deliberately changed the text. Equally, he may only have 'improved' on what he thought was a corrupt passage, or just copied it carelessly. In no way can we say that it was a simple accident. The change certainly reflects a new attitude, which was more favourable to private violence. The same custom was familiar to the Germanic peoples, and it was well established in their laws. They clearly assumed that the offenders were normally killed on the spot: only the Visigoths saw it worth while to lay down rules for the possibility that the pair had escaped their immediate death and a public enquiry was necessary. Frankish laws as usual defined statutory fines as an alternative, trying to prevent blood feuds.[22]

Thus it was now the husband himself or the woman's own relatives who were expected to carry out the punishment. It has been claimed that the compilers of the late Roman codes adopted this custom directly from their Germanic neighbours.[23] Some influence is admittedly possible, but it is important to notice that the development was quite natural for Roman society, too. Only from the beginning of the principate had the Roman state been strong enough to claim that it could guard citizens' morals and to demand the sole right of jurisdiction over adultery cases. When central government collapsed in the late fifth century, the state had to abandon formally a task which it had perhaps never really coped with. When exactly private retribution was made legal is uncertain. The Roman Law of Burgundy (LRB 25) referred to some statute of Majorian which had allegedly reintroduced this 'old rule' to Roman law. The statement is inaccurate at the very least but not totally impossible: there may have been a law which is no longer extant.[24]

In the eastern empire, central government continued to assert its jurisdiction and no similar development took place. In Justinian's reign the statutory penalty for adultery was death, probably both for the man and the woman. In 556 a new law ordered explicitly that only the man had to be executed and the woman

---

[22] LB 68; ER 211–13; LV 3. 4. 1–13; PLS 15; LRib 39; see also Greg. Tur. *franc.* 5. 32, 6. 36, 8. 19. Zeumer (1898) iii. 605–12.   [23] Thus e.g. Zeumer (1898) iii. 608.
[24] LRB 25 has also been thought to refer mistakenly to NMaj 9, see e.g. Meyer *ad* NMaj 9; this is possible but not wholly convincing.

shut in a monastery for the rest of her life unless her husband forgave her and took her back within two years.[25]

Three years later this rule may have been observed in Byzantine Italy: the pope, Pelagius, wrote to a subdeacon to shave the heads of an adulterous couple, to guard the woman in a safe place for possible reconciliation with her husband, and to deliver the adulterer to a state dignitary. In the same year Pelagius ordered another male adulterer to be shut in a monastery. This may have been a special case, though, because the culprit was a cleric. Only if he tried to escape should he pay the full penalty, which '*ecclesiastica moderatio*' had tempered and which seems to have been only exile.[26] What is notable in these cases is the active role which church officials take in the matter. It is just one more sign of how difficult it was for the late ancient state to enforce its laws. The church was the only organization which had wide authority, effective administration, and sufficient local connections to cope with the everyday problems of its members.

Reviewing the legislation on adultery from the principate to late antiquity, it is obvious that the statutory penalties were more severe in the later periods. The observation is not surprising as it conforms with the general evolution of Roman criminal law. Punishments were gradually becoming harsher and judicial savagery towards citizens increased. Evolution of penalties was accompanied by their differentiation according to social status, as we have seen. Reasons for this have been sought in the overall social and political developments of the empire.[27]

On the other hand, we have seen that statutory penalties do not tell the whole truth: legal theory and practice did not always coincide. As the evidence is so sparse, almost everything is conjectural but I do nevertheless suspect that changes were less clear in practice than in theory. Up to the end of the third century our sources are mainly interested in the uppermost classes, so they tend to give the penalty of the Julian law, *relegatio*, which was applicable to them. Silent humble folk could always expect

---

[25] CI 9. 9. 9, 29. 4; Inst. 4. 18. 4; Nov. 134. 10; Beaucamp (1990: 165–9; cf. 1992a: 342–3). Even Justinian allowed husbands a very limited right to kill the adulterer in specified circumstances, Nov. 117. 15. pr (542).

[26] Pel. I *ep.* 64, 54; cf. *ep.* 53. 8; Greg. M. *ep.* 3. 40, 42.

[27] Levy (1930/1) 75; Garnsey (1970) 103–52, 274, 278; MacMullen (1986a); see also Millar (1984).

more brutal treatment. From the fourth century, legislators tried
to take the mass of the population into account, presenting those
punishments which applied to the lower and middle class. In this
way death now became the 'statutory' penalty although members
of the nobility could still escape with exile. They faced execution
mostly in exceptional circumstances, as is attested for the reigns
of Caracalla, Maximin Daia, and Valentinian. In addition, offenders in all classes could normally hope with good reason that their
case would never be brought in front of an imperial court.

It is impossible to see how the laws on adultery in late antiquity
could be attributed to the influence of Christianity.[28] What little
we know of ecclesiastical attitudes through Augustine and Basil
shows that they did not wish the death penalty for their parishioners. Apart from that, it will become evident in the following
sections that, although the church was hostile not only towards
adultery but towards all extramarital relations, its teaching had
little effect on Roman morals or legislation.

It is true that Christian writers frequently condemned the
morals of pagan antiquity. They claimed that the secular world
was living in total debauchery and that they themselves were the
only ones to hold such virtues as *castitas* and *pudicitia* in high
esteem.[29] The truth of the first proposition is difficult to ascertain
but the second one was definitely false. It is sufficient to cite a few
laws from the third century, where pagan emperors declared that
they would guard just these virtues.[30] Diocletian (or Galerius) did
not hesitate to plead divine authority in his long and emotional
edict on honourable matrimony (Coll. 6. 4). There cannot be the
slightest doubt that adultery, in the sense of a woman's marital
infidelity, was always considered a very grave offence in Roman
society. Here Christianity made no difference at all. In fact, the
interests of church and state coincided although Diocletian did
not yet want to admit it.

The Double Standard

It was on the question of double standards where the views of
church and state diverged. According to Roman law, husbands

---

[28] Among the more recent proponents of this view is Bauman (1980) 190–2, 213.
[29] Thraede (1972) 240, with references; Brown (1988) 208.
[30] CI 9. 9. 9, 20, 27. See also Symm. *ep.* 9. 147–8.

were not required to be faithful (CI 9. 9. 1). Jerome regretted that
Roman men were freely permitted to lead a dissolute life with
prostitutes and slave girls:

*Aliae sunt leges Caesarum, aliae Christi, aliud Papinianus, aliud Paulus
noster praecipit. Apud illos in viris pudicitiae frena laxantur, et solo stupro
atque adulterio condemnato, passim per lupanaria' et ancillulas libido
permittitur, . . . Apud nos, quod non licet feminis, aeque non licet viris.*
(Hier. *ep.* 77. 3)

The laws of Caesars are different from the laws of Christ: Papinian
commands one thing, our Paul another. Among the Romans men's
unchastity goes unchecked; seduction and adultery are condemned, but
free permission is given to lust to range the brothels and to have slave
girls . . . With us what is unlawful for women is equally unlawful for
men. (tr. Wright, in Loeb)

   Demands for strict monogamy were not totally unheard of even
in pagan society. Male sexual freedom had been censured by
many Greek philosophers since Plato, and these ideas were
propounded in Rome mainly by Stoics.[31] The emperor Caracalla
considered it unjust that a man accused his wife of adultery if he
himself had shown a total lack of *pudicitia*: but with this he
clearly meant a sexual crime, rather than just occasional affairs
with slave girls.[32]
   We can conclude that cultured Romans were conscious of the
double standard and some may have been slightly embarrassed
about it but few abandoned it in their own life.[33] In this respect,
the unanimity and intransigence of Christian writers was in a
class of its own: they condemned absolutely the contemporary
male sexual freedom.[34] But these very same sermons reveal that

---

[31] Delling (1959a) 671–2; Veyne (1987) 45–9; Treggiari (1991a) 199–201, 221–2,
312–13.
[32] Augustine quoted Caracalla's words directly from the Gregorian Code, *adult.
conjug.* 2. 8. 7, CSEL 41. 389; a part of the same passage is cited also by Ulpian, D.
48. 5. 14. 5.
[33] Cf. e.g. Sen. *ep.* 94. 26; Gell. 10. 23. 5; Mart. 12. 58; Plut. *praec. conj.* 16–17
(140B–C); Aug. *nupt. et concup.* 1. 3. 4, CSEL 42. 214. For an inspiring discussion
of the whole theme, see now Treggiari (1991a) 299–319.
[34] E.g. Lact. *inst.* 6. 23–5, CSEL 19. 568; Ambr. *Abr.* 1. 25, CSEL 32. 1. 519;
Greg. Naz. *or.* 37. 6–7, PG 36. 289; Joh Chrys. *in I Thess.* 5. 2, PG 62. 425; *in II Tim.*
3. 3, PG 62. 617; Aug. *serm.* 82. 11, 132. 2–4, 153. 5. 6, 224. 3, PL 38. 511, 735, 828, 1095;
serm. 392. 4–5, PL 39. 1711.

the state paid no heed to their teaching. Christian emperors did nothing to restrict the traditional liberties of their male subjects.

When Constantine decreed that a man could repudiate his wife because of her adultery, he especially stressed that the rule did not work the other way round: a woman could not divorce only because her husband happened to have affairs with other women. Ninety years later there had been some progress. Now it was a mitigating factor if a woman was divorcing and could show *morum vitia* (not otherwise specified) in her husband. Still later, in 449, it was a ground for divorce if the husband was *adulter* (that is, condemned for adultery with a married woman and facing execution) or if he brought dissolute women into his own house and made love to them *in his wife's presence.*[35] It is hard to believe that husbands in pagan Rome would have often rendered themselves guilty of such insolence and, if they had, their wives would have been able to depart with their dowries at that very moment.

Male extramarital sex as such was never punishable in late antiquity. There are only two laws in the whole period which consider the matter as an offence against the wife, one from the Visigothic and another from the Ostrogothic government. They both state that a woman who has cohabited with a married man should be left to his wife's mercy. Of course, there was no question of any punishment for the man.[36] It is interesting that Salvian idealized Germanic chastity and contrasted it with (Christian) Roman immorality; but we should probably not give too much weight to this testimony.[37]

The bishops were clearly frustrated to find no response among their flock. Men could defend the double standard with the argument that their affairs did not endanger the purity of the family line.[38] Even Augustine himself could not totally dismiss the idea that monogamy was more natural for a woman than for a man.[39] The majority of Christians did not see any reason to change their habits: husbands boasted about their sexual

[35] CT 3. 16. 1–2; CI 5. 17. 8. 2; see Beaucamp (1990) 170–7, and above, Ch. 5, Sect. 3.
[36] LV.Ant 3. 4. 9; Cass. *var.* 9. 18. 7 (533/4); cf. Zeumer (1898) iii. 610–11.
[37] Salv. *gub.* 7. 23–7; cf. also 7. 64, CSEL 8. 162, 176.
[38] Aster. Amas. *hom.* 5; cf. Jul. *elog. in Const.* 38 (46D); Greg. Naz. *or.* 37. 8, PG 36. 292; Isid. Pelus. *ep.* 129, PG 78. 1212.
[39] Aug. *bon. conjug.* 17. 20, CSEL 41. 213; *nupt. et concup.* 1. 9. 10, CSEL 42. 222; *de serm. dom.* 1. 16. 49, PL 34. 1254.

exploits and got angry if someone tried to reproach them. Long after the 'victory' of Christianity, church leaders complained that all men made love to their female slaves and there were so many fornicators in any city that the bishop could not excommunicate them all.[40]

2. CONCUBINAGE

Wife or Concubine?

If a Roman man did not want to take a wife, nothing prevented him from taking a concubine instead, and sometimes this was even considered more proper. In fact, it was not always easy to tell whether a given relationship was marriage or concubinage. Public wedding, a dowry, or a written contract were unambiguous signs and so common in the upper classes that real confusion was probably rare, but none of these was a legal prerequisite to a valid marriage. If they were absent, the spouses' intent to be married was the only criterion. This could clearly cause uncertainty for jurists, perhaps also occasionally for the couple themselves.[41] It seems that, if the man and woman were socially equal, they were assumed to be married whereas concubinage was characterized by a social gap between them.[42]

The situation remained basically the same in the later empire. Public celebration, financial transfers, and accompanying documents usually showed that two people were legally married. In the lack of such evidence they could still be considered husband and wife if they were of the same social standing. Otherwise it was natural to assume that the woman was only a concubine.[43] There

---

[40] Basil. *ep.* 188. 9, 199. 21; Joh. Chrys. *virg.* 52. 7, SC 125. 296; Aug. *serm.* 9. 4, 9. 12, CCL 41. 115, 131; *adult. conjug.* 2. 8. 7, 2. 20. 21, CSEL 41. 388, 408; Innoc. *ep.* 6. 9–10, PL 20. 499; Salv. *gub.* 7. 17–20, CSEL 8. 160; Caes. Arel. *serm.* 41. 4, 42. 2–4, 43. 7, CCL 103. 182, 185, 193; *serm.* 189. 4, CCL 104. 773; Greg. Tur. *vit. patr.* 7. 1. See further Beaucamp (1992a) 352, for eastern writers.

[41] Quint. *inst.* 5. 11. 32; D. 23. 2. 24, 24. 1. 3. 1; 25. 7. 3. 4, 32. 49. 4, 35. 1. 15, 39. 5. 31. pr; 48. 5. 35; PS 2. 20. 1; CI 4. 6. 1 (215), 5. 4. 9 (Probus); etc. See Ehrhardt (1937) 1479–82, 1485–6; and esp. Treggiari (1981a) 60–4.

[42] Wolff (1945) 34–5; Treggiari (1981a) 59, 76; See e.g. D. 25. 7. 3; 39. 5. 31. pr.

[43] CT 3. 7. 3 (428 east); CI 2. 7. 23. 4 (506 east), 5. 4. 23. 7 (520/523 east); cf. LRB 37. 1–2; Hier. *ep.* 69. 5; Joh. Chrys. *in Matth.* 73. 4, PG 58. 678; Leo M. *ep.* 167. 4, PL 54. 1204; Cass. *var.* 7. 40; for the Syro-Roman Law Book L 35–6, see Selb (1964) 176 n. 38; for Augustine, Shaw (1987a) 34–6; and for the whole question, Kaser (1975) 169–71, with further references and literature.

were attempts in the western empire to make public wedding or dowry compulsory.[44] However, it is clear that this was mainly intended for well-to-do people, and in any case the law would have been very difficult to enforce in the lower classes. Nothing certain can be inferred from later western texts and codes, which variously adopted and adapted old rules.[45] The problem is also reflected in a Merovingian *formula* which may preserve Roman traditions: a man states that he has married a free woman but for some reason or another failed to have a written dowry agreement drawn up; now his children should according to law be bastards (*naturales*) but he is evidently able to remedy the situation with the present deed.[46]

In the east Justinian similarly tried to make a written document compulsory. He complained that people misused free-form marriage and decreed that the highest officials (the class of *illustres*) always had to give *dos* and *donatio*. This almost automatically guaranteed that some sort of document would be written. People below this class could, as an alternative, have their marriage certified by local clergy, but simple soldiers, farmers, and other humble people were still allowed to leave their marriages unrecorded. Only four years later Justinian changed his mind and again permitted marriage without documents for all citizens except *illustres*. It does not seem to have been rare in his reign.[47]

Thus concubinage normally existed when the woman was well beneath her partner's social status. It was possible that a free man lived together with someone else's slave though it would certainly have been degrading for a well-born man, and he could be expected to buy her in such a case.[48] If he did not do so, he was probably very poor. In that case it might be asked whether he should be reduced to slavery himself; as we will see, this is

---

[44] CT 4. 6. 7 + CI 5. 4. 21 (426 west), rejected by the eastern law CT 3. 7. 3 + 4. 6. 8 (428); but cf. below n. 87. NMaj 6. 9 (458).

[45] CT 3. 7. 3 + int. (in the *Breviarium*) and LRB 37. 1–2 are contradictory; GE 1. 4. pr is vague, while PS 2. 20. 1 was totally misunderstood later in the Visigothic interpretation, and still worse in the *Epitome Aegidii* (LRV PS 2. 21, p. 368). See also LV 3. 1. 9 (Ervig), with Zeumer (1898) iii. 587–8.

[46] *Cart. Sen. App.* 1a. Cf. *Form. Tur.* 14 with CT 3. 5. 2. int.

[47] Nov. 74. 4 (538), 117. 2–4 (542).

[48] CI 2. 20. 4 (294), 6. 27. 3 (293), 6. 59. 9 (294), 7. 16. 3 (225), 7. 16. 29 (294). See also CT 12. 1. 6 (319). A relationship where a slave was involved was more accurately called *contubernium*, see e.g. PS 2. 19. 6; Rawson (1974) 293–9; Treggiari (1981*b*), esp. 53–4.

what could happen to women in similar circumstances. For a long time emperors did not allow that.[49] But the status distinction between slaves and poor free was already being blurred, and between them had appeared the class of *coloni*, dependent farmers who were tied to the soil. From the mid-fifth century, western laws tried to regulate the case where a free man cohabited with an alien *colona* or female slave: although he did not lose his nominal freedom, he could no longer leave her master. This seems to have been a purely western development, and it appeared also in Frankish and Visigothic law.[50] If it ever surfaced in eastern practice, it was not recorded in our extant legal sources.[51]

We may surmise that concubinage often, perhaps predominantly, came into existence between a woman and her own master.[52] They could live thus for a long time or the man could eventually free her. In that case he could either marry her or continue to keep her as concubine: both alternatives were respectable in the principate.[53] Only senators had no option, as they were expressly forbidden to marry freedwomen.[54] On the other hand, even a freeborn woman could be a concubine, at least if she was of low birth. This was a delicate question, however, and there were always some who wanted to forbid it altogether—though with little success.[55]

Whatever her legal status, *concubina* in the strict sense of the

[49] CI 7. 16. 3 (225), 6. 59. 9 (294); see also CT 12. 1. 6 (319). On free women and slaves, see next section.

[50] NVal 31. 5 (451) + int; NMaj 7. pr (458); ET 64; LRB 37. 6; cf. Salv. *gub.* 4. 26, CSEL 8. 72; LV.Ant 3. 2. 3; PLS 13. 9, 25. 3; LRib 61. 15; but cf. ER 156 and 194; see Nehlsen (1972) 245, 307–12.

[51] There is a mysterious reference to it in a sermon of unknown date, Ps.Joh. Chrys. *de legisl.* 3 PG 56. 401. For Byzantine Italy, see Greg. M. *ep.* 9. 85 (the husband of a slave belonging to the Roman church obviously remains free).

[52] e.g. D. 20. 1. 8, 42. 5. 38, 49. 15. 21. pr; CT 4. 8. 7. (331); CI 7. 15. 3 (531); *Const. apost.* 8. 32. 12, SC 336. 238; Hier. *ep.* 69. 5; Lib. *or.* 48. 30; Max. Taur. *serm.* 88. 5, CCL 23. 361; Sidon. *ep.* 9. 6. 1; Caes. Arel. *serm.* 42. 5, CCL 103. 188; Pel. I *ep.* 47. For inscriptions, see Treggiari (1981a) 65.

[53] GI 1. 19; D. 12. 2. 16, 23. 2. 28, 29, 41, 51; 25. 7. 1. pr, 38. 1. 46, 40. 2. 13, 40. 9. 21, 48. 5. 14. pr; CI 6. 3. 9 (225). Concubinage between *patronus* and *liberta* is not very common in inscriptions but marriages are often attested; see Weaver (1972: 180–1; 1986: 149–50); Rawson (1974) 291; Treggiari (1981a) 66–8.

[54] Dio 54. 16. 2, 56. 7. 2; D. 23. 2. 16, 44; cf. e.g. Corbett (1930) 30–9. On CT 4. 6. 3 (336) and later legislation, extending this prohibition, see further below.

[55] D. 23. 2. 24, 25. 7. 1. 1, 3, 34. 9. 16. 1, 48. 5. 35; CI 7. 16. 34 (294); CI 5. 27. 5 (477); SHA *Aurel.* 49. In inscriptions freeborn *concubinae* are almost non-existent, Rawson (1974) 289; Treggiari (1981a) 66–8, 78–81.

word was not a casual mistress. Concubinage was a union of some duration and essentially monogamous. It was never considered proper to have a wife and a concubine simultaneously, whether in the principate or in the later empire.[56] Naturally this rule was not easy to enforce as all casual affairs were permitted and a man could not be prevented from regularly using the services of his own female slaves.[57]

Thus a concubine was usually taken either before or after marriage. It is easy to see one reason why an upper-class widower would have preferred concubinage to remarriage: if he already had a sufficient number of heirs, he did not want more legitimate children to divide the family estate. It was safer for him to take a dependent concubine to satisfy his sexual and emotional needs. This phenomenon is frequently attested in the principate, notably for some emperors.[58] In late antiquity it is sometimes mentioned, though not very often.[59]

It is the concubinage of younger men which is most prominent in late ancient sources. As we have so often noted, Roman males entered their first marriage relatively late, and it was not unnatural that they sought sexual pleasures well before that time. It seems to have been common in the upper and middle classes that a man in his youth took a concubine, often a slave, whom he could later reject when he found a bride of sufficient wealth and social status. Young Augustine himself is the best-known example of such behaviour. In these temporary unions children were naturally avoided, though not always with success.[60] It is strange that, although this kind of concubinage figures in republican

[56] D. 24. 2. 11. 2, 45. 1. 121. 1, 50. 16. 144; PS 2. 20. 1 (whether interpolated or not); CI 5. 26. 1 (326), 7. 15. 3. 2 (531); see Treggiari (1981*a*) 77–8; Evans Grubbs (1995) 294–300.

[57] See e.g. Aug. *serm.* 224. 3, PL 38. 1095; Hier. *ep.* 22. 2; Max. Taur. *serm.* 88. 5, CCL 23. 361; Joh. Chrys. *ad Stag.* 2. 3, PG 47. 452; Theodoret. *hist. rel.* 8. 13, SC 234. 400; Salv. *gub.* 4. 24–6, CSEL 8. 72; Greg. Tur. *franc.* 10. 8. For Egypt, see Beaucamp (1992*a*) 52–3. And cf. above, previous section.

[58] Suet. *Vesp.* 3; Dio 65. 14; Marc. Aur. 1. 17. 2; SHA *Marc.* 29. 10; *Ant. Pius* 8. 9; D. 31. 29. pr; but cf. 34. 9. 16. 1; Rawson (1974) 288; Treggiari (1981*a*) esp. 76; Gardner (1986) 143; Goody (1990) 418–20; Krause (1994*a*) 62–4.

[59] See Caes. Arel. *serm.* 42. 5, CCL 103. 188; Pel. I *ep.* 47 (559); *Conc. Aurel.* (538) 10, CCL 148A. 118; Nov. 12. 4 (535). Cf. also Aug. *ep.* 259, CSEL 57. 611 ff. ('*concubina*' used of a whole flock of kept women).

[60] Aug. *conf.* 4. 2, 6. 12. 21–6. 15. 25, CCL 27. 40, 87; *bon. conjug.* 5. 5, CSEL 41. 193; Joh. Chrys. *in I Thess.* 5. 3, PG 62. 426; Paul. Pell. 154–86, CSEL 16. 297; Sidon. *ep.* 9. 6; Caes. Arel. *serm.* 43. 4–5, CCL 103. 191.

comedies, it is not attested in the principate.[61] Perhaps it was so natural that it did not draw any attention before the church fathers started to attack it.

Both church and state thought that a young man who was living in concubinage did best if he stopped it and married legally. There were two possibilities: he could either marry the concubine or abandon her and take a wife with a higher social status. The first alternative had always been theoretically possible (except for senators).[62] However, there was the practical problem that concubines were usually of a very low social status. Even if they had been freed before the marriage, it was considered improper for a decent man to have legitimate children from such a union (see below). Thus it seems to have been a general feeling in late antiquity that the morally right thing to do was to send a humble concubine away with her children, if there were any, and to find a more suitable wife. The leaders of the church tacitly accepted this solution. They did not like unequal unions either, and they clearly did not expect their well-to-do fellow citizens to be willing to marry base-born women. The most important thing for the bishops was to stop concubinage, one way or another: the fate of poor women and their children was of secondary importance.[63]

In fact, concubinage was so popular that bishops had little hope of eradicating it, not even Caesarius of Arles, who waged a futile war against it in the early sixth century.[64] The bishops had to console themselves with the notion that monogamous concubinage was better than limitless debauchery.[65] It is ironic that the church itself had created an additional motive for living with a concubine when it had forbidden priests to marry. Suspicions of

---

[61] Treggiari (1981*a*) 76.

[62] D. 24. 1. 58, 39. 5. 31. pr, 48. 5. 14. 6; Aug. *bon. conjug.* 14. 17, CSEL 41. 209; Nov. 18. 11 (536). Similarly ER 222.

[63] See e.g. *Const. apost.* 8. 32. 13, SC 336. 238; Ambr. *Abr.* 1. 19, CSEL 32. 1. 515; Aug. *bon. conjug.* 5. 5, CSEL 41. 193; *fid. et oper.* 19. 35, CSEL 41. 81; Leo M. *ep.* 167. 4–6, PL 54. 1204; Sidon. *ep.* 9. 6. Evans Grubbs (1995) 309–16. Rare advice to free the concubine and marry her was given by Max. Taur. *serm.* 88. 5, CCL 23. 362.   [64] Caes. Arel. *serm.* 32. 4, 42. 5, 43. 2–5, CCL 103. 142, 188, 190.

[65] Basil. *ep.* 199. 26; Aug. *bon. conjug.* 5. 5, CSEL 41. 193; *Conc. Tolet.* I (400) 17; Salv. *gub.* 4. 25, CSEL 8. 72; *Conc. Aurel.* (538) 10, CCL 148A. 118.

clerical concubinage were discussed by Gregory the Great and by numerous Gallic and Spanish councils.[66]

It is likewise paradoxical that, although bishops and lawmakers disapproved of divorce in late antiquity, they had nothing against dissolution of a concubinage. The state was concerned only with the transmission of property and not with the sexual life of men as such. So concubinage continued as a licit and legally recognized practice both in the west and in the Byzantine empire.[67] It flourished in Merovingian society (where also open polygyny may sometimes have existed) and was still practised in the Carolingian period and later in the middle ages.[68]

In general, there is hardly any reason to envy those women who were kept as concubines. Especially as partners of well-born young men, they were purely sexual objects who were readily disposed of after they were no longer needed. There were naturally exceptions: a slave or freedwoman who cohabited with her widowed master could establish a satisfying relationship with him. The union offered her security and a standard of living which she could never have attained otherwise. In some cases she could even command respect and wield political influence. This was particularly true in the Merovingian period, when Frankish kings often married women from the lowest classes.[69]

Illegitimate Children

Most Roman men who lived in concubinage probably did it because they wanted to have sex without legitimate offspring. And, as we have seen, the state had nothing against this. It was only when a man took his relationship in earnest, attempting to take care of his concubine and illegitimate children, that problems arose. He could either try to legitimize them or at least leave them some property. This was something which the state wanted to regulate very strictly if not to forbid altogether.

---

[66] Greg. M. *ep.* 3. 44–5, 9. 111, 9. 219, 13. 36–7, 14. 16–17; *Conc. Agath.* (506) 11, CCL 148. 200; *Aurel.* (538) 4; *Asp.* (551) 2; *Conc. inc. loci* (*post* 614) 8, CCL 148A.115, 163, 287; *Conc. Gerund.* (517) 7; *Ilerd.* (523) 15; *Hisp.* (590) 3; *Tolet.* IV (633) 43; *Tolet.* IX (655) 10 (the most hostile of all, condemning children from such unions to slavery). See also Meyer (1895) 165, and Wemple (1981) 40–1.

[67] Cf. e.g. *'legitima coniunctio'*, CT 4. 6. 7 (426 west); *'licita consuetudo'*, CI 6. 57. 5. 2 (529 east); Meyer (1895) 157–68; Kaser (1975) 184; Karabelias (1988) 196–201.

[68] Meyer (1895) 165–7; Wemple (1981) 39–41, 75–83; Stafford (1983) 60–79; Herlihy (1985) 49, 62.

[69] Wemple (1981) 50, 56–7; Stafford (1983) 68 and *passim*.

Constantine confirmed that free men who were not imperial or local dignitaries could cohabit with slave women, though it was by no means honourable. But he had to stress that children from such unions remained slaves if they were not solemnly freed by the master—a self-evident fact in Roman law.[70] It is clear that, although Roman men often freed their slave concubines and children they did not always want to do so. In that case they remained slaves after his death. It was only Justinian in the east who changed the law and decreed that they would be automatically free if the master had not forbidden it in his will.[71]

The children of a slave concubine could thus be freed, or even freeborn if their mother had been freed early enough, but they were still illegitimate. In theory, they could be legitimized by adoption (in this case *arrogatio*). However, we have to remember that *arrogatio* was not a simple manœuvre or something which could be carried out at will. Outside Rome *arrogatio* was granted by the emperor himself (*per rescriptum principis*), and in late antiquity this was the only available method. Weighty arguments had to be adduced for *arrogatio*, and there had always been many restrictions which could prevent it from being used in a particular case: lack of other children was required, for example.[72] This meant that, if a high magistrate had tried to adopt his bastard son, he would certainly not have been allowed to do so, and as far as we know aristocrats in the early empire did not even try.[73] However, it is true that many tetrarchic emperors recognized their illegitimate children. Constantine himself and his eldest son Crispus were probably born of concubines.[74] Of course, most of these men had an obscure military background and none could be called an aristocrat.

[70] CT 12. 1. 6 (319), 4. 8. 7 (331). Evans Grubbs (1995) 277–83. Cf. CI 3. 32. 7 (245), 4. 19. 10, 13 (293), 7. 16. 29 (294).

[71] D. 20. 1. 8, 35. 2. 63. pr, 42. 5. 38, 42. 8. 17. 1, 49. 15. 21. pr; CI 4. 6. 6 (293), 7. 16. 12 (293); 7. 16. 29 (294); CT 4. 6. 7 (426 west); LRB 37. 3; CI 7. 15. 3 (531). See also *Fragm. Gaudenz.* 9 (LV, p. 470); Caes. Arel. *serm.* 42. 5, CCL 103. 188. For the inscriptional evidence (e.g. CIL vi. 23848, 27137) see Gardner (1989) 254–5.

[72] See e.g. GI 1. 98–100; D. 1. 7. 2, 17. 3, 46; CI 8. 47. 3, 6; and cf. Thomas (1967) 413–18; Kaser (1971: 347–8; 1975: 208–9); Gardner (1989), all with further references.

[73] Cf. Syme (1960) 323–5; Rawson (1974: 303 n. 74; 1989: 16–18); Gardner (1989) 243.

[74] See e.g. Drijvers (1992) 15–19, for Constantius; Ps.Aur. Vict. *epit.* 41. 4., with Demandt (1989) 70 n. 43, for Constantine; CT 4. 6. 2 for Licinius(?); Lact. *mort. pers.* 50. 2 for Galerius.

When Constantine came to power, he assumed a very traditional Roman upper-class attitude towards illegitimacy. He expressly declared that he would not permit any dignitaries to adopt or otherwise legitimize their children by lowborn mothers. It may have remained open for other people, although this question has been hotly debated.[75] In any case, the difficulties involved in obtaining an imperial rescript guaranteed that it remained irrelevant to the lower classes.[76] It was finally and definitely forbidden by Justin and Justinian.[77]

Legitimation was easiest to accept if the concubine was freeborn (*ingenua*) and there were no legitimate descendants whose inheritance would have been diminished. Constantine decreed that if such a couple married their existing children would be automatically legitimized. His original law is now lost, and it may have been only a temporary measure, but in 477 Zeno renewed it in the east.[78] In the sixth century the eastern emperors, especially Justinian, regularized the procedure and made it gradually more liberal, extending it to cover slaveborn concubines and well-born men, too. This was completed in 539 when Justinian generally abolished the distinction between *liberti* and *ingenui*.[79]

Most of this legislation was enacted after the two halves of the empire had been separated, and it had no direct counterpart in the west, as far as we know.[80] In the form which it received from Justinian it clearly made the situation of humble concubines' children more tolerable. Before that, it is very doubtful whether the laws really affected unequal unions at all: they applied to *ingenuae* whereas concubines in the upper classes were usually slaves and freedwomen. It seems that, if legitimation by subsequent matrimony was anything more than a mere curiosity, it

---

[75] CT 4. 6. 2, 3 (336). See e.g. Navarra (1988) 468–75; but her conclusions are not totally satisfying.   [76] Cf. Gardner (1986) 144.

[77] CI 5. 27. 7 (519); Nov. 74. 3, 89. 7, 89. 11. 2. It had been permitted by Anastasius, CI 5. 27. 6 (517).

[78] CI 5. 27. 5; Constantine's law was probably the missing CT 4. 6. 1. If it had not been included in the Theodosian Code, Marcian could hardly have referred to it in NMc 4. 4 (454 east).

[79] CI 5. 27. 6–7, 10–11; Nov. 12. 4, 18. 11, 19, 74. praef.-2, 78, 89. 8–11. On the equation of freeborn and freed (both called *ingenui*) in the west, see e.g. CT 4. 6. 4. int and *Fragm. Gaudenziana* 8–9 (LV, p. 470); in the Germanic codes it is commonplace.

[80] Cf. however Hier. *ep.* 69. 5; Cass. *var.* 7. 40; *Fragm. Gaudenz.* 8; *Cart. Sen. App.* 1a; and further below.

mainly helped those humbler freeborn couples who could have married but had not formally done so. They had perhaps lacked sufficient incentive, and they could never hope to obtain an imperial rescript to adopt the children afterwards. Constantine and Zeno certainly did not intend to encourage marriages across class boundaries.[81]

In the principate only senators were forbidden to marry freedwomen: almost all other unions were legal. Moreover, men were not forbidden to transfer property to their concubines and illegitimate children, although they were naturally not expected to neglect their legitimate family.[82] On these questions Constantine took a strong view. He extended the prohibition to marry lowborn women to cover not only senators but also equestrians and leading decurions of the cities. He also extended the circle of women who were to be avoided: in addition to slaves, freedwomen and women connected with the most shameful professions, it now included daughters of freedwomen, and even those who were *'humiles vel abiectae'*. We do not know what Constantine meant by these words nor how they were interpreted after him. In the mid-fifth century eastern courts wondered whether it meant that senators could not marry poor freeborn women. The emperor Marcian removed the ambiguity and rejected this interpretation, but it is no evidence of Constantine's original intentions.[83]

Constantine did not stop half-way: at the same time as he prohibited marriages between dignitaries and humble women he also attacked their quasi-marital unions. Men were not forbidden to have concubines but they were denied the right to donate or bequeath anything to their lowborn partners or their illegitimate children.

These were harsh rules, and they applied to a large number of people, not just the old aristocracy. It is no wonder that the emperor Valentinian in 371 had to relax the law's rigour: now a man could bequeath a quarter of his property to his concubine and illegitimate children if there were no legitimate descendants or ascendants, and one-twelfth if these existed (CT 4. 6. 4). I

---

[81] Cf. Navarra (1988) 459–68. On the whole issue of quasi-marital relationships, and esp. Constantine's legislation, see now Evans Grubbs (1995) 261–316.

[82] D. 28. 6. 45. pr, 31. 29. pr, 34. 9. 16. 1.

[83] CT 4. 6. 2, 3 (336); NMc 4 (454); Beaucamp (1990) 284–90.

suspect that a senator in the early empire would not have done much more than that.

We know further details of this legislation because it was a very important question personally for the famous rhetorician Libanius in Antioch. He never married but lived in concubinage with a slaveborn woman. From this union he had a son who could not inherit anything from him, according to Constantine's law. Libanius had in vain tried to procure an imperial dispensation from Julian and Jovian. Valentinian's law in 371 came to his aid although Valentinian's brother Valens confirmed it only grudgingly in the east, but soon it was again rescinded. In the end Libanius was able to receive a dispensation from Theodosius. Sadly, the son died before him.[84]

There are a number of interesting points in Libanius' story. First, he reveals that if he had not been able to bequeath his property to his son legally he would have done it illegally, through trusted friends. This was exactly what Constantine had suspected in his law of 336, and another example of how difficult it was to enforce laws in late antiquity.[85] Secondly, Libanius' efforts seem to have been supported by the *curia* of Antioch, who wanted to secure a new member to reinforce its dwindling ranks. Later the enrolment in the *curia* became a regular method in the east to enable illegitimate children to inherit their father's property.[86]

Thirdly, it was not uncommon to evade the prohibitions by acquiring an imperial dispensation. The same thing is attested also by Jerome:

Multos videmus ob nimiam paupertatem uxorum sarcinam declinare, et ancillulas suas habere pro uxoribus, susceptosque ex his liberos colere ut proprios; si forte ditati ab imperatore stolas illis meruerint . . . sin autem principale rescriptum eadem tenuitas inpetrare non quiverit . . . (ep. 69. 5)

We can see that many people decline the burden of wives because of their excessive poverty. In lieu of wives they keep their mean slave women, and children born from these they raise as if they were their proper

[84] Lib. *or.* 1. 145, 195–6, 283; 17. 37; *ep.* 1063. 5, 1064. 1, 1221. 6. See *Libanius' Autobiography*, ed. A. F. Norman (1965), esp. commentaries to paras. 145, 195, 258, 278, and 283. [85] Lib. *or.* 1. 195. See also Nov. 89. 12. 1.
[86] Lib. *or.* 1. 196; NTh. 22. 1 (442), 22. 2. 11 (443); CI 5. 27. 4 (470), 5. 27. 9 (528); Nov. 89. 2–6 (539); Kaser (1975) 221. See also Lib. *or.* 2. 36, 72; 48. 30; from the west NMaj 7. 2 (458); and cf. CT 12. 1. 6 (319). For earlier times, see Neesen (1981) 225.

offspring. If the men by chance get rich and thereafter the emperor grants their women the status of a wedded wife . . . But if their poverty prevents them from acquiring an imperial rescript . . .

The exact legal and social background of this passage is somewhat obscure. Is Jerome speaking of really poor people or is the alleged 'poverty' here only relative? He expressly refers to the legitimation of a wife, and only the upper classes were banned from marrying freedwomen. On the other hand, although Jerome (for his own purposes) stresses the woman's marital status, the procedure was certainly first and foremost aimed at improving the children's position.

It is clear that the legislation on illegitimate children was a very sensitive topic. After the law of Valentinian had been adopted in the east and then again rescinded under Theodosius, it was also revoked in the west in 397. Eight years later it was reintroduced in the east. In 426/7 there was a western law, the transmission of which is very fragmentary and uncertain. It seems to have declared that, if there were legitimate descendants, illegitimate children could inherit not just one-twelfth but one-eighth. It is uncertain whether this quota was afterwards adopted in the east and whether it applied also to those cases where no legitimate children existed. But there must have been continual dissension since only a little later an eastern law is once more found revoking something, although we do not know exactly what.[87]

If anything can be gleaned from this totally confusing story, it must be that there was no general agreement about the rights of illegitimate children. Adding to our confusion, contemporary bishops frequently stressed that children from an unequal union could not inherit: perhaps they only meant that bastards could not be made sole heirs. In any case, it is doubtful whether they could follow the constantly changing legislation.[88]

We would expect even less accuracy in later western sources. The Roman Law of Burgundy adopted the rule which may have

[87] CT 4. 6. 5–8; see also NTh 22. 1. int; CI 5. 27. 8. pr; cf. Gaudemet (1960) 417–19; Beaucamp (1990) 195–8. The relationship between CT 4. 6. 7 and 8 is very obscure. Before the law which is now numbered 8 there may have existed yet another which has not been preserved because the manuscript T breaks up in the middle of number 7 (and 8 is taken only from the *Breviarium*).

[88] Ambr. *Abr.* 1. 19, CSEL 32. 1. 515; Max. Taur. *serm.* 88. 5, CCL 23. 361; Aug. *serm.* 288, PL 39. 2291.

been the last confirmed in the Theodosian Code: illegitimate children could inherit one-eighth of the father's property. The same quota appeared also in the *Breviarium* in an interpretation to a Theodosian *novella*. However, this seems to have been a mere accident. From the main chapter of the Theodosian Code the *Breviarium* adopted only the law of Valentinian which established the quota as one-twelfth, or one-quarter if there were no legitimate children. The same rule is found also in a smaller Visigothic collection.[89] A contemporary sermon of bishop Caesarius does not conflict with this if we assume that he had the total property in mind:

quoscumque ipsae concubinae conceperint, non liberi, sed servi nascantur. Unde etiam post acceptam libertatem hereditatem patris nulla lege et nullo ordine accipere permittuntur. (*serm.* 42. 5, CCL 103. 188)

Should the concubines conceive, the children are not born free but slaves. Thus, even after they have received their freedom they are not legally nor properly permitted to receive their father's inheritance.

But, whatever the bishop thought about current law, he did not give an accurate picture of practices prevailing within the former western imperial territory. There is evidence from both Visigothic and Ostrogothic domains that fathers could obtain a royal rescript allowing them to make their illegitimate children heirs. Merovingian documents reveal that in Gaul it was later possible even without official authorization.[90] These dispensations certainly originated in Roman imperial chancelleries in the fifth century if not earlier. It is not clear whether they technically aimed at full legitimization or only enabled the children to inherit: in the less organized state of the society, and after the old system of inheritable names had collapsed, there was probably no real difference any more.

In the east, this distinction was at least theoretically preserved.[91] However, Justinian gradually improved the lot of ille-

[89] LRB 37. 4; NTh 22. 1. int; CT 4. 6. 4 (= LRV 4. 6. 1); *Fragm. Gaudenz.* 9 (LV, p. 470); the *Breviarium* incorporated also CT 4. 6. 8 (= LRV 4. 6. 2), a somewhat puzzling choice as it did not have any real meaning after it had been taken from its context.

[90] Cass. *var.* 7. 40; *Fragm. Gaudenz.* 8 (LV, p. 470); *Cart. Sen.* 42; *Cart. Sen. App.* 1a. Cf. above Hier. *ep.* 69. 5. See also Stafford (1983) 62–9, for the often dubious distinction between legitimacy and illegitimacy in the Frankish royal families.

[91] Cf. e.g. 'ad instar legitimi filii', CI 5. 27. 4 (470); 'legitimi successores', CI 5. 27. 9 (528); Nov. 89. 4, 12 (539).

gitimate children. He enabled them to inherit from their father's property, at first one-half and finally all, and one-sixth even on intestacy, all this in the absence of legitimate children, of course.[92] Moreover, he put *libertae* on a level with *ingenuae* and removed all prohibitions on marriages between upper and lower classes. After this, the law did not prevent anyone from marrying his concubine and retroactively legitimizing his children.[93]

It was naturally still the man who made the decision: his concubine and children could not compel him although they could refuse. It was another innovation of Justinian that the children were entitled to maintenance from their father or his legitimate heirs (Nov. 89. 12. 6, 13, 15). Furthermore, illegitimate children were not automatically outcasts in Byzantine society. They could climb to the highest imperial offices or become so rich that they did not want to be legitimized because their property would then have fallen under *patria potestas*.[94]

3. SEXUAL AFFAIRS OF UNMARRIED WOMEN

The Crime of Stuprum

The two preceding sections, on adultery and concubinage, have shown that Roman women were divided into two classes as far as sexual life and morals were concerned. First, there were those who were expected to bear legitimate children and whose chastity had to be guarded closely. They had the honourable status of a *materfamilias*. Intercourse with virgins, widows, and *divorcées* of this group was punishable as *stuprum*. On the other hand, there were those women who were used when men wanted sexual pleasures but no legitimate offspring. The sexual life of these females was not a moral issue for Roman lawmakers. They could be used as dependent concubines or casual mistresses or they could voluntarily establish a quasi-marital relationship with someone they had chosen.[95]

Although women in the latter class were usually slaves or

[92] CI 5. 27. 8 (528); Nov. 18. 5 (536); 89. praef, 12, 13, 15 (539); Beaucamp (1990) 199–201.   [93] Nov. 78. 2–3 (539), 117. 2, 6 (542); Beaucamp (1990) 280–3, 290–1.
[94] CI 5. 27. 9. pr (528); Nov. 74. praef. 2.
[95] Cf. D. 23. 2. 24, 47, 25. 7. 1, 3, 48. 5. 6. 1, 11, 14. 2, 35; 50. 16. 101. pr; CI 9. 9. 22 (290); CT 9. 7. 1 (326); CI 6. 57. 5 (529); ET 62. Cf. Beaucamp (1990) 22–3. For virgins as *matresfamilias*, see Tert. *virg. vel.* 11. 6, CCL 2. 1221.

freedwomen, the division was not an automatic one. Many freed couples married honourably. On the other hand, even freeborn women could live in concubinage, and a daughter of an otherwise respectable family could lose her reputation. So it was not always easy to tell if someone was a dignified matron or a loose woman. Ulpian presented the problem as follows:

'Matrem familias' accipere debemus eam, quae non inhoneste vixit: matrem enim familias a ceteris feminis mores discernunt atque separant. Proinde nihil intererit, nupta sit an vidua, ingenua sit an libertina: nam neque nuptiae neque natales faciunt matrem familias, sed boni mores. (D. 50. 16. 46. 1)

We ought to regard as *'materfamilias'* a woman who has not lived dishonorably; for her behavior separates and distinguishes a *materfamilias* from other women. It will make no difference whether she is currently married or a widow, freeborn or freed; for neither marriage nor birth make a *materfamilias* but good behavior. (the translation of the Philadelphia Digest slightly modified)

Women with illegitimate children (*spurii*) were certainly very common in Roman society.[96] If a female slave was freed but her partner was not, their subsequent children would be freeborn and illegitimate. There were perhaps humble mothers who had not cared to enter into a formal marriage because there had not been enough financial reasons to do so. There were former concubines who had been sent away with their children when the master had married a sufficiently rich woman. These women were naturally not considered suitable wives for upper-class males but they had done nothing illegal either, so they faced no sanctions, nor were the children threatened in any way. They caused a scandal only if upper-class property was involved, as we saw in the previous chapter.

There was probably no hard-and-fast rule to tell whether the sexual activities of a particular unmarried woman should actually be punished as *stuprum* or be tacitly condoned. It depended not only on her status and previous reputation but also on whether there was anyone who wanted to lay a charge against her. Near

[96] See e.g. D. 31. 77. 2, 38. 2. 18, 38. 8. 2, 8, 38. 10. 7, 38. 17. 1. 2, 2. 1, 40. 2. 20. 3; CI 6. 57. 5 (529). FIRA iii. 4 = P.Mich. iii. 169 (145); 5 = BGU vii. 1690 (131); 6 = SB i. 5217 (148); 28 = P.Harr. i. 68 = P.Diog. 18 (225); Rawson (1989). For inscriptions, see Rawson (1974) 300–4. Cf. also Gardner (1986) 143; and for Egypt, Bagnall and Frier (1994) 155–6.

relatives might wish to defend the family honour or some personal financial interests: aristocracy was in a special position. But
these considerations may not have weighed very heavily among
the urban population at large, where freed and freeborn intermingled. Moreover, if a family member indulged in an extramarital sexual relationship, it was much easier to correct her privately.
Thus prosecution for *stuprum* was hardly a frequent phenomenon
in Roman society.[97]

In any case, *stuprum* was not as grave an offence as adultery.
The punishment is never explicitly given in our extant sources
before Justinian. When it is alluded to, it seems to be connected
with aggravating circumstances. In the *Lex Julia de adulteris* the
penalty may originally have been the same as for adultery. It can
hardly have been more than exile at the end of the third century
and it was evidently not death under Constantine.[98] This applied
mainly to the upper classes, but humble people were probably a
rare sight at a trial for *stuprum* anyway.

In the reign of Valentinian when sheer terror was employed
against senators, a few noble women and men in Rome were
executed for *stuprum*. Ammianus clearly considered this punishment exceptional though he does not say that it was illegal. In the
late fifth-century west the penalty for *stuprum* among the upper
classes was certainly not more than *deportatio*. In Justinian's
Institutes, an upper-class offender only lost half his property,
while lower-class people were corporally punished and exiled.
Women probably received the same treatment.[99] Of course,
imperial law often did not come into play. Ecclesiastical courts
were a feasible alternative. When Gregory the Great discussed a
case in the 590s, he noted that the law prescribed a 'grave penalty',
but he suggested that the culprits should marry and, if the man
did not consent, he should be corporally chastised and shut in a
monastery for a lengthy time.[100]

---

[97] Cf. Gardner (1986) 121–5; CT 3. 16. 2. pr = CI 9. 9. 34, with Beaucamp (1990)
180–1; P.Masp. i. 67097 (567/579), with Beaucamp (1992a) 79–82.

[98] If PS 5. 4. 14 (= D. 47. 11. 1. 2) refers to ordinary *stuprum*, it conflicts with PS
5. 22. 5 (= D. 48. 19. 38. 3); Coll. 5. 2. 2 (= PS 2. 26. 13) obviously concerns a
homosexual relationship. CT 9. 8. 1 (326). See also Beaucamp (1990) 178–80.

[99] Amm. 28. 1. 28, 48–56; NAnth 1. 3 (468); Inst. 4. 18. 4 (not reliable for the
original *Lex Julia*); cf. 6. 57. 5 (529); ET 36–9, 60–2.

[100] Greg. M. *ep.* 3. 40, 42; cf. 4. 6, 4. 9; and Pel. I *ep.* 54. See also Beaucamp
(1992a) 339–42.

The bride's virginity at her first marriage was an important thing in the Mediterranean world. Premarital intercourse was strongly censured not only as a sexual offence but also because it challenged the parents' right to find a suitable partner for their daughter. Since Roman girls married so young, premarital sex must actually have been rare, and almost non-existent in the upper classes. During marriage sexual offences were punished as *adulterium*, so that in practice *stuprum* was more often connected with widows and *divorcées*. Thus, although it was officially condemned, it appears never to have preoccupied the authorities on the same scale as adultery. After all, widows were a class of their own, and the state had little incentive (or capability) to interfere in their life if the circumstances were not particularly shocking. True, consecrated virgins and ascetic widows may later have caused increasing problems.[101]

The pope Callistus (217–22) had, according to his enemy Hippolytus, allowed noble Christian women to cohabit informally with free or slave (Christian) men. The alleged reason for this concession was also surprising: if the ladies had legally married men of lesser birth, they would have lost their own inherited rank. At that time there were not enough noble Christian males to marry, and marriages with pagans were strongly condemned, so there is at least some logic in the story, and besides, Callistus was a former slave himself. But whether the account can really be taken literally remains doubtful. In any case, if senatorial women were concerned, there cannot have been many of them, and later churchmen definitely rejected such liberal attitudes.[102]

Free Women and Alien Slaves

Like concubinage between free men and slave women, a quasi-marital union between free women and slave men was possible. Of course, it was not something to be encouraged, and for respectable women it would have been totally degrading. The

---

[101] Cf. Krause (1994c) 80–93.

[102] Hipp. *phil.* 9. 12. 24–5. Cf. Tert. *uxor.* 2. 8. 3, CCL 1. 392; *Conc. Elib.* 15–17; D. 1. 9. 8; CI 5. 4. 10, 12. 1. 1. The interpretation is controversial at best, see Gaudemet (1955b); Chastagnol (1979) 21–2; Raepsaet-Charlier (1982); Evans Grubbs (1993a) 132–4. For later attitudes, see e.g. Hier. *ep.* 128. 4.

most natural case would have been *contubernium* between a freed-woman and her former partner who remained in slavery.[103]

There was one common type of union between male slaves and freeborn women, namely those which involved imperial slaves. In the principate, slaves belonging to the emperor constituted the administrative staff of the central governement and they continued in important positions after their manumission. Their social status seems to have been above that of humbler freeborn citizens, a fact which enabled them to 'marry' freeborn women. A great number of their attested partners in the inscriptions of the early empire were actually *ingenuae*, perhaps as many as two-thirds.[104] This marriage pattern was potentially dangerous for the government, which relied on house-born slaves (*vernae*) for the labour pool: according to Roman law, children from unequal unions followed their mother's status and thus remained free.

It was perhaps to solve this problem that a decree was passed in the reign of Claudius (the *senatusconsultum Claudianum*) and later modified by Hadrian. A woman who cohabited with an alien slave could now be reduced to slavery. It meant that her children would be slaves, too. This ensured the continuous supply of imperial slaves while the parents could expect manumission in due time. For many humbler freeborn women the prospect seems to have been inviting enough. But the *senatusconsultum* was applied also to women living with private slaves. The slave's master could either permit the woman (and children) to remain free or, after a solemn warning (*denuntiatio*), claim her as his slave.[105]

The *SC Claudianum* was not discussed in the Digest nor in the Justinian Code because it was no longer relevant when the *Corpus Iuris Civilis* was compiled. That is why very little is known about its practical operation in the third century.[106] Unions between freeborn women and slaves belonging to private owners are not easy to find in inscriptions. On the other hand, status confusion

[103] See PS 2. 21A. 11; and cf. Rawson (1966) 74–6; Weaver (1972: 185–8; 1986: 157).
[104] Weaver (1972: 112–36; 1986: 154–8).
[105] Tac. *ann*. 12. 53; GI 1. 84, 91, 160; UE 11. 11; PS 2. 21A, 4. 10. 2; *Fragm. de iure fisci* 12 (FIRA ii. 629); Tert. *uxor*. 2. 8. 1–2, CCL 1. 392. For more details, and inscriptions, see Weaver (1972: 156–78; 1986); and cf. e.g. Gardner (1986) 141–2.
[106] Cf. PS 2. 21A (theoretical scenarios); D. 16. 3. 27 (an imaginary example), 50. 2. 9; CI 5. 18. 3 (error of status), 6. 55. 6, 7. 16. 3; on these, see Evans Grubbs (1993a) 135–7.

was widespread in the lower classes, and unequal unions certainly existed in sufficiently large numbers to be more than a mere curiosity.[107] But we simply do not know whether slaveowners regularly made use of their right to enslave the free female partner. The practice may well have varied in different areas.[108]

In any case, the law remained basically the same until the end of the third century. After that, it began to vacillate. We have the relevant title almost complete as it existed in the Theodosian Code, but it clearly did not include all the pertinent laws in that period. What it had were heavily abridged, to leave us totally in the dark about the circumstances in which a particular edict was meant to be applied. The first laws are from the early part of Constantine's (and Licinius') reign. The point at issue was the woman's enslavement: would she lose her freedom automatically or only after three solemn warnings? The significance of the warnings was that they enabled her to evade enslavement if she could persuade the slave's master not to use his option. In the 320s there were three different rules, depending on who owned the slave. Female partners of municipal slaves would automatically become slaves themselves, while women married to private slaves would be enslaved only after due warning. On the contrary, the partner of an imperial slave would always remain free although her children would be born to the status of freedpeople. This was a Constantinian innovation. It clearly ran counter to fiscal interests, although imperial slaves no longer occupied influential positions in the administration.[109]

In 331 Constantine changed his mind and established that no warnings were needed to enslave the woman. He may have meant both private and public slaves although this can only be conjectured from later laws. Julian again revoked this and reintroduced the warnings, which were an essential part of the original *SC Claudianum*. However, this expressly applied only to private slaves. After Julian's death Valentinian enacted in a short time no fewer than three laws on the question but the sole fact which can be deduced from them is that warnings were again being used to

[107] See Rawson (1966) 76–7; Weaver (1972) 187–93; Treggiari (1981*b*); and esp. Evans Grubbs (1993*a*) 134–40.

[108] For the scant evidence from Egypt, see Taubenschlag (1955) 72–3, 91–2.

[109] CT 4. 12. 1–3; PS 2. 21A. 14. On this whole question see Evans Grubbs (1993a: 140–2; 1995: 263–72. Cf. Jones (1964) 564–6.

prevent free women from cohabiting with imperial slaves. By the
end of the century, after a hundred years' wavering back and
forth, the law seems to have returned to where it started, at least
in the eastern empire.[110] It is very difficult to make any sense out
of this or to discern motives behind individual enactments. They
recall the vicissitudes of the legislation on illegitimate children,
discussed in the preceding section.

It was not only the woman's status but that of her children, too,
which was at stake. Servile offspring were valuable to the owner,
be it imperial fisc or a private person. Whether moral considerations actually weighed heavily, as the wording of some laws would
suggest, remains open. According to the masculine way of thinking, cohabitation with slaves resulted from women's concupis-
cence (*libido* and *cupiditas*). This tragicomic explanation
notwithstanding, most unions were in reality lasting, quasi-marital relationships, with children.

It is natural that this legislation created confusion among the
simple people whom it concerned. Bishop Augustine himself had
to consult a legal expert to learn the standpoint of imperial law.[111]
The situation was further complicated when other nominally free
but practically dependent classes (like *coloni*) emerged between
the old categories of free people and slaves. The imperial legislation tried to cover all the possible combinations which were
bound to come into being when humble folk intermixed. It
attempted to ensure that people did not flee their hereditary
occupations or defraud their patrons of the valuable offspring.[112] The western government further added to the confusion by introducing exceptional rules for women of decurionate
origins.[113]

In these circumstances, the old *senatusconsultum Claudianum*
was evidently not easy to apply. It was systematically excluded
from the *Breviarium* although it appears in some later additions.[114]

[110] CT 4. 12. 4–7, 10. 20. 3, 10; Cons. 9. 7. See also Beaucamp (1990) 185–91. For
the Syro-Roman Law Book L 48; P 59; R 11. 75, see Selb (1964) 178 n. 50.
[111] Aug. *ep.* *24. 1, CSEL 88. 126.
[112] CT 5. 18. 1, 10. 19. 15, 10. 20. 3, 5, 10, 15, 17; 12. 19. 1, 14. 7. 1; CI 10. 32. 29, 11.
48. 13, 21, 11. 68. 4, 11. 69. 1; NVal 31. 5–6; ET 64–7. See also Sidon. *ep.* 5. 19; Pel. I
ep. 64. 3–6.
[113] CT 12. 1. 178–9 (415 west); NMaj 7. 5 (458); Evans Grubbs (1993a) 150.
[114] Omitted are CT 4. 12 and PS 2. 21A; the relevant passages of GI were not
included in GE. However, the laws of CT 4. 12 (except 4. 12. 4, which was not

Traces of it can also be seen in the wording of some Visigothic laws. The rule which seems to have replaced it in late western legal thinking was a very simple one: a free man or woman who cohabited with an unfree was permanently tied to the union, and their children always followed the status of the more lowly parent.[115] Germanic laws contained similar provisions with some variation, most codes punishing the woman by enslavement, some also permitting her killing.[116] In practice, however, the ancient Roman custom survived. A free woman in Merovingian Gaul who wanted to marry a slave could write a contract with his master, to secure freedom for herself and her children.[117] It is tempting to assume that such contracts dated back to Roman times and continued the tradition of the *SC Claudianum*, which enabled the woman to remain free if the slaveowner agreed to the union.

In the east, it was not until Justinian that the *SC Claudianum* was abolished. He attempted to forbid such unions altogether, but only the slave man was threatened with castigation. The law does not specify whether the woman should go free or be accused of *stuprum*. This is conceivable for it depended on her status. Although Justinian mentioned the possibility that the woman might have relatives decorated with honours he probably meant decurions at most, who at this time could be rather humble sorts of people.[118] Most free women who contemplated a relationship with an alien slave were so poor that their sexual conduct was not a moral issue.

considered relevant because it ran counter to the rest) received a Visigothic interpretation and are found in a manuscript which contains laws missing from the *Breviarium*, see Mommsen, *Prolegom.* CT p. lxxxvi–vii (his remark on CT 4. 12. 5 is obviously a mistake). See also *App. LRV* 1. 18 (FIRA ii. 672).

[115] LRB 37. 5–6; see also the addition in some manuscripts to CT 4. 8. 7. int; Isid. *orig.* 9. 5. 18; cf. NVal 31. 5–6; *Conc. inc. loci (post* 614) 14, CCL 148A. 288; and *Form. Marc.* 2. 29; etc. below.

[116] LV.Ant 3. 2. 3–4; LV 3. 2. 7, 4. 5. 7, 9. 1. 16; LB 35. 2–3; PLS 13. 8, 25. 4; LRib 61. 9–18; ER 193, 217, 221; LL 24; see Zeumer (1898) i. 455–7, iii. 592–4; Nehlsen (1972) 242–5, 306–12, 387–9; Wemple (1981) 36.

[117] *Form. Andec.* 59; *F.Marc.* 2. 29; *Cart. Sen.* 6; *F.Bign.* 11; *F.Sal.Merk.* 31; *F.Sal.Lind.* 20; cf. also LV.Ant 3. 2. 4; and see Wemple (1981) 71–3.

[118] CI 7. 24. 1; Inst. 3. 12. 1; cf. also CT 12. 1. 178–9; NMaj 7. 5. Beaucamp (1990) 191–5. Pel. I *ep.* 45 (559) seems to present a free daughter of an ecclesiastical slave, but the exact situation is unclear.

Women and their Own Slaves

It was not impossible that a woman of high social standing felt sexual desire or perhaps lasting, deep affection towards a man of servile birth. However, it would hardly have happened with a slave owned by someone else: opportunities were limited, she risked enslavement by the *SC Claudianum*, and even men were after all discouraged from cohabiting with other people's property. But while men could freely have affairs with their own servants, or manumit and marry them, the situation of women was not symmetrical. If an upper-class male had sex with his dependants, his authority was only enhanced. A woman in a similar situation was felt to lose her superiority: that idea is certainly very deeply embedded in human consciousness.

A female slaveowner could naturally free the man who had earned her love, but their problems were not over yet. First, female like male members of senatorial families were allowed to marry only freeborn people. This did not prevent jurists from speculating about unions between senatorial women and *liberti*, but we may assume that they were rare in any case.[119] Secondly, all female patronesses were forbidden to marry their own freedmen. It would have compromised their reputation unless they were very humble indeed, in which case their reputation did not concern anyone.[120] Here was a particularly clear example of the sexual asymmetry just discussed.

Thus a widowed and reputable matron could not legally contract a marriage with her former slave. There were only two possibilities: she could cohabit with him secretly, or try to conceal his servile origins. The latter alternative may have been realistic only in favourable circumstances. One such attempt is described in the Justinian Code. In this case the false claim of free birth was exposed after the woman's death by her daughter.[121]

The first alternative was certainly more common and not

---

[119] D. 1. 9. 9, 23. 1. 16, 23. 2. 16, 32, 44; 24. 1. 3. 1. The only known case is the story in SHA *Verus* 9. 3; see Evans Grubbs (1993*a*) 133–4; Flavia Speranda in ILCV 161 was hardly senatorial, nor need she have been Christian, see ICUR NS iii. 7599.

[120] CI 5. 4. 3 (196); D. 23. 2. 13, 62. 1, 40. 2. 14; PS 2. 19. 9; Sen. *contr.* 7. 6, with Evans Grubbs (1993*a*) 125–30. Marriages (or quasi-marriages) between *patronae* and *liberti* are sometimes attested in inscriptions, see e.g. CIL v. 6039, vi. 14014, 14462, 15106 (*ingenua*), xii. 682a, etc. Cf. Weaver (1972) 180–1, 185, 189; Evans Grubbs (1993*a*) 130–1, with further inscriptions.

[121] CI 7. 20. 1 (290), with Evans Grubbs (1993*a*) 137–9.

insuperably difficult to conceal. It was frequently suspected that unmarried women had secret affairs with their male servants but these insinuations were obviously impossible to prove.[122] Nobody could oversee a widow in her own house, except her slaves. If they remained faithful she had little to fear. True, this dependence may have undermined her domestic authority though our male sources hardly ever discuss such problems.[123] Therefore, although the Romans abhorred the idea of slave–mistress relationships and although they were punishable as *stuprum*, if not worse, there was often very little they could do about it.[124]

Constantine attacked the practice in a somewhat mysterious law in 326:

Si qua cum servo occulte rem habere detegitur, capitali sententia subiugetur tradendo ignibus verberone . . . Ante legem nupta tali consortio segregetur, non solum domo, verum etiam provinciae communione privata, amati abscessum defleat relegati. Filii etiam, quos ex hac coniunctione habuerit, exuti omnibus dignitatis insignibus in nuda maneant libertate, neque per se neque per interpositam personam quolibet titulo voluntatis accepturi aliquid ex facultatibus mulieris. (CT 9. 9. 1)

If any woman is revealed to have dealings with [her] slave in secret, she shall undergo a capital penalty, and the worthless scoundrel shall be handed over to the flames. . . . A woman married before this law shall be separated from this union and deprived not only of her home, but even of the community of her province, and shall lament the absence of her exiled beloved. The children also, whom she had from this union, stripped of all marks of rank, shall remain in bare freedom, nor will they receive anything from the woman's property, either through themselves or through an intermediary under any title of will. (tr. Evans Grubbs (1993*a*), 143)

These excerpts show the dualistic nature of the text. A secret affair with a slave is punished by death, and the man is to be

---

[122] Tert. *uxor.* 2. 8. 4, CCL 1. 392; Hier. *ep.* 79. 8; 128. 4. Affairs of married women were also hinted at: they were easier to detect, Petron. 45, 69, 75; Mart. 6. 39, 12. 58; Juv. 6. 279; D. 1. 12. 1. 5, 28. 5. 49. 2, 48. 2. 5, 48. 5. 34; Aug. *serm.* 9. 4, CCL 41. 115; etc.

[123] Cf. Cic. *Cael.* 23. 57; Hier. *ep.* 79. 8; Amm. 28. 1. 49; CT 9. 9. 1.

[124] CI 7. 20. 1 (290) is the only extant case in legal sources before Constantine. The lack of evidence has led some scholars to believe that slave–mistress relationships were not punished (or even punishable) in the principate, e.g. Crook (1967*a*) 7; Karabelias (1988) 191. See, however, Philostr. *vit. soph.* 610 (= 2. 25. 2). On abhorrence, see e.g. Muson. 12; Ps.Aug. *quaest. de utr. test.* 115. 74, CSEL 50. 344.

burnt. But a union contracted before the law and blessed with children is punished in a surprisingly mild way, only by relegation. Exile is a very strange punishment for a slave, hardly a punishment at all. Something is certainly missing from the text that we have, at least the preamble which presented the law's original context and purpose. It seems that the main part of the law, starting from '*Ante legem nupta*', does not refer to a clandestine affair but to a more permanent union, perhaps a marriage between a patroness and her former slave, contracted in good faith in ignorance of the ban on such alliances.[125]

It is no wonder that ordinary citizens did not know that women were forbidden to marry their own freedmen. In the late fifth century the western emperor Anthemius was equally unaware of past legislation. He confirmed all such marriages if already contracted and penalized them only thenceforth. Both the emperor and the woman who had appealed to him knew Constantine's law from the Theodosian Code. However, they thought that it did not apply to slaves who had been freed; of earlier legislation they knew apparently nothing. This illustrates well the problems of determining what was considered valid Roman law at any particular time.[126]

Slave–mistress relationships were later consistently condemned all over the Mediterranean area. Laws banning them were recorded in both western and eastern collections: affairs with slaves were punished by death, marriages with freedmen somewhat more lightly.[127] They are further reflected in a Visigothic and perhaps also in a Merovingian law. Even if the wording of these enactments was influenced by Roman models, their content was hardly anything new for the Germanic population.[128] To condone sex between a respectable woman and one of her dependants would have required a much more liberal attitude than any ancient society can be expected to have possessed.

---

[125] Cf. D. 48. 2. 12. 4; see also Evans Grubbs (1993*a*) 142–7.

[126] NAnth 1 (468); Evans Grubbs (1993*a*) 151–2.

[127] In the east CI 5. 4. 3 and 9. 11. 1 = CT 9. 9. 1; in the west CT 9. 9. 1 and PS 2. 19. 9 + int were included in the *Breviarium*, and NAnth 1 was added in many later manuscripts; see also ET 61.

[128] LV.Ant 3. 2. 2; LV 5. 7. 17; PLS 98 (69); cf. Zeumer (1898) iii. 589–92; Nehlsen (1972) 241–2, 308–11.

4. SUMMARY AND CONCLUSIONS

The Christian church in late antiquity had adopted a very hostile attitude towards sex in general and extramarital sex in particular. It did all it could to replace old values with new ones. But in spite of these aspirations, Roman sexual behaviour hardly changed over the course of time. Extramarital sex by women had always been punishable, at least in theory. Extramarital affairs of men never became an offence in public opinion, if they did not have sex with married women. Statutory penalties for adultery became later more severe, as did all penalties in Roman criminal law, but they were unevenly applied to upper and lower classes. Moreover, many, if not most, cases were never taken to court.

Premarital sex by women was probably rare in the Roman empire, at least in those areas where girls married soon after puberty. Postmarital sex by widows was illegal, but often impossible to detect. In practice, they could have affairs even with their own slaves, although by the double standard of a slave-holding society this was one of the worst things that could happen. It can be suspected that widows had much more freedom in their sexual life than our legal sources indicate. In any case, these laws were applied only to upper-class women. If a woman was sufficiently humble, the state did not show any interest in her morals.

Roman legislation expected chaste behaviour only from those women who were marriageable by upper-class standards because these women were used to produce legitimate descendants. Other females (prostitutes, slaves, and lowborn concubines) were needed for sexual satisfaction when males wanted to shirk responsibility for their partner and particularly to avoid begetting rightful heirs. The law reflected this distinction. It was neither illegal nor immoral to have concubines. The only scandalous thing was when some men did not want to take a wife from their own class at all, and thus failed to uphold the inherited social structure. These 'depraved' people were strongly condemned and were forbidden to transmit the family property to their genuine but lowborn descendants.

Roman society had always had rigid class distinctions: no one needed to tell Cicero that he could not legitimize the children which he might have with his female slaves. But social mobility increased in late antiquity, and old values were no longer taken

needs saying that Roman society was male-oriented and male-dominated. In the following we shall explore the role of women outside their family. How was the division of sexes expressed in Roman law? What were women forbidden to do, and what was thought proper behaviour for them?

1. RESTRAINTS AND PRIVILEGES

Legal Restrictions

We have few direct sources to tell what ordinary lay people in late antiquity thought about equality between the sexes. Only the church fathers have left a written record of their views. As the discussion of sexual morals has shown, it is by no means clear that they are representative of general opinion. However, in this case it seems that, apart from their theological emphasis and biblical arguments, Christian writers did not propagate any radical views. With natural personal variation, their attitudes concurred with those of earlier authors and with the standpoint of Roman law.

According to this inherited pattern of thought, women were a weaker form of the human race, with lesser talents and graver faults, and in practice without equal rights. Many leading Christian authorities concluded that in theory and originally both sexes were equal and capable of the same virtue. On the other hand, they could not get away from the idea that women were still somehow inferior, representing carnality, irrationality, and moral weakness. Augustine admitted that they had 'in their mind an equal nature of reasonable understanding', but he still called the male sex '*virilis sexus utique potior*' and '*sexus honorabilior*', while the females were '*imbecillior sexus*'.[3]

Of all Christian writers, Jerome perhaps best illustrates these conflicting tendencies. His works are full of statements which

---

[3] Aug. *conf.* 13. 32. 47, CCL 27. 270; *nupt. et concup.* 1. 11. 12, CSEL 42. 225; *divers. quaest.* 11, CCL 44A. 18; *serm.* 132. 2, PL 38. 735; further e.g. *c. Jul.* 6. 26, PL 45. 1566; Ps.Aug. *quaest.* 45. 3, CSEL 50. 83; Ambrosiast. *in Eph.* 5. 33, CSEL 81. 3. 119; Ps.Greg. Nyss. *in Gen.* 1. 26 or. 1, PG 44. 276; Theodoret. *cur. aff.* 5. 56–7, SC 57. 244; Pallad. *hist. laus.* 41. 1; Caes. Arel. *serm.* 94. 2, 120. 1, CCL 103. 387, 501; Ven. Fort. *vita Radeg.* 1. See Thraede (1972: 238–47, 254–8; 1990); for Chrysostom, Clark (1977*b*); for Augustine, Bavel (1989); and for all the eastern writers, Beaucamp (1992*a*) 280–3.

would be called misogynous today although they were only part
of the commonly accepted way of thinking in the Graeco-Roman
world. On the other hand, Jerome had a close personal relationship with several women. Their intellectual equality with men
was a practical fact which Jerome openly admitted and which was
reflected in his theoretical writing as well. It is no wonder that
these different elements produced very inconsistent attitudes
towards women in his works. He did not need to notice it
himself. For him it was not a major issue, and he probably never
considered this part of his production as a unity.[4]

It is important to note that there was nothing new in these
doubts about female mental and moral ability. Writers in the early
empire expressed themselves in very much the same terms.[5]
Maybe they were less inclined to present theoretical reasoning
and, of course, they did not seek their arguments in the Bible. It
was certainly not an exclusively male view; women, too, could
allude to the prevailing opinion. In the papyri they often pleaded
feminine weakness when they appealed to a magistrate for help or
explained why they were not able to perform a particular task. It
was a typical example of *captatio benevolentiae*, with no defined
legal import.[6]

A rational mind, like Gaius, was inclined to question this
argument. In his well-known statement he claimed that the
whole idea of women's mental weakness was 'specious rather
than true' (GI 1. 190, cited above, Ch. 4, Sect. 1). But his view
was not shared by all juridically trained men. Feminine *ignorantia*, *levitas*, *imbecillitas*, and especially *infirmitas* were frequently
mentioned in legal texts in the principate and later.[7] Although in
the fifth century *fragilitas* replaced *infirmitas* both in eastern and
western legal sources, the new term certainly did not signify any

[4] e.g. Hier. *ep.* 39. 1, 53. 7, 65. 1, 108. 26, 127. 5–7, 130. 17; *in eccles.* 7. 26, 27, CCL
72. 311; *in Is.* 15. 56. 6, 7, CCL 73A. 634; *in Tit.* 2. 3–5, PL 26. 615; see further Arjava
(1989); Clark (1979; 1989).
[5] Cf. e.g. Cic. *Mur.* 12. 27; Val. Max. 9. 1. 3; Sen. *const.* 1. 1; *ira* 2. 30. 1; Tac. *ann.*
3. 33–4; Thraede (1972) 215–18; Dixon (1984) 356–8.
[6] e.g. P.Oxy. xxxiv. 2713 (c.297); CPR vii. 15 (c.330?); MChr 95 = P.Lond. iii. 971
(4th c.). There are no cases after the late 4th c.; it might be due to the scarcity of
available documents; see Anagnostou-Cañas (1984) 357–9; Beaucamp (1992a) 45–9,
and cf. 280.
[7] e.g. GI 1. 144; UE 11. 1; D. 16. 1. 2, 49. 14. 18. pr; CI 4. 29. 5, 5. 35. 1 (both 224);
CT 9. 24. 1. pr (320). See Beaucamp (1976: 486ff.; 1990: 11–16), showing that such
passages cannot all have been interpolated; and cf. also Marshall (1989) 51–4.

change of attitude. Later non-legal writers used both words indiscriminately.[8]

In all, the attitude of Roman jurists towards women was somewhat ambivalent. Ulpian casually noted an established fact: '*maior dignitas est in sexu virili*' (D. 1. 9. 1; 'greater dignity inheres in the male sex'). And Papinian openly admitted:

In multis iuris nostri articulis deterior est condicio feminarum quam masculorum. (D. 1. 5. 9)

There are many points in our law in which the condition of females is inferior to that of males.

We do not know the context of Papinian's statement and thus cannot identify exactly what he meant. The general tenor of Roman law is nevertheless clear. As long as women looked after their own affairs, they were treated almost as equals, but they were not expected to act on other people's behalf or assume a more active public role. As a matter of course, civic offices remained always outside their reach:

Feminae ab omnibus officiis civilibus vel publicis remotae sunt et ideo nec iudices esse possunt nec magistratum gerere nec postulare nec pro alio intervenire nec procuratores existere. (Ulp. D. 50. 17. 2)[9]

Women are debarred from all civil and public functions and therefore cannot be judges or hold a magistracy or bring a lawsuit or intervene on behalf of anyone else or act as procurators.

This attitude is not historically surprising as such. Roman lawyers rarely tried to explain the restrictions. In the early third century, Paul reasoned that women were not by nature incapable of acting as judges: they did not lack sufficient judgement (*iudicium*), like insane or young persons. But it had nevertheless been commonly accepted that women, like slaves, did not hold public offices.[10] Three centuries later Justinian was still unable to find convincing justification for the ban:

---

[8] *Infirmitas* still in CT 16. 2. 28 (390 west), 12. 1. 137. 1 (393 east), 9. 14. 3 (397 east); and Nov. 97. 3 (539); see also *Conc. Carth.* (424/5), CCL 149. 171. *Fragilitas* in CT 4. 14. 1. 2 (424 east), 2. 16. 3. int, 3. 5. 3. int; and frequently in Justinian's laws. Jerome already favoured *fragilitas*, *ep.* 65. 1, 77. 9, 128. 3, etc.; Arjava (1989) 8–9. See also Beaucamp (1976) 505, with a collection of literary evidence; and for the 6th c., Caes. Arel. *serm.* 43. 1, CCL 103. 190; Leander *reg.* praef. PL 72. 880.

[9] On the word '*postulare*', see further below.

[10] D. 5. 1. 12. 2; see also 16. 1. 1. 1, 2. 1; cf. Dixon (1984) 356–71, esp. 370; and Gardner (1993) 85–9.

Sancimus mulieres suae pudicitiae memores et operum, quae eis natura permisit et a quibus eas iussit abstinere, licet summae atque optimae opinionis constitutae arbitrium in se susceperint vel, si fuerint patronae, inter libertos suam interposuerint audientiam, ab omni iudiciali agmine separari. (CI 2. 55. 6)

We order that women should keep in mind their bashfulness and the tasks which nature has permitted them to do and from which it has enjoined them to abstain. Although they had shown the best conceivable judgement and had assumed the role of an arbitrator or, if they are patronesses, had conducted a hearing among their freedmen, they should be completely excluded from the number of judges [or: from any judicial activity].

We shall return both to women's public functions and to their proper behaviour later.

There was thus a general principle that women should not intervene in other people's affairs. From that idea followed a number of rules, among them the ban on being a guardian, which was discussed earlier in connection with mothers and children. Furthermore, women were forbidden to represent others in court. This rule dated back to the republic, and in our period it was firmly entrenched in Roman law. Its essentials appear in legal sources repeatedly from the third to the sixth century, both in the east and in the west, and it seems to have been observed in practice, at least in Egypt.[11]

Women could usually not bring criminal charges either, except when they had a clear personal interest in the case. This rule was frequently stated throughout the third century, and in 322 Constantine stressed it again. In the sixth century earlier statutes were incorporated both in Justinian's *Corpus* and in the *Breviarium*. There is no serious reason to doubt that the ban remained in force at all times, in spite of changes in the criminal procedure. Of course, it may have been difficult to enforce in absolute form. Constantine's law itself seems to suggest that.[12]

Another edict of Constantine presents many more difficulties.

[11] D. 3. 1. 1. 5, 3. 3. 41, 54, 37. 1. 7. pr, 40. 12. 3. 2; CI 2. 12. 4 (207), 2. 12. 18 (294); PS 1. 2. 2 + int; CT 2. 12. 5 (393 east) + int, 9. 1. 3. int; LRB 11. 2; Inst. 4. 13. 11. For the alleged origins of this ban, see below, Ch. 7, Sect. 2; and for late Roman Egypt, Beaucamp (1992a) 21–8.

[12] For the 3rd c., see D. 26. 10. 1. 7, 43. 29. 3. 11, 47. 10. 2, 47. 23. 6, 48. 2. 1, 2, 8, 13; 48. 4. 8, 48. 12. 3. 1, 48. 16. 1. 10, 4, 49. 14. 16, 18. pr; CI 9. 1. 4, 5, 9, 12; 9. 20. 5, 9. 22. 19, 9. 45. 5, 9. 46. 2. Constantine's law: CT 9. 1. 3. Beaucamp (1990) 41–5.

Its subject was abduction marriage, but it contained the following curious remark:

. . . puellae . . . quam propter vitium levitatis et sexus mobilitatem atque consili a postulationibus et testimoniis omnibusque rebus iudiciariis antiqui penitus arcuerunt.[13]

. . . it was because of the fault of frivolity and the inconstancy of her sex and judgment that a girl was altogether excluded by the ancients from conducting suits in court and from giving testimony and from all matters pertaining to courts.

This seems to be an exaggeration. Although the word 'antiqui' is not too precise, it must refer to the classical Roman jurisprudence. As we just noted, women had not been forbidden to act in court except on behalf of other people. Furthermore, they had definitely been able to give evidence in court. It is true that they could not witness testaments, but Ulpian and Paul considered that an exception.[14]

Much depends on the interpretation of the word '*postulatio*'. It is difficult to translate accurately with one word. In classical law it seems to have meant about the same as 'to appear personally before a judicial magistrate (like the praetor) with a claim or rejoinder'. In the time of the formulary procedure, until the third century, this was an essential part of any litigation. If someone was not allowed or willing to do it personally he had to use an advocate.[15] Ulpian himself says once that women could not *postulare*. He cannot be taken literally because elsewhere he states quite clearly that the ban meant only *postulare pro aliis*.[16]

When the formulary process was gradually replaced by magisterial *cognitio*, the technical meaning of *postulatio* must have changed, too. It certainly had some role in later times both in civil and in criminal cases. But it is worth noting that both in the

[13] CT 9. 24. 1 (320), *De raptu virginum vel viduarum*; on this law generally, see Evans Grubbs (1989).
[14] D. 22. 5. 4, 18, 28. 1. 20. 6; UE 20. 7; on women witnesses in the courts of the early principate, see Marshall (1989) 51, with references. But cf. also Gell. 7. 7; Plut. *Popl.* 8.
[15] On the definition of *postulare* in classical law, D. 3. 1. 1; cf. also 39. 5. 31. 4, 48. 5. 32, 40. 8. See F. Leifer, 'Postulatio', *RE* 22. 1 (1953), 874–89; Kaser (1966) 150–1, 171–2.
[16] D. 50. 17. 2, cited above; *contra* D. 3. 1. 1. 5, and other passages mentioned above. Perhaps 50. 17. 2 has inadvertently been corrupted and the words *pro alio* should be placed before *postulare*.

Justinian and in the Theodosian Code the title '*De postulando*' dealt only with the activity of advocates (*advocatus, patronus, causidicus*). Thus the word seems to have become connected especially with representing others in court, that is: *postulare pro aliis.*[17] This possibly helps to explain the strange wording of CT 9. 24. 1. However, it may be easier to assume that whoever drafted the law (and it was hardly Constantine himself) was not very well versed in classical jurisprudence. He simply wanted to say to his contemporaries that women should have nothing to do with judiciary matters.

That raises the question whether he knew the law of his own time better. It is impossible to believe that any Roman statute at any time would have barred women generally from all legal action. The above mentioned CT 9. 1. 3 only two years later completely refutes this possibility.[18] Women were not forbidden to plead their case in person either. The Romans admittedly had a deep-rooted aversion to women in court sessions and probably always preferred male representatives. It is possible that our amateurish legislator was here influenced by popular legal usage. But in that case the custom varied because both the papyri and another law of Constantine himself unambiguously show women appearing personally before the court.[19] The only thing which we can say for certain is that the man behind CT 9. 24. 1 had a very low opinion of women.

CT 9. 24. 1. pr also claimed that women had not been accepted as witnesses. In view of the foregoing this report does not in itself inspire particular confidence. As we already noted, it was not true of classical law. In the fourth and fifth centuries the situation is less clear. There are no relevant passages in legal sources. Thus it is all the more interesting to find what the Christian 'Ambrosiaster' has to say about this matter. He argues that a woman cannot be the image of God because she has been subjected to man:

. . . *nec docere enim potest nec testis esse neque fidem dicere nec iudicare.* (Ps.Aug. *quaest.* 45. 3, CSEL 50. 83)

[17] CI 2. 6; CT 2. 10; see Beaucamp (1990) 35–40, esp. n. 44.
[18] See also e.g. Symm. *ep.* 4. 68, 4. 71; *rel.* 19, 39; Greg. M. *ep.* 3. 57, 9. 87; and next note.
[19] CT 8. 15. 1; Ambr. *in psalm. 118 serm.* 16. 7. 2, CSEL 62. 355; Beaucamp (1992a) 22–3; see further below, on women's seclusion and proper behaviour.

. . . for she cannot teach nor be a witness nor stand surety nor act as a judge.

We have seen in previous chapters that Ambrosiaster often commented on law and was obviously familiar with it. Moreover, he was right that a woman could not stand surety or act as a judge. We cannot reject his testimony out of hand. It is possible that in the fourth and fifth centuries women were despised as witnesses, perhaps in documents if not generally in court. It was natural to think that one could avoid 'untrustworthy' witnesses when one was planning to draw up a deed, whereas if an investigation was carried out all available evidence had to be used. Later Visigothic laws accepted female testimony in court without problems (LV 2. 4. 12–13). In the Digest Justinian adopted the classical rule that female witnesses were excluded only from wills. After Justinian, Byzantine commentaries reveal that the matter was still under dispute: women could be accepted in courts but not in contracts.[20]

The papyri suggest a similar custom. They show several women giving evidence in Egyptian courts while in the hundreds of existing contracts there is not a single female witness.[21] In late Italian papyri, thirty-five witnesses appear in wills and eighty-three in other documents, none of them a woman. A few Merovingian charters display an occasional female attestant, but hundreds of others do not.[22] It seems that, whether or not women in theory could witness documents in Gothic and Byzantine Italy and in Merovingian Gaul, it was in practice exceptional.

Protection of Women

In the reign of Claudius or Nero, the senate passed a decree which stated that women could not assume obligations on behalf of anyone else. In other words, they were not allowed to be guarantors or pledge their property on alien debts. This *senatus-*

---

[20] D. 22. 5. 18, 28. 1. 20. 6; *Basilica* 21. 1. 17 *sch.* (Scheltema B iv. 1242); Beaucamp (1990) 45, esp. n. 83 (though she does not discuss Ambrosiaster).

[21] P.Vidob.Tandem 8 (3rd/4th c.); P.Lips. 47 (332); PSI vii. 790 (6th c.); Beaucamp (1992a) 28–31. Similarly for the hellenistic period, Préaux (1959) 146.

[22] Pard. 241? (627), 490 (714), 516 (721); Pard. Add. 10 (699, the mother of the principals). However, in the latter half of the 8th c. the documents from Fulda (many of them drawn up in Mainz) show a fair number of female witnesses; they disappear soon after 800. I owe this information to Katrinette Bodarwé.

consultum Velleianum had been preceded by imperial edicts which prevented wives from undertaking an obligation (*'intercedere'*) on behalf of their husbands. The *senatusconsultum* itself did not differentiate between husbands and other people, but there are a number of rescripts from the third century which show that in actuality most problems arose from sureties within the family. We can easily believe that the ban was first and foremost motivated by the Roman fathers' genuine desire to protect their family property against their sons-in-law. The extension of the rule to other cases was a secondary effect. Of course, it was supported by the general sentiment that women should just mind their own business.[23]

Hasty promises of surety can certainly be dangerous, for both males and females. It is not surprising to find that Roman jurists regarded the *SC Velleianum* as a clearly positive measure which helped women (D. 16. 1). In all actual cases which appear in the Justinian Code (CI 4. 29) women themselves appealed to the decree. They had assumed an obligation which they wanted to get rid of. Sometimes they were not relieved of the obligation because they had acted with intent to defraud from the very beginning:

Infirmitas enim feminarum, non calliditas auxilium demeruit. (Ulp. D. 16. 1. 2. 3; cf. 50. 17. 110. 4)

For it was the vulnerability of women, not their cunning that deserved assistance.

It would have been impossible to use the decree against women. There was no penalty. If the female guarantor wanted to fulfil the obligation, none could prevent her; women were not forbidden from alienating their property. Of course, a payment for the husband would have constituted an invalid gift.[24] If the senate had wanted to curb women's economic activity, it would have been much more effective to forbid them to take on obligations on their own behalf. On the contrary, a woman could appeal to the *senatusconsultum* only if the creditor had clearly known that she was giving surety for someone else because no one would

[23] D. 16. 1. 2; CI 4. 29; CI 8. 27. 11; Nov. 134. 8; cf. Gardner (1986: 75–6; 1993: 97–100); Crook (1986*b*) 90–1.

[24] D. 16. 1. 4, 16. 1. 31, 32. 4; CI 4. 29. 9 (239); P.Col. 123. 18–20 with comm. pp. 63–5; Gaudemet (1959) 212–13. For gifts between spouses, see above, Ch. 4, Sect. 3.

otherwise have ventured to make normal contracts with women, according to Paul.[25]

The *SC Velleianum* does not figure in the extant parts of the Theodosian Code. However, the ban is mentioned in a late fifth-century *interpretatio* and in the *Edictum Theoderici*. Moreover, the relevant passages of Paul's Sentences with their *interpretationes* were included in the *Breviarium*. All these, together with the casual mention by Ambrosiaster, suggest that the decree had not fallen into desuetude during late antiquity. Later, it is difficult to believe that such legal niceties had much value in the western kingdoms. In the east the *SC Velleianum* appears in legal sources in the sixth century. Justinian accepted female *intercessio* as binding in certain cases but explicitly disapproved of it on behalf of husbands. How far the rules really affected the life of ordinary citizens is less clear. Among guarantors in Byzantine papyri males by far outnumber females: there are only about a dozen women, many of them widowed mothers. But the problem of the *senatusconsultum* never appears.[26]

Around the year 600 Sisivera, the Gothic freedwoman of another Gothic woman, donated a piece of land to the church of Ravenna. In the deed of gift she affirmed that she had transferred the ownership deliberately and of her own will, so that none could claim it back:

> *excluso erga me omnium legum beneficia, quae de revocandis donationibus et de sexu femineo Belliianus senatusconsultus mulieribus subvenire adsolet.* (P.Tjäder i. 20)

I waive all the legal privileges which the *SC Belliianus* grants to help women, concerning the revocation of gifts and the female sex.

There is no doubt that the scribe meant the *SC Velleianum* because at that time the letters B and V were easily confused. Of course, the decree had originally nothing to do with donations or their revocation, nor was it interpreted so in Justinian's law, which should have been in force in Byzantine Ravenna.

---

[25] D. 16. 1. 11; Medicus (1957) 79–82; cf. also Beaucamp (1990) 54–71.

[26] CT 2. 16. 3. int; ET 133; PS 2. 11. 1–2; Ps.Aug. *quaest.* 45. 3, CSEL 50. 83 (cited above). In the east, CI 4. 29. 21–5, 5. 35. 3; the Syro-Roman Law Book, L 55–6, 67; Selb (1964) 180–3. On husbands, Nov. 134. 8. See Medicus (1957) 66–77, 82–3; Kaser (1975) 461–2; Beaucamp (1990) 71–8. On the papyri, Beaucamp (1992a) 36–45; e.g. SP xx. 135 + SB viii. 9770 (511); SP xx. 139 (531); P.Lond. v. 1711. 77 = FIRA iii. 18 (566/573).

We might regard this as only an occasional lapse if there were not two other Italian papyri which show similar ideas.[27] Neither of them explicitly refers to the *SC Velleianum* but the other mentions a *senatusconsultum*. They both display the notion that women had a right to revoke their donations. Thus it seems that Italian scribes in the Byzantine and Langobardic period often inserted such a clause into documents where women made gifts. In those later times the phrases were taken rather mechanically from pattern books. Mistakes reveal that the scribes did not understand them very well, but the clauses themselves cannot be ascribed to mere notarial incompetence. A sales contract from seventh-century Egypt records a similar locution. The female sellers 'waive all the help of laws' and, after a gap, refer to a 'novel law' and to an '*exceptio intercessionis*'. Moreover, a like phenomenon reappears much later in medieval Byzantine notarial *formulae*: women renounce the aid of the *SC Velleianum* in acts which have nothing to do with sureties.[28]

Such phrases clearly had a common foundation. Otherwise it is impossible to explain their existence in so many different sources around the Byzantine empire. At some point an idea must have developed that women enjoyed a special privilege: they could reclaim their transactions and had to renounce this right in order to transfer the ownership permanently. How it was connected with the *SC Velleianum* is impossible to say. Perhaps some constitution (like Nov. 61. 1. 1) was misinterpreted and further developed in legal practice.

Although this was certainly a very late phenomenon in Roman law, it was not a totally illogical development. After all, the ancient *senatusconsultum* really had established a 'privilege' for women, by making certain of their acts void and revocable. It was also thought that because women were both 'fragile' and 'inexperienced' they might be excused some errors. In Roman law, as in all developed legal systems, only ignorance of facts, but not ignorance of law, normally constituted a valid excuse. The

---

[27] See P.Tjäder ii. 56 (613/641), with comm. pp. 308–9 (again a Gothic woman, and a very distorted phrase); the third document is mentioned in P.Tjäder i, p. 463 (AD 767). See also a related clause in a soldier's document, P.Tjäder i. 16 (*c*.600?); and cf. Frezza (1974) 10–11; P.Tjäder i, p. 265.

[28] P.Herm. 35 (7th c.); Beaucamp (1992*a*) 43–44; for later evidence, see Saradi-Mendelovici (1990).

Romans allowed certain exceptions: minors, soldiers, rustics, and women, could in special cases plead ignorance. The origins of this idea are obscure, but it appears frequently in early third-century juristic writings and was probably much older. However, it was by no means a general rule. In normal situations women had as little excuse as anyone else.[29]

Through the rescripts we gain some insight into the problems of ordinary imperial subjects. Both men and women approached the emperor incessantly, hoping to cancel a deal by which they claimed they had been defrauded. From only two years, 293 and 294, there are at least two dozen such petitions. Over and over again Diocletian had to explain how detrimental it would be for organized society if contracts could be annulled at will.[30]

In the fourth and fifth centuries imperial laws continued to stress that, if women had been heedless, they could not automatically escape the consequences by pleading ignorance. Particularly, adult women could not abrogate their contracts. The laws sometimes referred to special exceptions, like manifest fraud. But on the whole it is difficult to know how far exactly women's privileges went. Probably people of the time did not know either. It appears that the lawgivers sometimes considered legal usage to be more indulgent towards the weaker sex than was necessary.[31]

In criminal law, there was another way to favour women: they could be condemned to milder penalties. The idea is expressed in an eastern law from the year 397:

Mitior enim circa eas debet esse sententia, quas pro infirmitate sexus minus ausuras esse confidimus. (CT 9. 14. 3. 2)

For the sentence ought to be lighter in the case of those persons, who, We trust, will be less daring because of the frailty of their sex.

---

[29] D. 2. 8. 8. 2, 2. 13. 1. 5, 22. 3. 25. 1, 22. 6. 8, 9. pr, 23. 2. 57a, 25. 4. 2. 1, 48. 5. 39. 2–4, 48. 10. 15. 5, 49. 14. 2. 7; Coll. 6. 3. 3; CI 1. 18 (*De iuris et facti ignorantia*), esp. 1. 18. 3 (244), 6. 9. 6 (294); the person in 1. 18. 10 is not necessarily a woman. Most of these passages cannot be later interpolations; cf. Beaucamp (1976: 494–9; 1990: 79–87).

[30] See CI 4. 44 (*De rescindenda venditione*), and e.g. 2. 4 (*De transactionibus*), esp. 2. 4. 20, 39, and 8. 53. 10, 17; Huchthausen (1976) 67–70.

[31] CT 3. 5. 3 (330) + int, 2. 16. 3 (414 west) + int, 4. 14. 1. 2 (424 east); CI 1. 18. 13 (472 east), 5. 31. 11 (479 east); Nov. 12. 1 (535); Cass. *var.* 2. 11. 1 (507/511); Beaucamp (1990) 87–92.

In fact, this was a very special case because the women in question were not criminals themselves but only daughters of men who had conspired against the life of high officials. The plotters were executed, and their sons were condemned to perpetual poverty, but their daughters were allowed a modest living. The same notion appears also in two Constantinian laws. One of them stated that those who counterfeit money were to be punished 'according to their sex and social standing'. The other ruled that those who helped an abductor should be condemned 'without regard to their sex'. They give the impression that in the early fourth century it was normal to mete out different punishments to men and women.[32]

Such usage is not particularly well attested in earlier legal sources. There is only one passage in the Digest:

Sacrilegii poenam debebit proconsul pro qualitate personae proque rei condicione et temporis et aetatis et sexus vel clementius vel severius statuere. (Ulp. D. 48. 13. 7)

The proconsul ought to impose the penalty for sacrilege more or less severely, depending on the status, age, and sex of the person, the nature of the property, and the time.

The problem is that the words '*et aetatis et sexus*' could easily have been added to the text later. Thus Ulpian need not actually have formulated the rule. But the African bishop Cyprian records that in a mid-third-century persecution male Christians were condemned to death while females were only sent to exile. It is quite possible that already in the principate criminal courts had exercised their free discretion and had occasionally shown leniency towards the weaker sex. Unfortunately we know little about their functioning in practice, and in any case we may assume that social status influenced their decisions even more than age or sex.[33]

Of course, the 'favouritism' towards women was no sign of their strong position in contemporary society. In Frankish laws, if someone harmed or killed a woman, he had to pay a bigger compensatory fine (*wergeld*) than for a man, especially if she was of child-bearing age. This underlined her defencelessness and her

---

[32] CT 9. 21. 1 (319), 9. 24. 1. 5 (326?); cf. also 16. 5. 54. 3 (414 west); CI 9. 13. 1. 4 (533); Joh. Chrys. *in Ephes.* 15. 3, PG 62. 109, with Beaucamp (1992a) 277.
[33] Cypr. *ep.* 80. 1, CSEL 3. 2. 839; cf. also Sen. *ira* 3. 24. 3.

reproductive value rather than her elevated social status.[34] The modest privileges in Roman law reflected an all too correct male opinion that one should feel sorry for those who had been unfortunate enough to be born women. Justinian's chancellery in particular often wrote laws which express pity or even a kind of appreciation for women: they had to obey their husbands and face the dangers of childbirth. His legislation marked a new emphasis in the old discourse but offered no radical novelties. Although he carefully protected women's rights to their dowry and inheritance, he did little to change their social position.[35]

2. WOMEN IN PUBLIC

Seclusion and Proper Behaviour

Above we examined a law of Constantine (CT 9. 1. 3) which stated that women could not usually bring criminal charges. It did not introduce particular legal changes but rather expressed an established opinion about women's role in public life. We shall now look at three other laws from the early part of Constantine's reign. These texts do not *forbid* a woman to do anything. On the contrary, they say that she is *not compelled* to appear in public. For example, the relevant part of the first law reads as follows:

Maritus citra mandatum in rebus uxoris . . . intercedendi habeat liberam facultatem, ne feminae persequendae litis obtentu in contumeliam matronalis pudoris inreverenter inruant nec conventibus virorum vel iudiciis interesse cogantur. (315 CI 2. 12. 21)

The husband should have a free opportunity to intervene without mandate in his wife's (legal) affairs . . . so that women shall not, on the pretext that they would pursue a case, irreverently and insolently forsake their matronly bashfulness nor be compelled to attend assemblies of men or courts.

Another law forbids any judge to have a matron dragged forth into public from her home, where she secludes herself 'out of consideration for her sex' (CT 1. 22. 1). The third one allows women, 'on account of their modesty and bashfulness', to prove

[34] PLS 24. 8–9, 31. 1–2, 41. 15–19; LRib 12. 1; etc.; Ganshof (1962) 47–52; Wemple (1981) 29. Note that the Visigoths had an inverse rule, LV.Ant 8. 4. 16.
[35] e.g. CI 5. 3. 20, 8. 17. 12; Nov. 5. 2. pr, 18. 4. pr, 21; see Beaucamp (1990) 23–7.

their age in absence by documents or witnesses (CT 2. 17. 1. 1). Again, these enactments do not seem to have brought about sweeping changes in current legislation. Perhaps they only adapted earlier principles for new circumstances or recalled rules which had not been observed in practice.[36] What the passages have in common is the repeated assertion that women's bashfulness (*pudicitia, verecundia*) would require their staying at home as much as possible. Was this emphasis something new?

To answer the question, we have to go back to the old prohibition against female representatives in court. Ulpian claimed that it had been caused by a special incident which had induced the praetor to impose a general ban:

Et ratio quidem prohibendi, ne contra pudicitiam sexui congruentem alienis causis se immisceant, ne virilibus officiis fungantur mulieres: origo vero introducta est a Carfania improbissima femina, quae inverecunde postulans et magistratum inquietans causam dedit edicto. (D. 3. 1. 1. 5)

There is a reason for this prohibition, to prevent them from involving themselves in the cases of other people contrary to the modesty in keeping with their sex and to prevent women from performing the functions of men. Its introduction goes back to a shameless woman called Carfania who by brazenly making applications and annoying the magistrate gave rise to the edict.

It is open to doubt whether the prohibition can really be linked with this story, but that is not important here.[37] More noteworthy is Ulpian's general idea, which is expressed in the words *pudicitia* and *verecundia*: women should display a certain modesty and abstain from public activities, such as litigation. The same thought again emerges in a passage of Ambrose (*in psalm. 118 serm.* 16. 7. 2, CSEL 62. 355) which echoes the wording of Ulpian's and Constantine's statements.

The three constitutions of Constantine were written within a period of just a few years. Undeniably they stand apart among late ancient legal sources. We have to go as late as Justinian, over two hundred years later, to find anything similar.[38] Yet, as we

---

[36] For CT 1. 22. 1, cf. D. 2. 4. 18, 2. 4. 21 = 50. 17. 103; Tac. *ann.* 2. 34; and for CI 2. 12. 21, see D. 46.7.3.3.

[37] Carfania is undoubtedly the same person as C. Afrania in Val.Max. 8. 3. 2; but cf. also Marshall (1989) 43–7; Gardner (1986) 262–3.

[38] CI 2. 55. 6, 2. 58. 2. 1, 8. 37. 14. 1; Nov. 124. 1; cf. Beaucamp (1990) 136–8.

amounts of property for the relief of the poor and for the building of churches and monasteries. Their piety and wealth earned due respect just as in pagan times.[54]

Women's public functions were not limited to voluntary benefaction. It is obvious that when compulsory *munera* spread throughout the empire female citizens could not escape them. Ulpian said that they were immune from *corporalia munera* but what exactly he meant we do not know. Other statements make it clear that women were burdened by *munera patrimonii* in the same way as men. On the other hand, they were not thought capable of all *munera personalia* but only a part of them. It would be interesting to hear of some concrete examples but such are not given in legal sources.[55] We only hear that women could be liable for the collection of taxes; partnership in a company of tax collectors was hereditary.[56]

As far as we can tell from the papyri, women did not achieve titular municipal offices (*arkhai*) at all in hellenistic or Roman Egypt, nor are compulsory services (*leitourgiai*) attested in the first three centuries AD. There is some sparse evidence for the subsequent period. For example, women are mentioned in connection with the billeting of soldiers and the production of military clothing. Moreover, in the sixth century we encounter a few women who have attained offices like *pagarkhia*, *proedria*, *logisteia*, and *pateria* ('the father of the city'). Although these posts had been municipal magistracies in the fourth century, it seems that they had now become mere *munera patrimonii*. In other words, they were assigned to particular domains (*oikoi*), which females could inherit in the same way as males.[57]

---

[54] See Clark (1990); Consolino (1989); cf. Ward-Perkins (1984); and generally for women's ascetic movement, above, Ch. 5, Sect. 1. Euergetism was one of the main themes in the tenth international congress of Greek and Latin epigraphy at Nimes in October 1992. I have consulted its preliminary reports, esp. the contribution of C. Lepelley.

[55] D. 50. 1. 37. 2, 38. 3, 50. 4. 3. 3; CI 5. 71. 16, 10. 42. 9, 10. 52. 5, 10. 64. 1; CT 13. 3. 3 (333), 13. 3. 16 (414 east), 16. 2. 10, 14; Symm. *ep.* 7. 126, 9. 40. Cf. Neesen (1981) 208–9, 219; Beaucamp (1990: 31–4; 1992a: 273–4).

[56] D. 49. 14. 47. pr; cf. 17. 2. 59; Gardner (1986) 236; for one or two cases in Egypt, see Sijpesteijn (1985; 1986); Lewis (1990).

[57] See Préaux (1959) 137–9; Lewis (1982) 80–1, 94, 159–60; Anagnostou-Cañas (1984) 357–8; Sijpesteijn (1987b); and above all Beaucamp (1992a) 5–18; e.g. P.Lips. 45 and 60 (371); P.Oxy. l. 3581 (4/5th c.); P.Lond. v. 1660 (c. 553); P.Oxy. xxxvi. 2780 (553); CPR x. 127 (584); P.Oxy. xliv. 3204 (588); and cf. Bagnall (1993) 159–60.

It is interesting to find a similar phenomenon in the highest echelons of imperial aristocracy. In the fourth century the praetorship had become a very expensive and onerous office. If a designated praetor died before his term began, his heirs had to shoulder his responsibilities. What if he had no sons but only daughters? Constantine had decreed that women could not assume the office. Valentinian and Valens confirmed the decision in a later law (CT 6. 4. 17). However, they added that, if there were both sons and daughters, the girls had to share the expenses in proportion to their inheritance. In most cases the children of a designated praetor were very young, but it is notable that the emperors considered such an issue worthy of legislation. In the principate the inability of women to hold the praetorship did not need to be discussed at all. Of course, the once glorious office had by the fourth century lost all practical importance. It was just a kind of surtax on senatorial property.[58]

In 590 the Byzantine authorities in Italy ordered a widow to assume the local administrative office of *comes* after her late husband, though only until the end of the current tax period. What duties the task entailed is hopelessly obscure. We might suspect that it involved some financial burdens, at least responsibility for taxation. In any case, this must have been a very late development. A woman in office could not have been imagined as long as the old administrative structure survived.[59]

It is true that women had endowed their communities already at the time when it was purely voluntary, and they had attained honorific offices before *honores* had in reality become hated burdens. Thus their public role in late antiquity can perhaps partly, but not solely, be explained by the fact that times were growing harder and males wanted to shirk their responsibilities.[60] We do not even have any statistics to demonstrate if women in the later empire really performed more civic duties than before. However, that is what we would expect by reason of the hereditary nature of most occupations.

Women's participation in public life certainly caused embarrassment in the Mediterranean world. According to 'common

[58] Cf. CT 6. 4. 13, 25; Zos. 2. 38. 3; Olympiod. *frg.* 41. 2 (Blockley).
[59] Greg. M. *ep.* 1. 13; cf. Brown (1984) 57 n. 34.
[60] See esp. Van Bremen (1983) 233–7; cf. also Boatwright (1991) 258–60.

sense', they should have stayed at home, leaving all civic offices as a province of men.[61] Perhaps many of them really would have liked to do so. However, no community could afford to neglect the material resources which women commanded. That was the lasting dilemma of men in late antiquity: how to utilize women's wealth but not assign them tasks which required formal authority over their fellow citizens. For example, although the curial class was dwindling, and even men of dubious reputation were allowed to enter the city councils, women were never qualified. Thus female heiresses constantly drained the financial resources of this overburdened group; they 'took out' properties which ought to have been liable for curial duties. In the fifth century, daughters of councillors were encouraged to marry within their class. Otherwise they forfeited to the council one-quarter of their inheritance, later as much as three-quarters.[62]

Another group whose membership was strictly hereditary was the guild of bakers in Rome (that is, those people who owned and managed the bakeries). If someone married the daughter of a baker, they both became tied to the profession.[63] The inherent conflict between women's fortunes and their proper submissive role was probably often solved so that the heiress brought the property and her husband was responsible for its use. But this is only a conjecture as virtually nothing is known about real life.

In general, all those imperial and local offices which had real political significance remained closed to women. The administration of the later Roman empire was based on a hierarchically structured official machinery, consisting of thousands of male functionaries, from the great ministers down to the last underpaid clerks in distant provinces. The general efficiency of the imperial bureaucracy may be doubted. But it is clear that women were automatically shut off from a great part of the decisions which were taken every day in their society.

What political influence women had in the Roman empire was

[61] e.g. D. 50. 17. 2; Philo Alex. *leg. spec.* 3. 169–71; Arnob. *nat.* 7. 42; Lact. *epit.* 33. 5, SC 335. 142; Ambr. *parad.* 11. 50, CSEL 32. 1. 307; Beaucamp (1992a) 289–91; and cf. above, Ch. 4, Sect. 2.
[62] CT 12. 1. 137 (393 east); NTh 22. 2. 7–11 (443), later valid in the west, too; CI 10. 35. 3. 1 (528); Nov. 38. 4–5, 101. 4; Lib. *or.* 2. 36, 48. 30; Procop. *hist. arc.* 29. 17–25; Cass. *var.* 9. 4; Jones (1964) 737–57; Neesen (1981) 225; Demandt (1989) 408–10; Beaucamp (1990: 29–31; 1992a: 20). For Sijpesteijn (1987a), cf. Lewis (1990).
[63] CT 14. 3. 2 (355), 14. 3. 14 (372); Sirks (1988) 481–2.

strictly unofficial. Empresses and senatorial ladies could take part in high politics, in late antiquity as well as in the principate.[64] However, this depended on their personal qualities and informal authority since the Roman political system never recognized female rulers. In general, it seems that dynastic principles enhanced the role of women in the imperial government. Female members of the dominant families gained prestige as links in the important blood relationships. Moreover, dynastic succession was bound to result in long minorities during which female relatives could become virtual regents. Such strong figures were Julia Maesa, the grandmother of Elagabal and Alexander Severus, and Justina, the mother of Valentinian II. In the early fifth century Pulcheria in reality overshadowed her unenterprising brother Theodosius II in the eastern empire while their aunt, Galla Placidia, held the western realm for her minor son Valentinian III.[65]

Thus the blurring of women's private and public roles gave them access to political power. But this was possible only at the absolute top of late Roman society where the hereditary nature and mystification of the imperial office gave special weight to family ties. On all other levels political decision-making remained a male preserve. The collapse of the western empire brought about a change. Central bureaucracy, chosen officials, and formal competence lost their importance. In the Germanic kingdoms many more decisions were taken locally by people who had power through their family or through their personal resources. With or without their husbands, queens and noblewomen governed large areas in early medieval Europe. After a short period of Carolingian centralization, this trend again continued towards the end of the first millennium.[66]

3. SUMMARY AND CONCLUSIONS

In most European legal systems today it would be difficult to preclude women from activities which are open to men. Those few restrictions that have survived in modern societies have

[64] See e.g. Thraede (1972) 213–14.
[65] See e.g. Kettenhofen (1979); Holum (1982); Oost (1968).
[66] See McNamara and Wemple (1974); Nelson (1978); Wemple (1981) 58–70, 97–9, 122–3, 194–5; Stafford (1983); Ennen (1984) 48–75; Schulenburg (1988) 105.

usually been claimed to aid and protect women. Thus in many countries certain professions or working hours have been thought too dangerous or exhausting for the weaker sex. Often such prejudices have, in the course of time, turned out to be false. It has been seriously asked if they ever worked for the benefit of women. Perhaps they always had only negative effects; they not only excluded women from various profitable opportunities but also prevented them from testing and proving their competence, thus perpetuating the fallacy.

As we have seen, such questions are relevant in Roman society, too. The Romans justified many restrictions with feminine *imbecillitas* and *fragilitas*. Certain 'difficult' activities were thought to be a male preserve. True, even some men found it difficult to believe that all women needed protection, and it could hardly be claimed that witnessing a testament exposed them to any danger. In practice, protection and restraints were only two sides of the same coin, two aspects of the traditional idea of female nature which reinforced each other. As the statement of Gaius about *tutela* (GI 1. 190–2) shows, it was not altogether impossible to differentiate between selfish interests and altruistic care. But his contemporaries certainly did not often weigh their motives. Even in retrospect it is hard to draw the line. When males controlled women in order to defend them, it was not so much their personal safety which they had in mind but rather their property. On the other hand, even when such measures did not directly harm women, they nevertheless strengthened the idea of female inferiority.[67]

Did the legal capacity of women change in the period ranging from the early empire through late antiquity to the early middle ages? It is surprisingly difficult to provide an answer. Many basic facts are unknown or uncertain. We know that during the principate women were independent legal subjects and had almost the same rights as men. They could initiate proceedings, be witnesses, and appear personally in courts, although they probably did not do so very often. The only important restriction was that they could not represent others in legal matters. The guardianship survived as a formality which did not apply to most women,

---

[67] For a discussion of mentalities behind protection, cf. e.g. Medicus (1957) 4–9; Dixon (1984) 362–7; Crook (1986*b*); Beaucamp (1990) 68–71.

and it disappeared altogether in the fourth century. Justinian endorsed all these principles in his sixth-century compilation. The developments in the intervening period are much more obscure, but it seems unlikely that the imperial chancelleries enacted laws expressly to change the position of women. It is another question how various provincial courts applied the ancient statutes. If in some region women had a very limited freedom, they did not even try to take part in juridical affairs. But as far as Roman law is concerned, nothing in later western sources indicates that women's rights were significantly curtailed.

In late antiquity the basic attitude towards female public appearance was as negative as it always was in Roman history. But the seclusion of women always remained an ideal which was very imperfectly realized in the upper sections of the society. If we compare the descriptions of Rome by, for example, Tacitus and Jerome, we have to note that aristocratic women's life had changed little. They were free to move and travel and dispose of their inherited property. In the Romanized provincial upper and middle classes, women's financial resources were in late antiquity more than ever needed for public functions. Whether this directly affected their social position is impossible to say. Legal sources do not prove very helpful in such matters. As for the lower classes, we can only presume that they continued to live according to their local traditions.

8

General Conclusions

Is it possible to detect a general historical trend behind all the individual phenomena which have emerged from our examination? The answer seems to be no. No new ideal for female roles and behaviour was ever formulated. No grand theory alone can explain either the position of women in late Roman law and society, or all the changes which took place. To confirm this impression, we shall once more review the major cultural, social, and legal developments in late antiquity.

Taking Christianization first, the present study has indicated that it is often not meaningful to speak about Christian influence at all; the Christians simply did not have any distinctive behaviour pattern of their own. Sometimes the bishops preached new ideals but few people lived up to them. And even in those rare cases where Christian models were generally adopted it always has to be asked if there were other factors which helped to bring about the change.

All Romans expected good parents to love their children and good children to respect and obey their parents. It was assumed that a husband would take good care of his wife and the wife was advised to follow her husband's counsel. Women were responsible for domestic matters while men reserved public offices for themselves. By and large, Christian and pagan ideas did not differ from each other in this, although the opinions of individuals naturally varied. The church fathers did not even claim to teach anything new in such matters. On the contrary, they often asserted that similar views had been universally accepted by all men. At most the Christians could maintain that they practised the common ideals better than pagans, but as time went on this argument was not particularly justified either.

In regard to sex and marriage the Christian church propagated values which were less traditional. We have assessed the consequences of this teaching on three separate areas: extramarital sex, divorce, and ascetic celibacy. Each area illustrates in a different way how an ideological change was reflected in secular legislation and in the everyday life of women in late antiquity.

In pagan times there were two aspects to the problem of extramarital sex. First, respectable women were categorically forbidden to have relations outside wedlock. Secondly, respectable men could freely have affairs with prostitutes, slaves, or concubines. The church taught a much more egalitarian message: both men and women were subjected to the same strict rules. Now, we must ask: what effect did this change have on late Roman society? The answer is: none at all. In the Christian empire, the extramarital sex of men was never penalized. It was not even strongly disapproved of as long as the men took their sexual partners only from the lowest classes and did not try to transfer their family property to their illegitimate children. The sermons of bishops reveal that contemporary Christian males tended to follow the sexual behaviour of their pagan forefathers. At this point we have an ideological innovation which did not coincide with what males thought was sensible and desirable. Therefore it did not meet with any response.

Divorce is a much more complicated question. Again, the position of the church was fairly simple: divorce could not be tolerated and, if possible, it should be forbidden. What makes the question difficult is the fact that we are not well acquainted with the views of the pagans on this matter. We do not know if there were other, more secular, motivations which were running parallel to the bishops' teaching.

In any case, from the reign of Constantine onwards, the legislation on divorce was sometimes tightened, sometimes relaxed. For a long time, the laws remained much more liberal in the eastern empire than in the west. This suggests that religious conviction did not play the decisive role. It is difficult to believe that the eastern emperors or their advisers were less committed Christians than their western colleagues. On the other hand, even in the west, divorce remained legal if both parties agreed to it. This meant that there was always a wide gulf between what the ecclesiastical leaders demanded and what people actually did. In spite of all its authority, the church could not make its members believe that divorce was a great sin.

Remarriage is another issue in which Christian influence can be exaggerated. It has often been claimed that lawgivers in late antiquity tried to discourage remarriage by various penalties. This view has proved to be false. There can be no doubt that all Roman emperors, both pagan and Christian, wanted their subjects to marry and to remarry, and to beget legitimate children. The new legal rules affecting remarried persons were actually not penalties at all. They only tried to ensure that property was preserved and inherited in the direct line, thus reflecting a widespread sentiment in the Mediterranean world.

However, when the bishops recommended single life to their female audience, they used both religious and secular arguments. According to them, it was easier to live when one was free from the dangers of childbirth and from the rule of a husband. Obviously, many women found this to be true. There would certainly have been many independent widows even without the spread of Christian asceticism though perhaps not quite so many. For young girls to remain unmarried, the new religious movement was a condition *sine qua non*. Thus we can say that an ideological innovation made a new pattern of social behaviour possible.

The alternative to married life was the Christian church's most important contribution to women's history. How this change should be evaluated is a much debated question. Independent women were soon directed into convents. It is true that during the early middle ages a convent was often the only safe place for a solitary female. On the other hand, monastic celibacy was sometimes abused by parents who wanted to get rid of surplus daughters. The initial choice may thus not have been really free for the individual. And those who had taken the veil could no longer return to the world, however much they might have wished. Religious life could clearly be very different for different women, depending on personal circumstances.

These examples show that it is not easy to bring about a real social change. A new ideal alone is not enough. But, if it is combined with some other forces, it can affect the way people behave towards each other. Christianity, as recorded in the Bible, offered a wide range of alternative paths which later societies could follow—if they so chose.

260 General Conclusions

In the course of this study, continuities and very slow developments have dominated the scene. This has left little room or indeed reason to discuss the legislation of individual emperors. But it is impossible to disregard totally the role played by Constantine the Great. He tried to forbid divorce, took a firm stand against mixed marriages and aristocratic bastards, cruelly punished abduction marriage, and disapproved of women's appearance in court. Do these measures tell something about his legislative policy and the motives behind it?

Those things which attracted Constantine's attention had always been sore spots in Roman society if not forbidden outright. Ideologically his laws were not innovative although they display an unusual emphasis. It is difficult to avoid a comparision with Augustus. Both men had politically united the empire after long civil strife and subsequently tried to unite it internally behind common moral ideals. They were both concerned with the purity and well-being of upper-class families who produced legitimate children. They tried to carry out a policy of moral rearmament and the invigoration of old virtues by new legislation. But these same values could often be linked with fourth-century Christian teaching. In his efforts, Constantine found a welcome ally in the church, and we need not question his religious sincerity (although we can, of course).

It remains obscure as to how far Constantine pursued a systematic legislative policy. Roman emperors may often only have reacted to individual cases in a haphazard manner. Either way, he was a busy legislator and he had plenty of time, as his reign was the longest since Augustus. Julian claimed that Constantine was an innovator and a disturber of ancient laws and of traditional customs (Amm. 21. 10. 8). However, Julian may not have been thinking of family law in the first place, nor does this passage give the slightest hint that he referred to any religious connections. In any case, Constantine's family policy met the same fate as that of Augustus: his successors were less strenuous in their moral emphasis. In the later fourth century many of his laws were relaxed or repealed. It proved as futile to coerce a Christian society into moral rectitude as a pagan one.

After two centuries, women and their problems figure very prominently in the laws of Justinian. Again, we have an exceptionally long reign with busy legislative activity. It is perhaps true that Justinian's protective rhetoric was more conspicuous than his actual measures in favour of women. But he systematically preserved their ancient rights and even gave them new rights over their dowries. Moreover, he was the first Roman emperor to improve both the lot of those women who had been sexually exploited by upper-class males and the lot of their illegitimate children. Justinian was also concerned with the welfare of slaves and freedmen, although he did not dream of abolishing slavery itself. Do we finally have an emperor who wanted to put Christian teaching into practice already in this world?

If we are looking for a truly Christian legislator, Justinian is a far better candidate than Constantine. His laws appear clement and civilized compared with the ruthless enactments of the fourth century. It cannot simply be said that he mechanically copied classical models, for he was a great innovator in many respects. Did he try to change the world around him because he was a better Christian than his predecessors? Or was he a good Christian because the world had already changed? He ruled over a society which was politically and economically more stable than in Constantine's day. It also seems that he had at his service a better trained juridical staff. In fact, it would be very helpful to know who actually initiated the legal measures which go under Justinian's name. In general, his legislation well deserves fresh study.

*

How then did women's legal position change during late antiquity? A brief summary will show that no clear trend is visible. The most significant individual change seems to be the disappearance of *tutela mulierum* but, although this can probably be dated to the fourth century, we should not conclude that women's emancipation reached its zenith just at that moment. The slow adjustment of written law to social and economic developments is a well-known phenomenon in most cultures. Roman lawgivers, too, were reluctant to abolish time-honoured statutes even when they had become obsolete. There is every reason to believe that the guardianship had in real life been eroded already by the early principate. On the other hand, we do not know a single new statute in the later empire which would have curbed female economic activity. The legal and social position of propertied women does not appear to have varied much between the first and the sixth centuries AD.

Of course, there were other developments in Roman law which indirectly affected women. For example, when the public jurisdictional authority gradually waned, husbands regained the right to take revenge on their adulterous wives. This was not so much a change in the role of women as in the respective functions of the state and family. Similarly, the increasingly moralizing tone and aggravated penalties in late Roman criminal law were general phenomena which affected men and women alike. Moreover, in late Roman fiscal rules the importance of family ties seems to have increased. It was not so much because there was a new, stronger conception of the family but rather because the state desperately wanted to find someone who could be made responsible. For that reason even daughters, wives, and husbands had to fulfil the duties of their family members and to assume financial obligations which had earlier been assigned individually.

The cornerstone of the Roman family system was *patria potestas*. Not even the surge of new citizens from alien cultures after 212 could shatter the legal powers of the Roman father. It seems that in most parts of the later Roman empire people had sufficient familiarity with the doctrine of *patria potestas* to live with it or use the methods of Roman law to avoid it. Those who for one reason or another wanted to release their children from *potestas* could emancipate them. The paternal power survived in the east beyond Justinian and in the west as long as we can follow the sources before they fade out in the dark ages.

Patria potestas was a peculiarly Roman mixture of individual freedom and family responsibility. As long as he lived, the *pater* took care of his household and descendants. Since he made all the decisions within his little kingdom, the system permitted a maximum of flexibility and a minimum of public involvement. During the imperial period, the state assumed more and more the role of a general peace officer. It was no longer taken for granted that fathers or remarried widows would always look after their children's interests. In some specifically defined circumstances the law encroached upon the territory of the *paterfamilias*, restricting his freedom of action. Whether we want to say that *patria potestas* was 'eroded' in late antiquity remains a matter of taste. Although the Romans developed many ways to evade its individual consequences, they apparently never considered it obsolete. After all, it is only natural that the older generation of males were reluctant to forsake a system which gave them economic power over their descendants.

One consequence of the Roman family system was the weak legal tie between mother and children, especially the missing rights of succession and guardianship. Clearly the Romans themselves came to consider that unjust or impractical, so they very early allowed and even expected mothers to draw up wills in favour of their children. The natural development of this practice was the later emergence of intestate maternal succession under imperial law. Mothers could also unofficially participate in the guardianship of their children. That they achieved the formal right to do so only in late antiquity perhaps had several reasons. First, juridically they were not close relatives. Secondly, the guardianship was a public duty, not suitable for females, especially as they might be in *tutela* themselves. And thirdly, Roman widows were officially encouraged to remarry and thus to provide a stepfather for the orphans. The last two problems were removed in the fourth century. In all these developments the mother was not so much competing with the father, for his prerogatives were little diminished. It was the agnatic kin which gradually lost the last remains of its once important position.

The position of married women was yet another issue which was influenced by the father-centred system. In most other cultures, wives have been put under their husband's rule. We have seen that this idea was latently present in classical Roman society, too. The husband was always regarded as the most natural support for his spouse, but the force of *patria potestas* prevented it from being sanctioned in Roman law. The conflict of male interests, between fathers-in-law and sons-in-law, incidentally gave women more freedom: husbands had no statutory power, fathers were dead, and other guardians had little personal interest in women's affairs. Of course, the generally independent role of women in Roman society may also have contributed to their sovereignty in marriage.

It is possible that, when the old *tutela* had finally disappeared, it made room for the spread of unofficial arrangments. Many women may themselves have doubted that they could manage without male help. These people resorted to local practices, which usually meant that the husband had some kind of power over his wife. It is interesting that there is no trace of this development in Justinian's law although we know that husbands held a strong position in contemporary Egypt, and very probably in other parts of his realm, too. Perhaps the popular customs had not spread to the Constantinopolitan upper classes. Besides, as long as *patria potestas* was a living institution, married women could not automatically be subjected to their husbands. How much independence wives preserved in the west we do not know. It depended probably more on personal qualities than on existing legislation, though allegiance to Roman law may perhaps have retarded the development in some population groups.

Of course, it would be meaningless to speak of wifely independence if women did not inherit property of their own. Here again personal differences were great because heirship strategies of individual families varied. On the whole, discrimination against women was probably most obvious in poor families. The more wealth people had the more likely they were to divide it evenly among their children. The daughters' extensive hereditary rights were still a notable feature of late Roman society. How far they were kept alive in the early medieval world is one more question which we cannot answer.

In sum, as far as Roman law is concerned, the basic conception of the family remained surprisingly constant during the imperial period. The father retained his central position. In the relationship between the spouses no radical changes can be detected. The mother's legal role was slowly enhanced at the expense of the agnatic kin, but we may presume that the real social change had taken place much earlier.

What about the interplay between Roman law and provincial practices? It is difficult to assess the influence which the new masses of citizens might have exerted on imperial legislation. We do not know much about their original customs in the first place. There are few cases in which we can suspect a 'foreign' element in late Roman family law. The appearance of *donatio ante nuptias* is a possible example. The gradual recognition of the mother's role was quite natural from the standpoint of old Roman values, and it had started long before 212; it can be explained without any hellenistic or eastern impact. But in so far as the peregrine habits had any effect, they certainly reinforced the already existing trends within Roman society. On the other hand, many institutions of Roman family law, like *patria potestas*, *tutela*, and the *ius liberorum* appear well known around the empire. While the 'vulgarization' of Roman law remains a rather ill-defined phenomenon, the Romanization of provincial culture can at least in such cases be demonstrated. This is not to claim, of course, that ordinary people ever were familiar with the technical details of the law.

Inevitably, the position of women is in many ways connected with demographic factors, like nuptiality, fertility, and mortality. For example, the number of widowed women has an obvious relationship with the spouses' ages at marriage. In the Mediterranean world this age-gap tended to be quite large. We do not know whether all peoples within the empire followed the same patterns; probably they did not. And if these variables changed, even slowly, they had far-reaching effects on women's lives, perhaps greater than any juridical norms invented by males. Alas, we know too little of them even in the early empire, and still less after the fourth century. For the people themselves such demographic facts were self-evident truths whose slow changes were not noticed, let alone recorded.

*

The period extending from the late Roman republic to the end of the western empire (and beyond in Byzantium) was the heyday of individualism in ancient and medieval history. An established central government could secure the well-being of the urban upper and middle classes. Families did not altogether lose their importance as social and political units, but emphasis was less on relations between families and more on those between individuals and the state. Under peaceful conditions, even weaker members of the community could successfully manage their own affairs. Women did not need their agnatic family or their husband to protect them. They were treated as independent legal subjects with unimpaired ownership rights. Women living in the last centuries of the empire had a greater legal capacity than their sisters in any historical period before the twentieth century.

All this enhanced the role of women in Roman economic life.

On the other hand, the centralized administration remained a male prerogative, closing direct routes to political power for women. Paradoxically, the fall of the Roman empire caused a change in both these aspects. In the early middle ages, women again needed protection as it was difficult to preserve one's possessions without physical force. The ability to bear arms determined a person's role in the society. As both the state and the individual were weaker, the kindred assumed renewed importance. But it was precisely this weakening of government machinery and the increasing prominence of family ties which gave some women new power over others. If they came from a sufficiently rich family or married an influential prince, they could wield great authority. With perhaps some risk of over-simplification, I think that most ordinary women would have benefited from the opportunity to manage their own affairs in the relative peace of the Roman empire whereas an ambitious lady would have appreciated the early medieval opportunities to govern other people.

However, I would not like to stress such differences too much. In all periods, the most common field of women's activity was reproduction: children and domestic work. Rich or poor, as long as they did not take the veil they could never totally escape these responsibilities. The passage from antiquity to the middle ages was certainly a tremendous historical change, but I believe that it affected the role of women much less than the role of men. Among women, the change was mostly felt by urban propertied ladies. The less means a woman possessed, the less alternatives she had in her life. If she obtained her livelihood by subsistence agriculture, as most people did, she would hardly have noticed any difference.

BIBLIOGRAPHY

The following abbreviations have been used:

ARC VII   *Atti dell'Accademia Romanistica Costantiniana. VII convegno internazionale* (Perugia, 1988).

HRG   *Handwörterbuch zur deutschen Rechtsgeschichte*, ed. A. Erler, E. Kaufmann, and R. Schmidt-Wiegand (Berlin, 1971–).

RE   *Paulys Real-enzyklopädie der classischen Altertumswissenschaft*, rev. edn. by G. Wissowa, W. Kroll, K. Mitthaus, and K. Ziegler (Stuttgart, 1893–1972).

RIDA   *Revue Internationale des Droits de l'Antiquité.*

RLAC   *Reallexikon für Antike und Christentum*, ed. Th. Klauser, E. Dassmann *et al.* (Stuttgart, 1950–).

ZRG   *Zeitschrift der Savigny-Stiftung für Rechtsgeschichte. Romanistische Abteilung.*

AFFELDT, W. (1986*a*), 'Frühmittelalter und historische Frauenforschung', in Affeldt and Kuhn (1986), 10–30.

——(1986*b*), 'Geschichte der Frauen im Frühmittelalter: Bemerkungen zum Forschungsstand', in Affeldt and Kuhn (1986), 32–42.

——(1990) (ed.), *Frauen in Spätantike und Frühmittelalter: Lebensbedingungen—Lebensnormen—Lebensformen* (Sigmaringen).

——and KUHN, A. (1986) (eds.), *Frauen in der Geschichte*, vii. *Interdisziplinäre Studien zur Geschichte der Frauen im frühen Mittelalter* (Geschichtsdidaktik: Studien, Materialien, 39; Düsseldorf).

——and REITER, S. (1986), 'Die Historiae Gregors von Tours als Quelle für die Lebenssituation von Frauen im Frankenreich des sechsten Jahrhunderts', in Affeldt and Kuhn (1986), 192–208.

AMIRA, K. VON, and ECKHARDT, K. A. (1960), *Germanisches Recht*, i. *Rechtsdenkmäler*[4] (Grundriss der germanischen Philologie, 5: 1; Berlin).

ANAGNOSTOU-CAÑAS, B. (1984), 'La Femme devant la justice provinciale dans l'Égypte romaine', *Revue historique de droit français et étranger*, 62: 337–60.

ANNÉ, L. (1941), *Les Rites des fiançailles et la donation pour cause de mariage dans le Bas-Empire* (Diss. ad gradum Magistri in Facultate Juris Canonici, 2: 33; Louvain).

ARJAVA, A. (1988), 'Divorce in Later Roman Law', *Arctos*, 22: 5–21.

——(1989), 'Jerome and Women', *Arctos*, 23: 5–18.

——(1991), 'Zum Gebrauch der griechischen Rangprädikate des Senatorenstandes in den Papyri und Inschriften', *Tyche*, 6: 17–35.

——(1993), 'Women in the Christian Empire: Ideological Change and Social Reality', in E. A. Livingstone (ed.), *Studia Patristica*, xxiv (Louvain), 6–9.

ARVIZU, F. (1984), 'La Femme dans Le Code d'Euric', *Revue historique de droit français et étranger*, 62: 391–405.

BAGNALL, R. S. (1987), 'Church, State and Divorce in Late Roman Egypt', in K.-L. Selig and R. Somerville (eds.), *Florilegium Columbianum: Essays in Honor of P. O. Kristeller* (New York), 41–61.

——(1992), 'Landholding in Late Roman Egypt: The Distribution of Wealth', *J. of Roman Studies*, 82: 128–49.

——(1993), *Egypt in Late Antiquity* (Princeton).

——and Frier, B. W. (1994), *The Demography of Roman Egypt* (Cambridge Studies in Population, Economy and Society in Past Time, 23).

BARNES, T. (1975), 'Two Senators under Constantine', *J. of Roman Studies*, 65: 40–9.

BARONE-ADESI, G. (1988), '"Favor liberorum" e "veterum legum moderamen"', in *ARC VII*, 433–57.

BAUMAN, R. (1980), 'The "leges iudiciorum publicorum" and their Interpretation in the Republic, Principate and Later Empire', in H. Temporini and W. Haase (eds.), *Aufstieg und Niedergang der römischen Welt*, ii. 13 (Berlin, New York), 103–233.

BAVEL, T. (1989), 'Augustine's View on Women', *Augustiniana*, 39: 5–53.

BEAUCAMP, J. (1976), 'Le Vocabulaire de la faiblesse féminine dans les textes juridiques romaines du IIIe au VIe siècle', *Revue historique de droit français et étranger*, 54: 485–508.

——(1985), 'La Référence au veuvage dans les papyrus byzantins', *Pallas*, 32: 149–57.

——(1990), *Le Statut de la femme à Byzance (4e–7e siècle)*, i. *Le droit impérial* (Trav. et mém. du Centre de recherche d'histoire et civilisation de Byzance, monogr. 5; Paris).

——(1992a), *Le Statut de la femme à Byzance (4e–7e siècle)*, ii. *Les pratiques sociales* (Trav. et mém. du Centre de recherche d'histoire et civilisation de Byzance, monogr. 6; Paris).

——(1992b), 'L'Égypte byzantine: biens des parents, biens du couple?', in D. Simon (ed.), *Eherecht und Familiengut in Antike und Mittelalter* (Schriften des Historischen Kollegs, 22; Munich), 61–76.

BECKER, H.-J. (1971), 'Edictum Theoderici', *HRG*, i. 801–3.

BIONDI, B. (1952–4), *Il diritto romano cristiano*, 3 vols. (Milan).

BOATWRIGHT, M. T. (1991), 'Plancia Magna of Perge: Women's Roles and Status in Roman Asia Minor', in S. Pomeroy (ed.), *Women's History and Ancient History* (Chapel Hill, NC), 249–72.

BOSWELL, J. (1984), 'Expositio and Oblatio: The Abandonment of Children and the Ancient and Medieval Family', *American Historical Review*, 89: 10–33.

———(1988), *The Kindness of Strangers: The Abandonment of Children in Western Europe from Late Antiquity to the Renaissance* (London).

BRADLEY, K. R. (1991), *Discovering the Roman Family: Studies in Roman Social History* (Oxford, New York).

BREMMER, J. (1989), 'Why did Early Christianity Attract Upper-Class Women?', in A. A. R. Bastiaensen *et al.* (eds.), *Fructus Centesimus: Mélanges G. J. M. Bartelink* (Instrumenta Patristica, 19; Steenbrugge), 37–47.

———(1995), 'Pauper or Patroness: The Widow in the Early Christian Church', in J. Bremmer and L. van den Bosch (eds.), *Between Poverty and the Pyre: Moments in the History of Widowhood* (London), 31–57.

BROWN, P. (1987), 'Late Antiquity', in P. Veyne (ed.), *A History of Private Life*, i. *From Pagan Rome to Byzantium* (Cambridge, Mass.), 235–311.

———(1988), *The Body and Society: Men, Women and Sexual Renunciation in Early Christianity* (Lectures on the History of Religions, NS 13; New York).

BROWN, T. S. (1984), *Gentlemen and Officers: Imperial Administration and Aristocratic Power in Byzantine Italy AD 554–800* (British School at Rome).

BRUNDAGE, J. A. (1987), *Law, Sex, and Christian Society in Medieval Europe* (Chicago).

BRUNT, P. A. (1971), *Italian Manpower 225 BC–AD 14* (Oxford).

CAMERON, A. (1986), 'Redrawing the Map: Early Christian Territory after Foucault' (review article), *J. of Roman Studies*, 76: 266–71.

———(1989), 'Virginity as Metaphor: Women and the Rhetoric of Early Christianity', in A. Cameron (ed.), *History as Text: The Writing of Ancient History* (London), 184–205.

———(1993a), *The Later Roman Empire AD 284–430* (London).

———(1993b), *The Mediterranean World in Late Antiquity AD 395–600* (London).

CANTALAMESSA, R. (1976), 'Etica sessuale e matrimonio nel cristianesimo delle origini: Bilancio di una ricerca', in R. Cantalamessa (ed.), *Etica sessuale e matrimonio nel cristianesimo delle origini* (Studia Patristica mediolanensia, 5; Milan), 423–60.

CANTARELLA, E. (1991), 'Homicides of Honor: The Development of

Italian Adultery Law over Two Millennia', in Kertzer and Saller (1991), 229–44.

CARLETTI, C. (1977), 'Aspetti biometrici del matrimonio nelle iscrizioni cristiane di Roma', *Augustinianum*, 17: 39–51.

CARON, P. G. (1988), 'Consensu licite matrimonia posse contrahi, contracta non nisi misso repudio solvi (C. 5.17.8)', in *ARC VII*, 287–98.

CASTELLO, C. (1983), 'Norme conciliari e autonomia legislativa degli imperatori cristiani in tema di divorzio', in *Atti dell'Accademia Romanistica Costantiniana. V conv. int.* (Perugia), 263–73.

CHAMPLIN, E. (1991), *Final Judgements: Duty and Emotion in Roman Wills, 200 BC–AD 250* (Berkeley).

CHASTAGNOL, A. (1979), 'Les Femmes dans l'ordre sénatorial: titulature et rang social à Rome', *Revue historique*, 262: 3–28.

——(1983), 'La Législation du clarissimat féminin de Sévère Alexandre à la fin du IVe siècle', in *Atti dell'Accademia Romanistica Costantiniana. V conv. int.* (Perugia), 255–62.

CLARK, E. A. (1977a), 'John Chrysostom and the Subintroductae', *Church History* 46: 171–85. (Reprinted in Clark (1986): 265–90.)

——(1977b), 'Sexual Politics in the Writings of John Chrysostom', *Anglican Theol. Review*, 59: 3–20.

——(1979), *Jerome, Chrysostom and Friends: Essays and Translations* (New York).

——(1981), 'Ascetic Renunciation and Feminine Advancement: A Paradox of Late Ancient Christianity', *Anglican Theol. Review* 63: 240–57. (Reprinted in Clark (1986): 175–208.)

——(1985), 'Authority and Humility: A Conflict of Values in Fourth-Century Female Monasticism', *Byzantinische Forschungen*, 9: 17–33. (Reprinted in Clark (1986): 209–28.)

——(1986), *Ascetic Piety and Women's Faith: Essays on Late Ancient Christianity* (Studies in Women and Religion, 20; Lewiston, NY).

——(1989), 'Theory and Practice in Late Ancient Asceticism: Jerome, Chrysostom, and Augustine', *J. of Feminist Studies in Religion*, 5: 25–46.

——(1990), 'Patrons, Not Priests: Gender and Power in Late Ancient Christianity', *Gender & History*, 2: 253–73.

——(1991), 'Sex, Shame, and Rhetoric: En-gendering Early Christian Ethics', *J. of the American Academy of Religion*, 59: 221–45.

CLARK, G. (1993), *Women in Late Antiquity: Pagan and Christian Life-Styles* (Oxford).

CLASSEN, P. (1977), 'Fortleben und Wandel spätrömischen Urkundenwesens im frühen Mittelalter', in P. Classen (ed.), *Recht und Schrift im Mittelalter* (Vorträge und Forschungen, 23; Sigmaringen), 13–54.

COHEN, D. (1991), 'The Augustan Law on Adultery: The Social and Cultural Context', in Kertzer and Saller (1991), 109–26.

COLEMAN, E. (1976), 'Infanticide in the Early Middle Ages', in Stuard (1976), 47–70. (Also in *Annales: Économies, Sociétés, Civilisations,* 29 (1974), 315–35.)

CONRAD, H. (1954), *Deutsche Rechtsgeschichte,* i. *Frühzeit und Mittelalter* (Karlsruhe).

CONSOLINO, F. E. (1989), 'Sante o patrone? Le aristocratiche tardoantiche e il potere della carità', *Studi storici,* 30: 969–91.

COOPER, K. (1992), 'Insinuations of Womanly Influence: An Aspect of the Christianization of the Roman Aristocracy', *J. of Roman Studies,* 82: 150–64.

CORBETT, P. E. (1930), *The Roman Law of Marriage* (Oxford, repr. 1979).

CORBIER, M. (1991*a*), 'Divorce and Adoption as Roman Familial Strategies', in Rawson (1991), 47–78.

——(1991*b*), 'Constructing Kinship in Rome: Marriage and Divorce, Filiation and Adoption', in Kertzer and Saller (1991), 127–44.

——(1991*c*), 'Family Behavior of the Roman Aristocracy', in S. Pomeroy (ed.), *Women's History and Ancient History* (Chapel Hill, NC), 173–96.

COTTON, H. (1993), 'The Guardianship of Jesus Son of Babatha: Roman and Local Law in the Province of Arabia', *J. of Roman Studies,* 83: 94–108.

——(1994), 'A Cancelled Marriage Contract from the Judaean Desert', *J. of Roman Studies,* 84: 64–86.

CRACCO RUGGINI, L. (1989), 'Juridical Status and Historical Role of Women in Roman Patriarchal Society', *Klio,* 71: 604–19.

CROOK, J. (1967*a*), 'Gaius, Institutes I, 84–86', *Class. Review,* 17: 7–8.

——(1967*b*), 'Patria potestas', *Class. Quarterly,* 17: 113–22.

——(1967*c*), *The Law and Life of Rome* (London).

——(1986*a*), 'Women in Roman Succession', in Rawson (1986), 58–82.

——(1986*b*), 'Feminine Inadequacy and the Senatusconsultum Velleianum', in Rawson (1986), 83–92.

——(1990), '"His and Hers": What Degree of Financial Responsibility did Husband and Wife Have for the Matrimonial Home and their Life in Common, in a Roman Marriage?', in J. Andreau and H. Bruhns (eds.), *Parenté et stratégies familiales dans l'Antiquité romaine* (Coll. de l'École française de Rome, 129), 153–72.

DALLA, D. (1988), 'Aspetti della patria potestà e dei rapporti tra genitori e figli nell'epoca postclassica', in *ARC VII,* 89–109.

DASSMANN, E. (1986), 'Haus II (Hausgemeinschaft)', *RLAC,* xiii, 801–905.

DE ROBERTIS, F. M. (1988), 'Oscillazioni nella ermeneutica neotestamentaria sul divorzio e ripensamenti di Giustiniano', in *ARC VII*, 299–307.

DELLING, G. (1959*a*), 'Ehebruch', *RLAC*, iv. 666–77.

———(1959*b*), 'Eheleben', *RLAC*, iv. 691–707.

———(1959*c*), 'Ehescheidung', *RLAC*, iv. 707–19.

———(1978), 'Geschlechter', *RLAC*, x. 780–803.

DEMANDT, A. (1989), *Die Spätantike: Römische Geschichte von Diocletian bis Justinian 284–565 n. Chr.* (Handbuch der Altertumswissenschaft, iii. 6; Munich).

DILCHER, G. (1978), 'Langobardisches Recht', *HRG*, ii. 1607–18.

DIXON, S. (1984), 'Infirmitas Sexus: Womanly Weakness in Roman Law', *Tijdschrift voor Rechtsgeschiedenis*, 52: 343–71.

———(1985), 'Breaking the Law to Do the Right Thing: The Gradual Erosion of the Voconian Law in Ancient Rome', *Adelaide Law Review*, 9: 519–34.

———(1986), 'Family Finances: Tullia and Terentia', in Rawson (1986), 93–120. (Also in *Antichthon*, 18 (1984), 78–101.)

——— (1988), *The Roman Mother* (London).

———(1991), 'The Sentimental Ideal of the Roman Family', in Rawson (1991), 99–113.

———(1992), *The Roman Family* (Baltimore, London).

DREW, K. F. (1988), *Law and Society in Early Medieval Europe: Studies in Legal History* (Variorum Coll. Studies, 271; London).

DRIJVERS, J. W. (1987), 'Virginity and Asceticism in Late Roman Western Elites', in J. Blok and P. Mason (eds.), *Sexual Asymmetry: Studies in Ancient Society* (Amsterdam), 241–73.

———(1992), *Helena Augusta: The Mother of Constantine the Great and the Legend of her Finding of the True Cross* (Leiden).

DUPONT, C. (1937), *Les Constitutions de Constantin et le droit privé au debut du IVe siècle: Les Personnes* (Lille).

ECK, W. (1980), 'Die Präsenz senatorischer Familien in den Städten des Imperium Romanum bis zum späten 3. Jahrhundert', in *Studien zur antiken Sozialgeschichte: Festschrift F. Vittinghoff* (Cologne), 283–322.

EGGER, B. (1994), 'Women and Marriage in the Greek Novels: The Boundaries of Romance', in J. Tatum (ed.), *The Search for the Ancient Novel* (Baltimore), 260–80.

EHRHARDT, A. (1937), 'Nuptiae', *RE*, xvii. 1478–89.

———(1955), 'Constantin d. Gr. Religionspolitik und Gesetzgebung', *ZRG* 72: 127–90.

ENNEN, E. (1984), *Frauen im Mittelalter* (Munich).

ÉTIENNE, R. (1978), 'La Démographie des familles impériales et sénatoriales au IVe siècle après J.C.', in *Transformations et conflits au IVe siècle après J.-C.* (Antiquitas, 1: 29; Bonn), 133–68.

EVANS GRUBBS, J. (1989), 'Abduction Marriage in Antiquity: A Law of Constantine (CTh ix. 24. 1) and its Social Context', *J. of Roman Studies*, 79: 59–83.

——(1993*a*), 'Marriage more Shameful than Adultery: Slave–Mistress Relationships, "Mixed Marriages", and Late Roman Law', *Phoenix*, 47: 125–54.

——(1993*b*), 'Constantine and Imperial Legislation on the Family', in Harries and Wood (1993), 120–42.

——(1995), *Law and Family in Late Antiquity: The Emperor Constantine's Marriage Legislation* (Oxford).

EYBEN, E. (1980/1), 'Family Planning in Graeco-Roman Antiquity', *Ancient Society*, 11/12: 5–82.

——(1991), 'Fathers and Sons', in Rawson (1991), 114–34.

FALLETTI, L. (1966/7), 'De la condition de la femme pendant le haut moyen-âge', *Annali di storia del diritto: Rassegna internazionale*, 10/11: 91–115.

FEDELE, P. (1977), 'Vedovanza e seconde nozze', in *Il matrimonio nella società altomedievale* (Settimane di studio del Centro italiano di studi sull'alto medioevo, 24; Spoleto), 819–40

FORBIS, E. P. (1990), 'Women's Public Image in Italian Honorary Inscriptions', *Amer. J. of Philology*, 111: 493–512.

FORLIN PATRUCCO, M. (1976), 'Aspetti di vita familiare nel IV secolo negli scritti dei padri cappadoci', in R. Cantalamessa (ed.), *Etica sessuale e matrimonio nel cristianesimo delle origini* (Studia Patristica mediolanensia, 5; Milan), 158–79.

FREND, W. H. C. (1984), *The Rise of Christianity* (London).

FREZZA, P. (1974), 'L'influsso del diritto romano giustinianeo nelle formule e nella prassi in Italia', in *Ius Romanum Medii Aevi*, I 2 c ee (Milan).

GANSHOF, F. L. (1962), 'Le Statut de la femme dans la monarchie franque', in *Recueils de la Société Jean Bodin*, xii. 5–58.

GARCÍA GARRIDO, M. (1958), *Ius uxorium* (Rome, Madrid).

——(1988), 'Relaciones personales y patrimoniales entre esposos y coniuges en el derecho imperial tardío. Notas criticas', in *ARC VII*, 23–47.

GARDNER, J. F. (1984), 'A Family and an Inheritance: The Problems of the Widow Petronilla', *Liverpool Class. Monthly*, 9: 132–3.

——(1985), 'The Recovery of Dowry in Roman law', *Class. Quarterly*, 35: 449–53.

——(1986), *Women in Roman Law and Society* (London).

——(1987), 'Another Family and an Inheritance: Claudius Brasidas and his Ex-Wife's Will', *Liverpool Class. Monthly*, 12: 52–4.

——(1989), 'The Adoption of Roman Freedmen', *Phoenix*, 43: 236–57.

274 *Bibliography*

GARDNER, J. F. (1993), *Being a Roman Citizen* (London).

GARNSEY, P. (1967), 'Adultery Trials and the Survival of the Quaestiones in the Severan Age', *J. of Roman Studies*, 57: 56–60.

——(1970), *Social Status and Legal Privilege in the Roman Empire* (Oxford).

——and Saller, R. P. (1987), *The Roman Empire: Economy, Society and Culture* (London).

GAUDEMET, J. (1955a), 'Survivances romaines dans le droit de la monarchie franque du Ve au Xe siècle', *Tijdschrift voor Rechtsgeschiedenis*, 23: 149–206. (Reprinted in idem, *La Formation du droit canonique médieval* (Variorum Coll. Studies, 111; London, 1980).)

——(1955b), 'La Décision de Callixte en matière de mariage', in *Studi in onore di U. E. Paoli* (Florence), 333–44. (Reprinted in Gaudemet (1980), 104–15).

——(1959), 'Le Statut de la femme dans l'empire romain', in *Recueils de la Société Jean Bodin*, xi. 191–221.

——(1960), 'La Transmission des constitutions relatives au droit successoral au Bas-Empire et dans les royaumes barbares', *RIDA* 7: 399–435.

——(1962), 'Les Transformations de la vie familiale au Bas Empire et l'influence du Christianisme', *Romanitas: Revista de cultura romana*, 5: 58–85.

——(1965), 'Le Bréviaire d'Alaric et les Epitome', in *Ius Romanum Medii Aevi*, I 2 b aa β (Milan), 3–57. (Reprinted in idem, *La Formation du droit canonique médieval* (Variorum Coll. Studies, 111; London, 1980).)

——(1969), 'Familie I (Familienrecht)', *RLAC*, vii. 286–358.

——(1978), 'Tendances nouvelles de la législation familiale au IVe siècle', in *Transformations et conflits au IVe siècle après J.-C.* (Antiquitas, 1: 29; Bonn), 187–207.

——(1980), *Sociétés et mariage* (Strasburg).

——(1988), 'La Législation sur le divorce dans le droit impérial des IVe et Ve siècles', in *ARC VII*, 75–88.

GEARY, P. J. (1988), *Before France and Germany: The Creation and Transformation of the Merovingian World* (Oxford).

GERNER, E. (1954), *Beiträge zum Recht der Parapherna* (Münchener Beiträge zur Papyrusforschung und antiken Rechtsgeschichte, 38) (= *RE Suppl.*, viii. 401 ff.).

GIARDINA, A. (1988), 'Carità eversiva: Le donazioni di Melania la giovane e gli equilibri della società tardoromana', *Studi storici*, 29: 127–42.

GOETZ, H.-W. (1991) (ed.), *Weibliche Lebensgestaltung im frühen Mittelalter* (Cologne).

GOFFART, W. (1980), *Barbarians and Romans, AD 481–584: The Techniques of Accommodation* (Princeton).

GONZÁLEZ, J. (1986), 'The Lex Irnitana: A New Copy of the Flavian Municipal Law', *J. of Roman Studies*, 76: 147–243.

GOODY, J. (1983), *The Development of the Family and Marriage in Europe* (Cambridge).

——(1990), *The Oriental, the Ancient, and the Primitive: Systems of Marriage and the Family in the Pre-Industrial Societies of Eurasia* (Studies in Literacy, Family, Culture, and the State; Cambridge).

GRAY-FOW, M. J. G. (1988), 'The Wicked Stepmother in Roman Literature and History: An Evaluation', *Latomus*, 47: 741–57.

GRUPE, G. (1990), 'Die "Ressource Frau": Aussagemöglichkeiten der Biowissenschaften', in Affeldt (1990) 105–14.

GUEROUT, J. (1965), 'Le Testament de Sainte Fare: Matériaux pour l'étude et l'édition critique de ce document', *Revue d'histoire ecclésiastique*, 60: 761–821.

HÄGE, G. (1968), *Ehegüterrechtliche Verhältnisse in den griechischen Papyri Ägyptens bis Diocletian* (Cologne).

HALLET, J. P. (1984), *Fathers and Daughters in Roman Society: Women and the Elite Family* (Princeton).

HARRIES, J. (1984), '"Treasure in Heaven": Property and Inheritance among Senators of Late Rome', in E. M. Craik (ed.), *Marriage and Property* (Aberdeen), 54–70.

——(1988), 'The Roman Imperial Quaestor from Constantine to Theodosius II', *J. of Roman Studies*, 78: 148–72.

——and Wood, I. (1993) (eds.), *The Theodosian Code: Studies in the Imperial Law of Late Antiquity* (London).

HARRIS, W. V. (1994), 'Child-Exposure in the Roman Empire', *J. of Roman Studies*, 84: 1–22.

HARTMANN, L. M. (1894), 'Adulterium', *RE*, i. 432–5.

HAUBEN, H. (1993), 'Femmes propriétaires et locataires de navires en Égypte ptolémaïque', *J. of Juristic Papyrology*, 23: 61–74.

HEIDRICH, I. (1991), 'Besitz und Besitzverfügung verheirateter und verwitweter freier Frauen im Merovingischen Frankenreich', in Goetz (1991), 119–38.

HERLIHY, D. (1976), 'Land, Family and Women in Continental Europe, 701–1200', in Stuard (1976), 13–45. (Reprinted from *Traditio*, 18 (1962), 89–120.)

——(1985), *Medieval Households* (Cambridge, Mass.).

——(1990), *Opera Muliebria: Women and Work in Medieval Europe* (Philadelphia).

HERRIN, J. (1983), 'In Search of Byzantine Women: Three Avenues of

Approach', in A. Cameron and A. Kuhrt (eds.), *Images of Women in Antiquity* (London), 167–89.

HOBSON, D. (1983), 'Women as Property Owners in Roman Egypt', *Transactions of the Amer. Philol. Ass.* 113: 311–21.

——(1984), 'The Role of Women in the Economic Life of Roman Egypt: A Case Study from First Century Tebtunis', *Class. Views*, 28: 373–90.

HOCHSTETLER, D. (1992), *A Conflict of Traditions: Women in Religion in the Early Middle Ages 500–840* (Lanham, Md., New York, London).

HOLUM, K. G. (1982), *Theodosian Empresses: Women and Imperial Dominion in Late Antiquity* (Berkeley).

HONORÉ, T. (1979), '"Imperial" Rescripts AD 193–305: Authorship and Authenticity', *J. of Roman Studies*, 69: 51–64.

——(1986), 'The Making of the Theodosian Code', *ZRG* 103: 133–222.

——(1993), 'Some Quaestors of the Reign of Theodosius II', in Harries and Wood (1993), 68–94.

HOPKINS, K. (1965), 'The Age of Roman Girls at Marriage', *Population Studies*, 18: 309–27.

——(1966), 'On the Probable Age Structure of the Roman Population', *Population Studies*, 20: 245–64.

——(1983), *Death and Renewal* (Sociological Studies in Roman History, 2; Cambridge).

HUCHTHAUSEN, L. (1974), 'Herkunft und ökonomische Stellung weiblicher Adressaten von Reskripten des Codex Iustinianus (2. und 3. Jh. u. Z.)', *Klio*, 56: 199–228.

——(1976), 'Zu kaiserlichen Reskripten an weibliche Adressaten aus der Zeit Diocletians (284–305 u. Z.)', *Klio*, 58: 55–85.

HUGHES, D. O. (1978), 'From Brideprice to Dowry in Mediterranean Europe', *J. of Family History*, 3: 262–96.

HUMBERT, M. (1972), *Le Remariage à Rome: Étude d'histoire juridique et sociale* (Milan).

HUNT, E. D. (1982), *Holy Land Pilgrimage in the Later Roman Empire AD 312–460* (Oxford).

HUNTER, D. G. (1987), 'Resistance to the Virginal Ideal in Late Fourth Century Rome: The Case of Jovinian', *Theological Studies*, 48: 45–64.

——(1989), 'On the Sin of Adam and Eve: A Little Known Defence of Marriage and Childbearing by Ambrosiaster', *Harvard Theol. Review*, 82: 283–99.

JONES, A. H. M. (1964), *The Later Roman Empire 284–602: A Social, Economic and Administrative Survey*, 3 vols. (Oxford, repr. 1986).

JOXE, F. (1959), 'Le Christianisme et l'évolution des sentiments familiaux dans les lettres privées sur papyrus', *Acta Antiqua*, 7: 411–20.

JUST, R. (1989), *Women in Athenian Law and Life* (London).

KAJANTO, I. (1969), 'On Divorce among the Common People of Rome', *Revue des études latines*, 49 bis (Mélanges M. Durry): 99–113.

KAMMEIER-NEBEL, A. (1986), 'Empfängnisverhütung, Abtreibung, Kindestötung und Aussetzung im frühen Mittelalter', in Affeldt and Kuhn (1986), 136–51.

KARABÉLIAS, E. (1988), 'La Pratique du concubinat avec une femme libre, affranchie ou esclave dans le droit postclassique', in *ARC VII*, 183–201.

KASER, M. (1938), 'Der Inhalt der Patria Potestas', *ZRG* 58: 62–87.

———(1966), *Das römische Zivilprozessrecht* (Handbuch der Altertumswissenschaft X. 3.4: Munich).

———(1967), 'Vulgarrecht', *RE*, ix. 1283–1304.

———(1971), *Das römische Privatrecht*, i. *Das altrömische, das vorklassische und klassische Recht*[2] (Handbuch der Altertumswissenschaft, x. 3.3.1; Munich).

———(1972), *Zur Methodologie der römischen Rechtsquellenforschung* (Österreichische Akad. d. Wissenschaften, Philos.-hist. Klasse, Sitzungsberichte 277: 5; Vienna).

———(1975), *Das römische Privatrecht*, ii. *Die Nachklassischen Entwicklungen*[2] (Handbuch der Altertumswissenschaft, x. 3.3.2; Munich).

———(1979), 'Ein Jahrhundert Interpolationenforschung an den römischen Rechtsquellen', *Anzeiger d. phil.-hist. Klasse d. Österr. Akad. d. Wiss.* 116: 83–113.

KATZOFF, R. (1985), 'Donatio ante nuptias and Jewish Dowry Additions', *Yale Class. Studies*, 28: 231–44.

KAUFMANN, E. (1989), 'Sippe', *HRG*, iv. 1668–70.

KEENAN, J. G. (1989), 'Roman Criminal Law in a Berlin Papyrus Codex (BGU IV 1024–1027)', *Archiv für Papyrusforschung*, 35: 15–23.

KERTZER, D. I., and SALLER, R. P. (1991) (eds.), *The Family in Italy from Antiquity to the Present* (New Haven).

KETTENHOFEN, E. (1979), *Die syrischen Augustae in der historischen Überlieferung* (Antiquitas, 3:24; Bonn).

KING, P. D. (1972), *Law and Society in the Visigothic Kingdom* (Cambridge Studies in Medieval Life and Thought 3:5).

KIRSCHENBAUM, A. (1987), *Sons, Slaves and Freedmen in Roman Commerce* (Jerusalem).

KÖTTING, B. (1988), *Die Bewertung der Wiederverheiratung (der zweiten Ehe) in der Antike und in der frühen Kirche* (Rheinisch-Westfälische Akad. d. Wiss., Vorträge Reihe G, 292; Opladen).

KOTTJE, R. (1990), 'Eherechtliche Bestimmungen der germanischen Volksrechte (5.–8. Jahrhundert)', in Affeldt (1990), 211–20.

KRAEMER, R. (1980), 'The Conversion of Women to Ascetic Forms of Christianity', *Signs*, 6: 298–307.

KRAUSE, J.-U. (1991), 'Familien- und Haushaltsstrukturen im spätantiken Gallien', *Klio*, 73: 537–62.

——(1994a), *Witwen und Waisen im Römischen Reich*, i. *Verwitwung und Wiederverheiratung* (HABES 16; Stuttgart).

——(1994b), *Witwen und Waisen im Römischen Reich*, ii. *Wirtschaftliche und gesellschaftliche Stellung von Witwen* (HABES 17; Stuttgart).

——(1994c), 'Die Gesellschaftliche Stellung von Witwen im Römischen Reich', *Saeculum*, 35: 71–104.

KROESCHELL, K. (1960), 'Die Sippe im germanischen Recht', *ZRG Germ. Abt.* 77: 1–25.

——(1982), 'Söhne und Töchter im germanischen Erbrecht', in *Studien zu den germanischen Volksrechten: Gedächtnisschrift für W. Ebel* (Rechtshistorische Reihe 1; Frankfurt, Berne), 87–107.

KÜBLER, B. (1909; 1910), 'Über das Ius liberorum der Frauen und die Vormundschaft der Mutter. Ein Beitrag zur Geschichte der Rezeption des römischen Rechts in Ägypten', *ZRG* 30: 154–83, and 31: 176–95.

KUNKEL, W. (1930), 'Matrimonium', *RE*, xiv. 2259–86.

KUTZNER, E. (1989), *Untersuchungen zur Stellung der Frau im römischen Oxyrhynchos* (Europäische Hochschulschriften, 3:392; Frankfurt).

LEONHARD, R. (1901), 'Concubinatus', *RE*, iv. 835–8.

LEVY, E. (1929), 'Westen und Osten in der nachklassischen Entwicklung des römischen Rechts', *ZRG* 49: 230–59. (Reprinted in Levy (1963), i. 163–83.)

——(1930/1), *Die römische Kapitalstrafe* (Sitzungsberichte der Heidelberger Akad. d. Wiss., phil.-hist. Klasse, Jg. 1930/31, 5. Abh.). (Reprinted in Levy (1963), ii. 325–78.)

——(1935), 'Zum Wesen des weströmischen Vulgarrechtes', in *Atti del Congr. Intern. di Diritto Romano*, ii. 29–51. (Reprinted in Levy (1963), i. 184–200.)

——(1938), 'Gesetz und Richter im kaiserlichen Strafrecht. Erster Teil: Die Strafzumessung', *Bullettino 'Vittorio Scialoja'*, 45: 57–166. (Reprinted in Levy (1963), ii. 433–508.)

——(1942), 'The First "Reception" of Roman Law in Germanic States', *American Historical Review*, 48: 20–9. (Reprinted in Levy (1963), i. 201–9.)

——(1950), 'The Reception of Highly Developed Legal Systems by Peoples of Different Cultures', *Washington Law Review*, 25: 233–45. (Reprinted in Levy (1963), i. 210–19.)

——(1951a), *West Roman Vulgar Law: The Law of Property* (Memoirs of the Amer. Philos. Society, 29; Philadelphia).

——(1951b), 'Vulgarization of Roman Law in the Early Middle Ages', *Bull. dell'Istituto di diritto romano (Suppl. post bellum)*, 55–6: 222–58.

(Reprinted from *Medievalia et Humanistica*, 1 (1943), 14–40; reprinted again in Levy (1963), i. 220–47).

——(1959*a*), 'Römisches Vulgarrecht und Kaiserrecht', *Bull. dell'Istituto di diritto romano*, 62: 1–7. (Reprinted in Levy (1963), i. 289–94.)

——(1959*b*), 'West-östliches Vulgarrecht und Justinian', *ZRG* 76: 1–36. (Reprinted in Levy (1963), i. 264–88.)

——(1960), 'Oströmisches Vulgarrecht nach dem Zerfall des Westreiches', *ZRG* 77: 1–15. (Reprinted in Levy (1963), i. 295–304.)

——(1962), 'Besprechung (A. d'Ors, El Código de Eurico)', *ZRG* 79: 479–88. (Reprinted in Levy (1963), i. 305–13.)

——(1963), *Gesammelte Schriften*, 2 vols. (Cologne, Graz).

LEWIS, N. (1970), 'On Paternal Authority in Roman Egypt', *RIDA* 17: 251–8.

——(1982), *The Compulsory Public Services of Roman Egypt* (Papyrologica Florentina, 11; Florence).

——(1983), *Life in Egypt under Roman Rule* (Oxford).

——(1990), 'Notationes legentis: Women in Public Offices', *Bulletin of the Amer. Soc. of Papyrologists*, 27: 38–40.

LIGHTMAN, M., and ZEISEL, W. (1977), 'Univira: An Example of Continuity and Change in Roman Society', *Church History*, 46: 19–32.

LIZZI, R. (1989), 'Una società esortata all'ascetismo: misure legislative e motivazioni economiche nel IV-V secolo d.C.', *Studi storici*, 30: 129–53.

MACMULLEN, R. (1964), 'Social Mobility and the Theodosian Code', *J. of Roman Studies*, 54: 49–53.

——(1980), 'Woman in Public in the Roman Empire', *Historia*, 29: 208–18.

——(1986*a*), 'Judicial Savagery in the Roman Empire', *Chiron*, 16: 147–66.

——(1986*b*), 'What Difference did Christianity Make?', *Historia*, 35: 322–43.

MCNAMARA, J. A. (1976), 'Sexual Equality and the Cult of Virginity in Early Christian Thought', *Feminist Studies*, 3: 145–58.

——(1985), 'A Legacy of Miracles: Hagiography and Nunneries in Merovingian Gaul', in J. Kirschner and S. F. Wemple (eds.), *Women of the Medieval World: Essays in Honor of J. Mundy* (New York), 36–52.

——(1992) (ed.), *Sainted Women of the Dark Ages*, ed. and tr. J. A. McNamara and J. E. Halborg with E. G. Whatley (Durham, NC, London).

——and WEMPLE, S. (1974), 'The Power of Women through the Family in Medieval Europe: 500–1100', in M. Hartman and L. Banner (eds.), *Clio's Consciousness Raised: New Perspectives on the History of Women* (New York), 103–18. (Also in *Feminist Studies*, 2 (1973), 126–41.)

McNAMARA, J. A. and WEMPLE, S. (1976), 'Marriage and Divorce in the Frankish Kingdom', in Stuard (1976), 95–124.

MANFREDINI, A. D. (1990), 'Natalità e legislazione tardoimperiale', in *Atti dell'Accademia Romanistica Costantiniana. VIII conv. int.* (Perugia), 517–33.

MARKUS, A. (1989), *Tutela impuberis: Einfluss der Volksrechte auf das klassische Vormundschaftsrecht unter besonderer Berücksichtigung der gräko-ägyptischen Papyri* (Marburg).

MARSHALL, A. J. (1989), 'Ladies at Law: The Role of Women in the Roman Civil Courts', in C. Deroux (ed.), *Studies in Latin Literature and Roman History*, v (Coll. Latomus, 206; Brussels), 35–54.

MASIELLO, T. (1979), *La donna tutrice: modelli culturali e prassi giuridica fra gli Antonini e i Severi* (Naples).

MATTHEWS, J. (1993), 'The Making of the Text', in Harries and Wood (1993), 19–44.

MEDICUS, D. (1957), *Zur Geschichte des Senatus Consultum Velleianum* (Forschungen zum röm. Recht, 8; Cologne).

MEINHART, M. (1967), *Die Senatusconsulta Tertullianum und Orfitianum in ihrer Bedeutung für das klassische römische Erbrecht* (Wiener rechtsgeschichtliche Arbeiten, 9; Vienna).

MERKLEIN, A. (1967), *Das Ehescheidungsrecht nach den Papyri der byzantinischen Zeit* (Diss. Erlangen).

MEYER, P. (1895), *Der römische Konkubinat nach den Rechtsquellen und den Inschriften* (Leipzig).

MEYER-MARTHALER, E. (1975), 'Einflüsse des römischen Rechts in den Formeln und in der Praxis: Schweitz', in *Ius Romanum Medii Aevi*, I 2 b dd δ (Milan).

——(1978), 'Lex Romana Curiensis', *HRG*, ii. 1935–40.

MIGLIARDI ZINGALE, L. (1990), 'Rileggendo P.Med.inv. 41: legislazione Giustinianea e prassi in tema di dote e donazione nuziale', *J. of Juristic Papyrology*, 20: 109–12.

MILLAR, F. (1977), *The Emperor in the Roman World (31 BC–AD 337)* (London).

——(1981), 'The World of the Golden Ass', *J. of Roman Studies*, 71: 63–75.

——(1983), 'Empire and City, Augustus to Julian: Obligations, Excuses and Status', *J. of Roman Studies*, 73: 76–96.

——(1984), 'Condemnation to Hard Labour in the Roman Empire', *Papers of the British School at Rome*, 39: 124–47.

——(1986), 'A New Approach to the Roman Jurists' (review article), *J. of Roman Studies*, 76: 272–80.

MITTEIS, L. (1891), *Reichsrecht und Volksrecht in den östlichen Provinzen des römischen Kaiserreichs* (Leipzig, repr. 1935 and 1963).

MODRZEJEWSKI, J. M. (1970), 'Zum hellenistischen Ehegüterrecht im griechischen und römischen Ägypten', *ZRG* 87: 50–84.

———(1974), 'A propos de la tutelle dative des femmes dans l'Égypte romaine', in *Akten des XIII Int. Papyrologenkongresses* (Münchener Beiträge zur Papyrusforschung und antiken Rechtsgeschichte, 66; Munich), 263–92.

———(1988), '"La Loi des Égyptiens": le droit grec dans l'Égypte romaine', in *Proceedings of the XVIII Int. Congr. of Papyrology*, ii (Athens), 383–99.

MONTEVECCHI, O. (1936), 'Ricerche di sociologia nei documenti dell'Egitto greco-romano, ii. I contratti di matrimonio e gli atti di divorzio', *Aegyptus*, 16: 3–83.

MURRAY, A. C. (1983), *Germanic Kinship Structure: Studies in Law and Society* (Pontifical Institute of Medieval Studies, Studies and Texts, 65; Toronto).

MUSCA, D. A. (1988), 'La donna nel mondo pagano e nel mondo cristiano: le punte minime dell'età matrimoniale attraverso il materiale epigrafico (urbs Roma)', in *ARC VII*, 147–81.

NAVARRA, M. (1988), 'Testi costantiniani in materia di filiazione naturale', in *ARC VII*, 459–75.

NEESEN, L. (1981), 'Die Entwicklung der Leistungen und Ämter (Munera et honores) im römischen Kaiserreich des zweiten bis vierten Jahrhunderts', *Historia*, 30: 203–35.

NEHLSEN, H. (1972), *Sklavenrecht zwischen Antike und Mittelalter: Germanisches und römisches Recht in den germanischen Rechtsaufzeichnungen*, i. *Ostgoten, Westgoten, Franken, Langobarden* (Göttinger Studien zur Rechtsgeschichte, 7; Göttingen).

———(1977), 'Zu Aktualität und Effektivität der ältesten germanischen Rechtsaufzeichnungen', in P. Classen (ed.), *Recht und Schrift im Mittelalter* (Vorträge und Forschungen, 23; Sigmaringen), 449–502.

———(1978a), 'Lex Burgundionum', *HRG*, ii. 1901–15.

———(1978b), 'Lex Romana Burgundionum', *HRG*, ii. 1927–34.

———(1978c), 'Lex Visigothorum', *HRG*, ii. 1966–79.

———(1982), 'Alarich II. als Gesetzgeber: Zur Geschichte der Lex Romana Visigothorum', in *Studien zu den germanischen Volksrechten: Gedächtnisschrift für W. Ebel* (Rechtshistorische Reihe, 1; Frankfurt, Berne), 143–203.

NELSON, J. L. (1978), 'Queens as Jezebels: The Careers of Brunhild and Balthild in Merovingian History', in D. Baker (ed.), *Medieval Women: Dedicated and Presented to Professor Rosalind M. T. Hill* (Oxford), 31–77.

———(1990a), 'Women and the Word in the Earlier Middle Ages', in W.

J. Sheils and D. Wood (eds.), *Women in the Church* (Studies in Church History, 27; Oxford), 53–78.

NELSON, J. L. (1990*b*), 'Commentary on the Papers of J. Verdon, S. F. Wemple and M. Parisse', in Affeldt (1990), 325–32.

NICOLS, J. (1989), 'Patrona ciuitatis: Gender and Civic Patronage', in C. Deroux (ed.), *Studies in Latin Literature and Roman History*, v (Coll. Latomus, 206; Brussels), 117–42.

NOCERA, G. (1988), 'I rapporti tra cristianesimo e istituti familiari alla luce del diritto e della letteratura del tardo impero', in *ARC VII*, 111–45.

NOLTE, C. (1986), 'Klosterleben von Frauen in der frühen Merowingerzeit: Überlegungen zur Regula ad virgines des Caesarius von Arles', in Affeldt and Kuhn (1986), 257–71.

NONN, U. (1972), 'Merowingische Testamente', *Archiv für Diplomatik*, 18: 1–129.

——(1982), 'Erminethrud—eine vornehme neustrische Dame um 700', *Historisches Jahrbuch*, 102: 135–43.

NORDBERG, H. (1963), *Biometrical Notes: The Information on Ancient Christian Inscriptions from Rome Concerning the Duration of Life and the Dates of Birth and Death* (Acta Inst. Romani Finlandiae, II. 2; Helsinki).

NOY, D. (1988), 'The Senatusconsultum Gaetulicianum, Manus and Inheritance', *Tijdschrift voor Rechtsgeschiedenis* 56: 299–304.

——(1990), 'Matchmakers and Marriage-Markets in Antiquity', *Class. Views*, 34: 375–400.

——(1991), 'Wicked Stepmothers in Roman Society and Imagination', *J. of Family History*, 16: 345–61.

OLBERG, G. (1990), 'Aspekte der rechtlich-sozialen Stellung der Frauen in den frühmittelalterlichen Leges', in Affeldt (1990), 221–35.

OOST, S. I. (1968), *Galla Placidia Augusta: A Biographical Essay* (Chicago).

PARIS, P. (1891), *Quatenus feminae res publicas in Asia Minore, Romanis imperantibus, attigerint* (Paris).

PARKIN, T. G. (1992), *Demography and Roman Society* (Baltimore).

PATLAGEAN, E. (1969), 'Sur la limitation de la fécondité dans la époque byzantine', *Annales: Économies, Sociétés, Civilisations*, 24: 1353–69.

——(1977), *Pauvreté économique et pauvreté sociale à Byzance: 4e–7e siècles* (Paris).

——(1978), 'Familles chrétiennes d'Asie Mineure et histoire démographique du IVe siècle', in *Transformations et conflits au IVe siècle après J.-C.* (Antiquitas, 1: 29; Bonn), 169–86.

POMEROY, S. (1975), *Goddesses, Whores, Wives and Slaves: Women in Classical Antiquity* (New York).

——(1976), 'The Relationship of the Married Woman to her Blood Relatives in Rome', *Ancient Society*, 7: 215–27.

——(1981), 'Women in Roman Egypt: A Preliminary Study Based on Papyri', in H. Foley (ed.), *Reflections of Women in Antiquity* (New York), 303–22.

PRÉAUX, C. (1959), 'Le Statut de la femme à l'époque hellénistique, principalement en Égypte', in *Recueils de la Société Jean Bodin*, xi. 127–75.

RAEPSAET-CHARLIER, M.-TH. (1981), 'Clarissima Femina', *RIDA* 28: 189–212.

——(1981/2), 'Ordre sénatorial et divorce sous le Haut-Empire: un chapitre de l'histoire des mentalités', *Acta Class. Univ. Scient. Debrecen*, 17/18: 161–73.

——(1982), 'Tertullien et la législation des mariages inégaux', *RIDA* 29: 253–63.

——(1987), *Prosopographie des femmes de l'ordre sénatorial (Ier–IIe s.)* (Louvain).

——(1992), 'Le Mariage, indice et facteur de mobilité sociale aux deux premiers siècles de notre ère: l'exemple sénatorial', in E. Frézouls (ed.), *La Mobilité sociale dans le monde romain* (Strasburg), 33–53.

——(1993*a*), 'Les Femmes sénatoriales du IIIe siècle: Étude préliminaire', in W. Eck (ed.), *Prospographie und Sozialgeschichte* (Cologne), 147–63.

——(1993*b*), 'Nouvelles recherches sur les femmes sénatoriales du Haut-Empire romain', *Klio*, 75: 257–71.

——(1993*c*), 'La Femme, la famille, la parenté à Rome: thèmes actuels de la recherche', *L'antiquité classique*, 62: 247–53.

——(1994), 'La Vie familiale des élites dans la Rome impérial: Le Droit et la pratique', *Cahiers du Centre G. Glotz*, 5: 165–97.

RAWSON, B. (1966), 'Family Life among the Lower Classes at Rome in the First Centuries of the Empire', *Class. Philology*, 61: 71–83.

——(1974), 'Roman Concubinage and Other de facto Marriages', *Transactions of the Amer. Philol. Ass.* 104: 279–305.

——(1986) (ed.), *The Family in Ancient Rome: New Perspectives* (Ithaca, NY).

——(1989), 'Spurii and the Roman View of Illegitimacy', *Antichthon*, 23: 10–41.

——(1991) (ed.), *Marriage, Divorce, and Children in Ancient Rome* (Oxford).

REINSBERG, C. (1983), 'Concordia: Die Darstellung von Hochzeit und ehelicher Eintracht in der Spätantike', in *Spätantike und frühes Christentum: Ausstellungskatalog* (Frankfurt), 312–17.

RICHLIN, A. (1981), 'Approaches to the Sources on Adultery at Rome', in H. Foley (ed.), *Reflections of Women in Antiquity* (New York), 379–404.

RIST, J. M. (1965), 'Hypatia', *Phoenix* 19: 214–25.

ROBINSON, O. (1987), 'The Status of Women in Roman Private Law', *Juridical Review*, 143–62.

——(1988), 'The Historical Background', in S. McLean and N. Burrows (eds.), *The Legal Relevance of Gender: Some Aspects of Sex-Based Discrimination* (London), 40–60.

ROGERS, G. M. (1992), 'The Constructions of Women at Ephesos', *Zeitschrift für Papyrologie und Epigraphik*, 90: 215–23.

ROUCHE, M. (1987), 'The Early Middle Ages in the West', in P. Veyne (ed.), *A History of Private Life*, i. *From Pagan Rome to Byzantium* (Cambridge, Mass.), 411–549.

RUPPRECHT, H.-A. (1985), 'Zum Ehegattenerbrecht nach den Papyri', *Bull. of the Amer. Soc. of Papyrologists*, 22: 291–5.

——(1986), 'Zur Frage der Frauentutel im römischen Ägypten', in G. Wesener (ed.), *Festschrift für A. Kränzlein* (Graz), 95–102.

——(1987), 'Ehevertrag und Erbrecht', in S. Janeras (ed.), *Miscellània Papirològica Ramon Roca-Puig* (Barcelona), 307–11.

SABBAH, G. (1992), 'Présences féminines dans l'histoire d'Ammien Marcellin: Les Rôles politiques', in J. den Boeft, D. den Hengst and H. C. Teitler (eds.), *Cognitio Gestorum: The Historiographic Art of Ammianus Marcellinus* (Amsterdam), 91–105.

SACHERS, E. (1953), 'Potestas Patria', *RE*, xxii. 1046–1175.

SALLER, R. P. (1984*a*), 'Familia, Domus and Roman Conception of the Family', *Phoenix*, 38: 336–55.

——(1984*b*), 'Roman Dowry and the Devolution of Property in the Principate', *Class. Quarterly*, 34: 195–205.

——(1986), 'Patria potestas and the Stereotype of the Roman Family', *Continuity and Change*, 1: 7–22.

——(1987), 'Men's Age at Marriage and its Consequences in the Roman Family', *Class. Philology*, 82: 21–34.

——(1988), 'Pietas, Obligation and Authority in the Roman Family', in P. Kneissl and V. Losemann (eds.), *Alte Geschichte und Wissenschaftsgeschichte: Festschrift für K. Christ* (Darmstadt), 393–410.

——(1991*a*), 'Corporal Punishment, Authority, and Obedience in the Roman Household', in Rawson (1991), 144–65.

——(1991*b*), 'Roman Heirship Strategies in Principle and in Practice', in Kertzer and Saller (1991), 26–47.

——(1994), *Patriarchy, Property and Death in the Roman Family* (Cambridge Studies in Population, Economy and Society in Past Time, 25).

SALOMIES, O. (1992), *Adoptive and Polyonymous Nomenclature in the*

Roman Empire (Soc. Scientiarum Fennica, Commentationes Hum. Litterarum, 97; Helsinki).

SALZMAN, M. R. (1989), 'Aristocratic Women: Conductors of Christianity in the Fourth Century', *Helios*, 16: 207–20.

SARADI-MENDELOVICI, H. (1990), 'A Contribution to the Study of the Byzantine Notarial Formulas: The infirmitas sexus of Women and the sc. Velleianum', *Byzantinische Zeitschrift*, 83: 72–90.

SARGENTI, M. (1985), 'Matrimonio cristiano e società pagana: Spunti per una ricerca', *Studia et documenta historiae et iuris*, 51: 367–91. (Reprinted in *ARC VII*, 49–74).

SCHAPS, D. M. (1979). *Economic Rights of Women in Ancient Greece* (Edinburgh).

SCHMIDT-WIEGAND, R. (1978a), 'Lex Ribuaria', *HRG*, ii. 1923–7.

——(1978b), 'Lex Salica', *HRG*, ii. 1949–62.

——(1990), 'Der Lebenskreis der Frau im Spiegel der volkssprachigen Bezeichnungen der Leges barbarorum', in Affeldt (1990), 195–209.

SCHOTT, C. (1978), 'Lex Alamannorum', *HRG*, ii. 1879–86.

——(1979), 'Der Stand der Leges-Forschung', *Frühmittelalterliche Studien*, 13: 29–55.

SCHOULER, B. (1985), 'Hommages de Libanios aux femmes de son temps', *Pallas*, 32: 123–48.

SCHULENBURG, J. T. (1988), 'Female Sanctity: Public and Private Roles, ca. 500–1100', in M. Erler and M. Kowaleski (eds.), *Women and Power in the Middle Ages* (Athens, Ga.), 102–25.

——(1989), 'Women's Monastic Communities 500–1100: Patterns of Expansion and Decline', *Signs*, 14: 261– 92.

SEALEY, R. (1990), *Women and Law in Classical Greece* (Chapel Hill, NC).

SELB, W. (1964), *Zur Bedeutung des Syrisch-Römischen Rechtsbuchs* (Münchener Beiträge zur Papyrusforschung und antiken Rechtsgeschichte, 49; Munich).

——(1992), 'Zur Christianisierung des Eherechts', in D. Simon (ed.), *Eherecht und Familiengut in Antike und Mittelalter* (Schriften des Historischen Kollegs, 22; Munich), 1–14.

SHAW, B. D. (1984), 'Latin Funerary Epigraphy and the Family Life in the Later Roman Empire', *Historia*, 33: 457–97.

——(1987a), 'The Age of Roman Girls at Marriage: Some Reconsiderations', *J. of Roman Studies*, 77: 30–46.

——(1987b), 'The Family in Late Antiquity: The Experience of Augustine', *Past & Present*, 115: 3–51.

SIEMS, H. (1978), 'Lex Romana Visigothorum', *HRG*, ii. 1940–9.

SIJPESTEIJN, P. J. (1965), 'Die χωρὶς κυρίου χρηματίζ ουσαι δικαίῳ τέκνων in den Papyri', *Aegyptus*, 45: 171–89.

SIJPESTEIJN P. J. (1985), 'A Female Tax Collector', *Zeitschrift für Papyrologie und Epigraphik*, 61: 71–3.

———(1986), 'Another Female Tax Collector', *Zeitschrift für Papyrologie und Epigraphik*, 64: 121–2.

———(1987*a*), 'A Female βουλευτής', *Bull. of the Amer. Soc. of Papyrologists*, 24: 141–2.

———(1987*b*), 'The Title πατὴρ (τῆς) πόλεως and the Papyri', *Tyche*, 2: 171–4.

SIMON, D. (1969), 'Aus dem Kodexunterricht des Thalelaios, A. Methode', *ZRG* 86: 334–83.

SIRKS, B. (1988), 'The Administration and Family Law: 4th Century Interference with the Bakers of the Corpus at Rome', in *ARC VII*, 477–86.

———(1993), 'The Sources of the Code', in Harries and Wood (1993), 45–67.

SIVAN, H. (1988), 'Who Was Egeria? Piety and Pilgrimage in the Age of Gratian', *Harvard Theological Review*, 81: 59–72.

SPAGNUOLO VIGORITA, T. (1988), '"Inminentes legum terrores": L'abrogazione delle leggi caducarie augustee in età costantininana', in *ARC VII*, 251–65.

STAFFORD, P. (1978), 'Sons and Mothers: Family Politics in the Early Middle Ages', in D. Baker (ed.), *Medieval Women: Dedicated and Presented to Professor Rosalind M. T. Hill* (Oxford), 79–100.

———(1983), *Queens, Concubines and Dowagers: The King's Wife in the Early Middle Ages* (London).

———(1993), 'Women and Landholding in England *c*.800 to *c*.1000 AD', unpublished paper.

STEINWENTER, A. (1951), 'Zum Problem der Kontinuität zwischen antiken und mittelalterlichen Rechtsordnungen', *Iura*, 2: 15–43.

STERNBERG, TH. (1985), 'Reskripte des Kaisers Alexander Severus an weibliche Adressaten', *Klio*, 67: 507–27.

STUARD, S. M. (1976) (ed.), *Women in Medieval Society* (Philadelphia).

SYME, R. (1960), 'Bastards in the Roman Aristocracy', *Proceedings of the Amer. Philosophical Society*, 104: 323–7.

TAUBENSCHLAG, R. (1916), 'Die Patria potestas im Recht der Papyri', *ZRG* 37: 177–230. (Reprinted in Taubenschlag (1959), 261–321.)

———(1929), 'Die Materna potestas im gräko-ägyptischen Recht', *ZRG* 49: 115–28. (Reprinted in Taubenschlag (1959), 323–37.)

———(1938), 'La Compétence du κύριος dans le droit gréco-égyptien', *Archives d'histoire du droit oriental*, 2: 293–314. (Reprinted in Taubenschlag (1959), 353–77.)

———(1955), *The Law of Greco-Roman Egypt in the Light of the Papyri*² (Warsaw).

——(1959), *Opera Minora*, ii (Warsaw).

THOMAS, J. A. C. (1967), 'Some Notes on adrogatio per rescriptum principis', *RIDA* 14: 413–27.

THOMAS, Y. (1992), 'The Division of the Sexes in Roman Law', in P. S. Pantel (ed.), *A History of Women in the West*, i. *From Ancient Goddesses to Christian Saints* (Cambridge, Mass.), 83–137.

THOMPSON, E. A. (1982), *Romans and Barbarians: The Decline of the Western Empire* (Madison).

THRAEDE, K. (1972), 'Frau', *RLAC*, viii. 197–269.

——(1987), 'Der mündigen Zähmung: Frauen im Urchristentum', in E. Olshausen (ed.), *Die Frau in der Gesellschaft* (Hum. Bildung XI Stuttgart Hist. Inst. der Univ.), 93–121.

——(1990), 'Zwischen Eva und Maria: das Bild der Frau bei Ambrosius und Augustin auf dem Hintergrund der Zeit', in Affeldt (1990), 129–39.

TREGGIARI, S. (1976), 'Jobs for Women', *Amer. J. of Ancient History*, 1: 76–104.

——(1979), 'Lower Class Women in the Roman Economy', *Florilegium*, 1: 65–86.

——(1981a), 'Concubinae', *Papers of the British School at Rome*, 49: 59–81.

——(1981b), 'Contubernales in CIL 6', *Phoenix*, 35: 42–69.

——(1982), 'Consent to Roman Marriage: Some Aspects of Law and Reality', *Class. Views*, 26: 34–44.

——(1985), 'Iam Proterva Fronte: Matrimonial Advances by Roman Women', in J. W. Eadie and J. Ober (eds.), *The Craft of the Ancient Historian, Essays in Honor of Ch. G. Starr* (Lanham, Md.), 331–52.

——(1991a), *Roman Marriage: Iusti Coniuges from the Time of Cicero to the Time of Ulpian* (Oxford).

——(1991b), 'Divorce Roman Style: How Easy and How Frequent Was it?', in Rawson (1991), 31–46.

——(1991c), 'Ideals and Practicalities in Matchmaking in Ancient Rome', in Kertzer and Saller (1991), 91–108.

TROJESEN, K. J. (1992), 'In Praise of Noble Women: Asceticism, Patronage and Honor', *Semeia*, 57: 41–64.

TURPIN, W. (1985), 'The Law Codes and Late Roman Law', *RIDA* 32: 339–53.

——(1987), 'The Purpose of the Roman Law Codes', *ZRG* 104: 620–30.

——(1988), 'Adnotatio and Imperial Rescript in Roman Legal Procedure', *RIDA* 35: 285–307.

——(1991), 'Imperial Subscriptions and the Administration of Justice', *J. of Roman Studies*, 81: 101–18.

VAN BREMEN, R. (1983), 'Women and Wealth', in A. Cameron and A. Kuhrt (eds.), *Images of Women in Antiquity* (London), 223–42.

VAN MINNEN, P. (1986), 'A Woman "naukleros" in P.Tebt. II 370', *Zeitschrift für Papyrologie und Epigraphik*, 66: 91–2.

VERDON, J. (1990), 'Les Femmes laïques en Gaule au temps des Mérovingiens: Les Réalités de la vie quotidienne', in Affeldt (1990), 239–61.

VEYNE, P. (1978), 'La Famille et l'amour sous le haut-empire romain', *Annales: Économies, Sociétés, Civilisations*, 33: 35–63.

——(1987), 'The Roman Empire', in P. Veyne (ed.), *A History of Private Life*, i. *From Pagan Rome to Byzantium* (Cambridge, Mass.), 5–233.

VISMARA, G. (1977), 'I rapporti patrimoniali tra coniugi nell'alto medioevo', in *Il matrimonio nella società altomedievale* (Settimane di studio del Centro italiano di studi sull'alto medioevo, 24; Spoleto), 633–91.

VOCI, P. (1980), 'Storia della patria potestas da Augusto a Diocleziano', *Iura*, 31: 37–100.

——(1985), 'Storia della patria potestas da Costantino a Giustiniano', *Studia et documenta historiae et iuris*, 51: 1–72.

VOLTERRA, E. (1966), 'Il senatoconsulto Orfiziano e la sua applicazione in documenti egiziani del III secolo d.C.', in *Atti dell'XI congresso intern. di papirologia* (Milan), 551–85.

——(1971), 'Il problema del testo delle costituzioni imperiali', in *Atti del II Congr. intern. della Soc. Italiana di storia del diritto* (Venice), 821–1097.

WALLACE-HADRILL, A. (1981), 'Family and Inheritance in the Augustan Marriage Laws', *Proceedings of the Cambridge Philol. Soc.* 27: 58–80.

WARD-PERKINS, B. (1984), *From Classical Antiquity to the Middle Ages: Urban Public Building in Northern and Central Italy AD 300–850* (Oxford).

WATSON, A. (1973), 'Private Law in the Rescripts of Carus, Carinus and Numerianus', *Tijdschrift voor Rechtsgeschiedenis*, 41: 19–34.

——(1977), *Society and Legal Change* (Edinburgh).

WEAVER, P. R. C. (1972), *Familia Caesaris: A Social Study of the Emperor's Freedmen and Slaves* (Cambridge).

——(1986), 'The Status of Children in Mixed Marriages', in Rawson (1986), 145–69.

WEISS, E. (1908), 'Beiträge zum gräko-ägyptischen Vormundschaftsrecht', *Archiv für Papyrusforschung*, 4: 73–94.

WEMPLE, S. F. (1981), *Women in Frankish Society: Marriage and the Cloister, 500–900* (Philadelphia).

WIEACKER, F. (1972), 'Zur Effektivität des Gesetzesrechts in der späten Antike', in *Festschrift für H. Heimpel*, iii (Veröffentlichungen des

Max-Planck-Instituts für Geschichte, 36/III; Göttingen), 546–66. (Reprinted in idem, *Ausgewählte Schriften*, i (1983), 222–40.)

——(1983), '"Vulgarrecht" und "Vulgarismus"', in idem, *Ausgewählte Schriften*, i (Frankfurt), 241–54.

——(1988), *Römische Rechtsgeschichte*, i (Handbuch der Altertumswissenschaft, x. 3. 1. 1; Munich).

WOESS, F. VON (1911), *Das römische Erbrecht und die Erbanwärter* (Berlin).

WOLFF, H.-J. (1939), *Written and Unwritten Marriages in Hellenistic and Postclassical Roman Law* (Haverford).

——(1945), 'The Background of the Postclassical Legislation on Illegitimacy', *Seminar*, 3: 21–45.

——(1950), 'Doctrinal Trends in Postclassical Roman Marriage Law', *ZRG* 67: 261–319.

——(1955), 'Zur Geschichte der Parapherna', *ZRG* 72: 335–47.

WOOD, I. (1986), 'Disputes in Late Fifth- and Sixth-Century Gaul: Some Problems', in W. Davies and P. Fouracre (eds.), *The Settlement of Disputes in Early Medieval Europe* (Cambridge), 7–22.

——(1990), 'Administration, Law and Culture in Merovingian Gaul', in R. McKitterick (ed.), *The Uses of Literacy in Early Medieval Europe* (Cambridge), 63–81.

——(1993), 'The Code in Merovingian Gaul', in Harries and Wood (1993), 161–77.

——(1994), *The Merovingian Kingdoms 450–751* (London).

YARBROUGH, A. (1976), 'Christianization in the Fourth Century: The Example of Roman Women', *Church History*, 45: 149–65.

YARON, R. (1966), 'Syro-Romana', *Iura*, 17: 114–64.

ZEUMER, K. (1898), 'Geschichte der westgotischen Gesetzgebung, i–iv', *Neues Archiv der Gesellschaft für ältere deutsche Geschichtskunde*, 23 (1898) 419–516; 24 (1899) 39–122 and 571–630; 26 (1901) 91–149.

A GLOSSARY OF LATIN LEGAL
TERMS

adulterium, intercourse of a currently married woman with someone other than her husband.

agnati, nearest paternal relatives linked through males; e.g brothers and sisters, paternal uncles and aunts, brothers' and uncles' children (but not aunts' and sisters' children).

arr(h)a, earnest-money; in marriage law (from the 4th c. AD), money or items given to ratify an engagement.

arrogatio, the form of adoption which was used when the person to be adopted was *sui iuris* (q.v.).

bona materna, property inherited from the mother by children who were still in *patria potestas* (q.v.); the inheritance legally accrued to the father, but in late Roman law he was forbidden to alienate it.

capitalis poena, capital penalty; this was usually death, but it could also mean *deportatio* (q.v.).

cognati, any blood relations within six degrees.

collatio dotis, the procedure by which the dowry of a daughter had to be taken into account if she wanted to receive her share from her father's estate on intestacy.

curator, the guardian of a young male from the age of 14 to 25 and of a female between 12 and 25.

curia, the local ruling council of a town; its members constituted the curial class, which was in practice hereditary.

deportatio, exile with loss of citizenship.

dominium, full ownership of a property.

donatio ante nuptias, bridegift, given from the groom's side to the bride's side, recognized in Roman law in the 4th c. AD.

dos, dowry, given from the bride's side to the groom's side.

edictum, ordinance of a magistrate, especially the annual edict of the praetor (to the 2nd c. AD); in the later empire, the term was used for imperial enactments of general application, as opposed to *rescriptum* (q.v.).

emancipatio, a fictitious sale which a *paterfamilias* could use to release his descendants from *patria potestas* (q.v.).

familia, all persons in the household of a single *paterfamilias* (q.v.), including his children and slaves; occasionally the word could include also *agnati* (q.v.).

fideicommissum, bequest given to someone with a request to transfer it to a third person.

filiusfamilias, a male living under *patria potestas* (q.v.); the female equivalent is *filiafamilias*.

formulae, stereotyped model documents, collected in pattern books (formularies) and used by scribes to draft actual documents.

ingenuus, freeborn; in the early middle ages the term comprised also freedpeople.

intercessio, financial intervention on behalf of someone else, especially by standing surety for an alien debt; *intercessio* by women was forbidden by the *SC Velleianum* in the mid-1st c. AD.

interpretationes, longer or shorter résumés of Roman legal texts, mainly of the Theodosian Code and its *novellae*; they were included in the *Lex Romana Visigothorum* in AD 506, but their origin is unknown.

ius (trium) liberorum, 'right of (three) children', a privilege granted to women who had given three live births, from which they derived certain legal benefits, like exemption from guardianship.

kyrios, Greek word for the guardian of an adult woman.

libertus, freed slave.

manus, the legal power which the husband acquired over his wife, if the marriage was concluded *cum manu*; in the imperial period, most marriages were *sine manu* ('without *manus*') and the husband consequently had no power.

materfamilias, a woman *sui iuris* (q.v.), of whatever age, either married or single, freeborn or freed, if only she lived honourably.

morgengabe, Germanic word for a gift from the husband to the wife after the wedding night; in the sources it cannot always be clearly distinguished from *donatio ante nuptias* (q.v.).

mundium, right of protection and control over a Germanic woman, exercised by her father, husband, or some other relative, or even by the king.

novella, 'new law', used for laws enacted after the promulgation of a major collection, like after the Theodosian and Justinian Codes.

parapherna, property brought by the wife to the matrimonial home but not included in her dowry.

paterfamilias, the male head of a family, wielding an extensive power over his sons, daughters, and sons' children (but not daughters' children) until his own death or until *emancipatio* (q.v.).

patria potestas, the power of a *paterfamilias* over his descendants linked through males; people who were *in patria potestate* did not have independent ownership rights because everything belonged to their *paterfamilias*.

patronus, the former owner of a freed slave; a *patronus* continued to have certain rights over his freedmen.

peculium, money or other property which a *paterfamilias* (q.v.) could give to his child or slave and which they could control independently of him unless he reclaimed it.

postulare, 'to appear personally before a judicial magistrate with a claim or rejoinder'; this was an essential part of litigation in the classical formulary procedure, but in the later empire its meaning is obscure.

pupillus, a child under *tutela impuberum* (q.v.).

querela inofficiosi testamenti, 'complaint of unduteous will', available to near relatives who had not been left at least a quarter of their intestate share; a successful claim broke the will.

relegatio, exile without loss of citizenship; this was not a *capitalis poena* (q.v.).

rescriptum, the emperor's written answer to a private petition or to a letter from an official; although it might set a legal precedent, it did not necessarily have any general validity.

res mancipi, the most important type of property in classical Roman law, the alienation of which required a more difficult procedure than otherwise; *res mancipi* included land in Italy, slaves, and cattle, but not land outside Italy; Justinian finally abolished the distinction between *res mancipi* and *res nec mancipi*.

retentiones, deductions made from the dowry when the husband returned it after divorce; permissible reasons were the existence of children and the wife's immoral behaviour.

senatusconsultum (*sc*), resolution of the senate; they were an important means of new legislation up to the Severan period (*c.* AD 200).

stuprum, illicit intercourse of a currently unmarried honourable woman; intercourse with a lowborn woman was not forbidden, and the distinction was sometimes difficult to draw.

subscriptio, the emperor's short answer, written beneath a legal petition from a subject.

sui iuris, independent citizen, not being in anyone's *patria potestas* (q.v.).

tutela, guardianship over under-age children, up to the age of 14 for boys and 12 for girls (*tutela impuberum*); also the guardianship over adult women (*tutela mulierum*).

tutor legitimus, 'legitimate guardian', the nearest agnatic (q.v.) male relative, who automatically became the guardian if there was no testamentary one; the legitimate guardianship over women was abolished in the mid-1st c. AD, and it survived only for under-age boys.

usucapio, the acquisition of full ownership rights by long use; the

required period was one year for moveables and two years for immove-
ables.

ususfructus, the right of use and enjoyment of someone else's property,
including its yield.

INDEX OF SOURCES

A. LEGAL SOURCES

Codex Euricianus
319: 137, 175
321: 51, 103, 104–5, 173, 175
327: 71, 96, 107, 175
336: 51, 107

Codex Gregorianus
2. 2: 55, 58
2. 4: 53, 64
3. 6. 5: 140, 145
13. 14: 99

Codex Iustinianus
1. 3. 54: 35, 46
1. 18: 240–1
2. 4. 18: 195
2. 4. 26: 85
2. 12. 18: 90, 91, 234
2. 12. 21: 144, 243–5
2. 18. 13: 134
2. 55. 6: 234, 244
3. 28: 46–7, 86, 95, 106
4. 29: 98, 142, 237–9
5. 1. 5: 34, 56
5. 1. 6: 30
5. 4. 3: 225, 227
5. 4. 8: 32, 36
5. 4. 10: 124, 220
5. 4. 11: 44, 45
5. 4. 12: 29, 30
5. 4. 14: 178
5. 4. 20: 35–7
5. 9. 1: 168
5. 9. 4: 175
5. 9. 6: 170, 173
5. 10. 1: 174–5
5. 12. 23: 142
5. 12. 24: 178, 187
5. 12. 31: 67
5. 14. 8, 11: 138, 144–5
5. 16: 136
5. 16. 2: 135
5. 17. 5: 44, 45, 178

5. 17. 8: 131, 168, 175, 181, 186, 204
5. 17. 9: 168, 181–2
5. 17. 11: 32, 35, 36, 182
5. 17. 12: 46, 50
5. 18. 7: 43–4
5. 24: 87
5. 25: 86–7, 172
5. 27. 5–7: 212
5. 27. 8–9: 214–15, 216–17
5. 30. 3: 116–17
5. 31: 89
5. 34. 2: 141
5. 37. 12: 115
6. 40: 167, 170
6. 55. 12: 96
6. 56: 105–7, 168
6. 58: 63
6. 60. 4: 103, 170, 173
6. 61: 101, 103–4, 170
7. 15. 3: 211
7. 16. 1: 85
7. 20. 1: 225–6
7. 24. 1: 224
8. 17. 12: 60, 64–7, 134
8. 38. 2: 178
8. 46. 4: 85
8. 47. 5: 88
8. 51: 81
9. 9. 1: 202–3
9. 9. 4: 194
9. 9. 9: 195, 200–1, 202
9. 9. 27: 198, 202
9. 9. 29: 196, 200–1
12. 1. 1: 124

Codex Theodosianus
1. 22. 1: 243–5
2. 1. 7: 124–5
2. 12. 4: 144–5, 150
2. 12. 21: 144
2. 17. 1: 117, 243–5
2. 21. 1–2: 64, 95

Codex Theodosianus (cont.)

3. 1. 3: 143, 145
3. 5. 2: 29, 34, 42, 55
3. 5. 6: 55–6
3. 5. 11: 33, 36, 56
3. 6. 1: 56
3. 7. 1: 29, 30, 36, 37, 42
3. 7. 3: 56, 205, 206
3. 8. 1: 168
3. 8. 2–3: 107, 174–5
3. 9. 1: 174–5
3. 10. 1: 34, 37, 56
3. 13. 3: 175
3. 16. 1–2: 16, 46, 56, 168, 178–82, 204, 219
3. 17. 2: 116–17
3. 17. 4: 91–2, 94, 117–18, 174
4. 6. 2–4: 211, 212, 213, 216
4. 6. 5–6: 215
4. 6. 7: 206, 210, 211, 215
4. 6. 8: 206, 215, 216
4. 8. 7: 211, 224
4. 12: 222–3
5. 1. 1–8: 79, 96, 106–7, 175
5. 1. 4: 70, 96
5. 1. 9: 125, 135, 136
5. 9–10: 81, 125
6. 4. 17: 252
8. 13: 85–6, 174
8. 15. 1: 236, 245
8. 16. 1: 78–9, 126, 135
8. 17: 80, 118, 126
8. 18. 1: 101, 104
8. 18. 2: 50, 104
8. 18. 3: 101–3, 173
8. 18. 4: 97
8. 18. 5–7: 101
8. 18. 9: 51, 104
8. 18. 10: 175
8. 19. 1: 51, 58, 101
8. 19. 2: 86
9. 1. 3: 234, 236
9. 7. 1: 217
9. 7. 2: 196, 197–8
9. 9. 1: 16, 226–7
9. 14. 3: 241–2
9. 21. 1: 242, 248
9. 24. 1: 16, 34, 35, 38, 39, 232, 235–6, 242
9. 25: 165
9. 38: 4
9. 40. 1: 195, 196
9. 42. 1: 134–5, 144
11. 27: 81

11. 36. 4: 196, 198, 199
12. 1. 6: 206, 211, 214
13. 5. 12: 249
14. 3. 2, 14: 253
16. 2. 20: 160
16. 2. 27–8: 160, 232–3

Collatio Mosaicarum et Romanarum legum

4: 194
6. 4: 12, 16, 30, 202

Consultatio veteris cuiusdam iurisconsulti

1: 140, 145
2: 145
8: 145
9: 12, 16

Decretum Childeberti

1: 97

Digesta

1. 5. 9: 233
1. 9. 1: 124, 233
3. 1. 1: 234–5, 244
3. 2. 1: 168
3. 5. 3: 230
5. 1. 12: 233
5. 2: 46–7, 95
16. 1: 136, 142, 237–9
22. 5. 18: 235, 237
23. 2. 1: 124
23. 2. 2: 29, 30, 35
23. 3. 9: 137–9
24. 1. 1–3: 135, 146
25. 3–4: 168
25. 3. 5: 86–7
26. 1: 89–90
26. 2. 26: 90, 92
26. 6: 89–90
27. 10. 4: 84
28. 1. 20. 6: 235, 237
48. 5. 14: 203
48. 5. 23: 194
48. 5. 33: 194
48. 13. 7: 242
48. 16. 8–9: 4
50. 16. 46: 218
50. 17. 2: 233, 235, 252–3

Edictum Theoderici

17–20: 38, 39
38–9: 198
54: 60, 175, 182
133: 239

Edictus Rothari
158–60: 48, 71
167: 61, 153
181–3: 61, 71, 170
192: 61, 183
199: 61, 71
211–13: 200

Fragmenta vaticana
1: 113, 116
110: 113, 116, 141
120: 178, 186
202: 113, 116, 141
254: 86, 98, 138
259: 113, 116
325–7: 116, 245

Fragmenta Gaudenziana
8–9: 211, 212, 216

Gaius, Institutiones
1. 55: 48
1. 84: 221
1. 91: 221
1. 104: 88
1. 114–15: 113
1. 115a: 95
1. 144: 112, 232
1. 145: 78, 114
1. 157: 117
1. 160: 221
1. 190–2: 112–14
1. 193: 140
2. 112–13: 95, 113
2. 118–22: 113

Institutiones Iustiniani
1. 11. 10: 88
4. 18. 4: 200–1, 219

Leges Liutprandi
5: 48, 71
65: 48, 71
102: 48, 61, 71
113: 48, 173

Lex Burgundionum
1: 48, 51, 175
12: 39, 40
14: 61, 71, 153
24: 48, 51, 107, 152, 170, 175
34: 182–3
42: 61, 175
51: 48, 51, 71
52: 61, 183
59: 94, 152
74: 172, 175

75: 48, 51, 71
78: 51, 71
85: 94, 152
100: 151

Lex Irnitana
21–2: 48
28: 113
86: 48

Lex Ribuaria
71. 1: 21

Lex Romana Burgundionum
9: 38, 39
10: 71, 96, 107
14: 51
16: 168, 175
21: 60, 182
22: 51, 60, 96, 101, 104–5
25: 199, 200
26: 51, 60, 104–5, 175
36: 79, 89, 94, 96
37: 60, 205, 206, 207, 211, 215–16, 224
45: 48, 71, 107

Lex Salica (PLS)
13: 39, 183, 207, 224
25: 207, 224
44: 97, 170
59: 71, 97, 107
98: 227
100–1: 61, 105, 153, 170, 175

Lex Visigothorum
2. 4. 12–13: 237
3. 1. 3: 56, 183
3. 1. 4: 151, 170
3. 1. 5: 61, 137
3. 2. 2: 227
3. 2. 3: 207, 224
3. 4: 200, 204
3. 6: 182–3
4. 2. 2: 51, 107
4. 2. 13: 51, 103, 173, 175
4. 2. 18: 96, 97
4. 3. 1: 89, 94
4. 3. 3: 94, 174
4. 5. 5: 51, 94
5. 2. 3: 151, 153
5. 2. 4–5: 137, 153, 170, 175
5. 2. 7: 137, 151

Novellae Anthemii
1: 219, 227

Novellae Iustiniani
  18. 3: 174–5
  21: 54, 57, 70
  22. 3–19: 182
  22. 18: 65–7, 88, 168
  22. 19: 29, 46
  22. 32: 174–5
  22. 43–4: 167, 171
  22. 47: 80, 107
  74. praef. 2: 50, 104, 212, 217
  74. 3: 212
  74. 4: 135, 206
  89: 212, 214, 217
  97: 42, 57, 58, 66, 68, 135, 153, 232
  115. 3: 35, 37, 46–7
  117. 1: 104
  117. 2–4: 206, 217
  117. 7: 87, 182
  117. 10: 182
  117. 14: 131, 182
  117. 15: 201
  134. 8: 238–9
  134. 10: 196, 200–1
  140: 182
  155: 92, 173, 174
Novellae Maioriani
  6: 46, 57, 60, 70, 161–3, 164–5, 170, 175, 206
  7: 214, 223, 224
  9: 198–9, 200
Novellae Marciani
  4: 212, 213
  5: 160
Novellae Theodosii
  11: 89, 92, 174

  12: 181–2
  14: 58, 59, 101, 104, 153, 175, 181
  22. 1: 214, 215, 216
  22. 2: 144, 214, 253
Novellae Valentiniani
  14: 145–6
  21. 1: 80, 126
  31: 223, 224
  35: 51, 57, 59, 60, 104–5, 181
Pauli Sententiae
  2. 19. 2: 40, 44
  2. 20. 1: 206, 208
  2. 21A: 220–3
  2. 26. 7: 199–200
  2. 26. 14: 195, 199
  4. 9: 78
Praeceptum Chlothari
  4: 22
Syro-Roman Law Book
  L 1: 65, 107
  L 40: 42, 50
  L 55–6: 239
  L 67: 239
  L 88: 36, 37
  L 114–15: 181
Tituli Ulpiani (UE)
  6: 44, 52, 178
  11: 112–13, 232
  14–18: 77
  26: 78, 83–4, 123
  29: 77–8, 114

B.   LITERARY SOURCES

Ambrose
  Abr.
    1. 19: 209, 215
    1. 91: 35, 37
  ep.
    35: 30–1
    58–9: 30
  hex.
    5. 18. 58: 47, 62, 81, 83
  in Luc.
    8: 87, 172, 180
  parad.
    11. 50: 128, 252–3

  in psalm. 118 serm.
    16. 7. 2: 236, 244–5
  vid.
    13. 81: 162
  virg.
    1. 58: 36, 159
    1. 62–6: 35, 46, 159

Ambrosiaster (Ps.Aug.)
  quaest.
    45. 3: 231, 236–7, 239
    115: 179–80, 183, 226

Ammianus Marcellinus
  14. 6. 19–20: 158
  21. 10. 8: 260
  28. 1. 16, 28, 48–56: 196–7, 219, 226
Apuleius
  apol.
    77: 44
    92: 128, 188
Asterius of Amaseia
  hom.
    5: 127, 172, 180, 204
Augustine
  adult. conjug.
    2. 8. 7: 178, 203, 204–5
    2. 14–17: 189, 197
  bon. conjug.
    1. 1: 127, 132
    5. 5: 208, 209
  conf.
    2. 2. 4: 31
    4. 2: 208
    9. 9. 19: 33, 130–1
  ep.
    252–5: 30, 36–7, 165
    262: 50, 84, 87, 146, 159
    *3: 165
    *24: 223
  nupt. et concup.
    1. 15. 17: 62, 83
  in psalm.
    44. 11: 42
  serm.
    45. 2: 50, 51
    332. 4: 130
    355–6: 46–7, 68–9, 125, 161, 172
    392. 4: 130, 146, 203
Basil the Great
  ep.
    199. 22: 36, 38
    199. 26: 197, 209
    199. 30: 37, 38
    199. 34: 197–8
Caesarius of Arles
  serm.
    42: 208, 209, 211
    43: 39, 204–5, 208, 209, 232–3
    52. 4: 63, 83
Cassiodorus
  var.
    4. 10. 2: 135, 145
    7. 40: 205, 212, 216

    9. 18. 7: 204
Conc. Hipp. (393)
  1–2: 32, 50, 51
Conc. Tolet. I (398)
  7: 131
Cyprian
  ep.
    80. 1: 242
Dio Cassius
  54. 16. 2: 81, 207
  77. 16. 4: 195
Gerontius
  vita Melan.
    12: 35, 43, 159
Gregory the Great
  ep.
    1. 13: 124, 171, 252
    3. 40, 42: 197–8, 201, 219
    4. 36: 105, 149
Gregory of Nazianzus
  carm.
    2. 2. 6: 127, 146, 247
  ep.
    144: 45, 180
  or.
    37: 50, 84, 180, 203, 204
Gregory of Nyssa
  vita Macr.
    20: 69
Gregory of Tours
  franc.
    1. 47: 56, 60
    4. 25–6: 172, 183
    6. 36: 40, 200
    9. 20: 60, 72
    9. 33: 40, 107, 245
    10. 8: 39, 72, 131, 182, 208
Hippolyt
  phil.
    9. 12. 24–5: 220
Isidor of Seville
  orig.
    5. 25. 5: 51
Jerome (Hieronymus)
  ep.
    22: 160–3, 208, 246
    52: 160
    54: 33, 132, 146, 158, 159, 161, 162, 171–3, 247
    69: 212, 214, 216

Jerome (Hieronymus) (*cont.*)
77: 159, 162, 163, 203, 232–3, 247
123: 171
127: 36, 95, 130, 158, 159, 162, 163, 171, 180, 232
in Eph.
3. 5. 22–33: 128, 131, 132, 133
in Tit.
2. 3–5: 128, 232

John Chrysostom
in acta
49. 4: 129–30, 146, 171
in Coloss.
1. 3: 41, 180
in I Thess.
5: 30, 203, 208
lib. rep.
1: 127–8, 169, 180
in Matth.
73. 4: 29–30, 129–30, 205
non iter. conjug.
6: 92, 173
qual. duc. ux.
2: 50, 59, 125
3: 30, 127
4: 58, 127, 128, 130, 188
virg.
52: 161, 197, 199, 204–5
53–5: 129–30, 131
57: 30, 34, 161

John Lydus
mag.
3. 28: 66

Lactantius
mort. pers.
39–40: 37, 168, 196

Leo (pope)
ep.
167: 35, 165, 205, 209

Libanius
or.
1. 195–6: 214
2. 36: 144, 214, 253
48. 30: 207, 214, 253

Maximus of Turin
serm.
88. 5: 207, 208, 209, 215

Paulinus of Pella
176–81: 30, 31, 208

Pelagius I
ep.
45: 224
47: 207, 208
54: 197–8, 201, 219
64: 182, 201, 223

Plutarch
conjug. praec.
11: 129
20: 139

Salvian
gub.
4. 24–6: 207, 208, 209

Sidonius Apollinaris
ep.
2. 2. 3: 60, 153
7. 2: 31, 33, 36, 50, 51, 60
9. 6: 207, 208, 209

Symmachus
ep.
6. 3: 30, 123–4
rel.
39: 12, 69, 116

Tertullian
apol.
6. 6: 184, 246
ux.
2. 8: 29, 220, 221, 226

C. DOCUMENTARY SOURCES

BGU
iv. 1049: 147
vii. 1578: 46, 49
vii. 1690: 218
Cart. Senon.
45: 72

CIL
vi. 1527, 37053: 139, 141, 184
vi. 10230: 173, 177
vi. 10231: 113
vi. 10247: 114, 120

CPL
206: 42
221: 90

CPR
i. 19: 121
i. 30 II: 34, 36, 56, 57, 130
vi. 78: 49, 100

FIRA iii.
4, *see* P.Mich. iii. 169
5, *see* BGU vii. 1690
6, *see* SB i. 5217
14, *see* CPL 206
15, *see* P.Masp. i. 67097
16, *see* P.Oxy. ix. 1206
17, *see* P.Mich. vii. 434
18, *see* P.Lond. v. 1711
20, *see* P.Mich. vii. 442
21, *see* P.Oxy. i. 129
22, *see* P.Flor. i. 93
23, *see* P.Lond. v. 1731
24, *see* P.Oxy. iv. 720
26, *see* P.Lond. ii. 470
27, *see* P.Oxy. xii. 1467
28, *see* P.Harr. i. 68
30, *see* SB v. 7558
47, *see* CPL 221
51, *see* P.Oxy. vi. 907
52, *see* P.Ant. 1
59, *see* PSI ix. 1027
61, *see* SB i. 1010
63, *see* P.Oxy. viii. 1114
67, *see* P.Lond. v. 1727
69, *see* CIL vi. 1527, 37053
70, *see* CIL vi. 10230
93, *see* CIL vi. 10231
95, *see* CIL vi. 10247
175, *see* P.Lips. 33
184, *see* P.Monac. i. 1

Form. Andec.
1: 60, 130, 152
12, 16: 245
34, 40: 60, 30, 152
41: 126–7, 137
54: 58, 60, 130, 152, 176
57: 182
59: 150, 224

Form. Marc.
1. 12: 126–7, 137
2. 7–8: 126–7, 137
2. 9: 60, 105, 152, 176
2. 10: 61, 72, 97–8
2. 12: 72

2. 16: 39, 60, 152
2. 17: 72, 126–7, 130, 174, 176
2. 30: 182

Form. Tur.
14: 34, 60, 130, 152, 176, 206
16: 39, 40
17–18: 126–7, 136, 137, 176
19: 182
20: 150
22: 61, 72, 98

Form. Vis.
14–20: 34, 60, 130, 152, 176
23–4: 126–7, 137
34: 51–2

MChr
361 (= P.Oxy. iv. p. 202): 147

Pard.
257 (will of Burgundofara): 23, 72

P.Ant.
1: 125

P.Cair.Preis.
2–3: 36, 187

P.Coll.Youtie.
ii. 83: 120, 121

P.Flor.
i. 93: 87, 185

P.Harr.
i. 68 (= P.Diog. 18): 49, 90, 218

P.Herm.
35: 240

P.Lips.
28: 50, 85
29: 121
33: 69
41: 36

P.Lond.
ii. 470: 141
iii. 971: 232
v. 1711: 34, 130, 187, 239
v. 1724: 147
v. 1727: 69, 125, 176
v. 1731: 87, 173

P.Masp.
i. 67005: 36, 37
i. 67006v: 34, 50
i. 67097: 47, 69
ii. 67156: 69, 147
iii. 67340r: 37, 130, 187

P.Mich.
iii. 169: 113, 218
vii. 434: 34
vii. 442: 113
viii. 507: 245

P.Monac.
i. 1: 69

P.Ness.
iii. 18: 34, 50, 57, 130

P.Oxy.
i. 129: 45, 50
ii. 237: 44–5, 46, 48, 49
iv. 720: 119
vi. 907: 69, 90, 143–4
viii. 1114: 49, 100
ix. 1206: 85
ix. 1208: 49, 100
x. 1273: 34, 36, 130
xii. 1466: 119
xii. 1467: 114, 119
xviii. 2187: 106
xxxiv. 2710: 119
l. 3581: 38, 87, 131, 185, 251
liv. 3758: 50, 120
liv. 3770: 36, 58, 87, 185, 187

P.Princ.
ii. 38: 120, 121, 141, 144

P.Ross.Georg.
iii. 28: 34, 130

P.Sakaon
37 (=P.Thead. 18): 90, 93

38 (= P.Flor. i. 36): 45, 55, 58

PSI
ix. 1027: 90, 113
xii. 1238: 119, 120

P.Strasb.
i. 29: 49, 100
iii. 131: 34, 130

P.Tjäder
i. 7–8: 93, 171
i. 13: 72, 149
i. 20: 72, 149, 239–40
ii. 30: 72, 93, 125, 149
ii. 37: 125, 149
ii. 55: 125
ii. 56: 240

P.Vind.Bosw.
5: 34, 36

SB
i. 1010: 49, 100
i. 5217: 218
v. 7558: 90
v. 7996: 50, 103
xvi. 12230: 57, 58, 66

SP
xx. 117: 147

Tablettes Albertini
1: 34, 60
11, 15, 18, 24, 27: 93, 149, 172

TAM
iii. 383, 482, 669, 705, 714: 119

SUBJECT INDEX

abduction 37–41
abortion 81, 83
adoption 85, 88, 211–12
adultery 69, 193–204
agnates 28, 89, 92–4, 95–7, 105–7, 112, 117
arra sponsalicia 55–6
Augustus, marriage laws of 77–8, 81, 114, 155, 167, 177

betrothal 54–6, 183
  see also bridegift, marriage
Breviarium of Alaric 13–14, 18, 22
bridegift 34, 52–62, 68, 152–3, 174–6, 181

celibacy:
  involuntary 164–6, 179–82, 187–8
  voluntary 26, 79, 81–2, 127–8, 148, 157–67, 190–1, 246, 259
children:
  abandonment and killing of 81, 83, 166
  illegitimate 86, 208–17, 218
  succession to 105–7
  see also guardianship
Christianity, influence of 3–6, 26, 31, 79, 127–8, 131–3, 157–72, 175–7, 183–5, 189–92, 202–5, 228–9, 246–7, 257–61
Codex Euricianus 19, 22
Codex Gregorianus 11, 13
Codex Iustinianus 13
Codex Theodosianus 11, 13–15, 18, 22 n., 23
coloni, colonae 207, 223
concubines 205–18
Constantine 3, 5, 78–9, 100–2, 143–4, 178–9, 243–6, 260–1
Constitutio Antoniniana (AD 212) 2
courts, women in 234–7, 243–5
curator 115–16, 141, 143–4
curial class 144, 213–14, 223, 253

Digesta 9–10
Diocletian 11, 16, 202

disinheritance 35, 37, 40, 46–8, 53, 64, 86
divorce 44–6, 86–7, 177–92, 258
donatio ante nuptias, see bridegift
double standard, *see* sexual morals
dowry (*dos*) 44, 52–62, 63–69, 98–9, 134, 153, 177–81, 186–8

Edictum Theoderici 19
Edictus Rothari 20
emancipatio 41–2, 45–6, 49, 50–2, 99–100, 104, 105–6, 113
empresses 254
equestrian class 9, 108–9, 213

family planning 62, 81–4, 164–6, 190–1, 208
father 28–52, 84–7, 113, 173, 194
  succession to 52–3, 62–75, 213–17
  see also *patria potestas*
fertility 77–84, 122, 166, 190–1
Formularies 23
Fragmenta vaticana 116
freedmen and freedwomen 77, 78, 113, 115
  sexual relationships with 194, 207, 210–18, 225–7

Gaius, *Institutiones* 9
gifts, see *arra*, bridegift, spouses
guardianship:
  over children 35–6, 49, 89–94, 112, 115–17, 141, 143–4
  over women 95, 112–23, 140–1, 147–56

infirmitas sexus 231–3
inheritance, *see* children, disinheritance, father, mother, spouses, wills
interpolations 9–10, 13, 90, 86 n., 88 n., 123, 141 n., 178 n., 195, 199–200, 208 n., 232 n.
ius liberorum 77–80, 84, 105–7, 114–15, 119–23, 126

Julian (emperor) 143, 179, 222, 260
Justinian 9, 16, 60, 96, 216–17, 243, 260–1

labour, gender division of 128, 248–9, 252–3
Leges Liutprandi 20
legislation, methods of 8–23
Lex Burgundionum 19
Lex Irnitana 48
Lex Julia de adulteris 194–5
Lex Julia de maritandis ordinibus 77–8
   see also Augustus
Lex Ribuaria 20
Lex Romana Burgundionum 19
Lex Romana Visigothorum, see *Breviarium* of Alaric
Lex Salica (Pactus) 20
Lex Visigothorum 19
Lex Voconia 69 n.

marriage:
   age at 31–3
   between close kin 30
   consent to 29–41, 158–60
   contract 34, 59, 130, 186–7, 205–6
   definition of 205–6
   with *manus* 94–5, 105, 108, 123–4
   prohibitions on 30, 207, 213, 225–7
   see also quasi–marital unions
mortality 32, 41, 81–3
mother 84–110, 263
   as a guardian 89–94, 174
   and the marriage of children 31–7
   succession to 94–105, 106, 108–10
   see also fertility
munera (civic obligations) 144, 249–53

novellae 13, 181

offices, women in 233–4, 250–4

parapherna 53, 137–8, 145
patria potestas 28, 41–52, 73–4, 94, 98–105, 155, 262–5
peculium 43, 51, 58, 64 n., 99, 102–3, 137–8
penalties 77, 179–82, 241–2
   death and exile 38–9, 179, 181, 182, 195–202, 219, 226–7, 242
   detention in a monastery 200–1, 219
   fines 20–1, 40, 131, 195, 200, 219, 242

quasi–marital unions 205–17, 220–9

rape, see abduction

remarriage 77, 87, 91–2, 101–3, 128, 158, 160–3, 167–77, 189–90, 259

seclusion and proper behaviour 243–7
senatorial class 9, 79, 108–9, 159–60
   dowries among 64, 67
   family behaviour of 31, 32–3, 44, 81–4, 124, 207, 213, 220, 225
senatus consultum 8
   Claudianum 221–5
   Orfitianum 95, 106
   Pisonianum 64 n.
   Tertullianum 105–6
   Velleianum 141–2, 237–40
sexual morals 3, 31, 202–5, 225, 228–9, 258
slaves 10, 248
   imperial 221–3
   sexual relationships with 194, 203–5, 206–16, 220–9
spouses 123–56
   choice of 29–40, 129–30
   gifts between 98–9, 135–7, 238
   love between 29–30, 37–8, 127, 130, 134–5
   property relations between 52–3, 129, 133–56, 238, 253
   succession between 77, 79–80, 99, 125–7, 137, 174–7
   see also wives
step-parents 88, 172–4
stuprum 217–20, 224, 226
Syro–Roman Law Book 24–5

Tablettes Albertini 24
Theodosius the Great 3, 160, 168
tutor, see guardianship

virginity:
   premarital 220
   lifelong, see celibacy
vulgar law 16–18, 22, 24

widows 37, 85, 89–94, 125–7, 132–3, 147–56, 158–63, 171–2, 220, 225–6
   see also remarriage
wills 63, 72, 95, 121, 125–7, 137
   see also disinheritance
witnesses, women as 235–7
wives:
   subordination of 128–33, 154–5, 161–2, 188, 263–4
   violence towards 130–2, 185, 193–4, 199–200
   see also spouses